NEGIMA! 19

Ken Akamatsu

TRANSLATED BY
Toshifumi Yoshida

ADAPTED BY
Ikoi Hiroe

LETTERING AND RETOUCH BY
Steve Palmer

DEL REY

BALLANTINE BOOKS · NEW YORK

Negima! volume 19 is a work of fiction. Names, characters, places, and incidents are the products of the author's imagination or are used fictitiously. Any resemblance to actual events, locales, or persons, living or dead, is entirely coincidental.

A Del Rey Manga/Kodansha Trade Paperback Original

Published in the United States by Del Rey Books, an imprint of The Random House Publishing Group, a division of Random House, Inc., New York.

DEL REY is a registered trademark and the Del Rey colophon is a trademark of Random House, Inc.

Publication rights arranged through Kodansha Ltd.

First published in Japan in 2007 by Kodansha Ltd., Tokyo

ISBN 978-0-345-50526-2

Printed in the United States of America

www.delreymanga.com

9 8 7 6 5 4 3 2 1

Translator—Toshifumi Yoshida
Adapter—Ikoi Hiroe
Lettering and retouch—Steve Palmer

Honorifics Explained

Throughout the Del Rey Manga books, you will find Japanese honorifics left intact in the translations. For those not familiar with how the Japanese use honorifics and, more important, how they differ from American honorifics, we present this brief overview.

Politeness has always been a critical facet of Japanese culture. Ever since the feudal era, when Japan was a highly stratified society, use of honorifics—which can be defined as polite speech that indicates relationship or status—has played an essential role in the Japanese language. When addressing someone in Japanese, an honorific usually takes the form of a suffix attached to one's name (example: "Asuna-san"), is used as a title at the end of one's name, or appears in place of the name itself (example: "Negi-sensei," or simply "Sensei!").

Honorifics can be expressions of respect or endearment. In the context of manga and anime, honorifics give insight into the nature of the relationship between characters. Many English translations leave out these important honorifics and therefore distort the feel of the original Japanese. Because Japanese honorifics contain nuances that English honorifics lack, it is our policy at Del Rey not to translate them. Here, instead, is a guide to some of the honorifics you may encounter in Del Rey Manga.

-san: This is the most common honorific and is equivalent to Mr., Miss, Ms., or Mrs. It is the all-purpose honorific and can be used in any situation where politeness is required.

-sama: This is one level higher than "-san" and is used to confer great respect.

-dono: This comes from the word "tono," which means "lord." It is an even higher level than "-sama" and confers utmost respect.

-kun: This suffix is used at the end of boys' names to express familiarity or endearment. It is also sometimes used by men

among friends, or when addressing someone younger or of a lower station.

-chan: This is used to express endearment, mostly toward girls. It is also used for little boys, pets, and even among lovers. It gives a sense of childish cuteness.

Bōzu: This is an informal way to refer to a boy, similar to the English terms "kid" and "squirt."

Sempai/Senpai: This title suggests that the addressee is one's senior in a group or organization. It is most often used in a school setting, where underclassmen refer to their upperclassmen as "sempai." It can also be used in the workplace, such as when a newer employee addresses an employee who has seniority in the company.

Kohai: This is the opposite of "sempai" and is used toward underclassmen in school or newcomers in the workplace. It connotes that the addressee is of a lower station.

Sensei: Literally meaning "one who has come before," this title is used for teachers, doctors, or masters of any profession or art.

Anesan (or *nesan*): A generic term for a girl, usually older, that means sister.

Ojōsama: A way of referring to the daughter or sister of someone with high political or social status.

-[blank]: This is usually forgotten in these lists, but it is perhaps the most significant difference between Japanese and English. The lack of honorific means that the speaker has permission to address the person in a very intimate way. Usually, only family, spouses, or very close friends have this kind of permission. Known as *yobisute*, it can be gratifying when someone who has earned the intimacy starts to call one by one's name without an honorific. But when that intimacy hasn't been earned, it can be very insulting.

A Word from the Author

Following in the footsteps of the animation and video games, *Negima!* is finally becoming a live-action drama series!

Now as to what kind of show it's going to be…!?

For more information, please look online, including on my own home page.

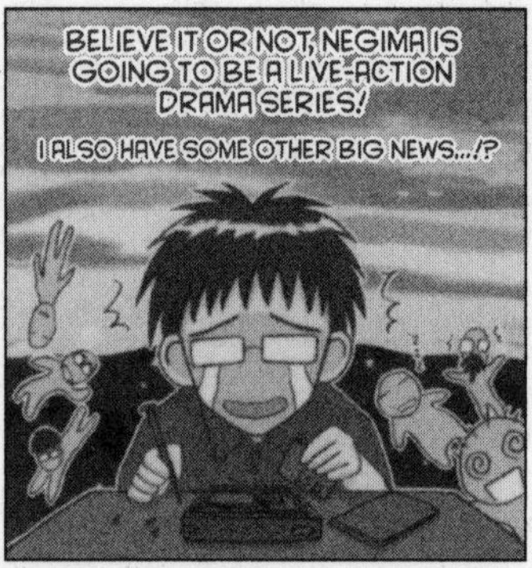
BELIEVE IT OR NOT, NEGIMA IS GOING TO BE A LIVE-ACTION DRAMA SERIES!
I ALSO HAVE SOME OTHER BIG NEWS...!?

On the manga front, as of volume 19, we enter into the summer vacation chapters, and a whole new story arc is about to begin. Please look forward to what I have in store for the Negi party and the other classmates in the chapters to come!

Ken Akamatsu
www.ailove.net

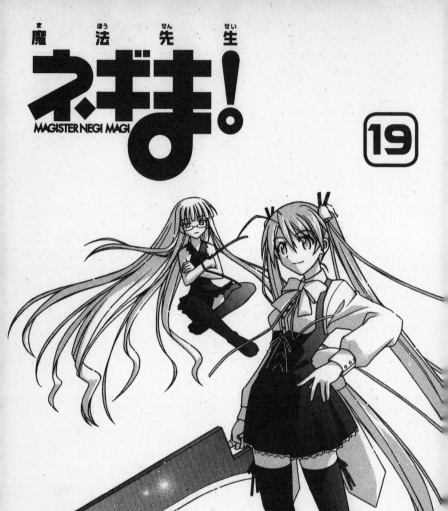

魔法先生 ネギま!

MAGISTER NEGI MAGI

19

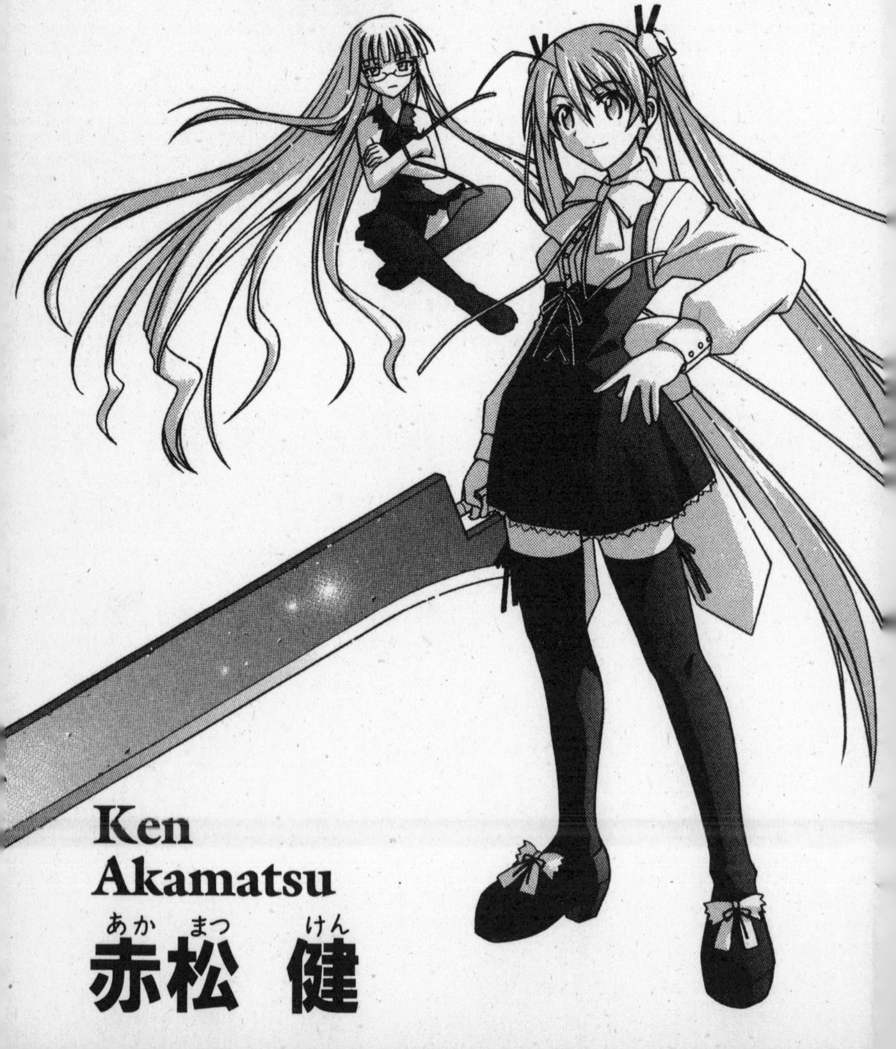

Ken
Akamatsu

赤松 健

DIARIUM EJ

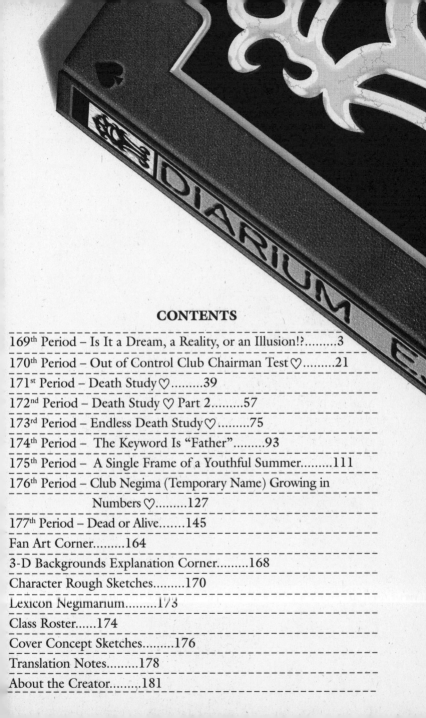

CONTENTS

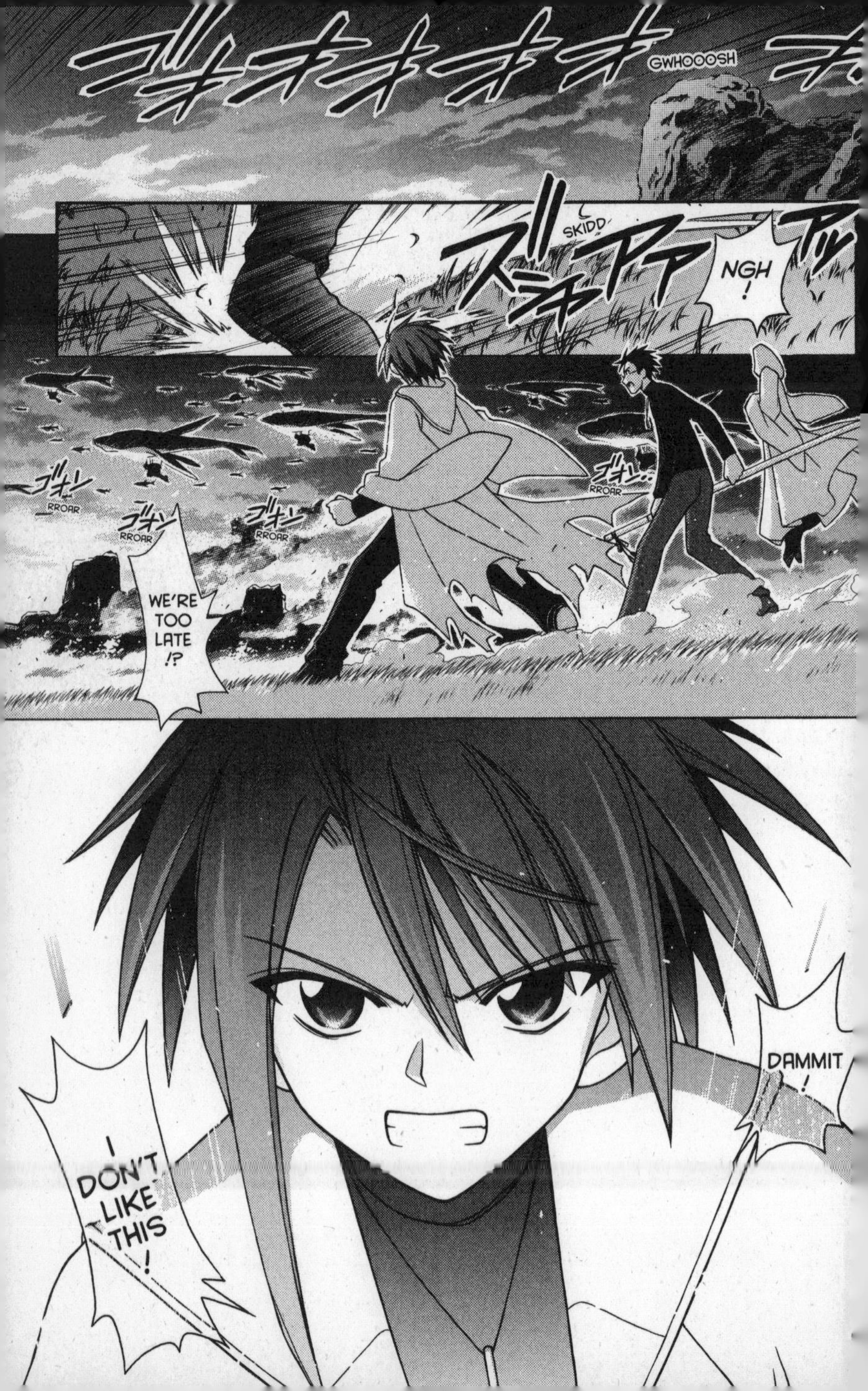
ゴオオオオオ
GWHOOOSH
ズシャアアッ
SKIDD
NGH!
ゴオン
RROAR
ゴオン
RROAR
ゴオン
RROAR
ゴオン
RROAR
WE'RE TOO LATE!?
DAMMIT!
I DON'T LIKE THIS!

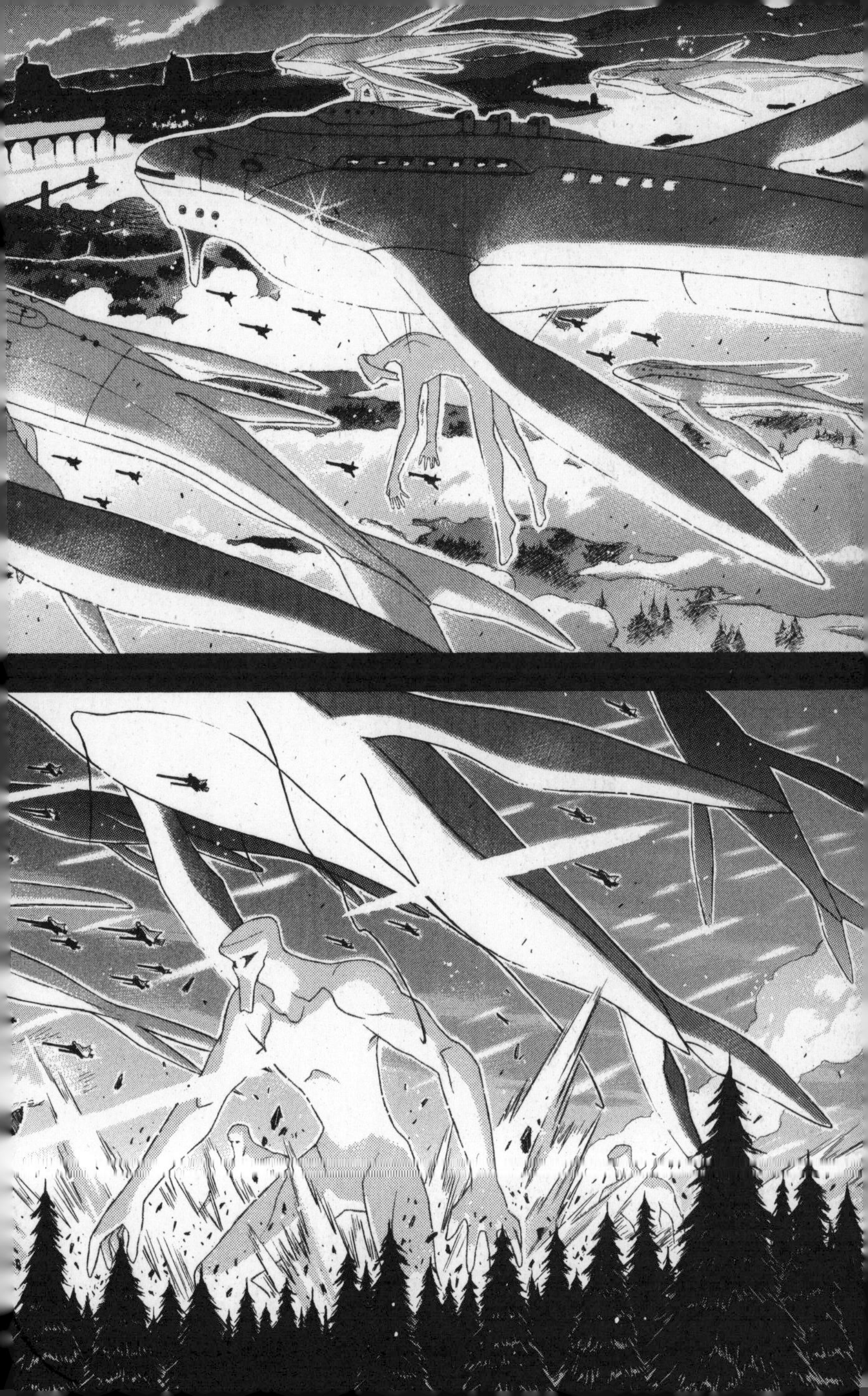

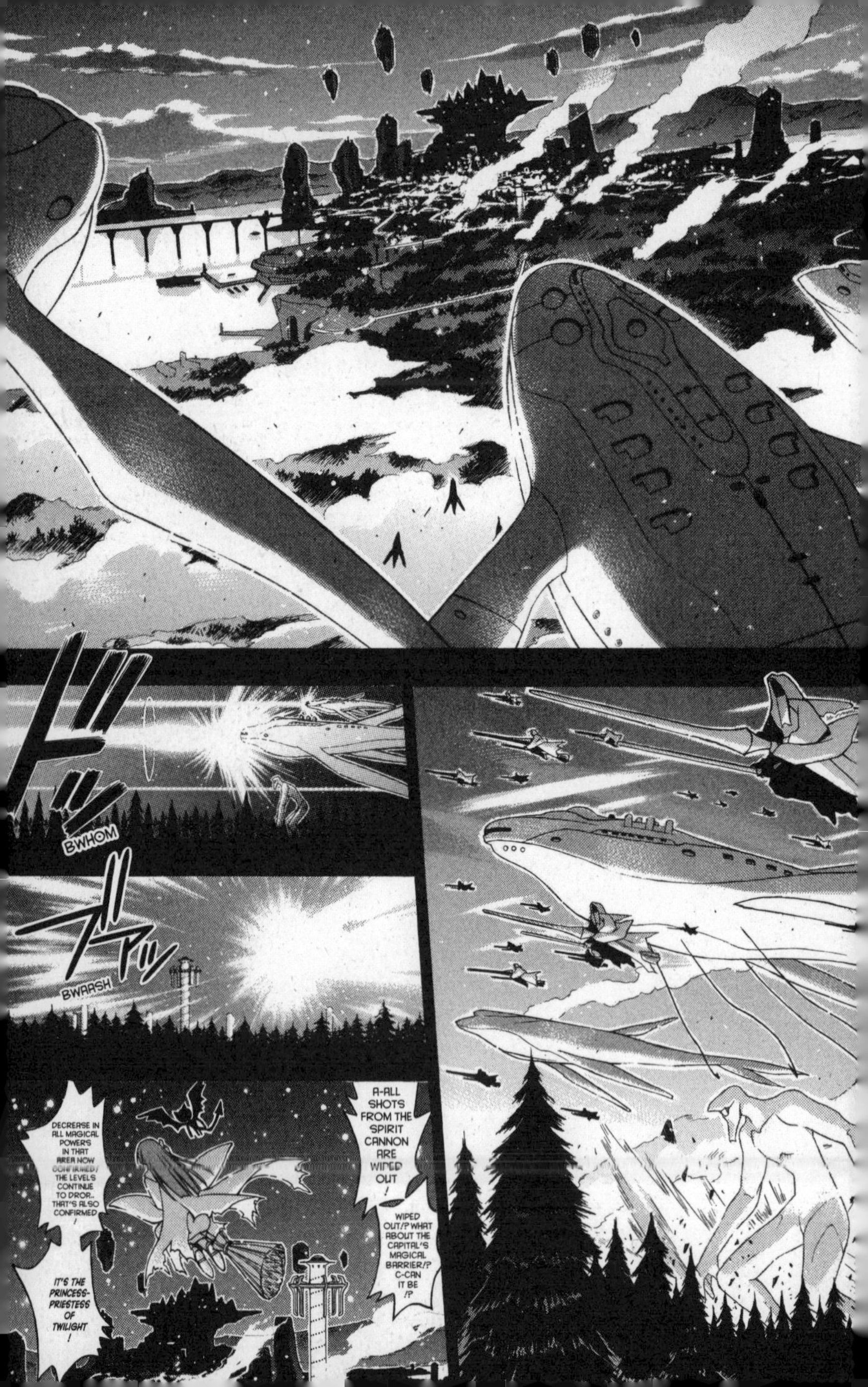
BWHOM
BWARSH
A-ALL SHOTS FROM THE SPIRIT CANNON ARE WIPED OUT!
WIPED OUT!? WHAT ABOUT THE CAPITAL'S MAGICAL BARRIER!? C-CAN IT BE!?
DECREASE IN ALL MAGICAL POWERS IN THAT AREA NOW CONFIRMED! THE LEVELS CONTINUE TO DROP... THAT'S ALSO CONFIRMED!
IT'S THE PRINCESS-PRIESTESS OF TWILIGHT!

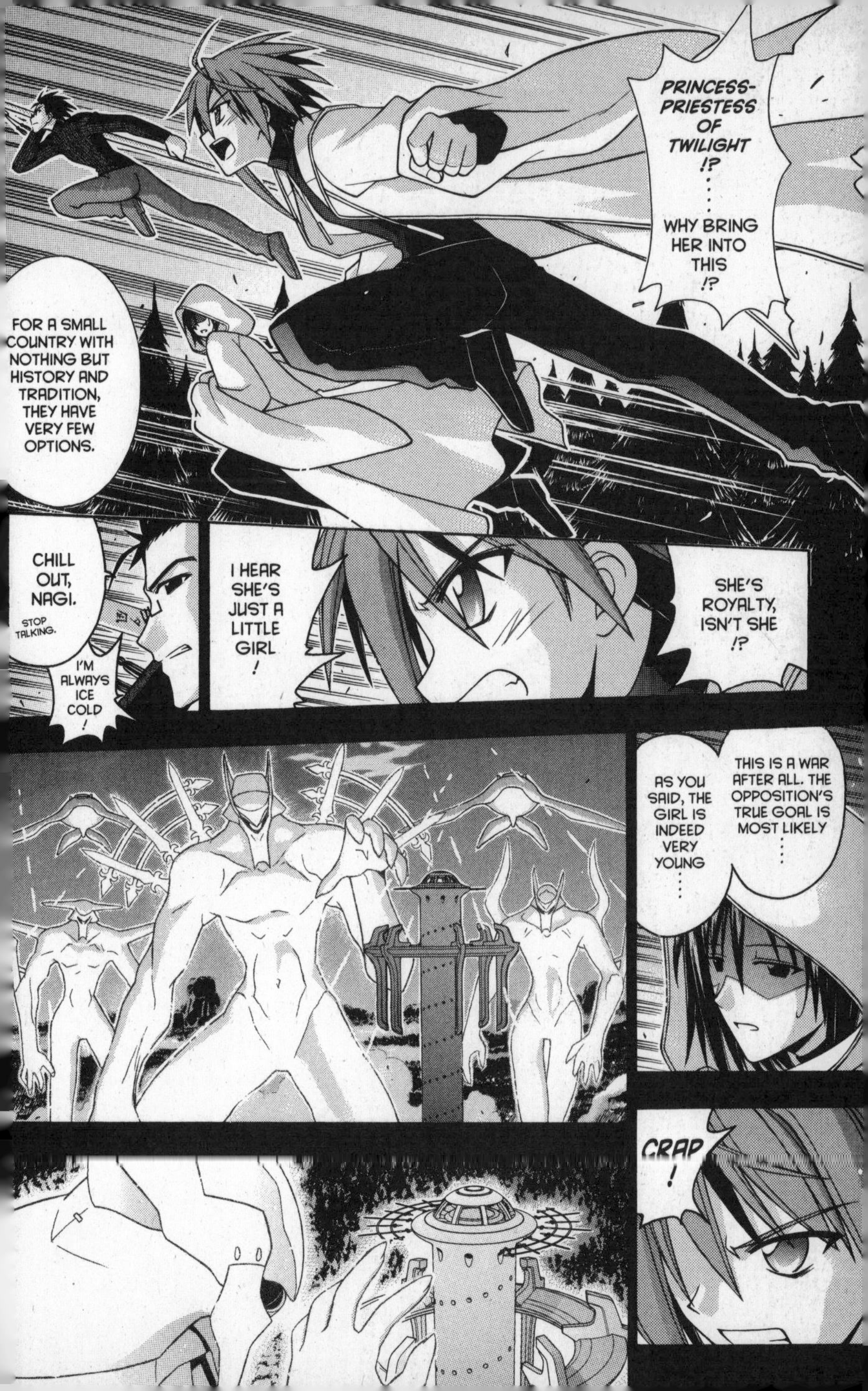
PRINCESS-PRIESTESS OF TWILIGHT !? ...... WHY BRING HER INTO THIS !?
FOR A SMALL COUNTRY WITH NOTHING BUT HISTORY AND TRADITION, THEY HAVE VERY FEW OPTIONS.
SHE'S ROYALTY, ISN'T SHE !?
I HEAR SHE'S JUST A LITTLE GIRL !
CHILL OUT, NAGI.
STOP TALKING.
I'M ALWAYS ICE COLD !
THIS IS A WAR AFTER ALL. THE OPPOSITION'S TRUE GOAL IS MOST LIKELY ....
AS YOU SAID, THE GIRL IS INDEED VERY YOUNG ....
CRAP !

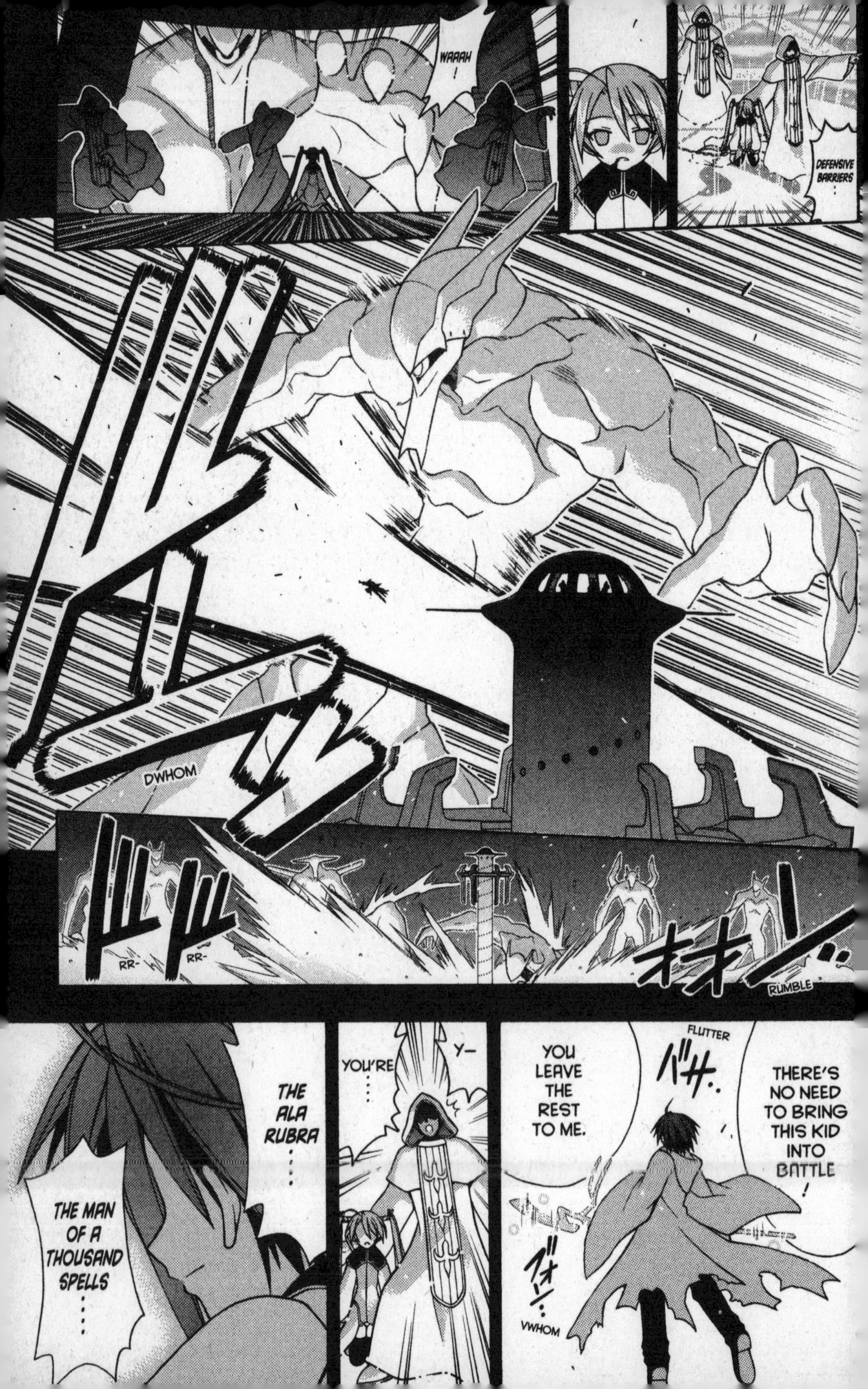
DEFENSIVE BARRIERS...
WAAAH!
DWHOM
RUMBLE
RR-
RR-
THERE'S NO NEED TO BRING THIS KID INTO BATTLE!
FLUTTER
YOU LEAVE THE REST TO ME.
VWHOM
Y—
YOU'RE...
THE ALA RUBRA...
THE MAN OF A THOUSAND SPELLS...

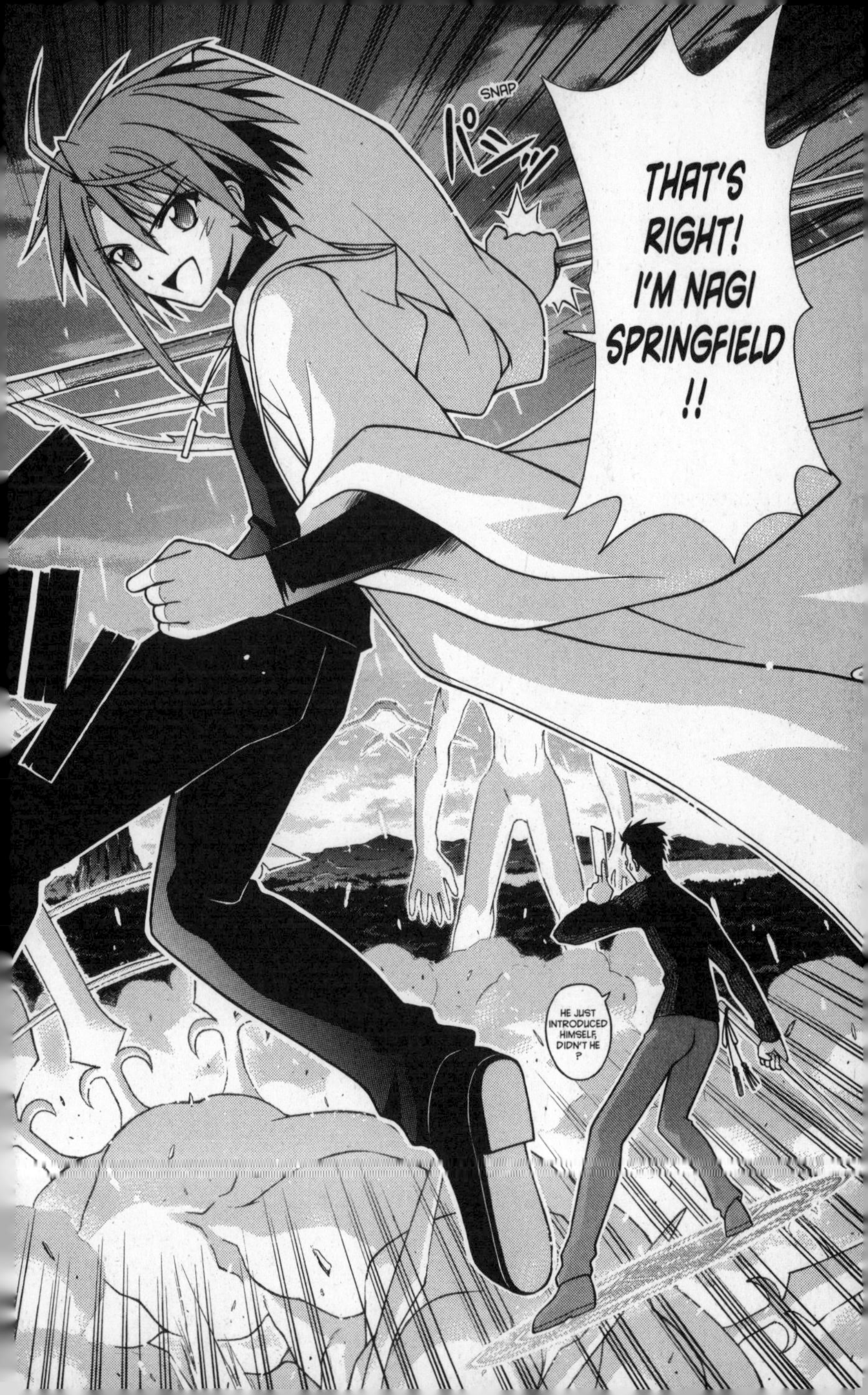
SNAP
パッ
THAT'S RIGHT! I'M NAGI SPRINGFIELD !!
HE JUST INTRODUCED HIMSELF, DIDN'T HE ?

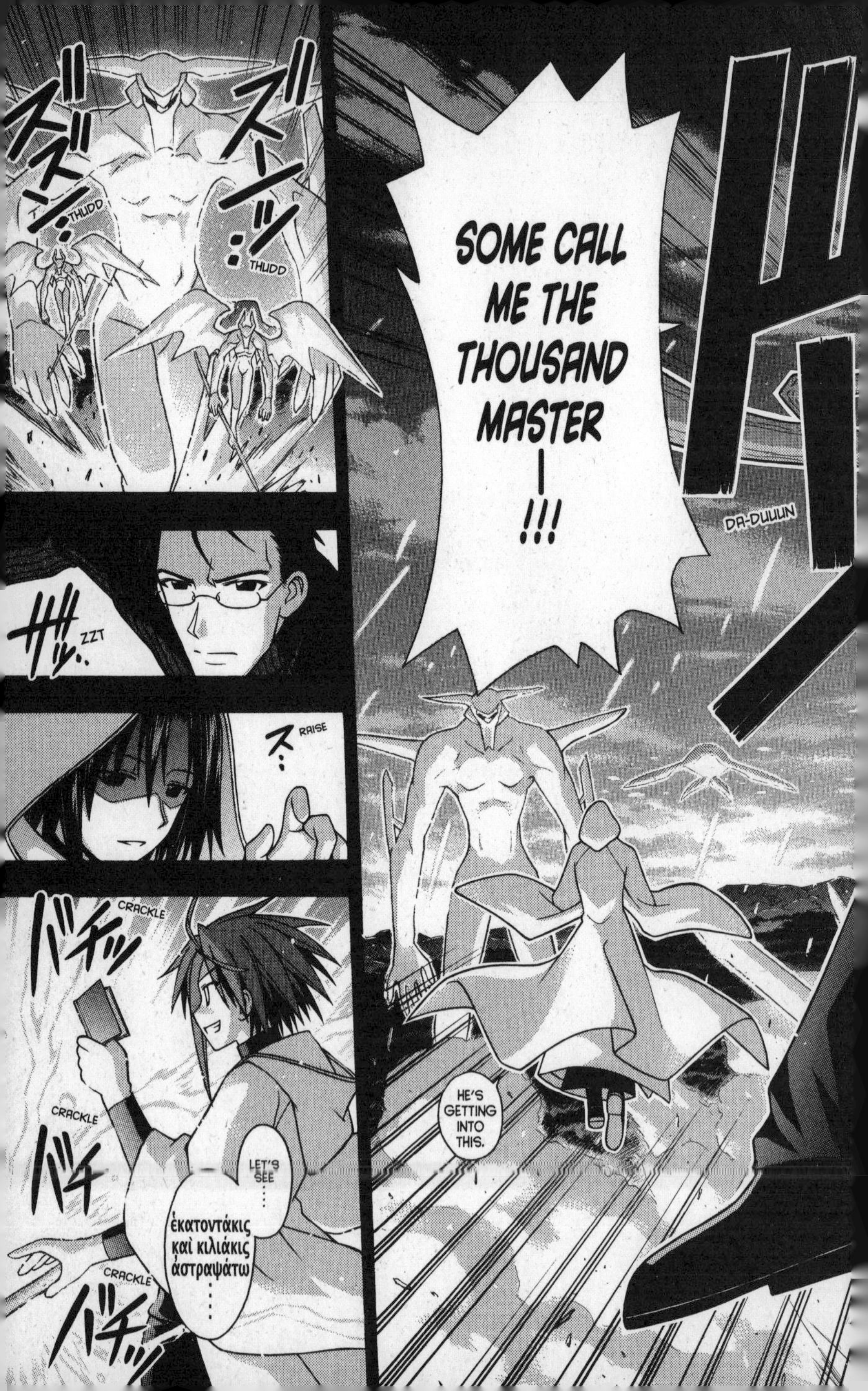
SOME CALL ME THE THOUSAND MASTER—!!!
DA-DUUUN
HE'S GETTING INTO THIS.
THUDD
THUDD
ZZT
RAISE
CRACKLE
CRACKLE
LET'S SEE.....
ἑκατοντάκις καὶ κιλιάκις ἀστραψάτω....
CRACKLE

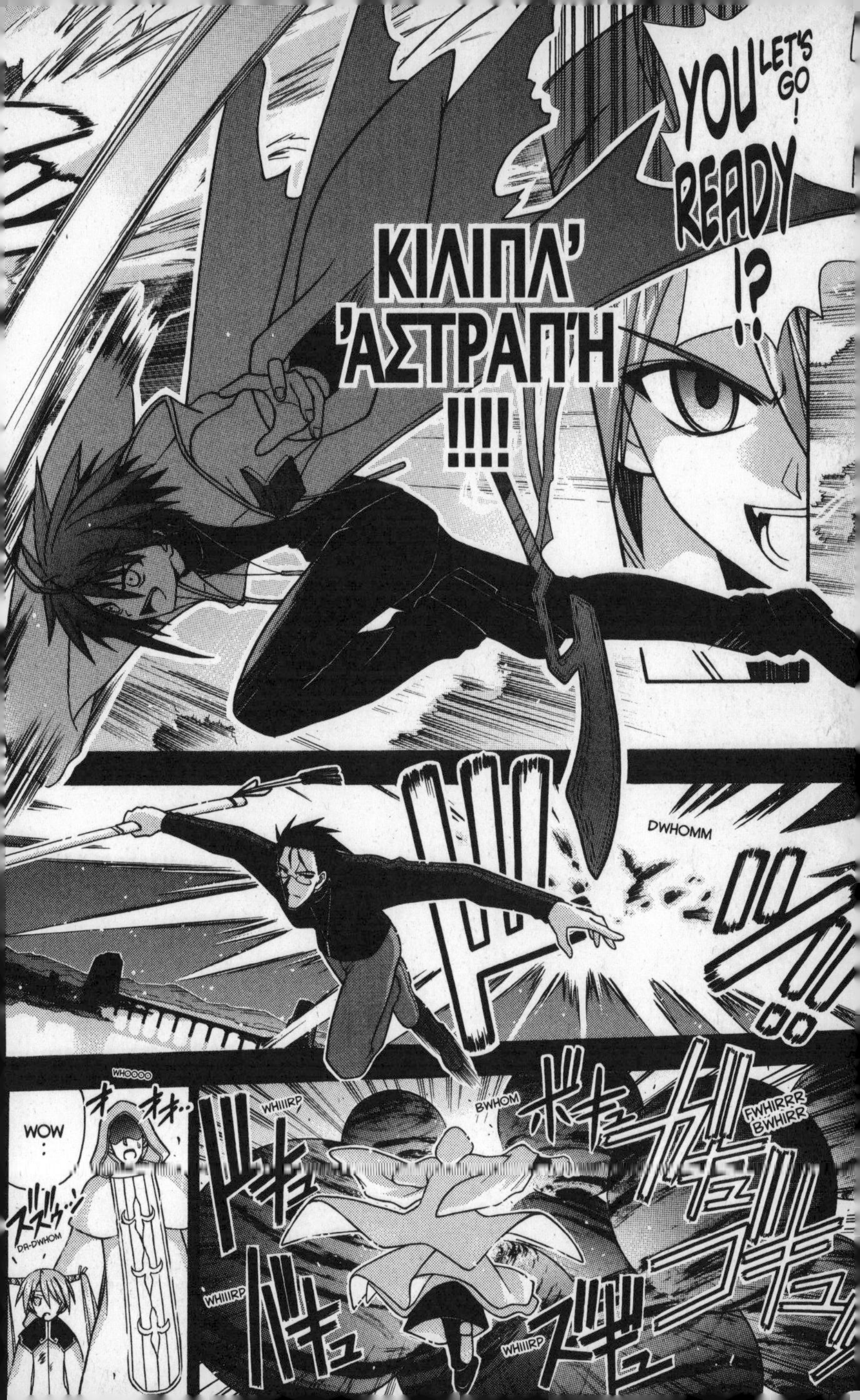
LET'S GO!
YOU READY!?
ΚΙΛΙΠΛ' 'ΑΣΤΡΑΠΉ!!!!!
DWHOMM
FWHIRRR BWHIRR
BWHOM
WHIIIRP
WHIIIRP
WHIIIRP
WHOOOO
WOW...
DR-DWHOM

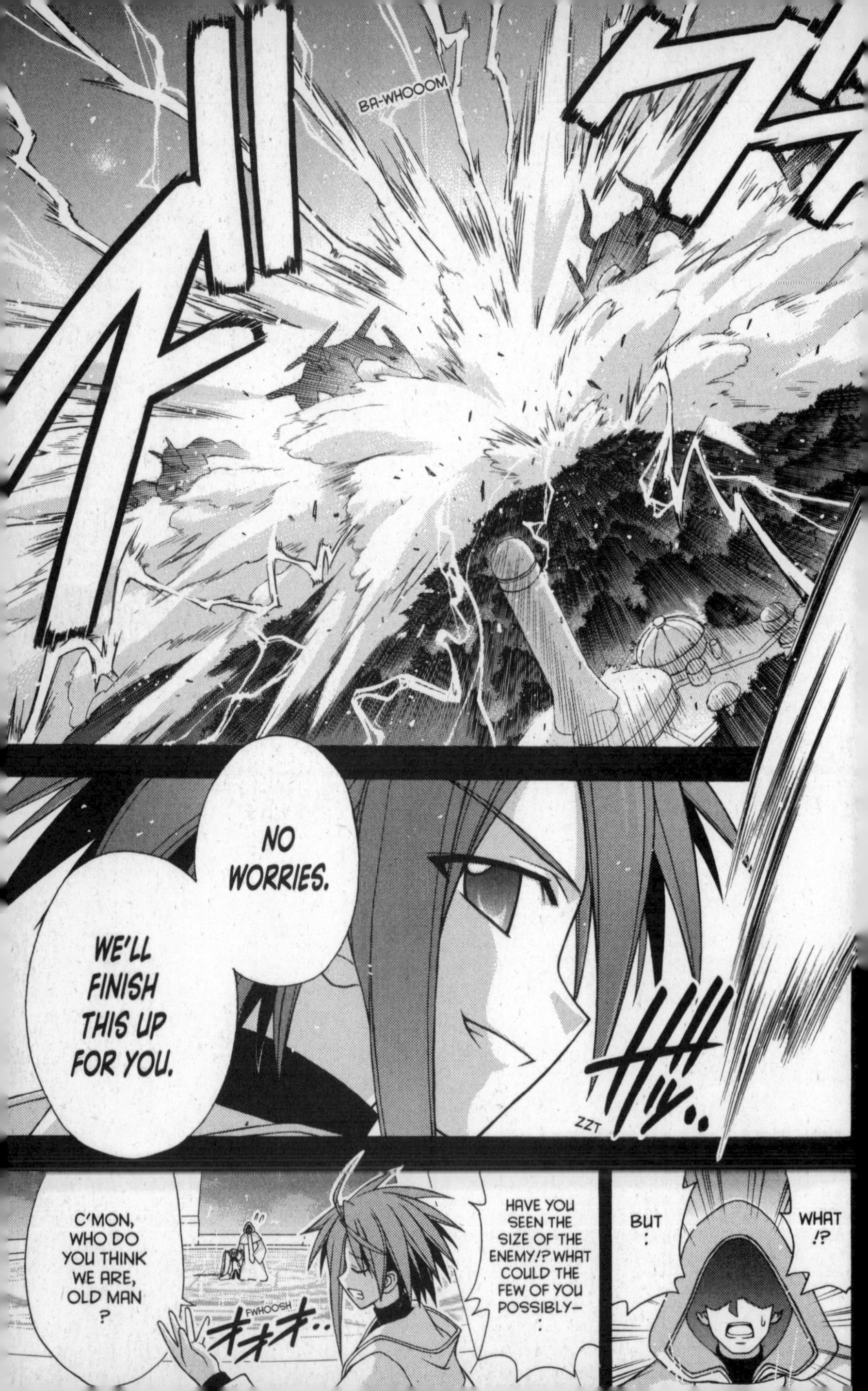
BA-WHOOOM
NO WORRIES.
WE'LL FINISH THIS UP FOR YOU.
ZZT
WHAT!?
BUT...
HAVE YOU SEEN THE SIZE OF THE ENEMY!? WHAT COULD THE FEW OF YOU POSSIBLY—...
C'MON, WHO DO YOU THINK WE ARE, OLD MAN?
FWHOOSH

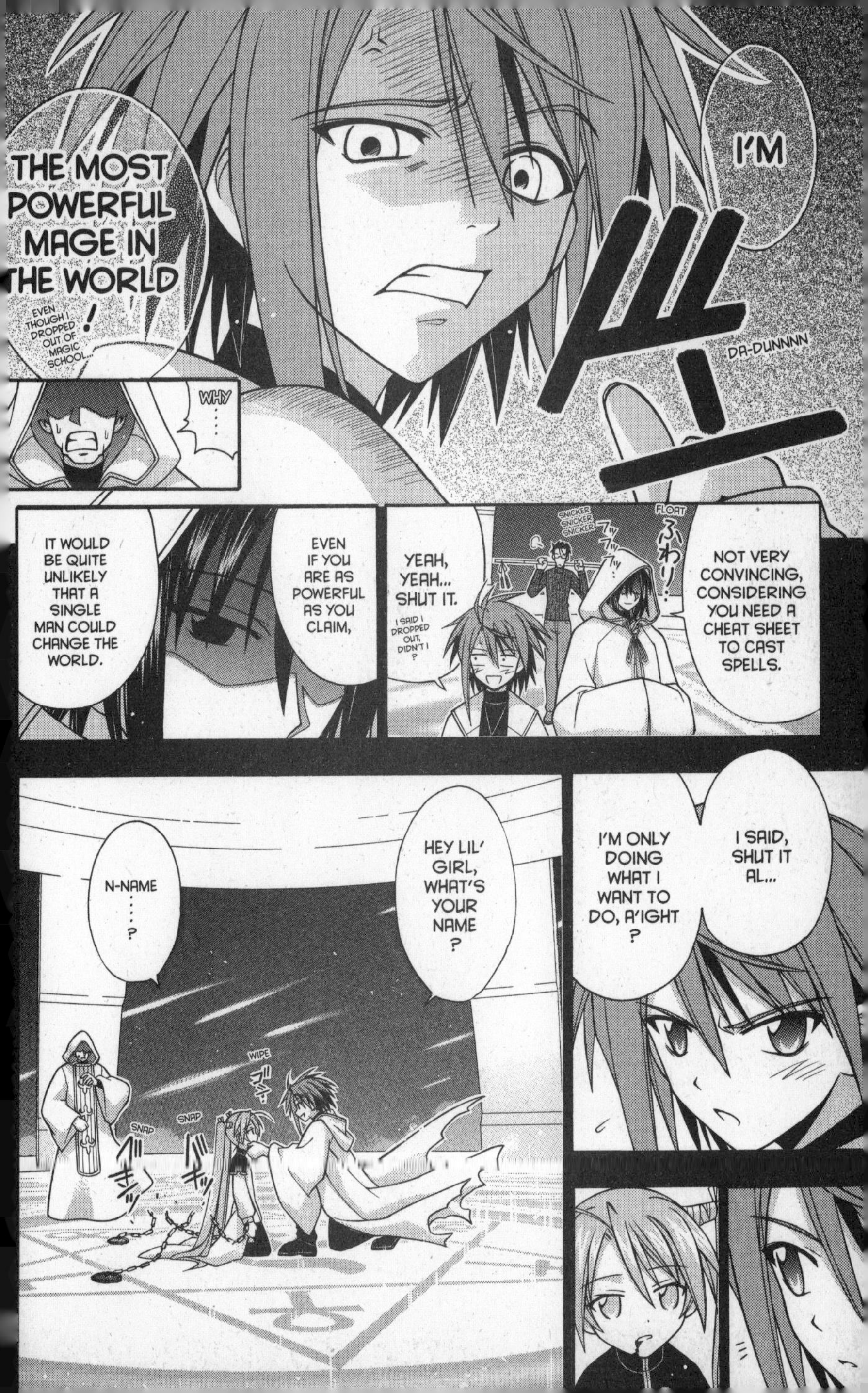

I'M
THE MOST POWERFUL MAGE IN THE WORLD!
EVEN THOUGH I DROPPED OUT OF MAGIC SCHOOL...
DA-DUNNNN
WHY....
NOT VERY CONVINCING, CONSIDERING YOU NEED A CHEAT SHEET TO CAST SPELLS.
FLOAT
SNICKER SNICKER SNICKER
YEAH, YEAH... SHUT IT.
I SAID I DROPPED OUT, DIDN'T I?
EVEN IF YOU ARE AS POWERFUL AS YOU CLAIM,
IT WOULD BE QUITE UNLIKELY THAT A SINGLE MAN COULD CHANGE THE WORLD.
I SAID, SHUT IT AL...
I'M ONLY DOING WHAT I WANT TO DO, A'IGHT?
HEY LIL' GIRL, WHAT'S YOUR NAME?
N-NAME....?
WIPE
SNAP
SNAP

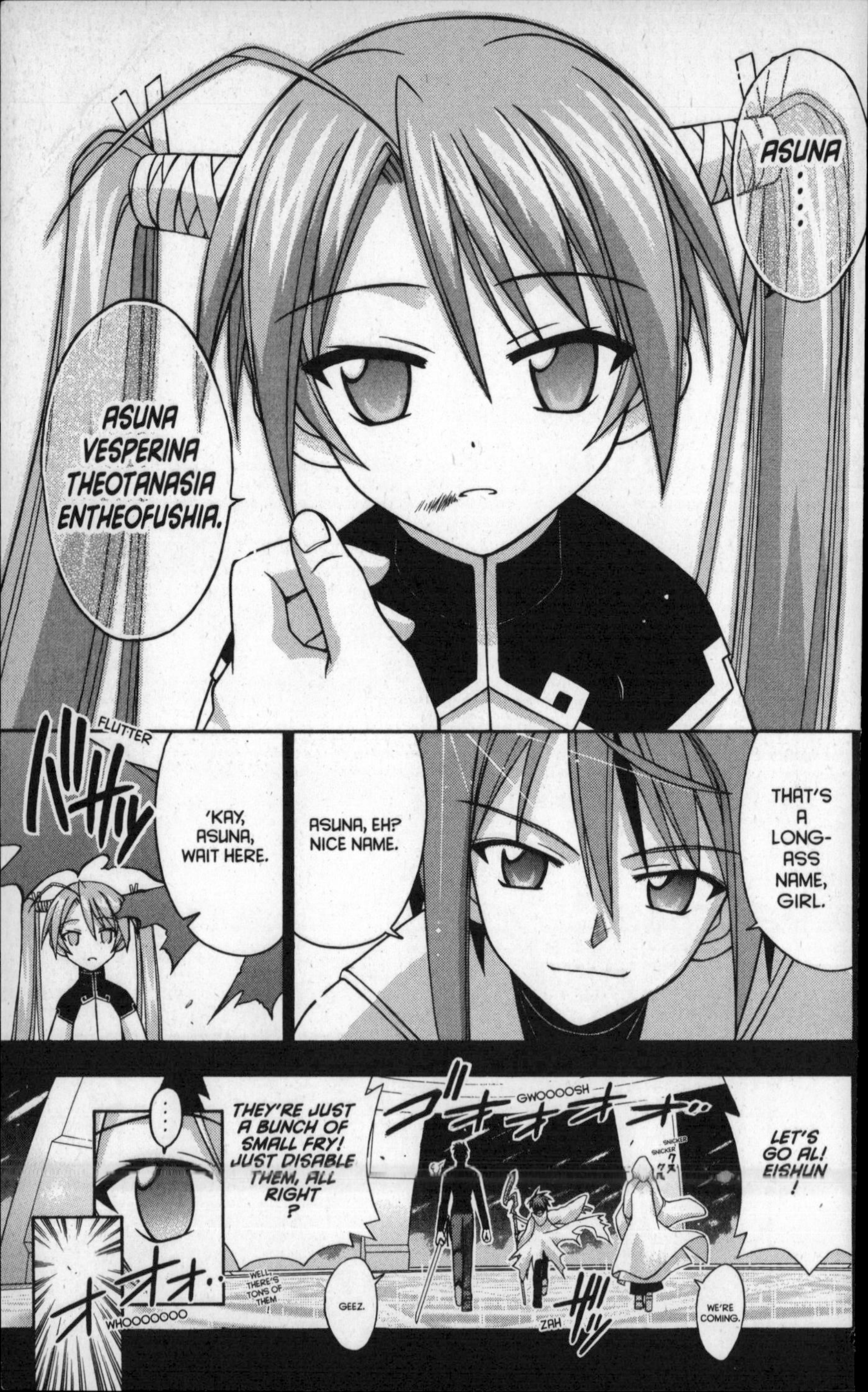
ASUNA ....
ASUNA VESPERINA THEOTANASIA ENTHEOFUSHIA.
THAT'S A LONG-ASS NAME, GIRL.
ASUNA, EH? NICE NAME.
FLUTTER
'KAY, ASUNA, WAIT HERE.
LET'S GO AL! EISHUN!
SNICKER SNICKER
GWOOOOSH
THEY'RE JUST A BUNCH OF SMALL FRY! JUST DISABLE THEM, ALL RIGHT?
WE'RE COMING.
ZAH
GEEZ.
WELL, THERE'S TONS OF THEM
...
WHOOOOOOO

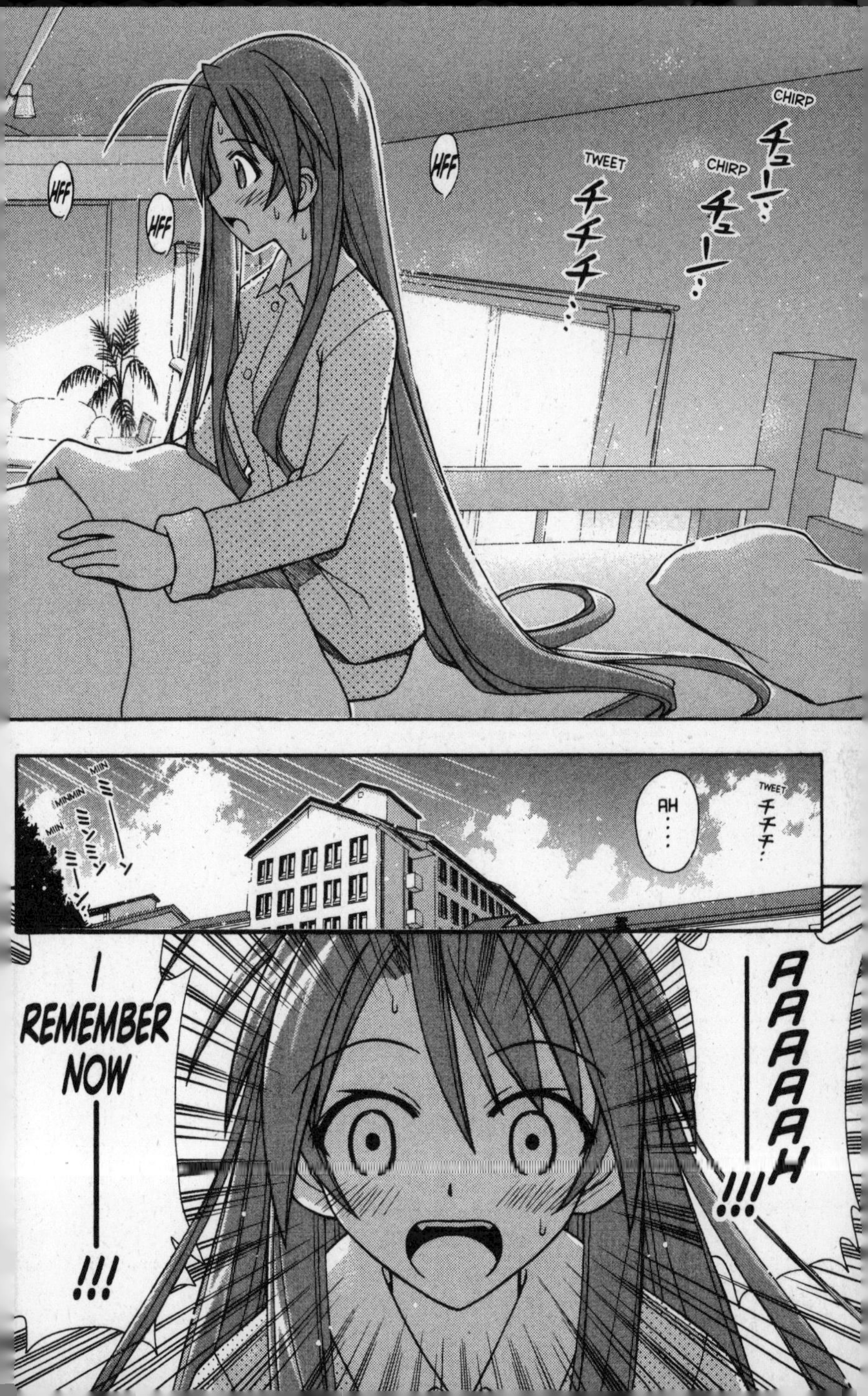
CHIRP
チュ〜ッ…
CHIRP
チュ〜ッ…
TWEET
チチチ…
HFF
HFF
HFF
TWEET
チチチ…
AH…..
MIIN
ミーン
MINMIN
ミンミン
MIIN
ミーン
AAAAAAH—!!!
I REMEMBER NOW——!!!

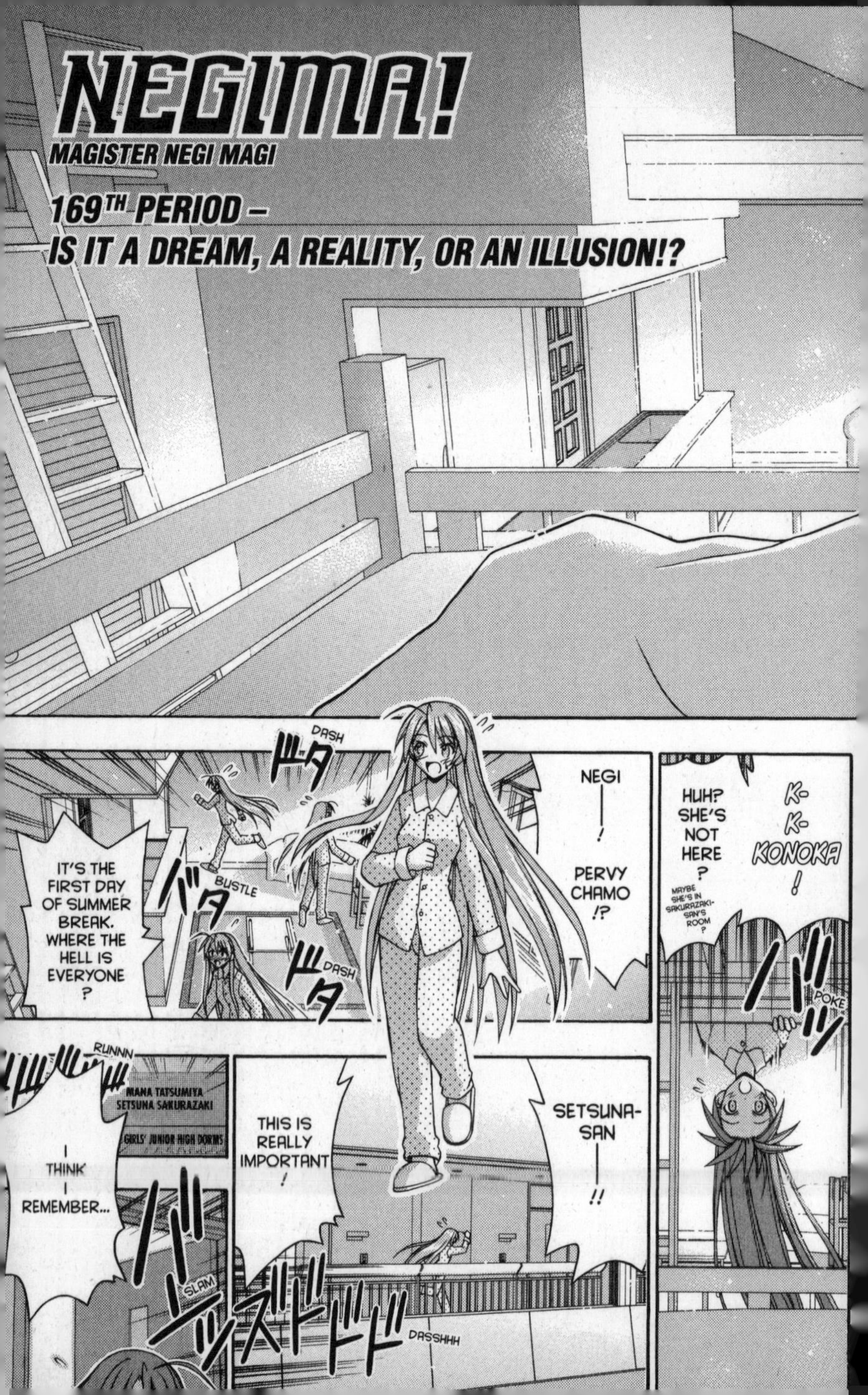
NEGIMA!
MAGISTER NEGI MAGI
169TH PERIOD – IS IT A DREAM, A REALITY, OR AN ILLUSION!?
HUH? SHE'S NOT HERE?
K-K-KONOKA!
MAYBE SHE'S IN SAKURAZAKI-SAN'S ROOM?
POKE
NEGI—!
PERVY CHAMO!?
DASH
IT'S THE FIRST DAY OF SUMMER BREAK. WHERE THE HELL IS EVERYONE?
BUSTLE
DASH
SETSUNA-SAN—!!
THIS IS REALLY IMPORTANT!
DASSHHH
RUNNN
MANA TATSUMIYA
SETSUNA SAKURAZAKI
GIRLS' JUNIOR HIGH DORMS
I THINK I REMEMBER...
SLAM

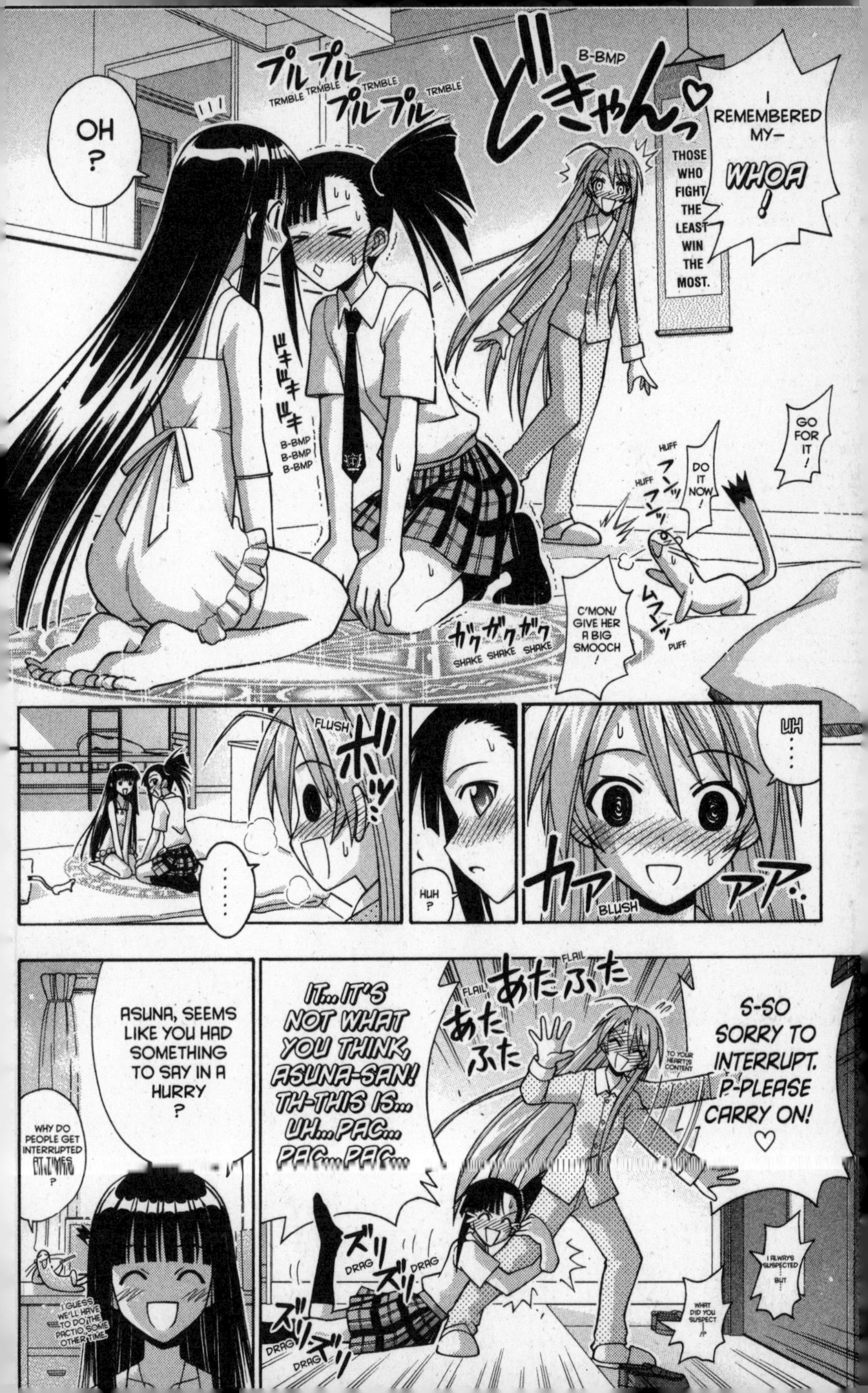
I REMEMBERED MY—
WHOA!
THOSE WHO FIGHT THE LEAST WIN THE MOST.
どきゅんっ♡
B-BMP
プルプル
TRMBLE TRMBLE
プルプル
TRMBLE TRMBLE
OH?
ドキドキドキ
B-BMP B-BMP B-BMP
GO FOR IT!
DO IT NOW!
フンッフンッ
HUFF HUFF
C'MON/ GIVE HER A BIG SMOOCH!
ムフンッ
PUFF
ガクガクガク
SHAKE SHAKE SHAKE
UH.....
カァァ
BLUSH
HUH?
ボッ
FLUSH
......
S-SO SORRY TO INTERRUPT. P-PLEASE CARRY ON! ♡
TO YOUR HEART'S CONTENT
あたふた あたふた
FLAIL FLAIL
IT...IT'S NOT WHAT YOU THINK, ASUNA-SAN! TH-THIS IS... UH...PAC... PAC...PAC...
I ALWAYS SUSPECTED... BUT
WHAT DID YOU SUSPECT!?
ズリズリ
DRAG DRAG
ズリズリ
DRAG DRAG
ASUNA, SEEMS LIKE YOU HAD SOMETHING TO SAY IN A HURRY?
WHY DO PEOPLE GET INTERRUPTED AT TIMES?
I GUESS WE'LL HAVE TO DO THE PACTIO SOME OTHER TIME.

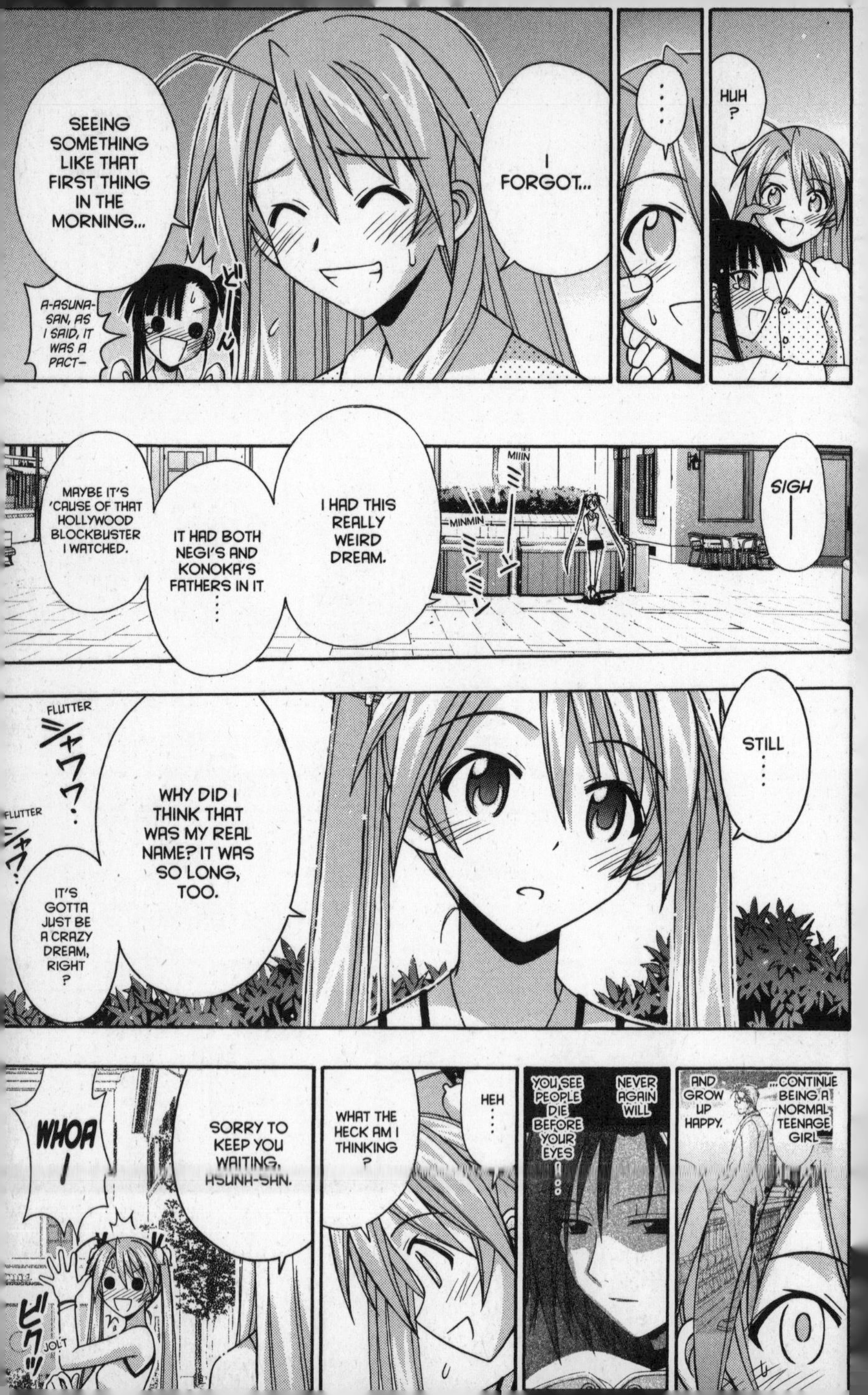
HUH ?
....
I FORGOT...
SEEING SOMETHING LIKE THAT FIRST THING IN THE MORNING...
A-ASUNA-SAN, AS I SAID, IT WAS A PACT–
SIGH
MIIIN
MINMIN
I HAD THIS REALLY WEIRD DREAM.
IT HAD BOTH NEGI'S AND KONOKA'S FATHERS IN IT ....
MAYBE IT'S 'CAUSE OF THAT HOLLYWOOD BLOCKBUSTER I WATCHED.
STILL ....
WHY DID I THINK THAT WAS MY REAL NAME? IT WAS SO LONG, TOO.
FLUTTER
FLUTTER
IT'S GOTTA JUST BE A CRAZY DREAM, RIGHT ?
...CONTINUE BEING A NORMAL TEENAGE GIRL
AND GROW UP HAPPY.
NEVER AGAIN WILL
YOU SEE PEOPLE DIE BEFORE YOUR EYES !!...
HEH ....
WHAT THE HECK AM I THINKING ?
SORRY TO KEEP YOU WAITING, ASUNA-SAN.
WHOA !
JOLT

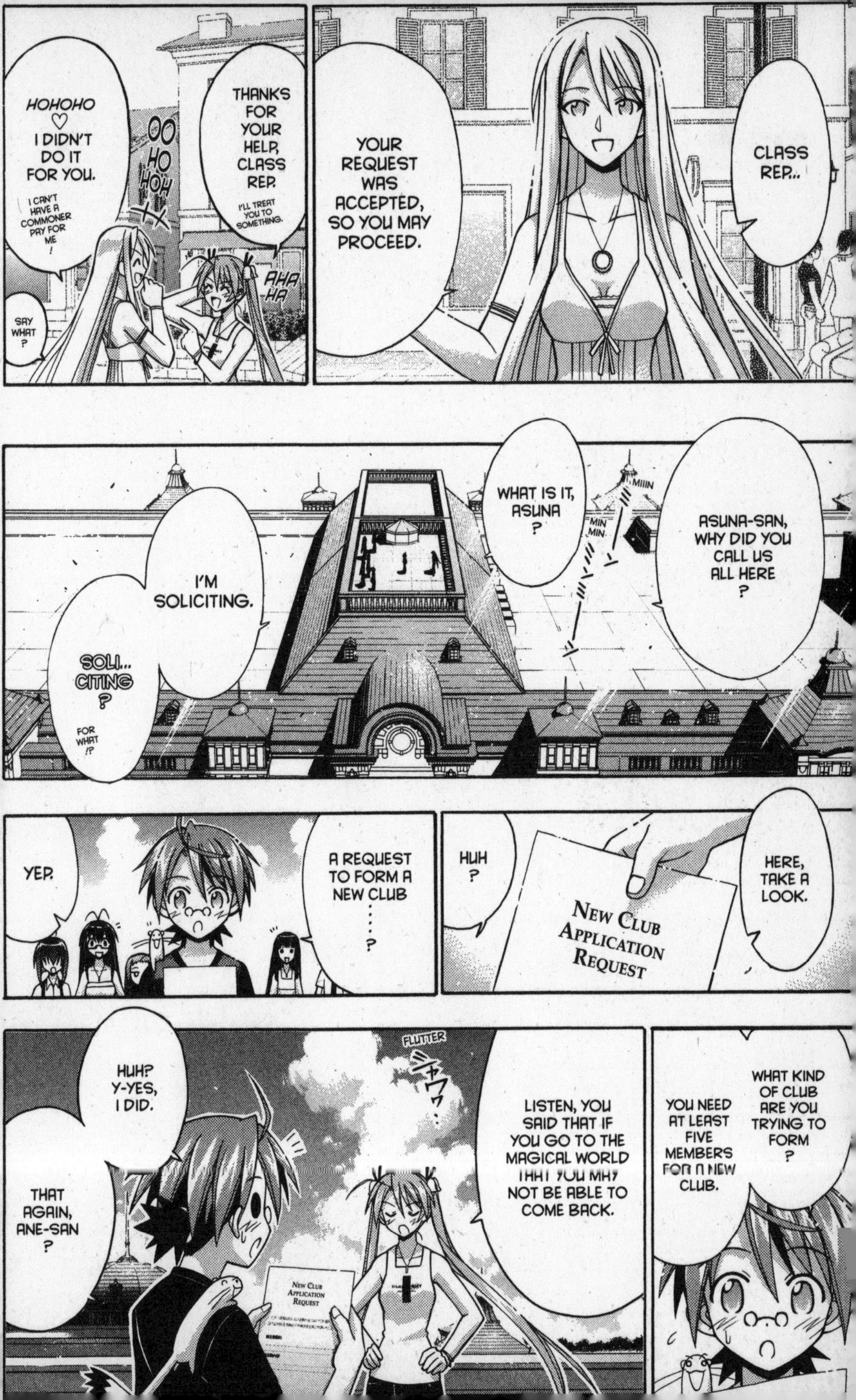

CLASS REP...
YOUR REQUEST WAS ACCEPTED, SO YOU MAY PROCEED.
THANKS FOR YOUR HELP, CLASS REP.
I'LL TREAT YOU TO SOMETHING.
OO HO HOH
HOHOHO ♡ I DIDN'T DO IT FOR YOU.
I CAN'T HAVE A COMMONER PAY FOR ME!
AHA HA
SAY WHAT?
ASUNA-SAN, WHY DID YOU CALL US ALL HERE?
MIIIN
MIN MIN
WHAT IS IT, ASUNA?
I'M SOLICITING.
SOLI... CITING?
FOR WHAT!?
HERE, TAKE A LOOK.
NEW CLUB APPLICATION REQUEST
HUH?
A REQUEST TO FORM A NEW CLUB.....?
YEP.
WHAT KIND OF CLUB ARE YOU TRYING TO FORM?
YOU NEED AT LEAST FIVE MEMBERS FOR A NEW CLUB.
LISTEN, YOU SAID THAT IF YOU GO TO THE MAGICAL WORLD THAT YOU MAY NOT BE ABLE TO COME BACK.
FLUTTER
HUH? Y-YES, I DID.
NEW CLUB APPLICATION REQUEST
THAT AGAIN, ANE-SAN?

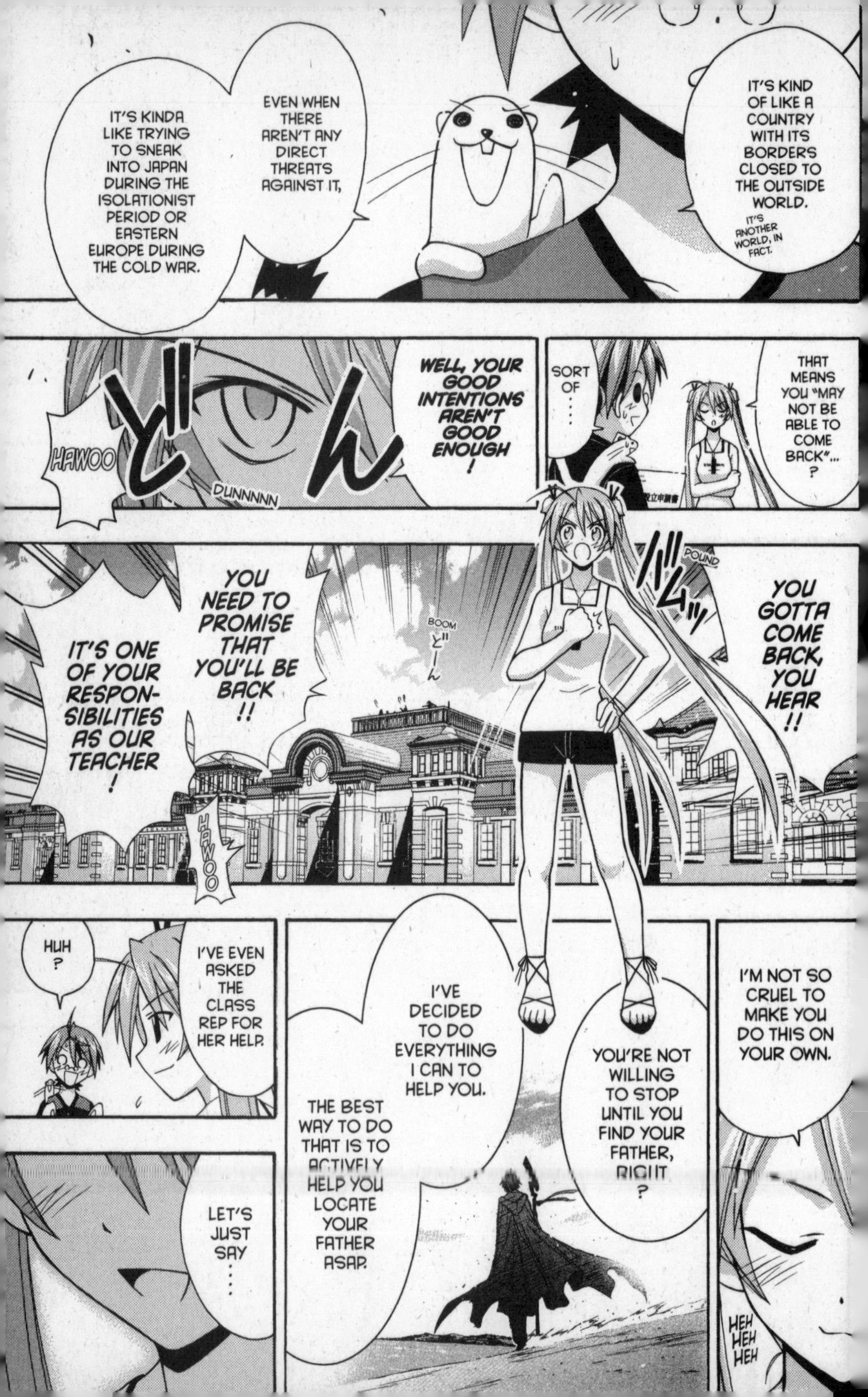

IT'S KIND OF LIKE A COUNTRY WITH ITS BORDERS CLOSED TO THE OUTSIDE WORLD.
IT'S ANOTHER WORLD, IN FACT.
EVEN WHEN THERE AREN'T ANY DIRECT THREATS AGAINST IT,
IT'S KINDA LIKE TRYING TO SNEAK INTO JAPAN DURING THE ISOLATIONIST PERIOD OR EASTERN EUROPE DURING THE COLD WAR.
THAT MEANS YOU "MAY NOT BE ABLE TO COME BACK"...?
SORT OF....
WELL, YOUR GOOD INTENTIONS AREN'T GOOD ENOUGH!
HAWOO
どん
DUNNNNN
ドム
POUND
YOU GOTTA COME BACK, YOU HEAR!!
BOOM
どーん
YOU NEED TO PROMISE THAT YOU'LL BE BACK!!
IT'S ONE OF YOUR RESPONSIBILITIES AS OUR TEACHER!
HAWOO
I'M NOT SO CRUEL TO MAKE YOU DO THIS ON YOUR OWN.
HEH HEH HEH
YOU'RE NOT WILLING TO STOP UNTIL YOU FIND YOUR FATHER, RIGHT?
I'VE DECIDED TO DO EVERYTHING I CAN TO HELP YOU.
THE BEST WAY TO DO THAT IS TO ACTIVELY HELP YOU LOCATE YOUR FATHER ASAP.
I'VE EVEN ASKED THE CLASS REP FOR HER HELP.
HUH?
LET'S JUST SAY....

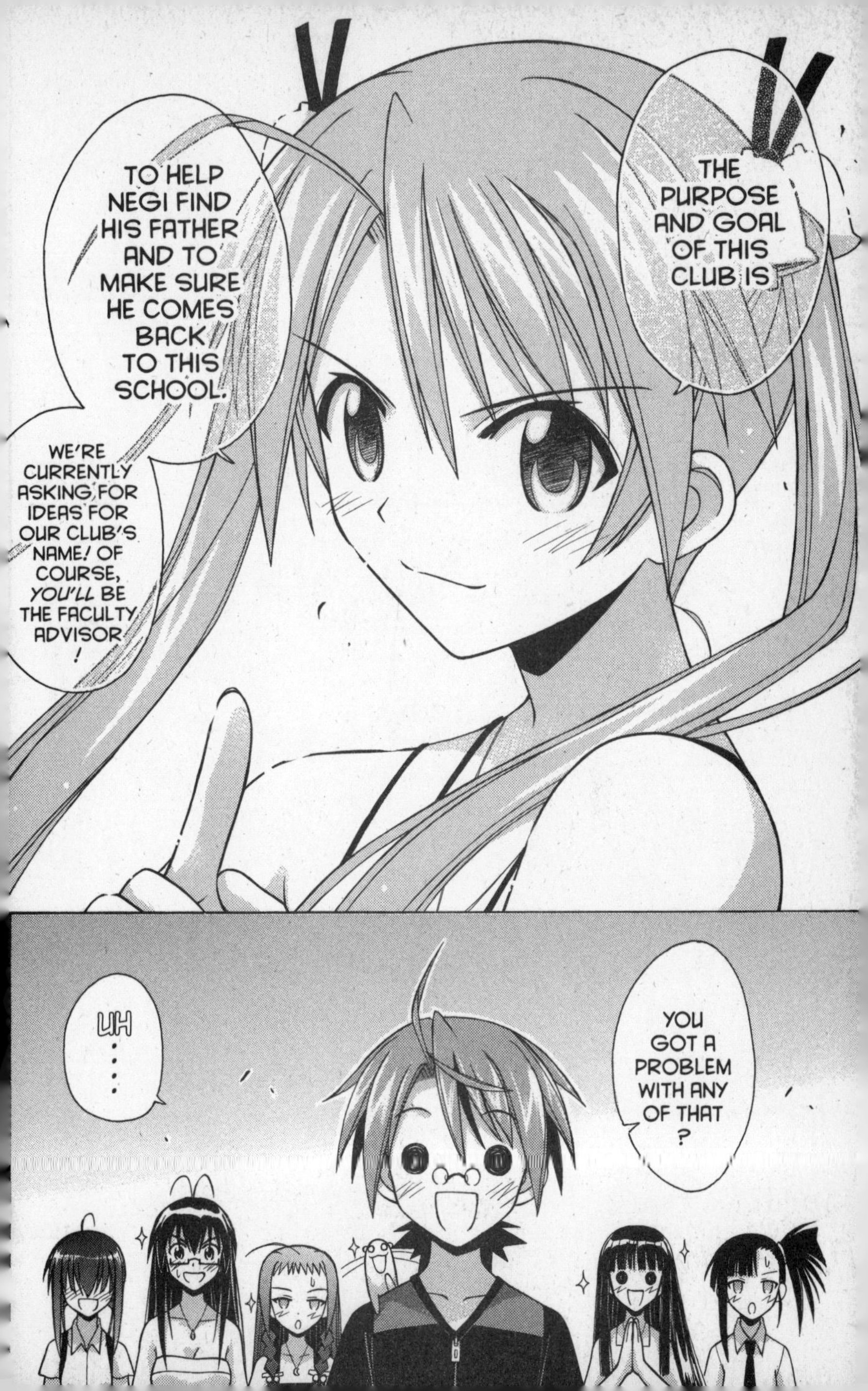
THE PURPOSE AND GOAL OF THIS CLUB IS
TO HELP NEGI FIND HIS FATHER AND TO MAKE SURE HE COMES BACK TO THIS SCHOOL.
WE'RE CURRENTLY ASKING FOR IDEAS FOR OUR CLUB'S NAME! OF COURSE, *YOU'LL* BE THE FACULTY ADVISOR!
YOU GOT A PROBLEM WITH ANY OF THAT?
UH....

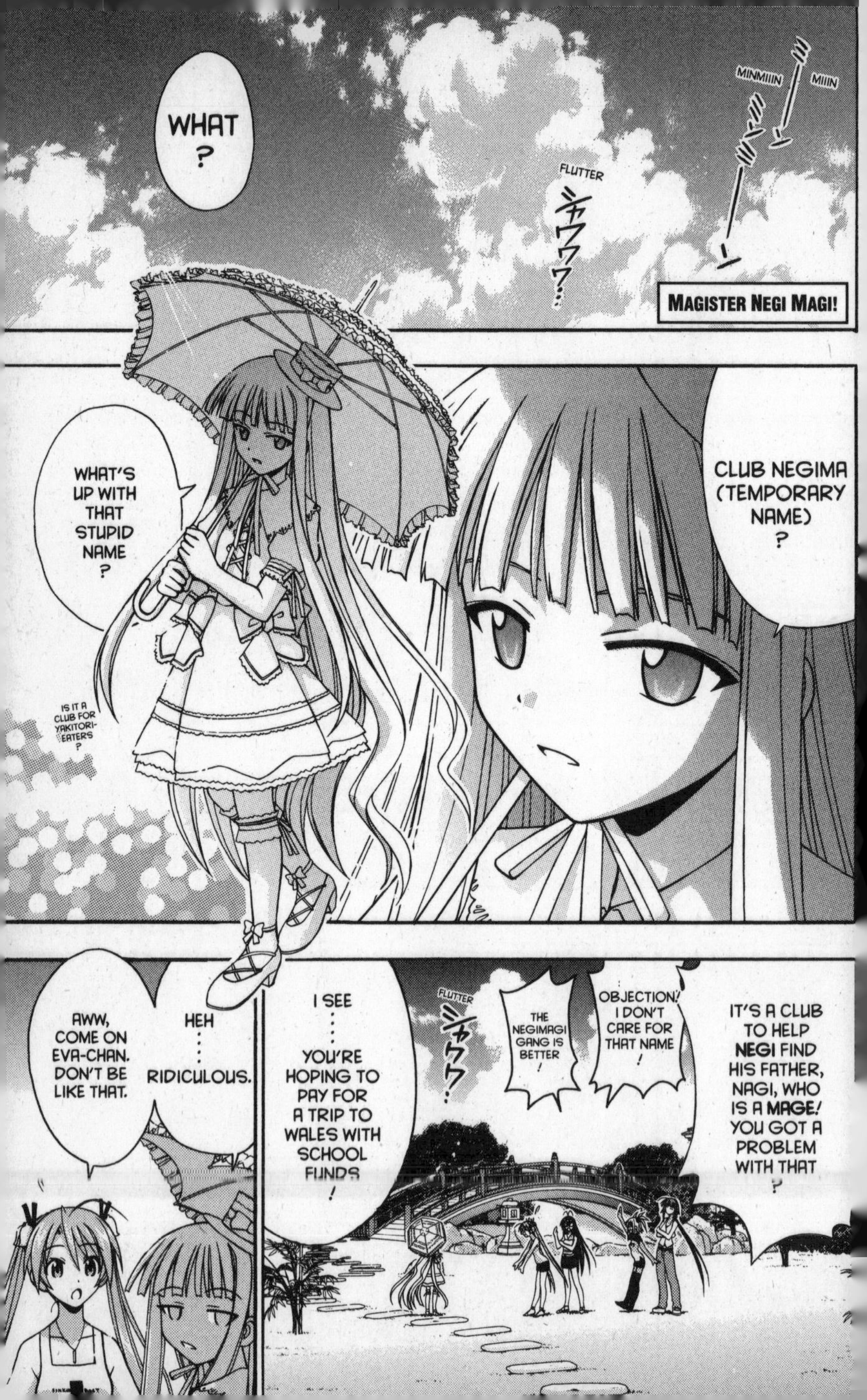
MINMIIN
MIIN
FLUTTER
シャワワワ…
WHAT?
MAGISTER NEGI MAGI!
CLUB NEGIMA (TEMPORARY NAME)?
WHAT'S UP WITH THAT STUPID NAME?
IS IT A CLUB FOR YAKITORI-EATERS?
IT'S A CLUB TO HELP NEGI FIND HIS FATHER, NAGI, WHO IS A MAGE! YOU GOT A PROBLEM WITH THAT?
OBJECTION! I DON'T CARE FOR THAT NAME!
THE NEGIMAGI GANG IS BETTER!
FLUTTER
シャワワ…
I SEE… YOU'RE HOPING TO PAY FOR A TRIP TO WALES WITH SCHOOL FUNDS!
HEH… RIDICULOUS.
AWW, COME ON EVA-CHAN. DON'T BE LIKE THAT.

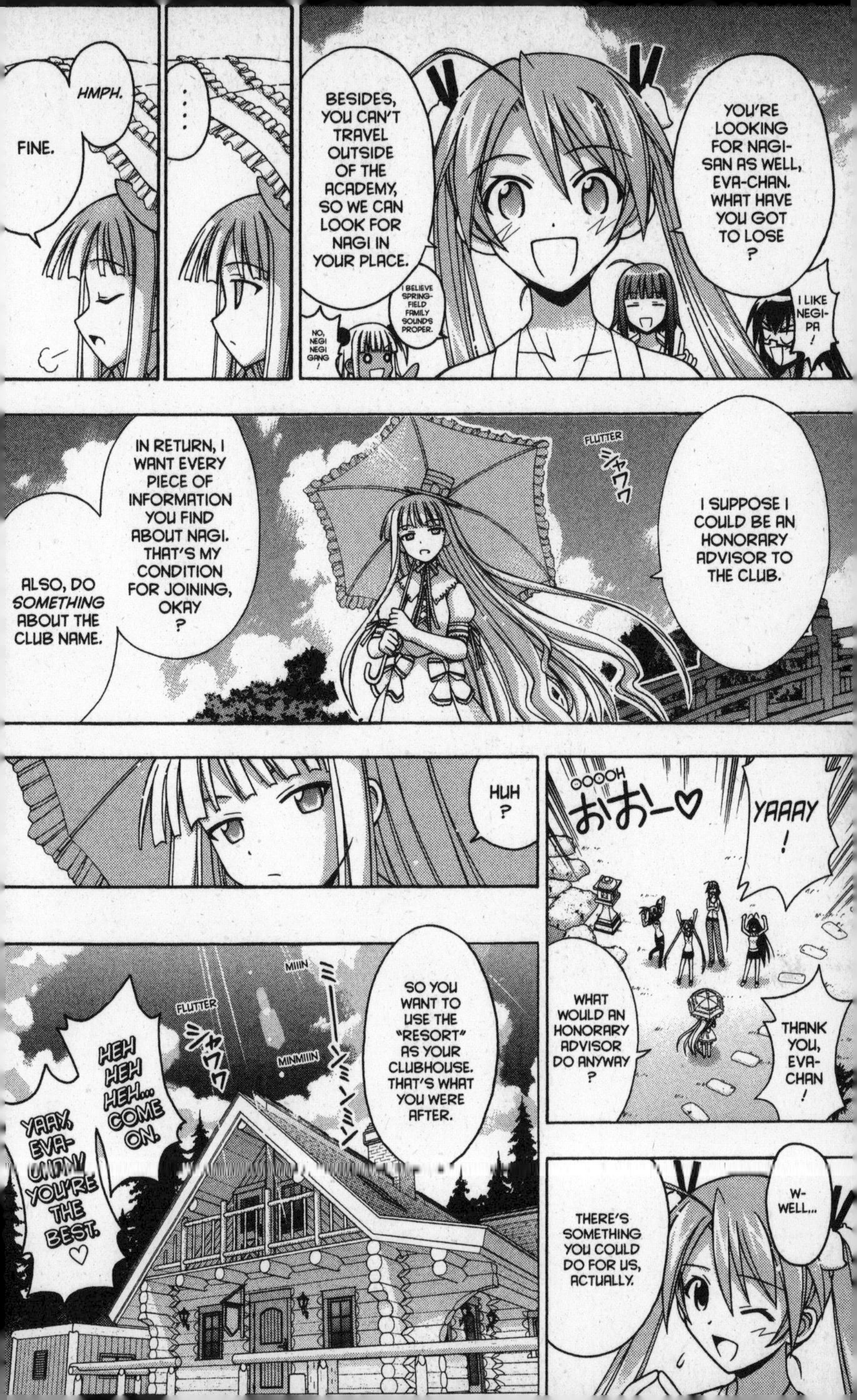
YOU'RE LOOKING FOR NAGI-SAN AS WELL, EVA-CHAN. WHAT HAVE YOU GOT TO LOSE?
I LIKE NEGI-PA!
BESIDES, YOU CAN'T TRAVEL OUTSIDE OF THE ACADEMY, SO WE CAN LOOK FOR NAGI IN YOUR PLACE.
I BELIEVE SPRING-FIELD FAMILY SOUNDS PROPER.
NO, NEGI NEGI GANG!
....
HMPH.
FINE.
I SUPPOSE I COULD BE AN HONORARY ADVISOR TO THE CLUB.
FLUTTER
シャワワ
IN RETURN, I WANT EVERY PIECE OF INFORMATION YOU FIND ABOUT NAGI. THAT'S MY CONDITION FOR JOINING, OKAY?
ALSO, DO *SOMETHING* ABOUT THE CLUB NAME.
OOOOH
おおー♡
YAAAY!
THANK YOU, EVA-CHAN!
WHAT WOULD AN HONORARY ADVISOR DO ANYWAY?
HUH?
W-WELL...
THERE'S SOMETHING YOU COULD DO FOR US, ACTUALLY.
SO YOU WANT TO USE THE "RESORT" AS YOUR CLUBHOUSE. THAT'S WHAT YOU WERE AFTER.
MIIIN
MINMIIIN
ミーンミンミン
FLUTTER
シャワワ
HEH HEH HEH... COME ON.
YAAY, EVA-CHAN! YOU'RE THE BEST. ♡

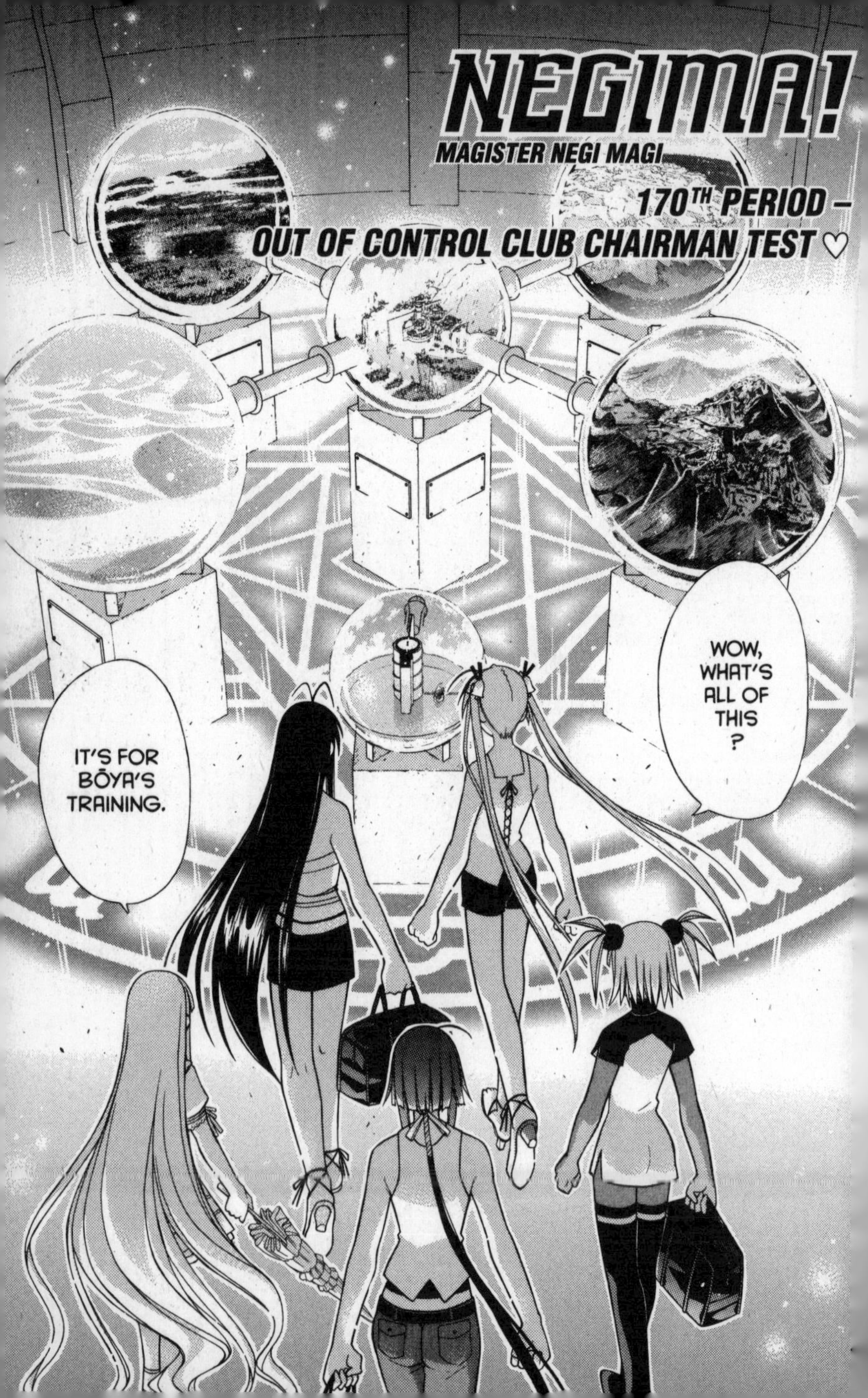
NEGIMA!
MAGISTER NEGI MAGI
170TH PERIOD – OUT OF CONTROL CLUB CHAIRMAN TEST ♡
WOW, WHAT'S ALL OF THIS?
IT'S FOR BŌYA'S TRAINING.

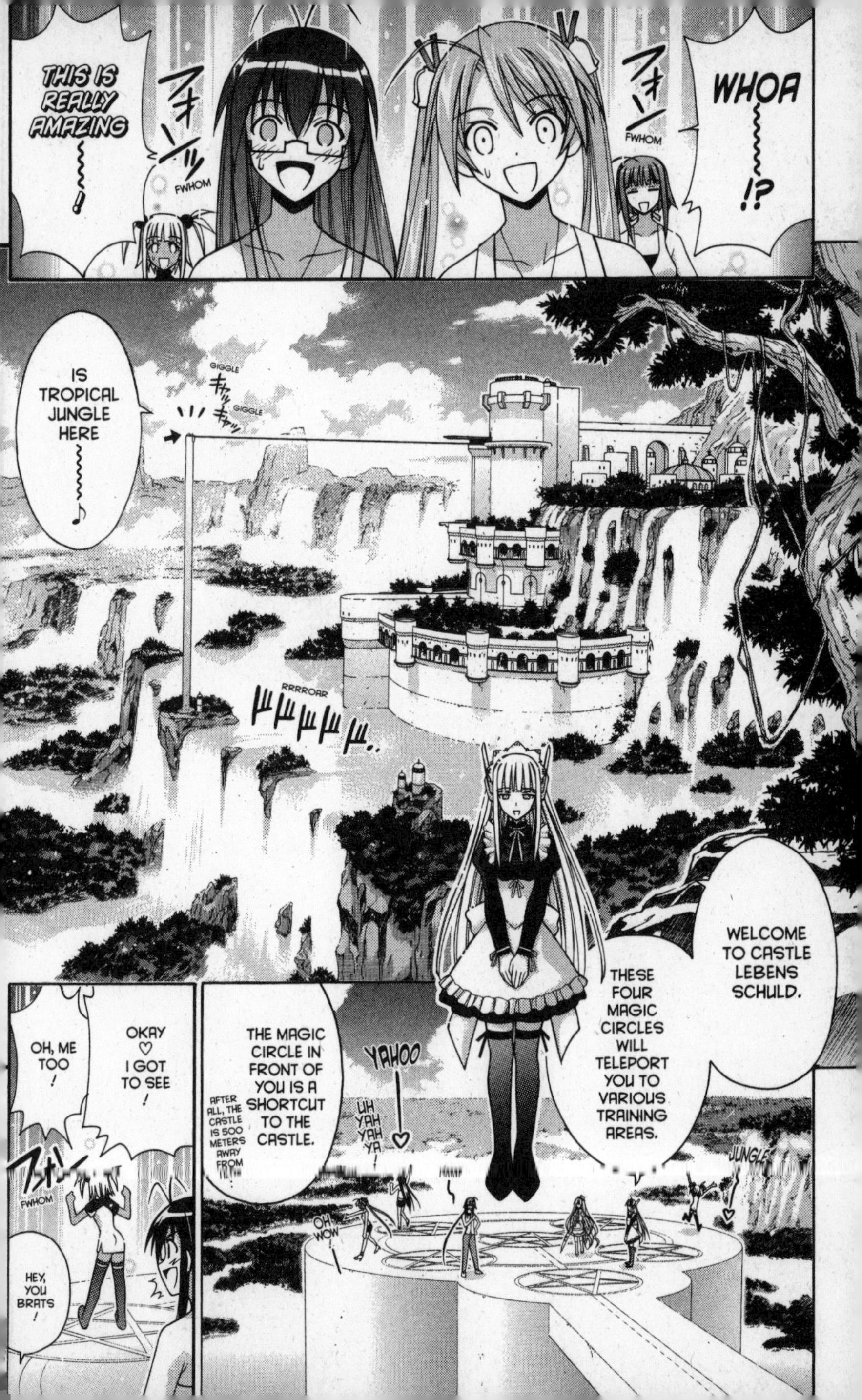
WHOA ~~~~!?
FWHOM
THIS IS REALLY AMAZING ~~~!
FWHOM
IS TROPICAL JUNGLE HERE ~~~♪
GIGGLE
GIGGLE
RRRROAR
WELCOME TO CASTLE LEBENS SCHULD.
THESE FOUR MAGIC CIRCLES WILL TELEPORT YOU TO VARIOUS TRAINING AREAS.
JUNGLE
YAHOO
UH YAH YAH YA ♥
OH WOW!
THE MAGIC CIRCLE IN FRONT OF YOU IS A SHORTCUT TO THE CASTLE.
AFTER ALL, THE CASTLE IS 500 METERS AWAY FROM
OKAY ♡ I GOT TO SEE!
OH, ME TOO!
FWHOM
HEY, YOU BRATS!

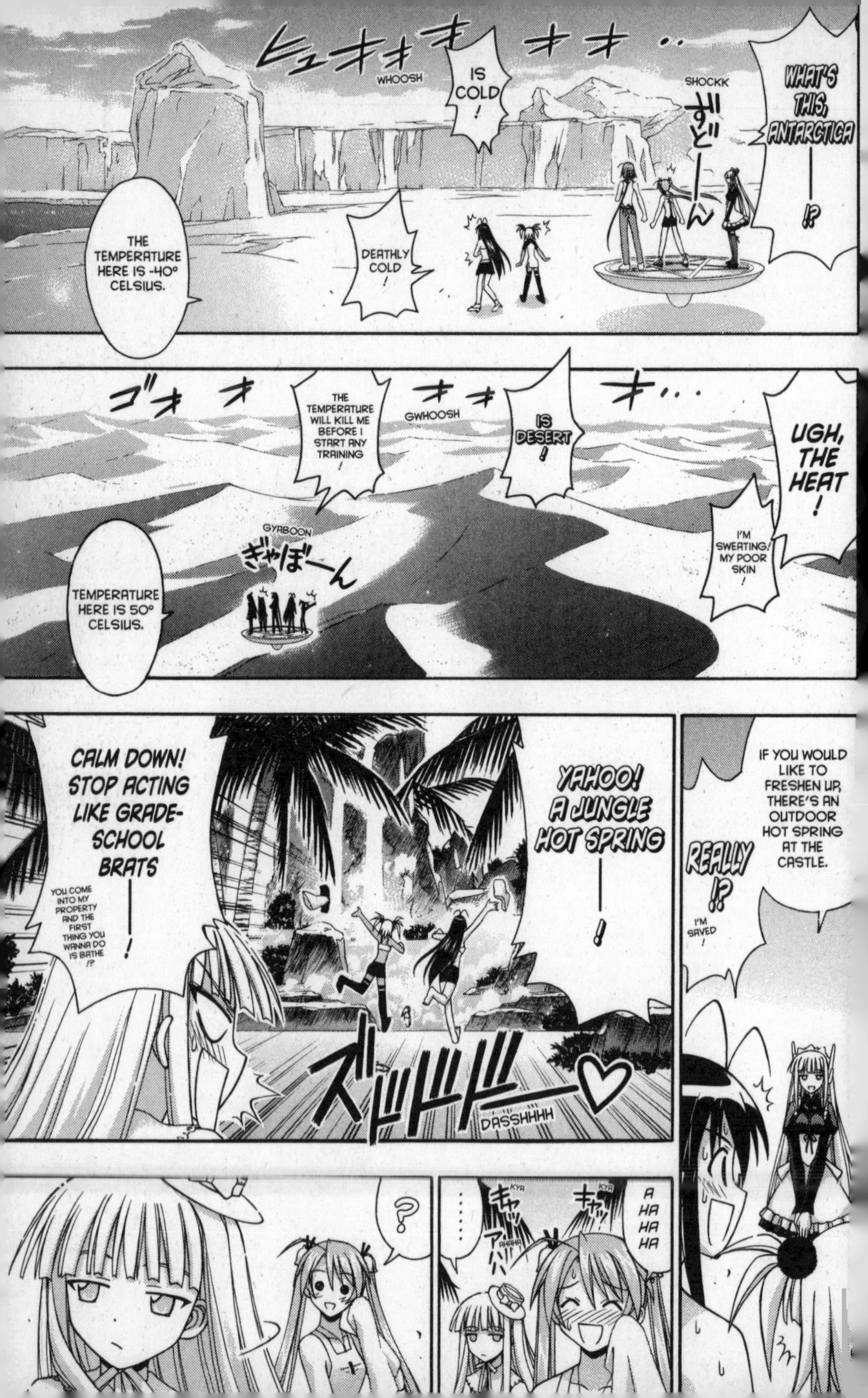
WHAT'S THIS, ANTARCTICA—!?
ずどーん
SHOCKK
IS COLD!
ヒュオォォ オオ..
WHOOSH
DEATHLY COLD!
THE TEMPERATURE HERE IS -40° CELSIUS.
UGH, THE HEAT!
I'M SWEATING! MY POOR SKIN!
IS DESERT!
ゴォォォ...
GWHOOSH
THE TEMPERATURE WILL KILL ME BEFORE I START ANY TRAINING!
ぎゃぼーん
GYABOON
TEMPERATURE HERE IS 50° CELSIUS.
IF YOU WOULD LIKE TO FRESHEN UP, THERE'S AN OUTDOOR HOT SPRING AT THE CASTLE.
REALLY!?
I'M SAVED!
YAHOO! A JUNGLE HOT SPRING—!
ズドドドドー
DASSHHHH
CALM DOWN! STOP ACTING LIKE GRADE-SCHOOL BRATS—!
YOU COME INTO MY PROPERTY AND THE FIRST THING YOU WANNA DO IS BATHE!?
A HA HA HA
キャッ
KYA
キャッ
KYA
アハハ
AHAHA
......
?

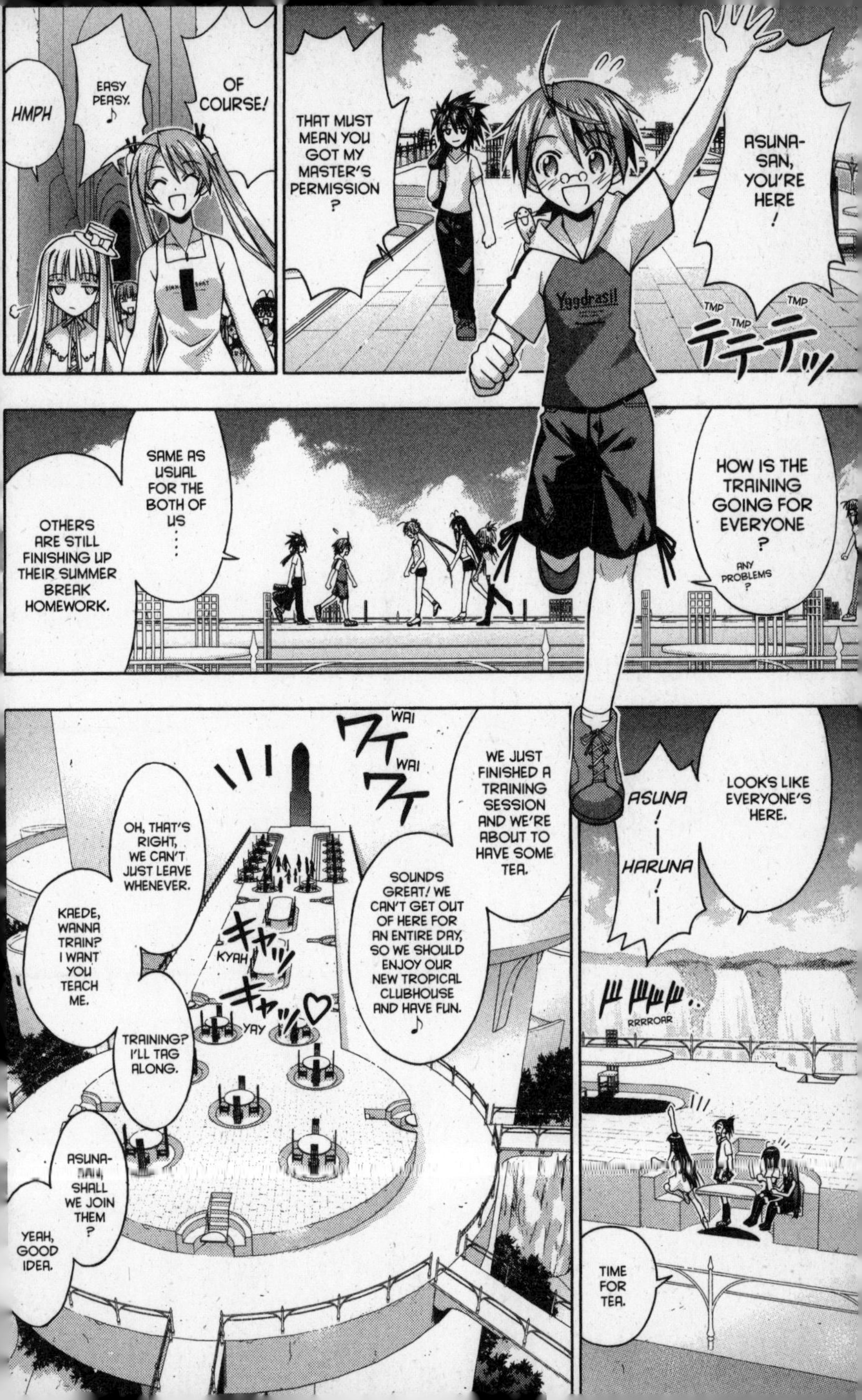
ASUNA-SAN, YOU'RE HERE!
TMP TMP TMP
THAT MUST MEAN YOU GOT MY MASTER'S PERMISSION?
OF COURSE!
EASY PEASY. ♪
HMPH
HOW IS THE TRAINING GOING FOR EVERYONE?
ANY PROBLEMS?
SAME AS USUAL FOR THE BOTH OF US...
OTHERS ARE STILL FINISHING UP THEIR SUMMER BREAK HOMEWORK.
LOOKS LIKE EVERYONE'S HERE.
ASUNA!
HARUNA!
RRRROAR
TIME FOR TEA.
WE JUST FINISHED A TRAINING SESSION AND WE'RE ABOUT TO HAVE SOME TEA.
WAI WAI
SOUNDS GREAT! WE CAN'T GET OUT OF HERE FOR AN ENTIRE DAY, SO WE SHOULD ENJOY OUR NEW TROPICAL CLUBHOUSE AND HAVE FUN. ♪
OH, THAT'S RIGHT, WE CAN'T JUST LEAVE WHENEVER.
KYAH
YAY
KAEDE, WANNA TRAIN? I WANT YOU TEACH ME.
TRAINING? I'LL TAG ALONG.
ASUNA-
SHALL WE JOIN THEM?
YEAH, GOOD IDEA.

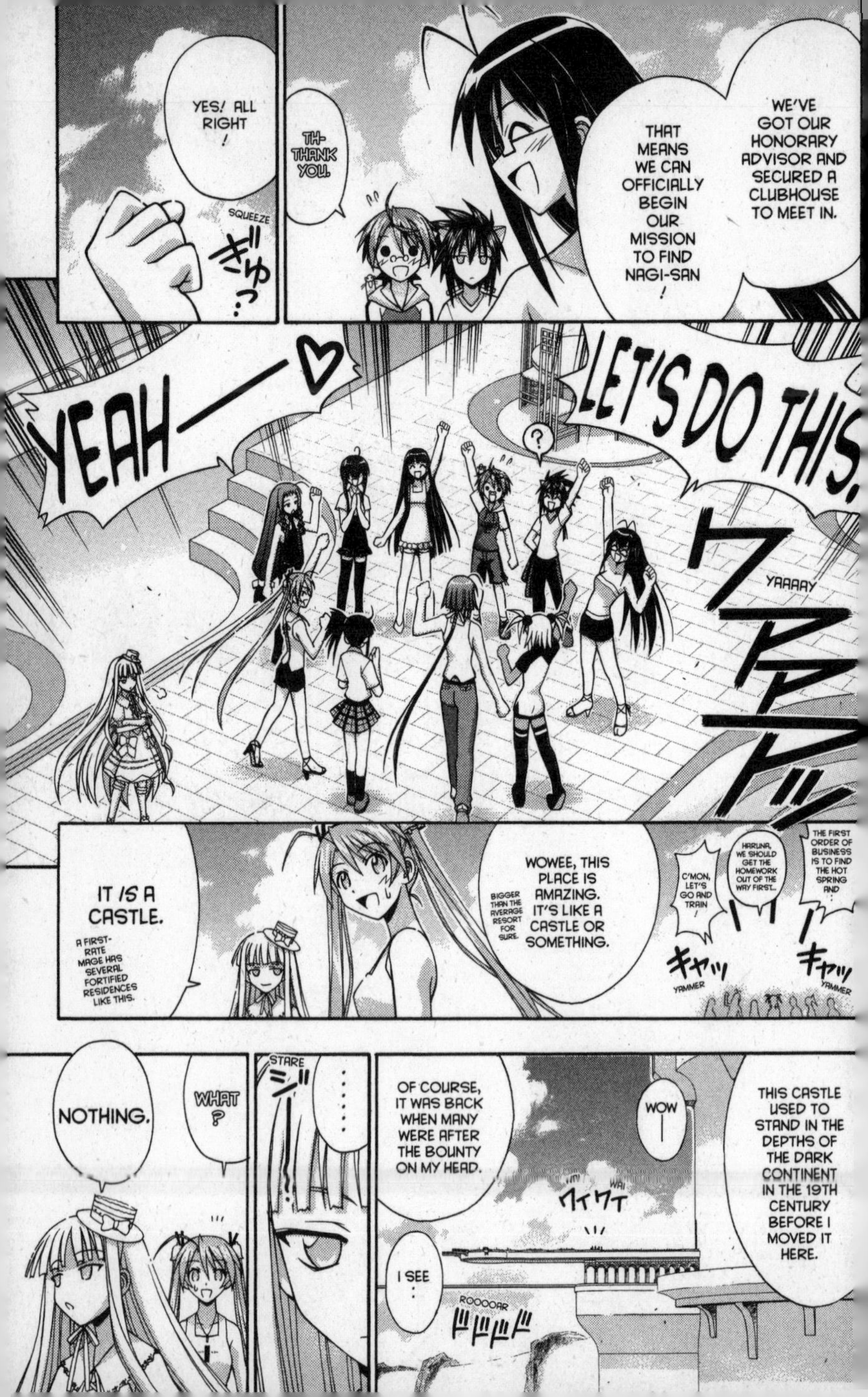
WE'VE GOT OUR HONORARY ADVISOR AND SECURED A CLUBHOUSE TO MEET IN.
THAT MEANS WE CAN OFFICIALLY BEGIN OUR MISSION TO FIND NAGI-SAN!
TH-THANK YOU.
YES! ALL RIGHT!
SQUEEZE
ぎゅっ...
LET'S DO THIS,
YEAH—♥
?
ワアアッ
YAAAAY
THE FIRST ORDER OF BUSINESS IS TO FIND THE HOT SPRING AND:
HARUNA, WE SHOULD GET THE HOMEWORK OUT OF THE WAY FIRST...
C'MON, LET'S GO AND TRAIN!
キャッ
YAMMER
キャッ
YAMMER
WOWEE, THIS PLACE IS AMAZING. IT'S LIKE A CASTLE OR SOMETHING.
BIGGER THAN THE AVERAGE RESORT FOR SURE.
IT IS A CASTLE.
A FIRST-RATE MAGE HAS SEVERAL FORTIFIED RESIDENCES LIKE THIS.
THIS CASTLE USED TO STAND IN THE DEPTHS OF THE DARK CONTINENT IN THE 19TH CENTURY BEFORE I MOVED IT HERE.
WOW—
WAI WAI
ワイワイ
OF COURSE, IT WAS BACK WHEN MANY WERE AFTER THE BOUNTY ON MY HEAD.
I SEE..
ROOOOAR
ドドドド
STARE
ジー
......
WHAT?
NOTHING.

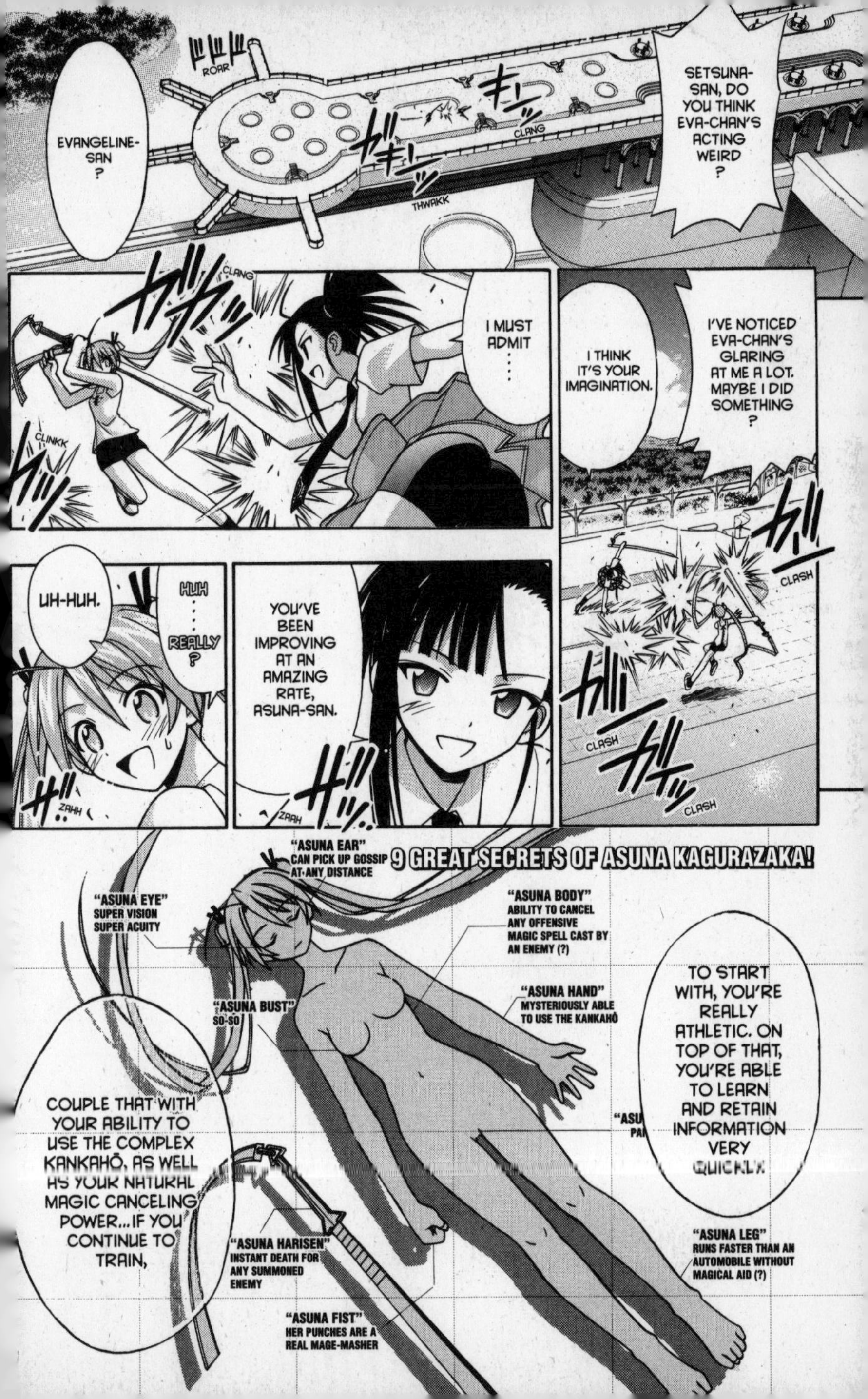
SETSUNA-SAN, DO YOU THINK EVA-CHAN'S ACTING WEIRD?
CLANG
THWAKK
ROAR
EVANGELINE-SAN?
I'VE NOTICED EVA-CHAN'S GLARING AT ME A LOT. MAYBE I DID SOMETHING?
I THINK IT'S YOUR IMAGINATION.
CLASH
CLASH
CLASH
I MUST ADMIT ...
CLANG
CLINKK
YOU'VE BEEN IMPROVING AT AN AMAZING RATE, ASUNA-SAN.
ZAHH
HUH ... REALLY?
UH-HUH.
ZAHH
9 GREAT SECRETS OF ASUNA KAGURAZAKA!
TO START WITH, YOU'RE REALLY ATHLETIC. ON TOP OF THAT, YOU'RE ABLE TO LEARN AND RETAIN INFORMATION VERY QUICKLY.
"ASUNA EAR" CAN PICK UP GOSSIP AT ANY DISTANCE
"ASUNA BODY" ABILITY TO CANCEL ANY OFFENSIVE MAGIC SPELL CAST BY AN ENEMY (?)
"ASUNA EYE" SUPER VISION SUPER ACUITY
"ASUNA HAND" MYSTERIOUSLY ABLE TO USE THE KANKAHŌ
"ASUNA BUST" SO-SO
"ASUNA LEG" RUNS FASTER THAN AN AUTOMOBILE WITHOUT MAGICAL AID (?)
"ASUNA HARISEN" INSTANT DEATH FOR ANY SUMMONED ENEMY
"ASUNA FIST" HER PUNCHES ARE A REAL MAGE-MASHER
COUPLE THAT WITH YOUR ABILITY TO USE THE COMPLEX KANKAHŌ, AS WELL AS YOUR NATURAL MAGIC CANCELING POWER...IF YOU CONTINUE TO TRAIN,

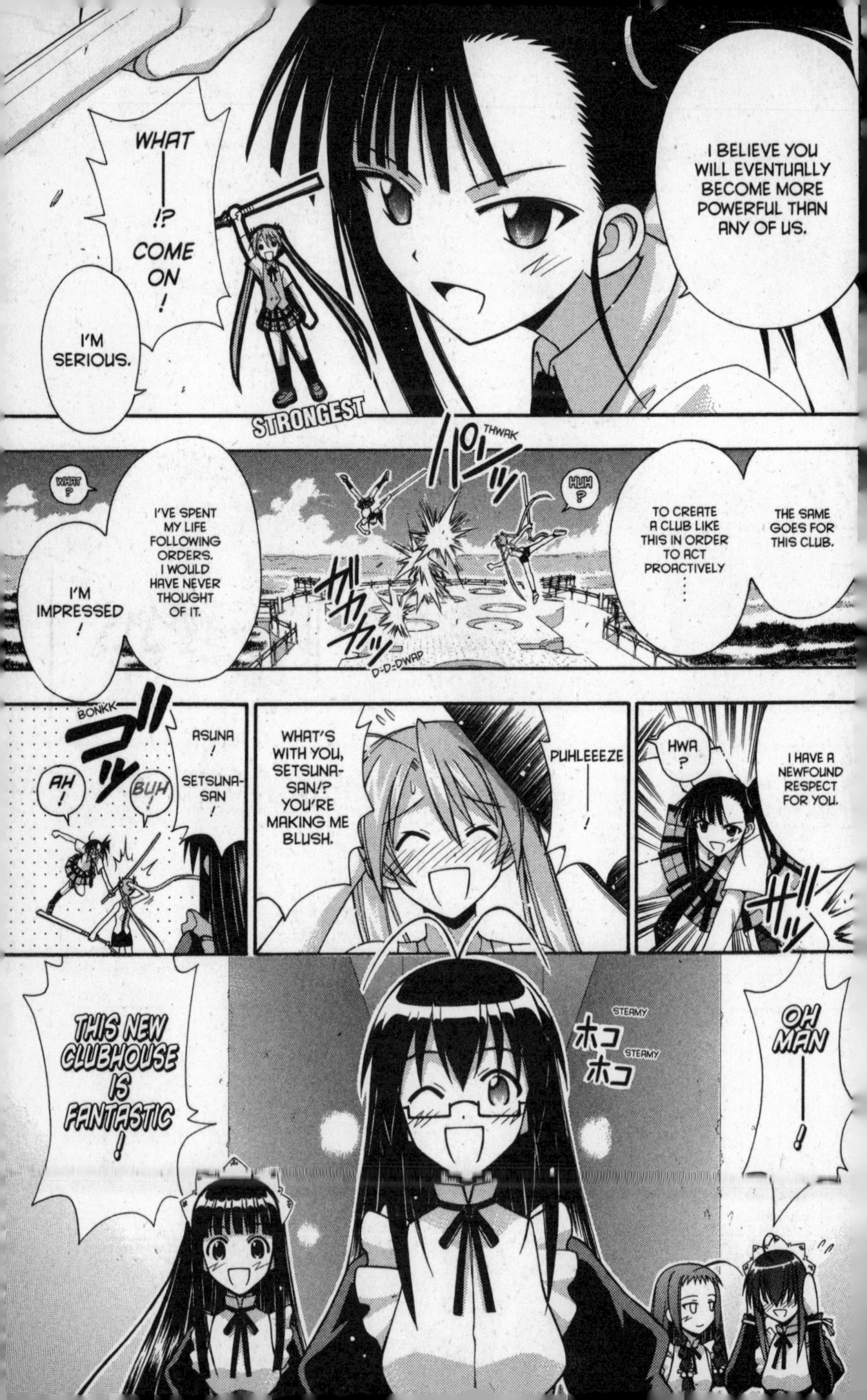
I BELIEVE YOU WILL EVENTUALLY BECOME MORE POWERFUL THAN ANY OF US.
WHAT —— !? COME ON!
I'M SERIOUS.
STRONGEST
THE SAME GOES FOR THIS CLUB.
TO CREATE A CLUB LIKE THIS IN ORDER TO ACT PROACTIVELY...
HUH?
THWAK
I'VE SPENT MY LIFE FOLLOWING ORDERS. I WOULD HAVE NEVER THOUGHT OF IT.
WHAT?
I'M IMPRESSED!
D-D-DWAP
I HAVE A NEWFOUND RESPECT FOR YOU.
HWA?
PUHLEEEZE ——!
WHAT'S WITH YOU, SETSUNA-SAN!? YOU'RE MAKING ME BLUSH.
ASUNA!
SETSUNA-SAN!
BUH!
AH!
BONKK
OH MAN ——!
STEAMY
STEAMY
THIS NEW CLUBHOUSE IS FANTASTIC!

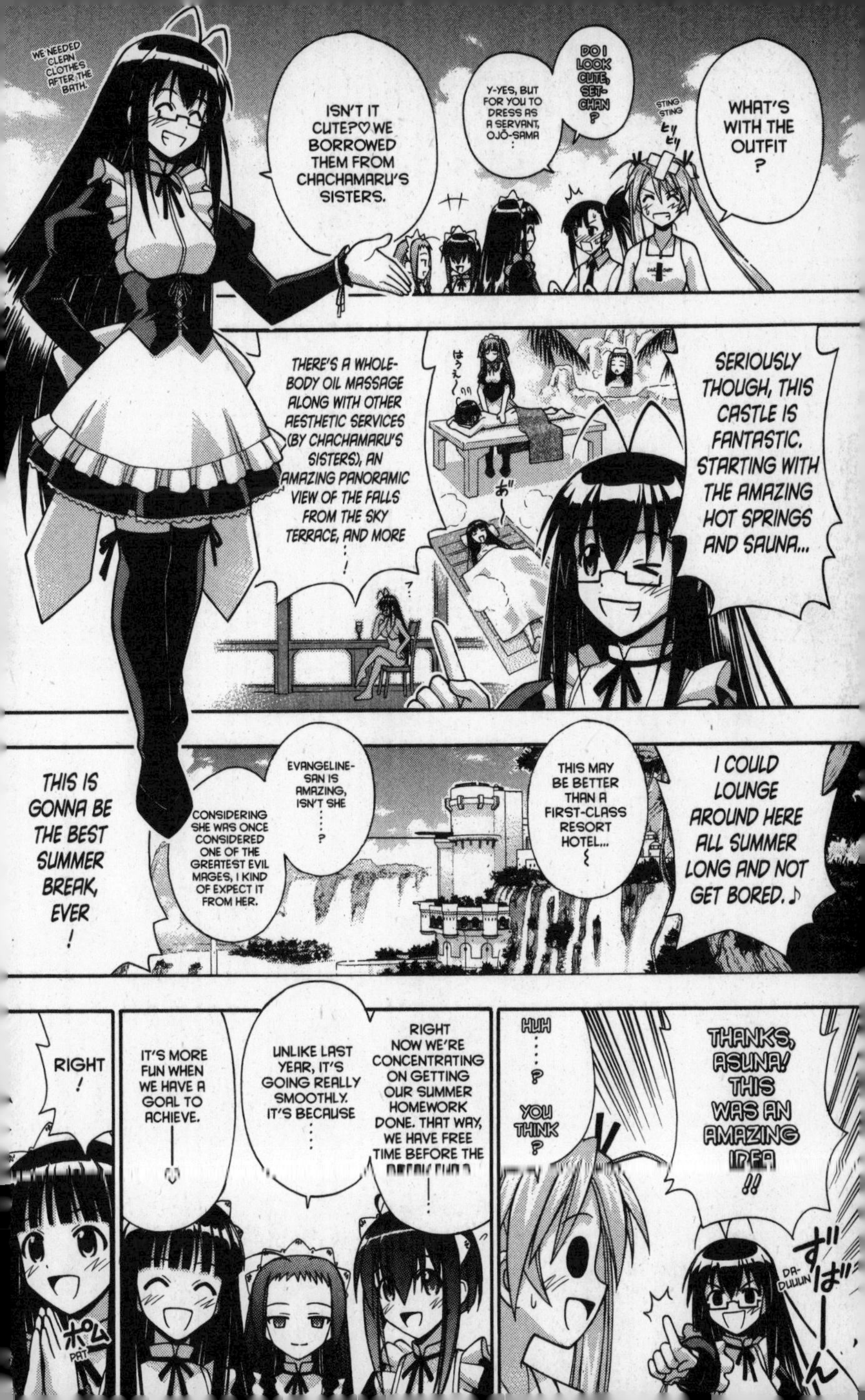
WHAT'S WITH THE OUTFIT?
STING STING
DO I LOOK CUTE, SET-CHAN?
Y-YES, BUT FOR YOU TO DRESS AS A SERVANT, OJŌ-SAMA...
ISN'T IT CUTE?♡ WE BORROWED THEM FROM CHACHAMARU'S SISTERS.
WE NEEDED CLEAN CLOTHES AFTER THE BATH.
SERIOUSLY THOUGH, THIS CASTLE IS FANTASTIC. STARTING WITH THE AMAZING HOT SPRINGS AND SAUNA...
THERE'S A WHOLE-BODY OIL MASSAGE ALONG WITH OTHER AESTHETIC SERVICES (BY CHACHAMARU'S SISTERS), AN AMAZING PANORAMIC VIEW OF THE FALLS FROM THE SKY TERRACE, AND MORE...!
I COULD LOUNGE AROUND HERE ALL SUMMER LONG AND NOT GET BORED.♪
THIS MAY BE BETTER THAN A FIRST-CLASS RESORT HOTEL...~
EVANGELINE-SAN IS AMAZING, ISN'T SHE...?
CONSIDERING SHE WAS ONCE CONSIDERED ONE OF THE GREATEST EVIL MAGES, I KIND OF EXPECT IT FROM HER.
THIS IS GONNA BE THE BEST SUMMER BREAK, EVER!
THANKS, ASUNA! THIS WAS AN AMAZING IDEA!!
DA-DUUUN
HUH...? YOU THINK?
RIGHT NOW WE'RE CONCENTRATING ON GETTING OUR SUMMER HOMEWORK DONE. THAT WAY, WE HAVE FREE TIME BEFORE THE
UNLIKE LAST YEAR, IT'S GOING REALLY SMOOTHLY. IT'S BECAUSE...
IT'S MORE FUN WHEN WE HAVE A GOAL TO ACHIEVE.
RIGHT!
PAT

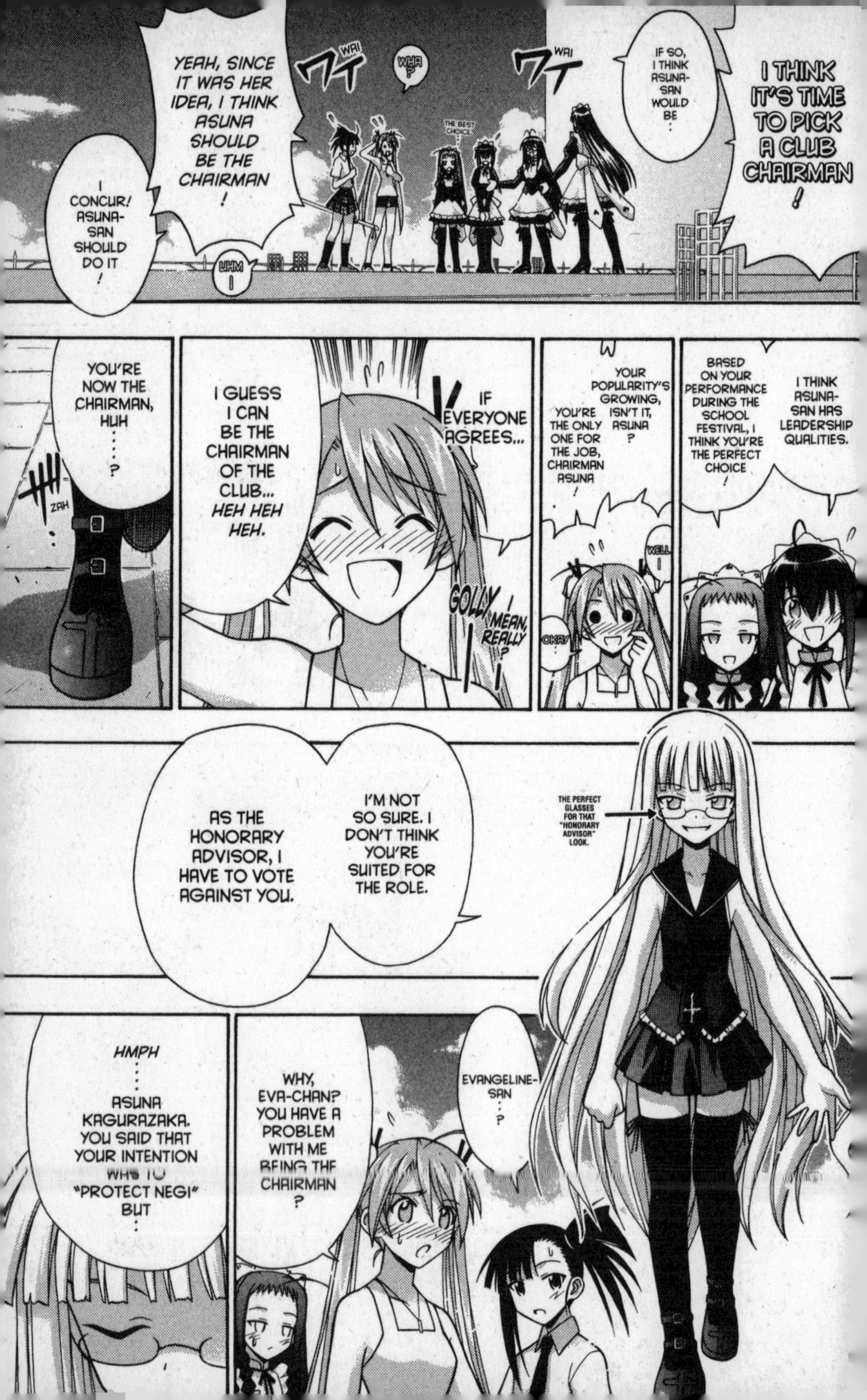
I THINK IT'S TIME TO PICK A CLUB CHAIRMAN!
IF SO, I THINK ASUNA-SAN WOULD BE...
WAI
THE BEST CHOICE.
WHA?
WAI
YEAH, SINCE IT WAS HER IDEA, I THINK ASUNA SHOULD BE THE CHAIRMAN!
I CONCUR! ASUNA-SAN SHOULD DO IT!
UHM
I THINK ASUNA-SAN HAS LEADERSHIP QUALITIES.
BASED ON YOUR PERFORMANCE DURING THE SCHOOL FESTIVAL, I THINK YOU'RE THE PERFECT CHOICE!
YOUR POPULARITY'S GROWING, ISN'T IT, ASUNA?
YOU'RE THE ONLY ONE FOR THE JOB, CHAIRMAN ASUNA!
WELL
OKAY
IF EVERYONE AGREES...
I GUESS I CAN BE THE CHAIRMAN OF THE CLUB... HEH HEH HEH.
GOLLY
I MEAN, REALLY?
YOU'RE NOW THE CHAIRMAN, HUH....?
ZAH
THE PERFECT GLASSES FOR THAT "HONORARY ADVISOR" LOOK.
I'M NOT SO SURE. I DON'T THINK YOU'RE SUITED FOR THE ROLE.
AS THE HONORARY ADVISOR, I HAVE TO VOTE AGAINST YOU.
EVANGELINE-SAN...?
WHY, EVA-CHAN? YOU HAVE A PROBLEM WITH ME BEING THE CHAIRMAN?
HMPH... ASUNA KAGURAZAKA. YOU SAID THAT YOUR INTENTION WAS TO "PROTECT NEGI" BUT...

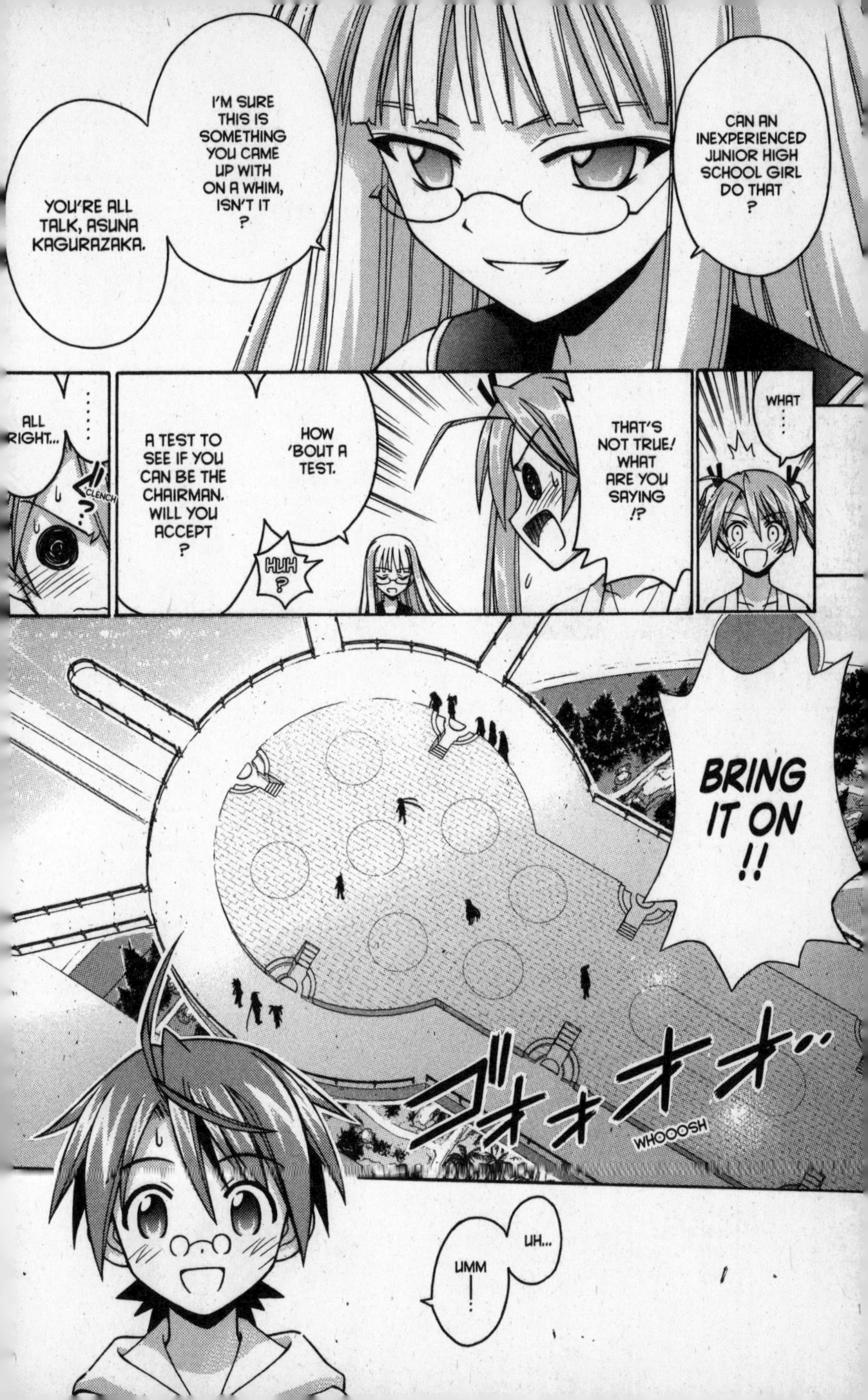

CAN AN INEXPERIENCED JUNIOR HIGH SCHOOL GIRL DO THAT?
I'M SURE THIS IS SOMETHING YOU CAME UP WITH ON A WHIM, ISN'T IT?
YOU'RE ALL TALK, ASUNA KAGURAZAKA.
WHAT......
THAT'S NOT TRUE! WHAT ARE YOU SAYING!?
HUH?
HOW 'BOUT A TEST.
A TEST TO SEE IF YOU CAN BE THE CHAIRMAN. WILL YOU ACCEPT?
......
ALL RIGHT...
CLENCH
?
BRING IT ON!!
ゴォォオオ
WHOOOSH
UH...
UMM!

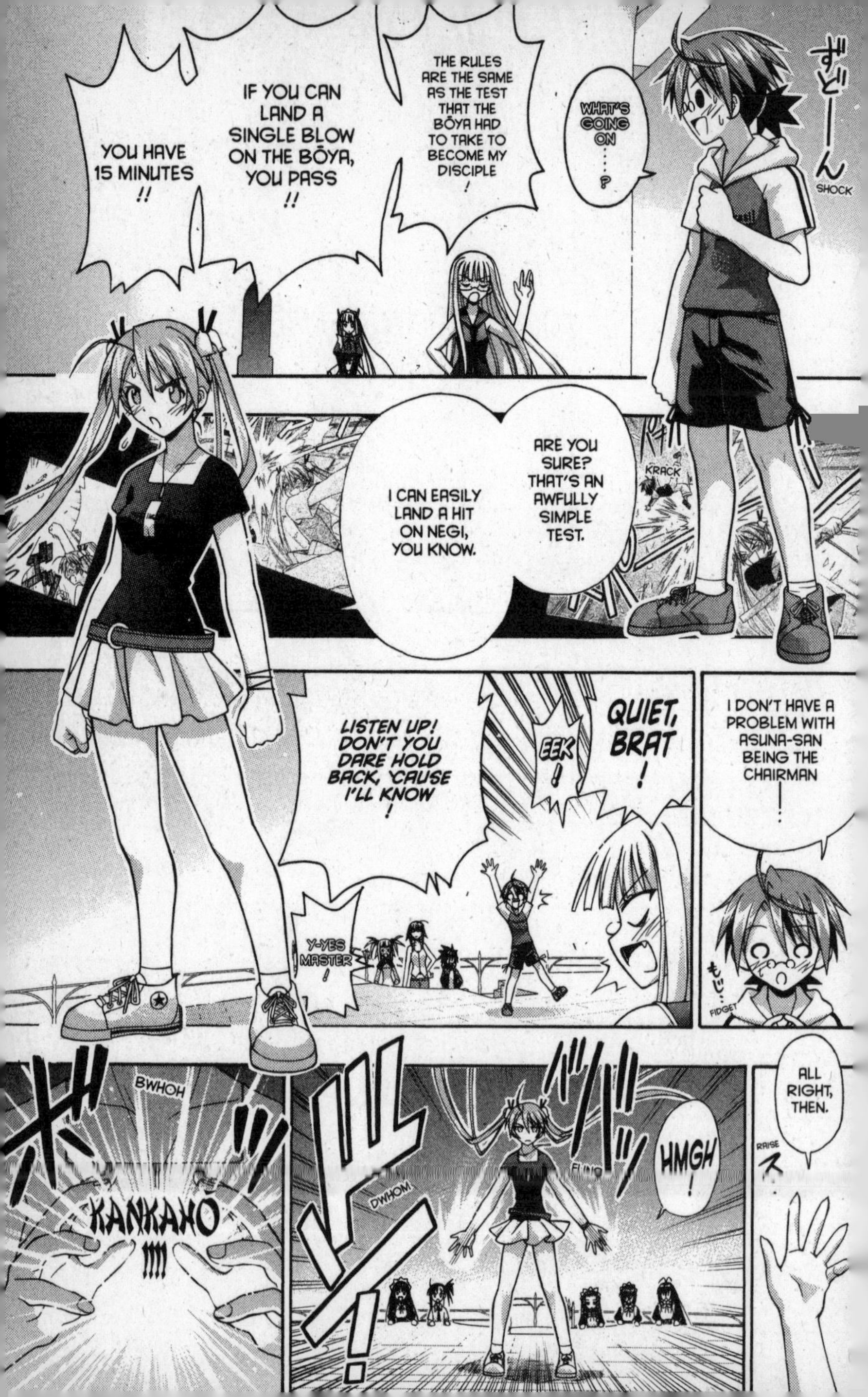
ずどーん
SHOCK
WHAT'S GOING ON......?
THE RULES ARE THE SAME AS THE TEST THAT THE BŌYA HAD TO TAKE TO BECOME MY DISCIPLE!
IF YOU CAN LAND A SINGLE BLOW ON THE BŌYA, YOU PASS!!
YOU HAVE 15 MINUTES!!
ARE YOU SURE? THAT'S AN AWFULLY SIMPLE TEST.
I CAN EASILY LAND A HIT ON NEGI, YOU KNOW.
KRACK
I DON'T HAVE A PROBLEM WITH ASUNA-SAN BEING THE CHAIRMAN...!
もじ…
FIDGET
QUIET, BRAT!
EEK!
LISTEN UP! DON'T YOU DARE HOLD BACK, 'CAUSE I'LL KNOW!
Y-YES MASTER!
ALL RIGHT, THEN.
RAISE
ス
HMGH!
FLING
DWHOM
BWHOH
KANKAHŌ!!!!

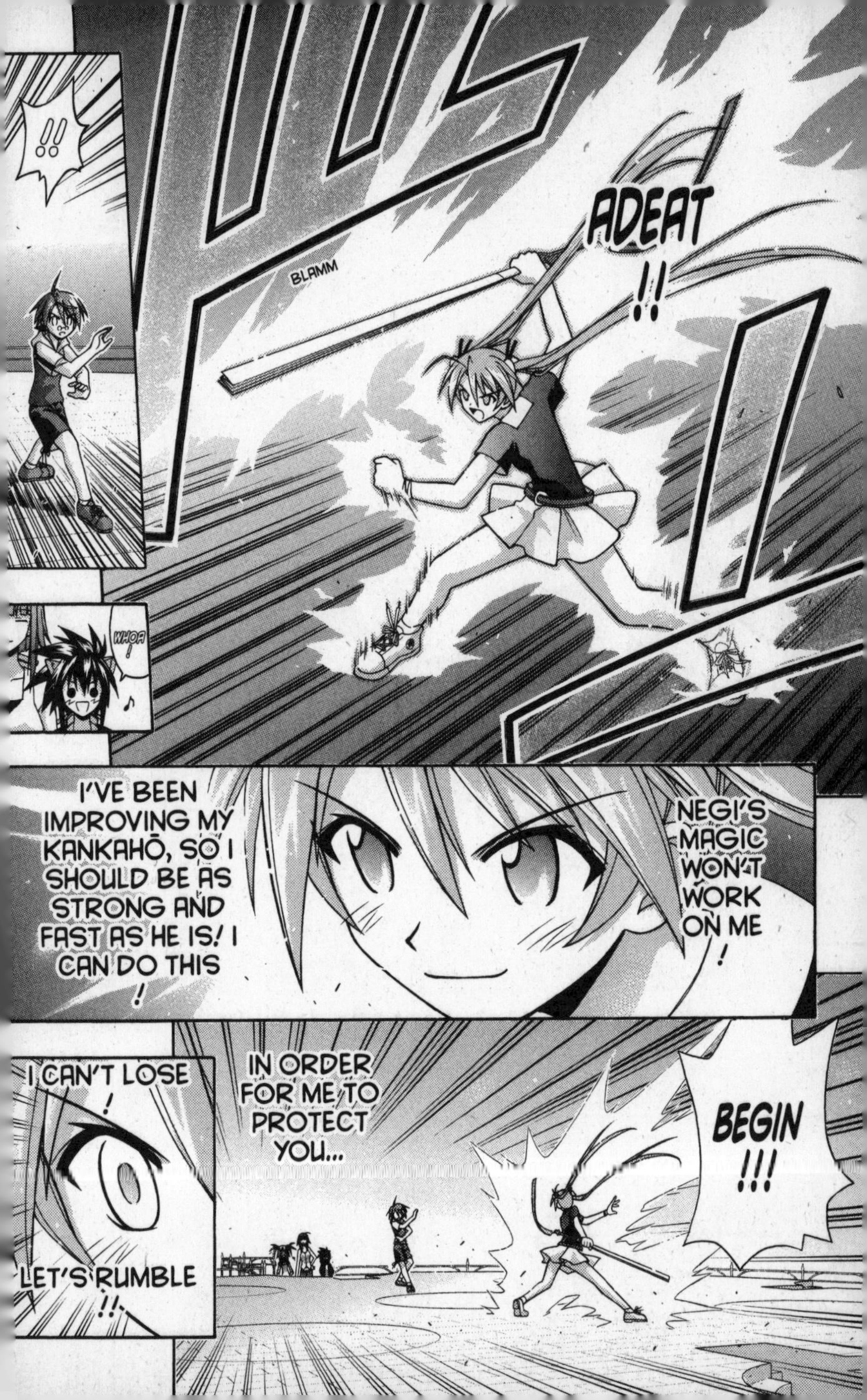

ADEAT!!
BLAMM
!!
WHOA!
NEGI'S MAGIC WON'T WORK ON ME!
I'VE BEEN IMPROVING MY KANKAHŌ, SO I SHOULD BE AS STRONG AND FAST AS HE IS! I CAN DO THIS!
BEGIN!!!
IN ORDER FOR ME TO PROTECT YOU...
I CAN'T LOSE!
LET'S RUMBLE!!

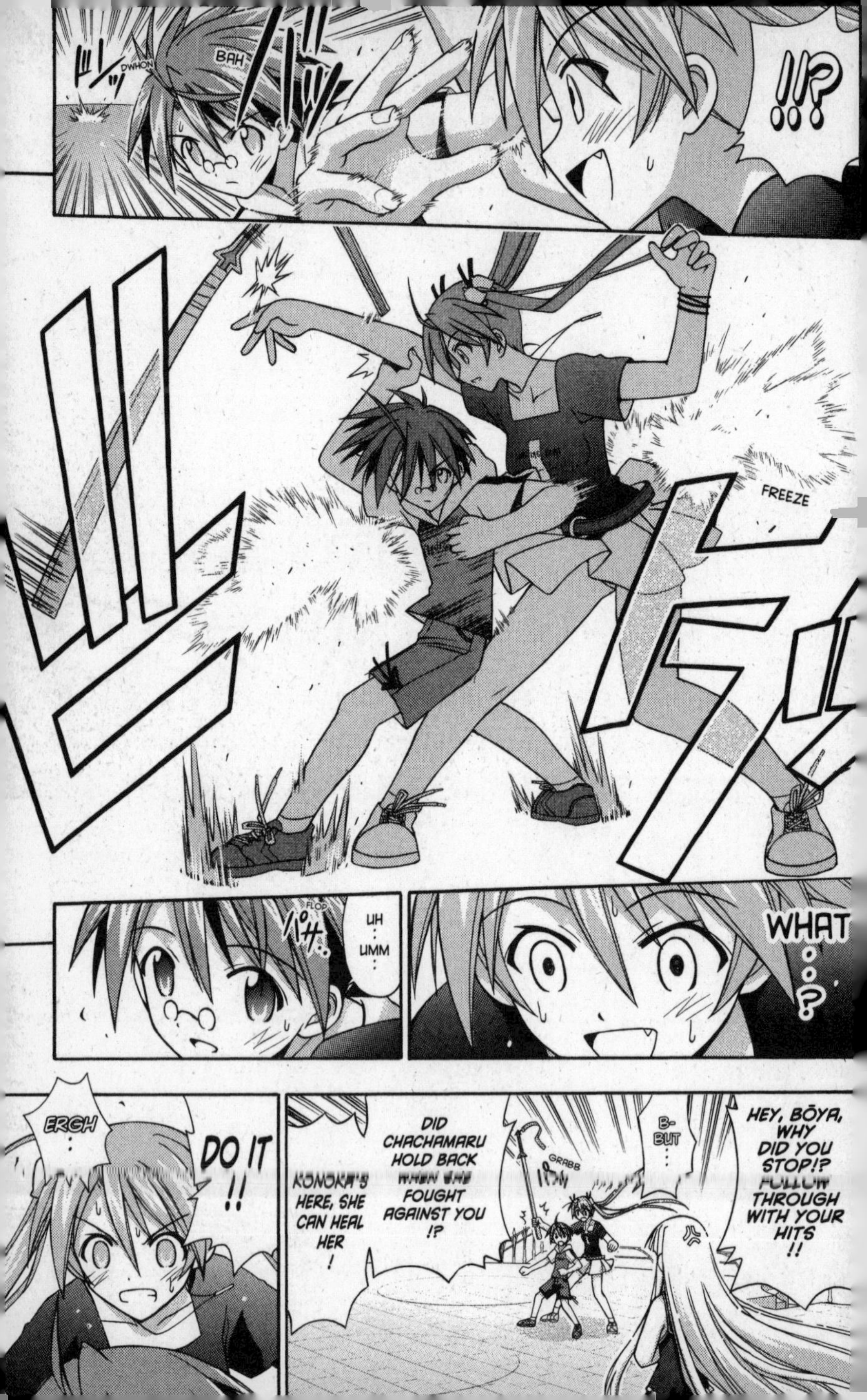
!!?
BAH
DWHON
FREEZE
WHAT...?
FLOP
UH... UMM...
HEY, BŌYA, WHY DID YOU STOP!? FOLLOW THROUGH WITH YOUR HITS!!
B-BUT...
GRABB
DID CHACHAMARU HOLD BACK WHEN SHE FOUGHT AGAINST YOU!?
KONOKA'S HERE, SHE CAN HEAL HER!
DO IT!!
ERGH...

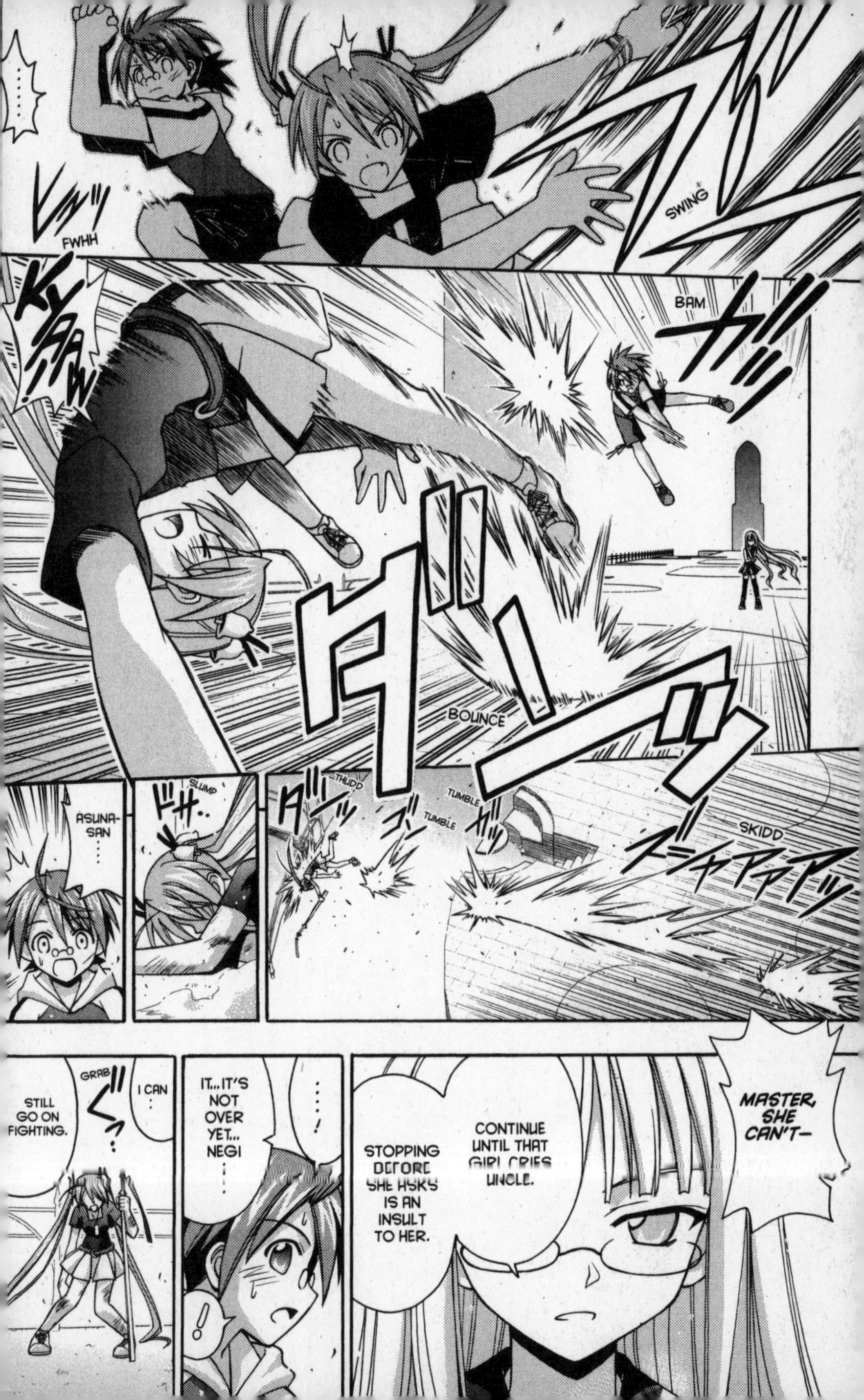
SWING
……!
FWHH
BAM
KYAAAW!
BOUNCE
SKIDD
TUMBLE
TUMBLE
THUDD
SLUMP
ASUNA-SAN……
MASTER, SHE CAN'T—
CONTINUE UNTIL THAT GIRL CRIES UNCLE.
STOPPING BEFORE SHE ASKS IS AN INSULT TO HER.
……!
IT…IT'S NOT OVER YET… NEGI……
!
I CAN…
GRAB
STILL GO ON FIGHTING.

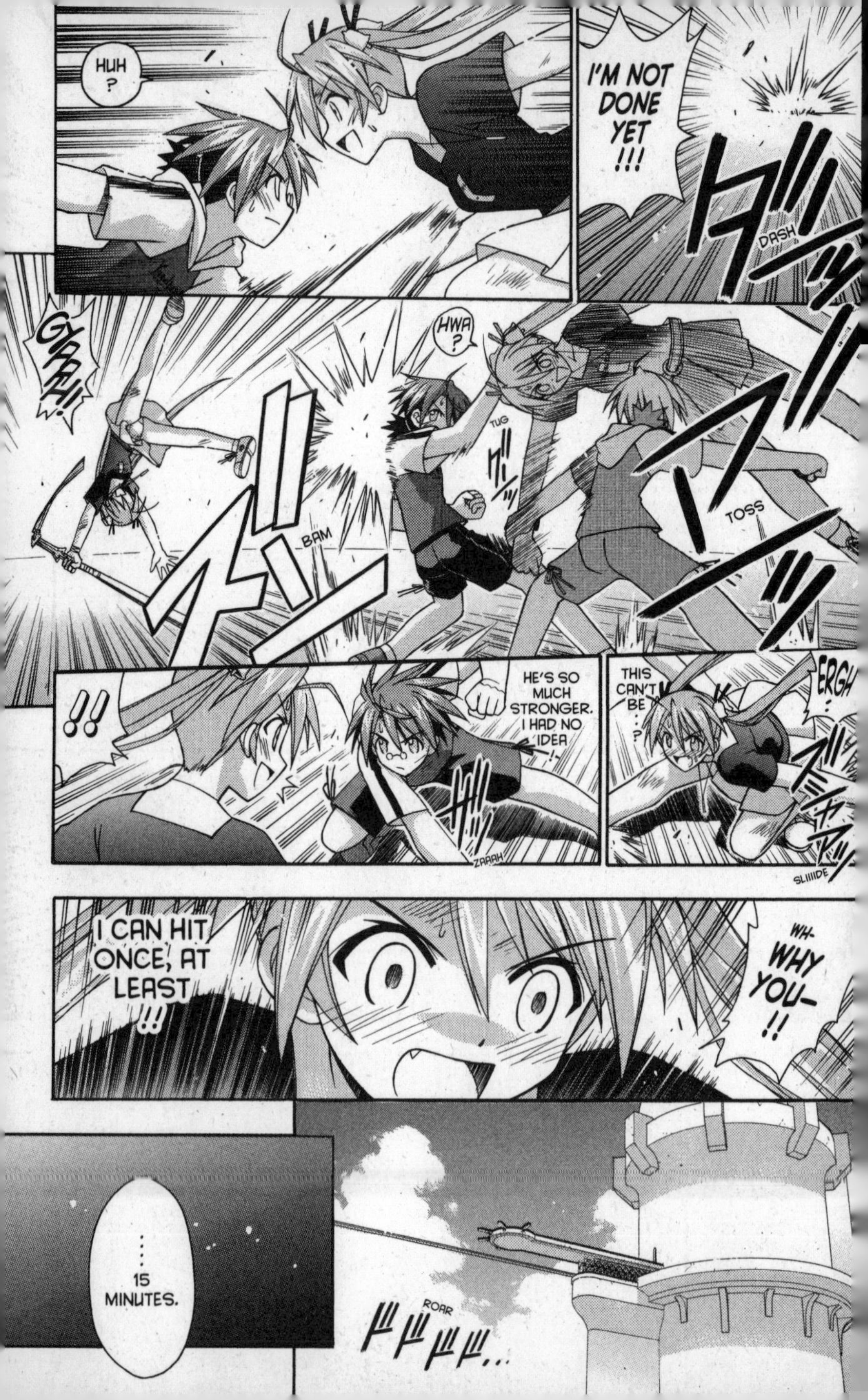
I'M NOT DONE YET !!!
DASH
HUH ?
HWA ?
TOSS
TUG
BAM
GYAAAH!!
ERGH !
THIS CAN'T BE . . . ?
SLIIIIDE
HE'S SO MUCH STRONGER. I HAD NO IDEA !
ZAAAAH
!!
WH- WHY YOU- !!
I CAN HIT ONCE, AT LEAST !!
ROAR
. . . . 15 MINUTES.

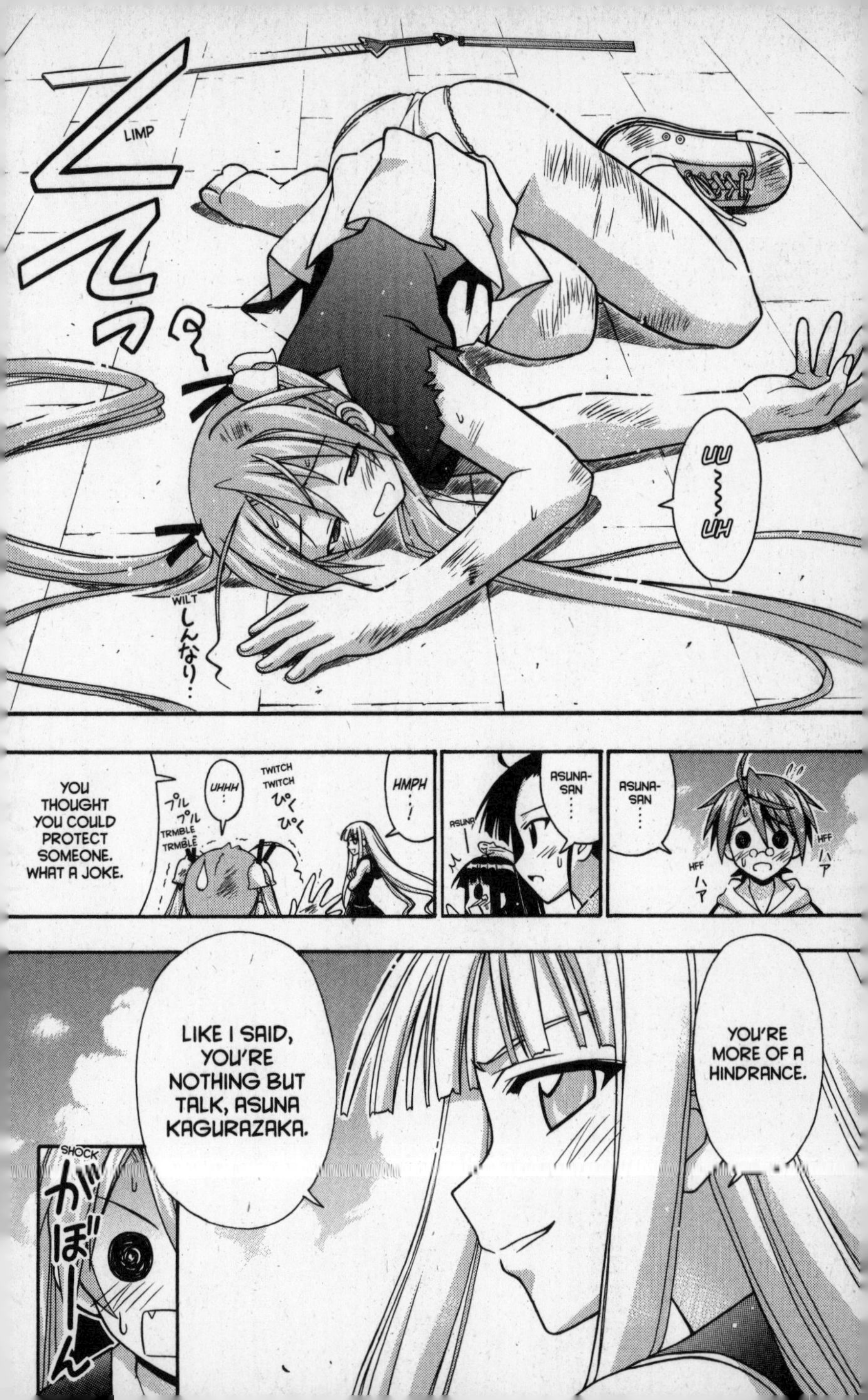
ズぇっ
LIMP
UU~~UH
WILT
しんなり…
ASUNA-SAN......
HFF ハァ
HFF ハァ
ASUNA-SAN......
ASUNA
HMPH...!
TWITCH TWITCH
ぴくぴく
UHHH...
プルプル
TRMBLE TRMBLE
YOU THOUGHT YOU COULD PROTECT SOMEONE. WHAT A JOKE.
YOU'RE MORE OF A HINDRANCE.
LIKE I SAID, YOU'RE NOTHING BUT TALK, ASUNA KAGURAZAKA.
SHOCK
がぼーん

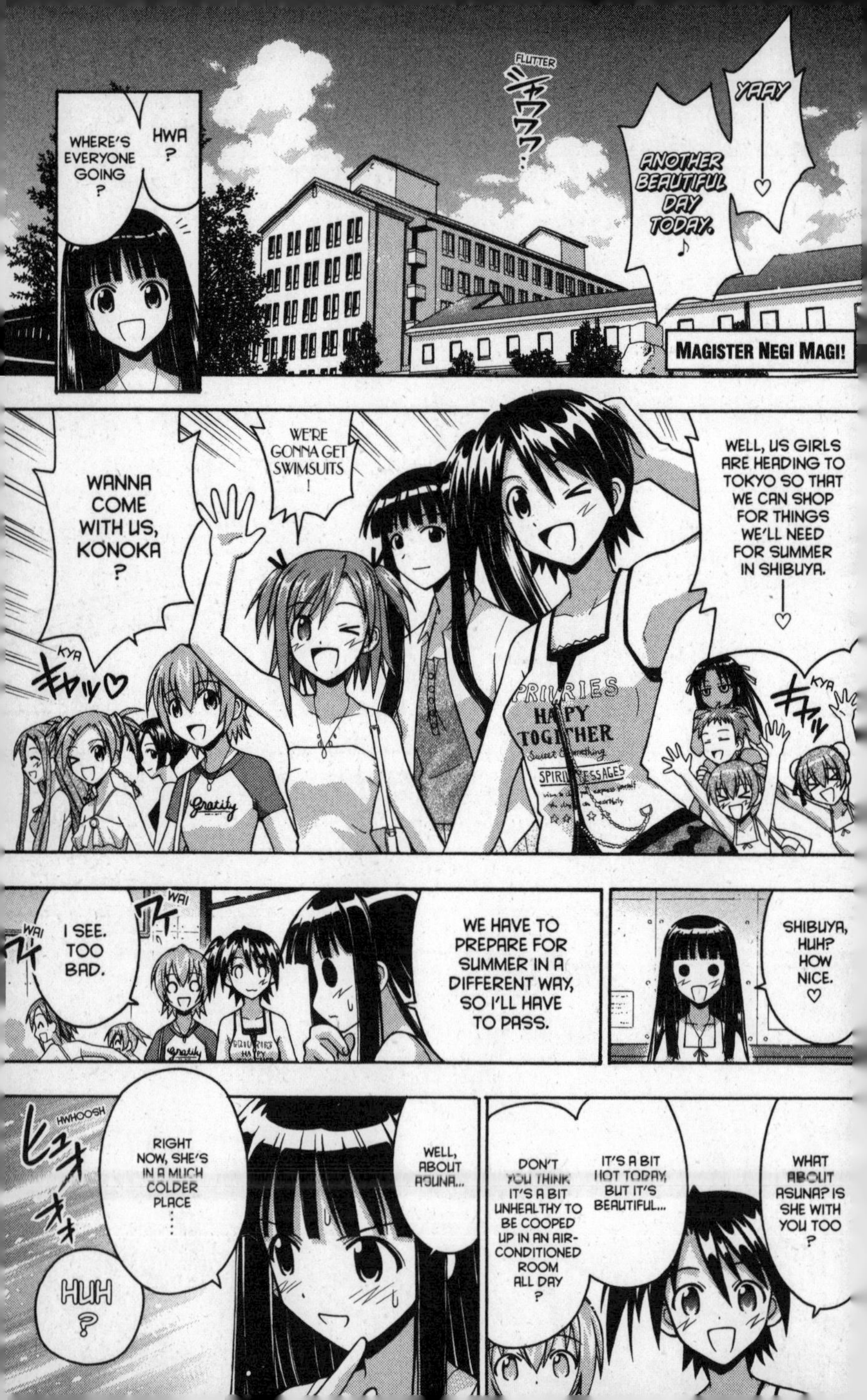

YAAY ♡
ANOTHER BEAUTIFUL DAY TODAY. ♪
FLUTTER
MAGISTER NEGI MAGI!
HWA?
WHERE'S EVERYONE GOING?
WELL, US GIRLS ARE HEADING TO TOKYO SO THAT WE CAN SHOP FOR THINGS WE'LL NEED FOR SUMMER IN SHIBUYA. ♡
KYA
WE'RE GONNA GET SWIMSUITS!
WANNA COME WITH US, KONOKA?
KYA
SHIBUYA, HUH? HOW NICE. ♡
WE HAVE TO PREPARE FOR SUMMER IN A DIFFERENT WAY, SO I'LL HAVE TO PASS.
I SEE. TOO BAD.
WAI
WAI
WHAT ABOUT ASUNA? IS SHE WITH YOU TOO?
IT'S A BIT HOT TODAY, BUT IT'S BEAUTIFUL...
DON'T YOU THINK IT'S A BIT UNHEALTHY TO BE COOPED UP IN AN AIR-CONDITIONED ROOM ALL DAY?
WELL, ABOUT ASUNA...
RIGHT NOW, SHE'S IN A MUCH COLDER PLACE.....
HWHOOSH
HUH?

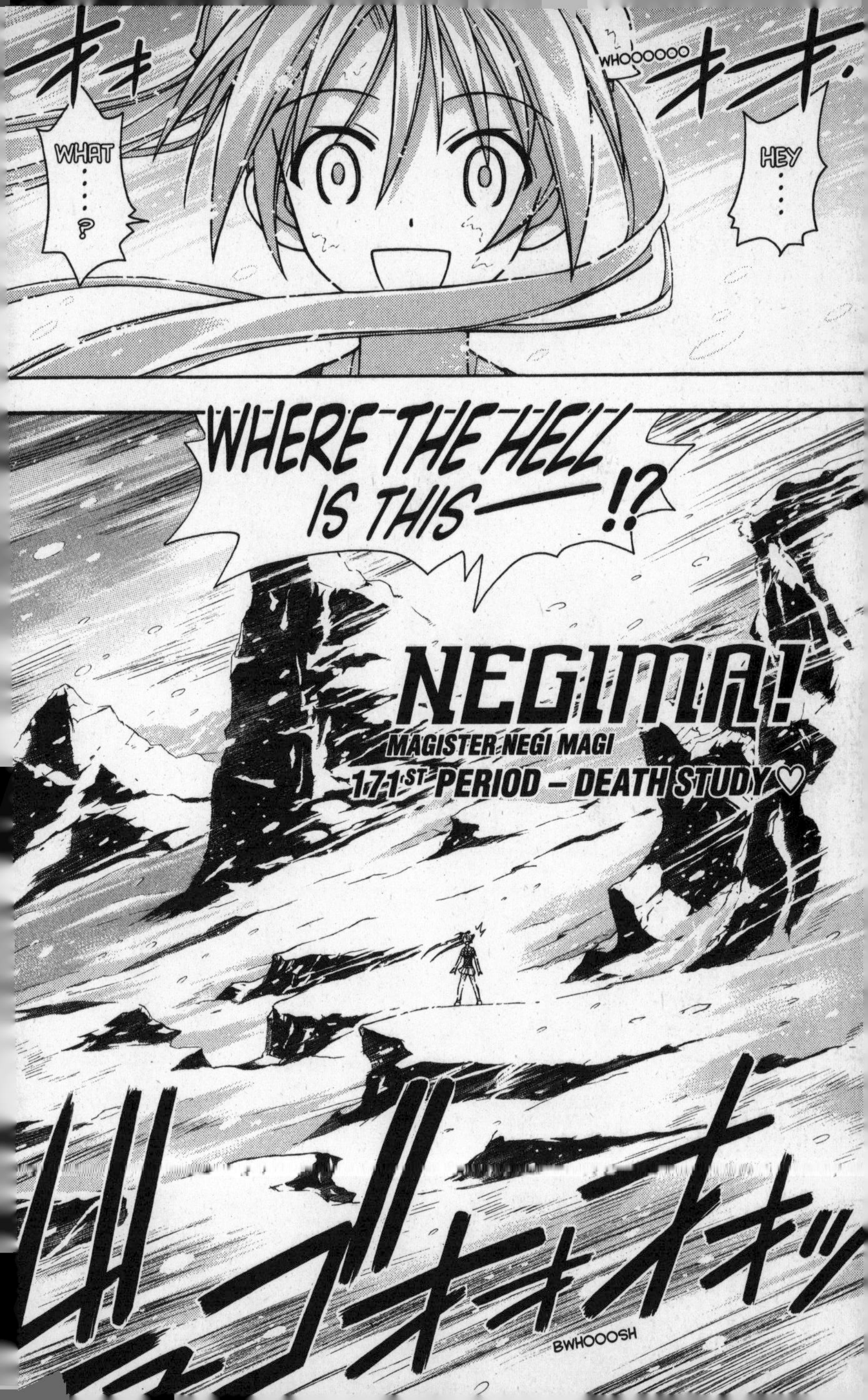
WHOOOOOO
HEY.....
WHAT.....?
WHERE THE HELL IS THIS——!?
NEGIMA!
MAGISTER NEGI MAGI
171ST PERIOD – DEATH STUDY♡
BWHOOOSH

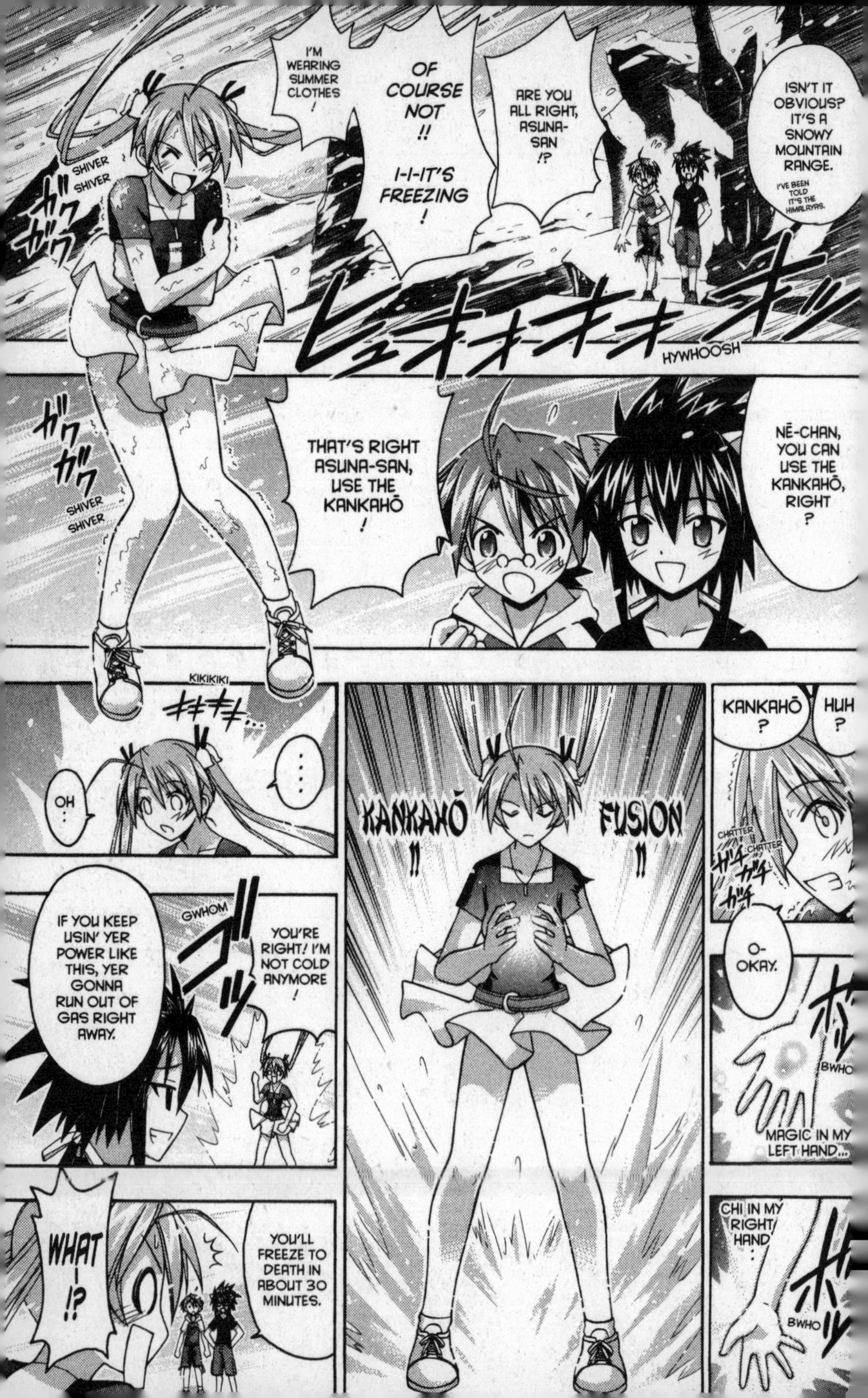
ISN'T IT OBVIOUS? IT'S A SNOWY MOUNTAIN RANGE.
I'VE BEEN TOLD IT'S THE HIMALAYAS.
ARE YOU ALL RIGHT, ASUNA-SAN!?
OF COURSE NOT!!
I-I-IT'S FREEZING!
I'M WEARING SUMMER CLOTHES!
SHIVER SHIVER
HYWHOOSH
NĒ-CHAN, YOU CAN USE THE KANKAHŌ, RIGHT?
THAT'S RIGHT ASUNA-SAN, USE THE KANKAHŌ!
SHIVER SHIVER
HUH?
KANKAHŌ?
CHATTER CHATTER
O-OKAY.
BWHO
MAGIC IN MY LEFT HAND...
CHI IN MY RIGHT HAND
BWHO
KANKAHŌ!!
FUSION!!
....
OH...
KIKIKIKI
YOU'RE RIGHT! I'M NOT COLD ANYMORE!
GWHOM
IF YOU KEEP USIN' YER POWER LIKE THIS, YER GONNA RUN OUT OF GAS RIGHT AWAY.
YOU'LL FREEZE TO DEATH IN ABOUT 30 MINUTES.
WHAT!?

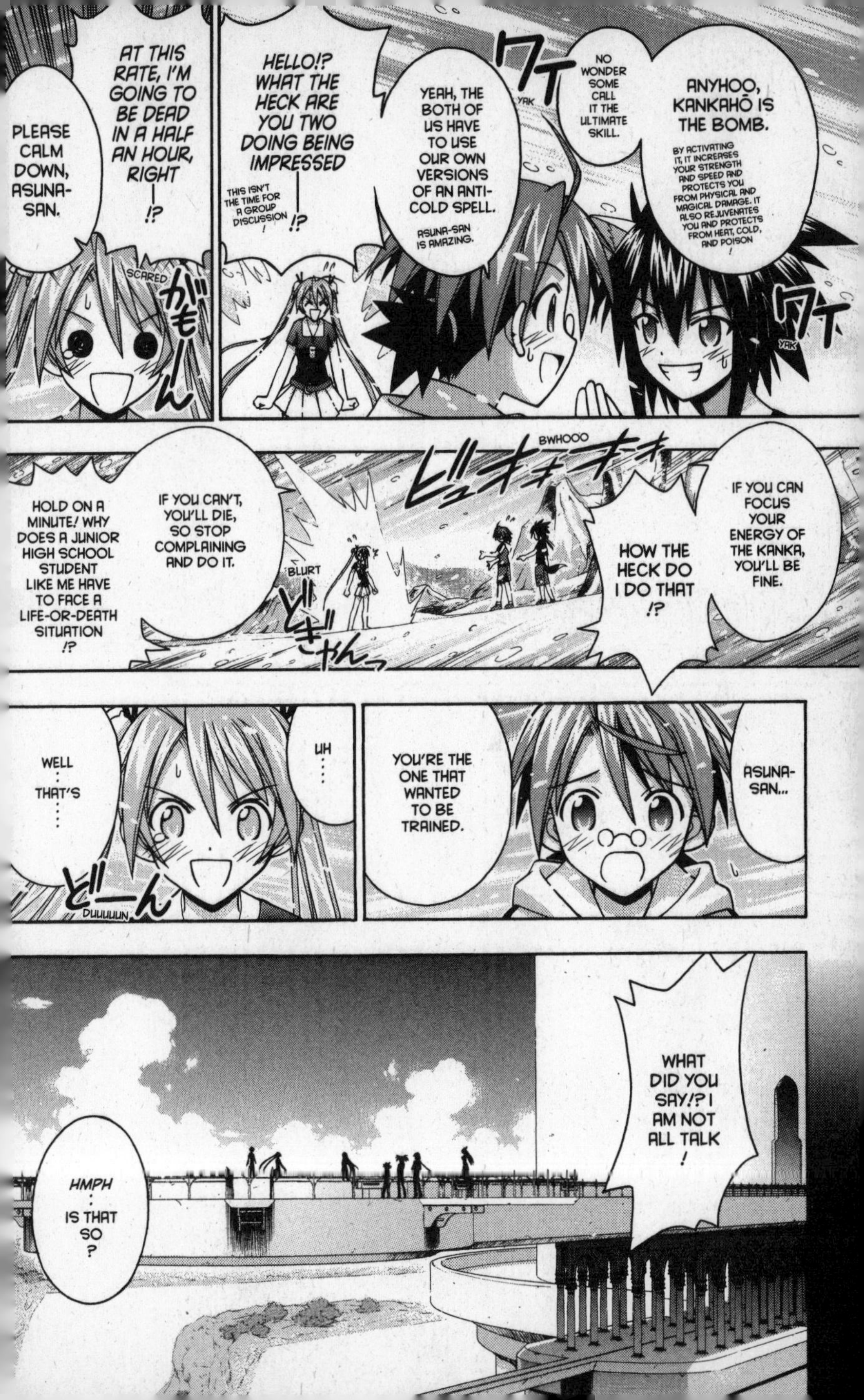

ANYHOO, KANKAHŌ IS THE BOMB.
BY ACTIVATING IT, IT INCREASES YOUR STRENGTH AND SPEED AND PROTECTS YOU FROM PHYSICAL AND MAGICAL DAMAGE. IT ALSO REJUVENATES YOU AND PROTECTS FROM HEAT, COLD, AND POISON!
YAK
NO WONDER SOME CALL IT THE ULTIMATE SKILL.
YAK
YEAH, THE BOTH OF US HAVE TO USE OUR OWN VERSIONS OF AN ANTI-COLD SPELL.
ASUNA-SAN IS AMAZING.
HELLO!? WHAT THE HECK ARE YOU TWO DOING BEING IMPRESSED—!?
THIS ISN'T THE TIME FOR A GROUP DISCUSSION!
AT THIS RATE, I'M GOING TO BE DEAD IN A HALF AN HOUR, RIGHT—!?
SCARED
PLEASE CALM DOWN, ASUNA-SAN.
IF YOU CAN FOCUS YOUR ENERGY OF THE KANKA, YOU'LL BE FINE.
HOW THE HECK DO I DO THAT!?
BWHOOO
BLURT
IF YOU CAN'T, YOU'LL DIE, SO STOP COMPLAINING AND DO IT.
HOLD ON A MINUTE! WHY DOES A JUNIOR HIGH SCHOOL STUDENT LIKE ME HAVE TO FACE A LIFE-OR-DEATH SITUATION!?
ASUNA-SAN...
YOU'RE THE ONE THAT WANTED TO BE TRAINED.
UH...
WELL... THAT'S...
DUUUUUN
WHAT DID YOU SAY!? I AM NOT ALL TALK!
HMPH... IS THAT SO?

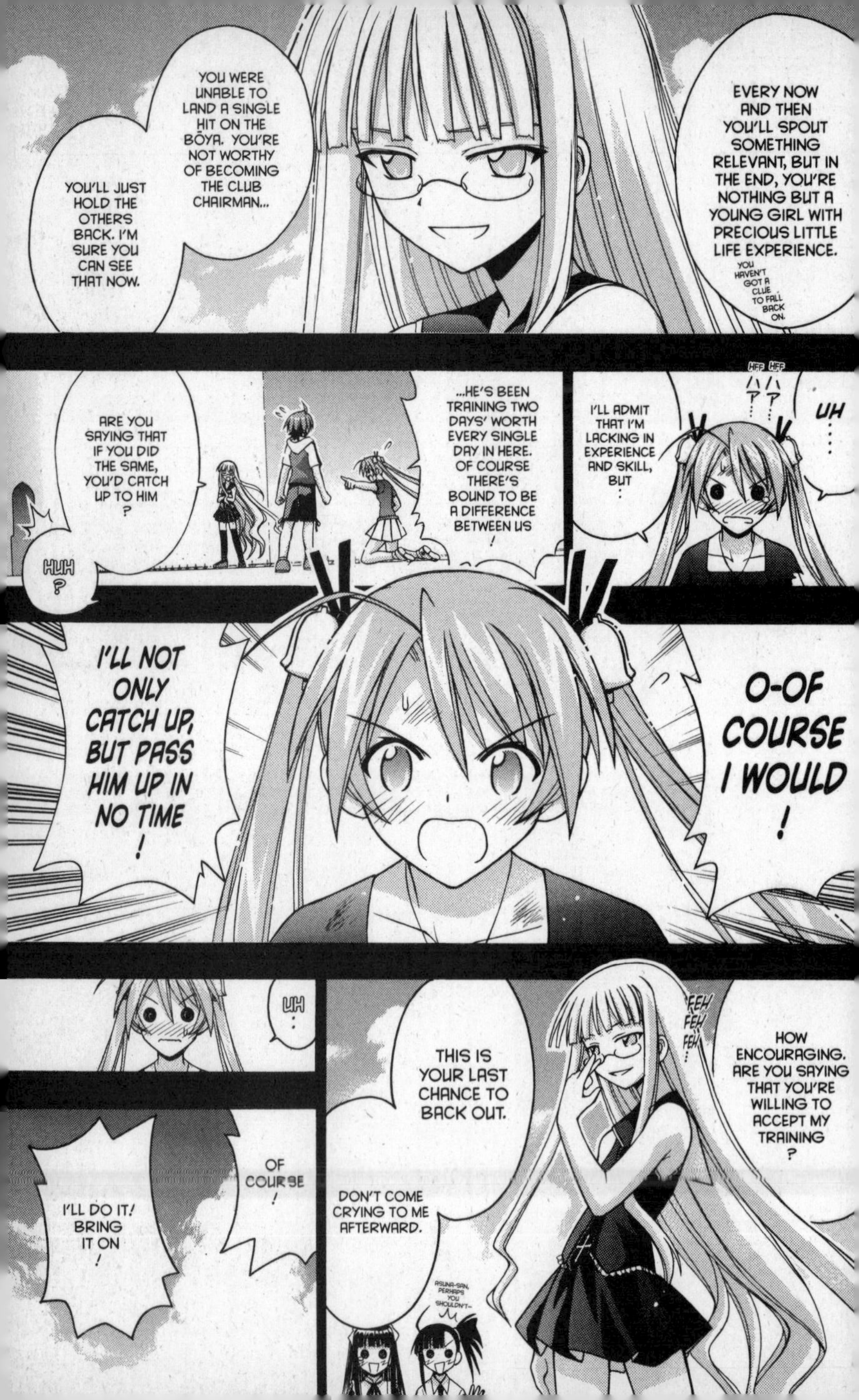
EVERY NOW AND THEN YOU'LL SPOUT SOMETHING RELEVANT, BUT IN THE END, YOU'RE NOTHING BUT A YOUNG GIRL WITH PRECIOUS LITTLE LIFE EXPERIENCE.
YOU HAVEN'T GOT A CLUE TO FALL BACK ON.
YOU WERE UNABLE TO LAND A SINGLE HIT ON THE BŌYA. YOU'RE NOT WORTHY OF BECOMING THE CLUB CHAIRMAN...
YOU'LL JUST HOLD THE OTHERS BACK. I'M SURE YOU CAN SEE THAT NOW.
HFF HFF
UH...
I'LL ADMIT THAT I'M LACKING IN EXPERIENCE AND SKILL, BUT...
...HE'S BEEN TRAINING TWO DAYS' WORTH EVERY SINGLE DAY IN HERE. OF COURSE THERE'S BOUND TO BE A DIFFERENCE BETWEEN US!
ARE YOU SAYING THAT IF YOU DID THE SAME, YOU'D CATCH UP TO HIM?
HUH?
O-OF COURSE I WOULD!
I'LL NOT ONLY CATCH UP, BUT PASS HIM UP IN NO TIME!
HOW ENCOURAGING. ARE YOU SAYING THAT YOU'RE WILLING TO ACCEPT MY TRAINING?
FEH FEH FEH...
THIS IS YOUR LAST CHANCE TO BACK OUT.
DON'T COME CRYING TO ME AFTERWARD.
ASUNA-SAN, PERHAPS YOU SHOULDN'T–
UH...
OF COURSE!
I'LL DO IT! BRING IT ON!

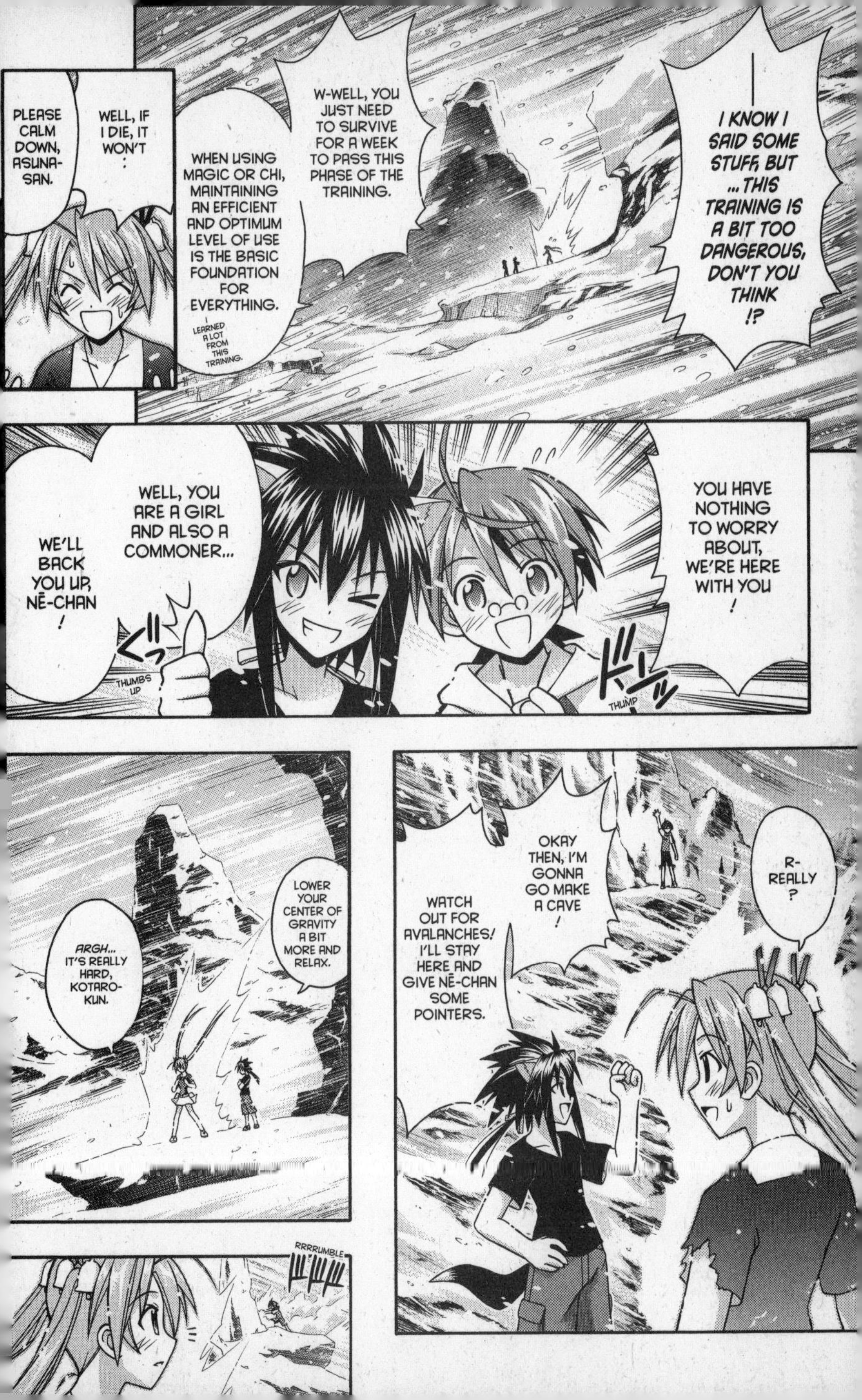

I KNOW I SAID SOME STUFF, BUT ...THIS TRAINING IS A BIT TOO DANGEROUS, DON'T YOU THINK!?
W-WELL, YOU JUST NEED TO SURVIVE FOR A WEEK TO PASS THIS PHASE OF THE TRAINING.
WHEN USING MAGIC OR CHI, MAINTAINING AN EFFICIENT AND OPTIMUM LEVEL OF USE IS THE BASIC FOUNDATION FOR EVERYTHING.
I LEARNED A LOT FROM THIS TRAINING.
WELL, IF I DIE, IT WON'T :
PLEASE CALM DOWN, ASUNA-SAN.
YOU HAVE NOTHING TO WORRY ABOUT, WE'RE HERE WITH YOU!
THUMP
WELL, YOU ARE A GIRL AND ALSO A COMMONER...
WE'LL BACK YOU UP, NĒ-CHAN!
THUMBS UP
R-REALLY?
OKAY THEN, I'M GONNA GO MAKE A CAVE!
WATCH OUT FOR AVALANCHES! I'LL STAY HERE AND GIVE NĒ-CHAN SOME POINTERS.
LOWER YOUR CENTER OF GRAVITY A BIT MORE AND RELAX.
ARGH... IT'S REALLY HARD, KOTARO-KUN.
RRRRUMBLE

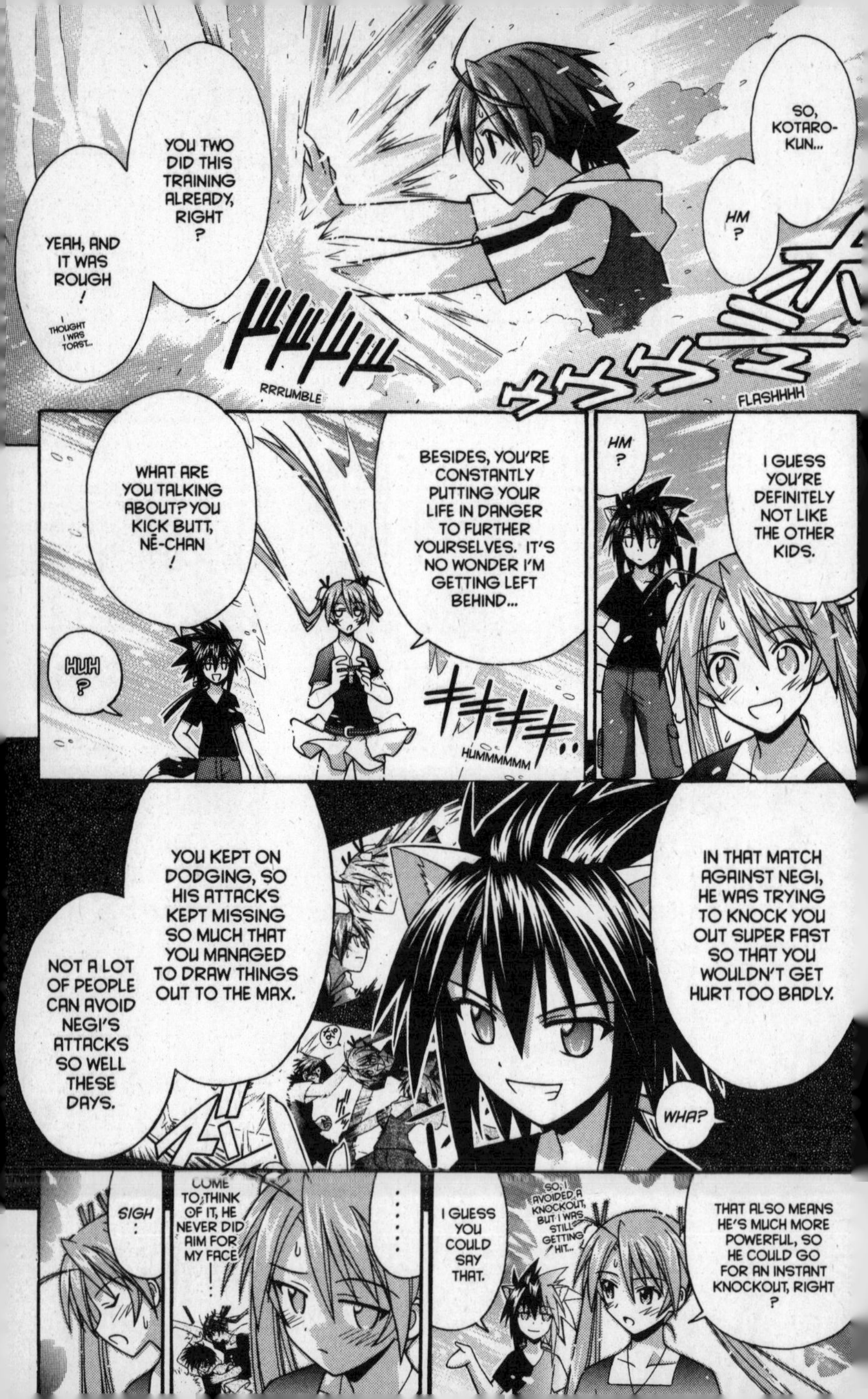
SO, KOTARO-KUN...
HM?
FLASHHHH
YOU TWO DID THIS TRAINING ALREADY, RIGHT?
YEAH, AND IT WAS ROUGH!
I THOUGHT I WAS TOAST...
RRRUMBLE
I GUESS YOU'RE DEFINITELY NOT LIKE THE OTHER KIDS.
HM?
BESIDES, YOU'RE CONSTANTLY PUTTING YOUR LIFE IN DANGER TO FURTHER YOURSELVES. IT'S NO WONDER I'M GETTING LEFT BEHIND...
HUMMMMMM
WHAT ARE YOU TALKING ABOUT? YOU KICK BUTT, NĒ-CHAN!
HUH?
IN THAT MATCH AGAINST NEGI, HE WAS TRYING TO KNOCK YOU OUT SUPER FAST SO THAT YOU WOULDN'T GET HURT TOO BADLY.
WHA?
YOU KEPT ON DODGING, SO HIS ATTACKS KEPT MISSING SO MUCH THAT YOU MANAGED TO DRAW THINGS OUT TO THE MAX.
NOT A LOT OF PEOPLE CAN AVOID NEGI'S ATTACKS SO WELL THESE DAYS.
THAT ALSO MEANS HE'S MUCH MORE POWERFUL, SO HE COULD GO FOR AN INSTANT KNOCKOUT, RIGHT?
SO, I AVOIDED A KNOCKOUT, BUT I WAS STILL GETTING HIT...
I GUESS YOU COULD SAY THAT.
.....
COME TO THINK OF IT, HE NEVER DID AIM FOR MY FACE...!
SIGH...

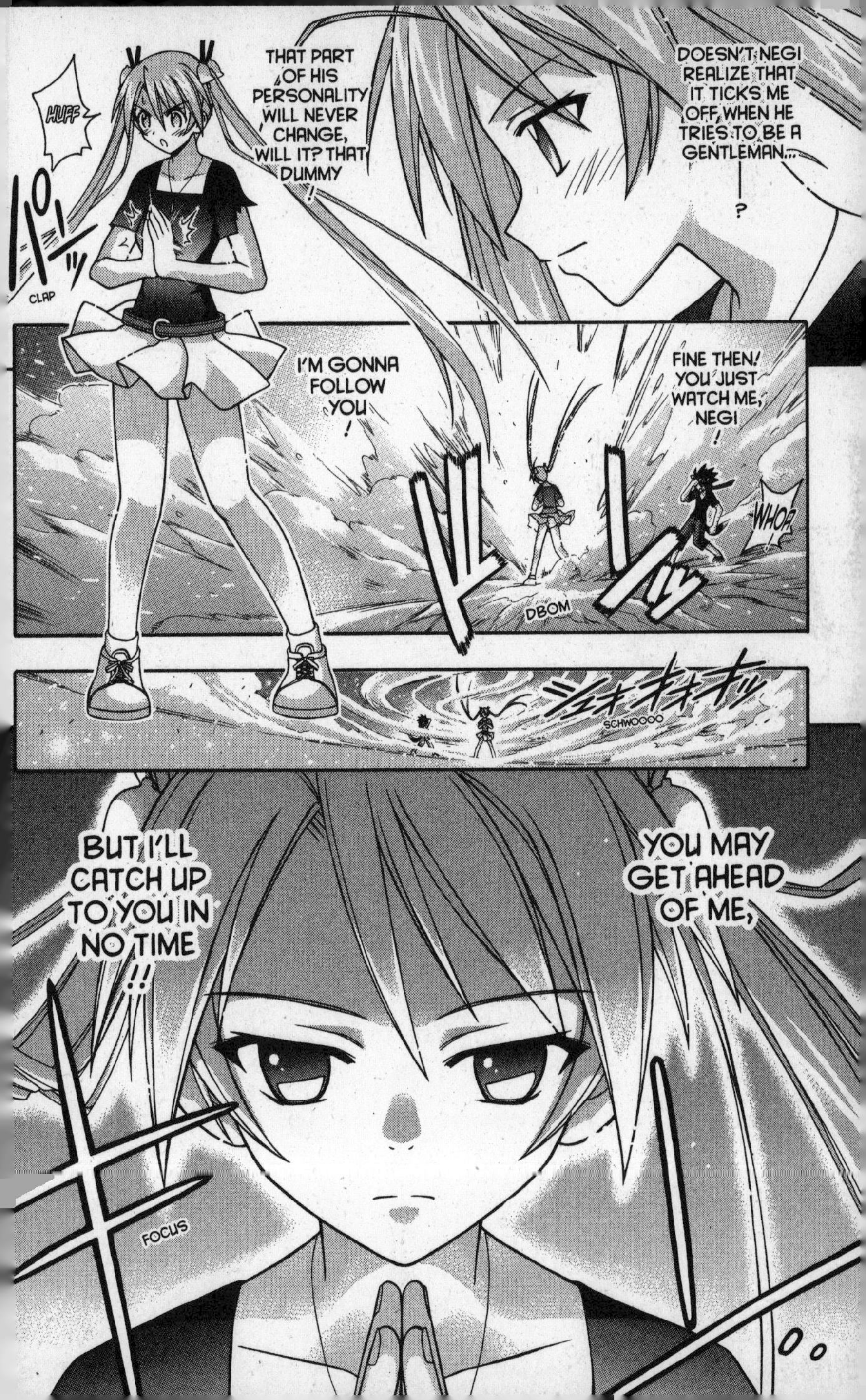
DOESN'T NEGI REALIZE THAT IT TICKS ME OFF WHEN HE TRIES TO BE A GENTLEMAN...!?
THAT PART OF HIS PERSONALITY WILL NEVER CHANGE, WILL IT? THAT DUMMY!
HUFF
CLAP
FINE THEN! YOU JUST WATCH ME, NEGI!
WHOP
I'M GONNA FOLLOW YOU!
DBOM
SCHWOOOO
YOU MAY GET AHEAD OF ME,
BUT I'LL CATCH UP TO YOU IN NO TIME!!
FOCUS

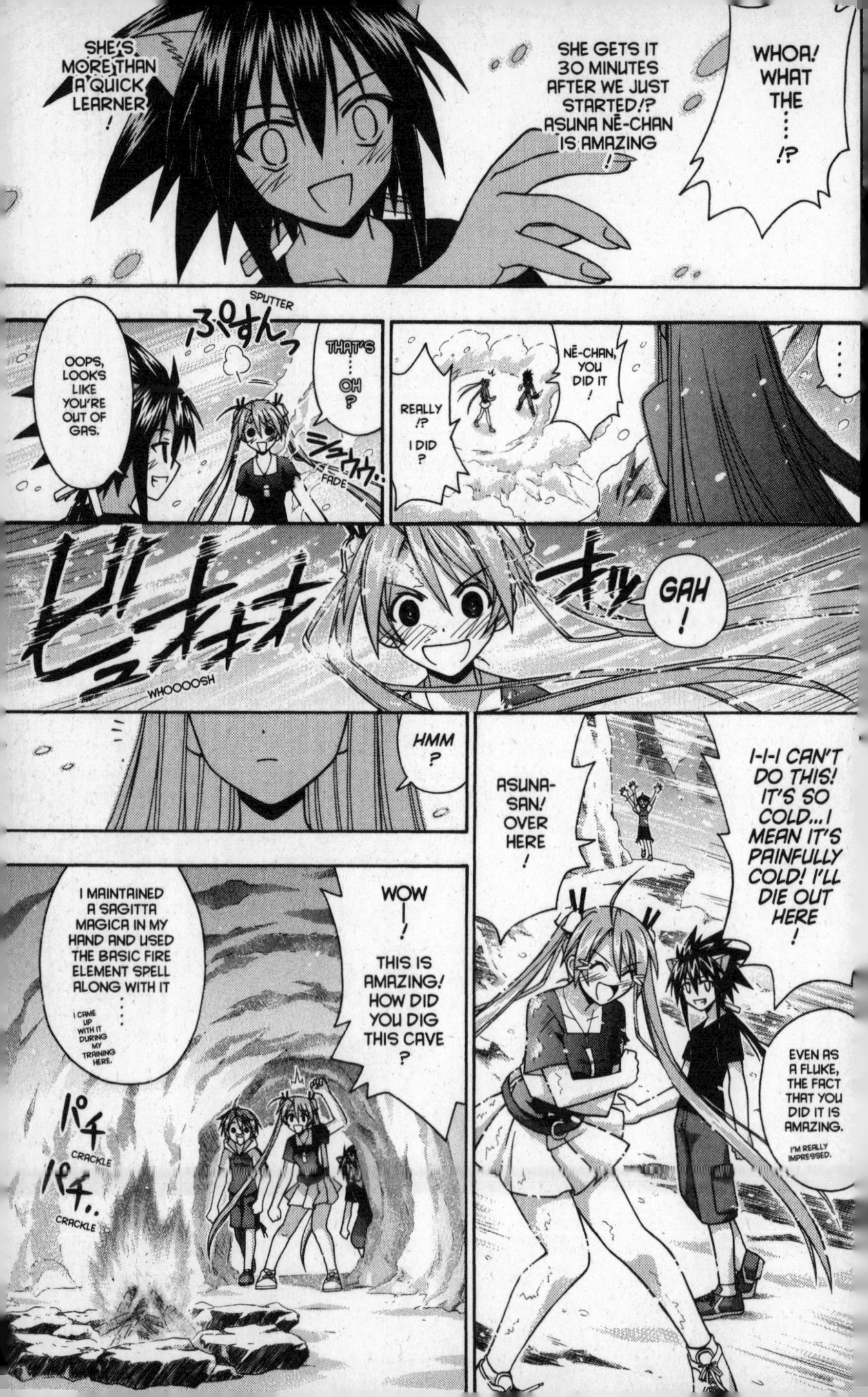

WHOA! WHAT THE......!?
SHE GETS IT 30 MINUTES AFTER WE JUST STARTED!? ASUNA NĒ-CHAN IS AMAZING!
SHE'S MORE THAN A QUICK LEARNER!
...
NĒ-CHAN, YOU DID IT!
REALLY!? I DID?
THAT'S... OH?
ぷすんっ
SPUTTER
シュウウ
FADE
OOPS, LOOKS LIKE YOU'RE OUT OF GAS.
GAH!
WHOOOOSH
I-I-I CAN'T DO THIS! IT'S SO COLD...I MEAN IT'S PAINFULLY COLD! I'LL DIE OUT HERE!
ASUNA-SAN! OVER HERE!
EVEN AS A FLUKE, THE FACT THAT YOU DID IT IS AMAZING.
I'M REALLY IMPRESSED.
HMM?
WOW! THIS IS AMAZING! HOW DID YOU DIG THIS CAVE?
I MAINTAINED A SAGITTA MAGICA IN MY HAND AND USED THE BASIC FIRE ELEMENT SPELL ALONG WITH IT...
I CAME UP WITH IT DURING MY TRAINING HERE.
パチ
CRACKLE
パチ..
CRACKLE

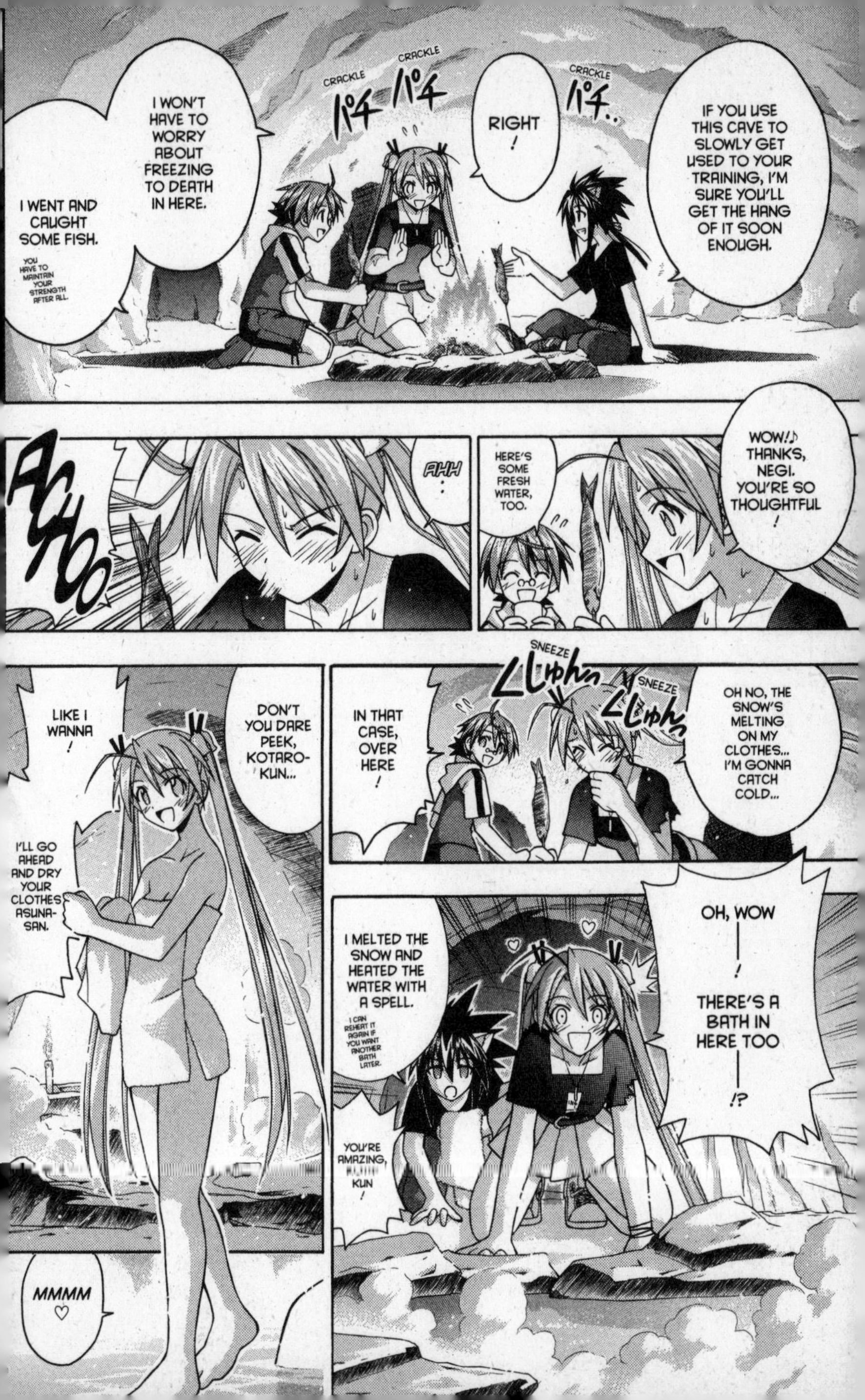
IF YOU USE THIS CAVE TO SLOWLY GET USED TO YOUR TRAINING, I'M SURE YOU'LL GET THE HANG OF IT SOON ENOUGH.
CRACKLE
パチ..
RIGHT!
CRACKLE
パチ
CRACKLE
パチ
I WON'T HAVE TO WORRY ABOUT FREEZING TO DEATH IN HERE.
I WENT AND CAUGHT SOME FISH.
YOU HAVE TO MAINTAIN YOUR STRENGTH AFTER ALL.
WOW!♪ THANKS, NEGI. YOU'RE SO THOUGHTFUL!
HERE'S SOME FRESH WATER, TOO.
AHH...
ACHOO
OH NO, THE SNOW'S MELTING ON MY CLOTHES... I'M GONNA CATCH COLD...
SNEEZE
くしゅん
SNEEZE
くしゅん
IN THAT CASE, OVER HERE!
OH, WOW—! THERE'S A BATH IN HERE TOO—!?
I MELTED THE SNOW AND HEATED THE WATER WITH A SPELL.
I CAN REHEAT IT AGAIN IF YOU WANT ANOTHER BATH LATER.
YOU'RE AMAZING,
KUN!
DON'T YOU DARE PEEK, KOTARO-KUN...
LIKE I WANNA!
I'LL GO AHEAD AND DRY YOUR CLOTHES, ASUNA-SAN.
MMMM♡

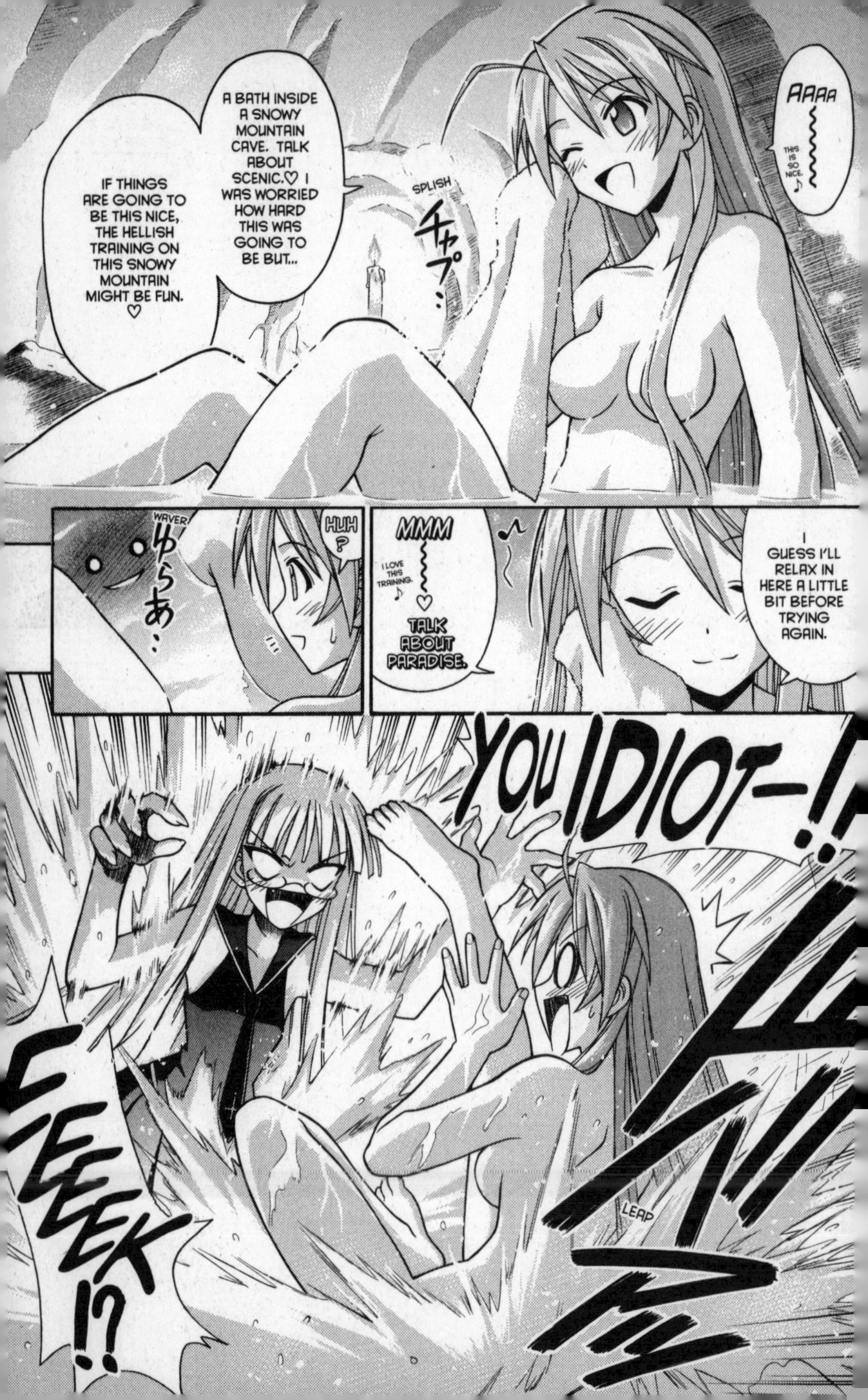
AAAA~~
THIS IS SO NICE. ♪
SPLISH
チャプ…
A BATH INSIDE A SNOWY MOUNTAIN CAVE. TALK ABOUT SCENIC.♡ I WAS WORRIED HOW HARD THIS WAS GOING TO BE BUT...
IF THINGS ARE GOING TO BE THIS NICE, THE HELLISH TRAINING ON THIS SNOWY MOUNTAIN MIGHT BE FUN. ♡
I GUESS I'LL RELAX IN HERE A LITTLE BIT BEFORE TRYING AGAIN.
MMM~ ♡
I LOVE THIS TRAINING. ♪
TALK ABOUT PARADISE.
HUH?
WAVER
ゆらあ…
YOU IDIOT—!!
LEAP
EEEEEK!?

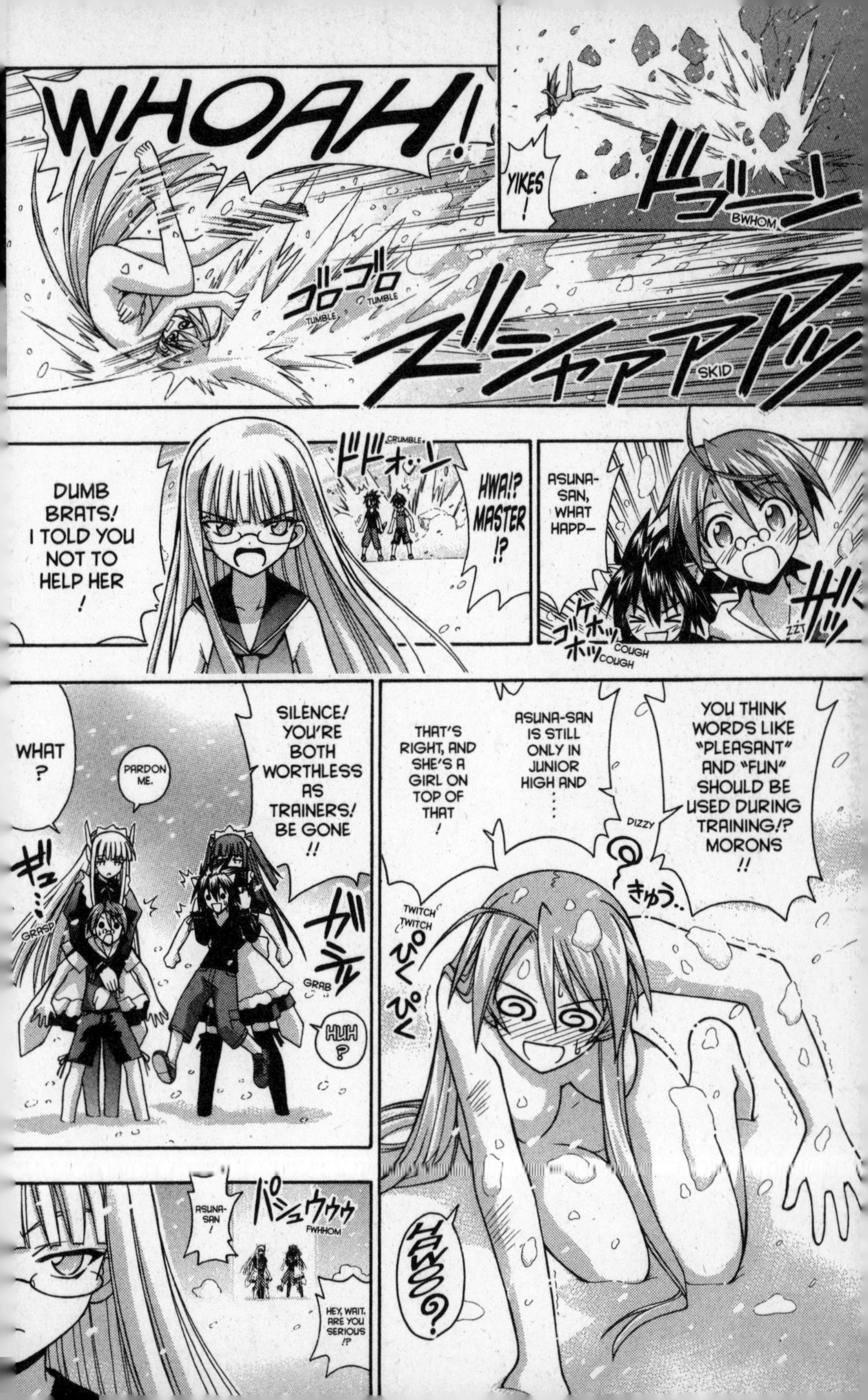
YIKES!
ドゴーン
BWHOM
WHOAH!
ゴロゴロ
TUMBLE TUMBLE
ズシャアアッ
SKID
ASUNA-SAN, WHAT HAPP—
ザッ
ZZT
ゲホッゴホッ
COUGH COUGH
ドドオッ
CRUMBLE
HWA!? MASTER!?
DUMB BRATS! I TOLD YOU NOT TO HELP HER!
YOU THINK WORDS LIKE "PLEASANT" AND "FUN" SHOULD BE USED DURING TRAINING!? MORONS!!
ASUNA-SAN IS STILL ONLY IN JUNIOR HIGH AND......
THAT'S RIGHT, AND SHE'S A GIRL ON TOP OF THAT!
きゅう..
DIZZY
ぴくぴく
TWITCH TWITCH
HAUU?
SILENCE! YOU'RE BOTH WORTHLESS AS TRAINERS! BE GONE!!
PARDON ME.
WHAT?
ガシッ
GRAB
HUH?
ギュ...
GRASP
パシュウウウ
FWHHOM
ASUNA-SAN!
HEY, WAIT. ARE YOU SERIOUS!?

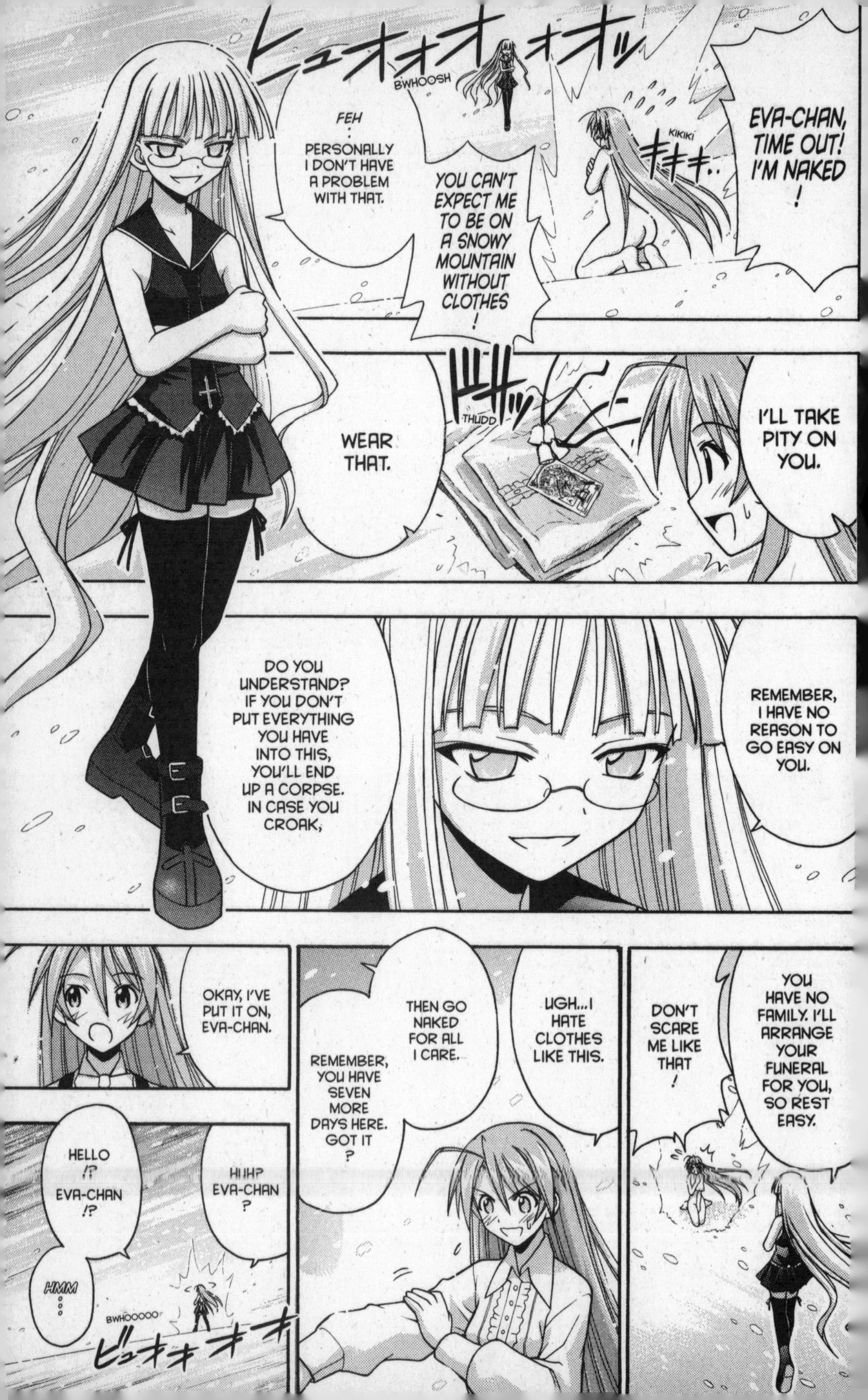
ヒュオオオオオッ
BWHOOSH
KIKIKI
キキキ..
EVA-CHAN, TIME OUT! I'M NAKED!
YOU CAN'T EXPECT ME TO BE ON A SNOWY MOUNTAIN WITHOUT CLOTHES!
FEH... PERSONALLY I DON'T HAVE A PROBLEM WITH THAT.
I'LL TAKE PITY ON YOU.
ドサッ
THUDD
WEAR THAT.
REMEMBER, I HAVE NO REASON TO GO EASY ON YOU.
DO YOU UNDERSTAND? IF YOU DON'T PUT EVERYTHING YOU HAVE INTO THIS, YOU'LL END UP A CORPSE. IN CASE YOU CROAK,
YOU HAVE NO FAMILY. I'LL ARRANGE YOUR FUNERAL FOR YOU, SO REST EASY.
DON'T SCARE ME LIKE THAT!
UGH...I HATE CLOTHES LIKE THIS.
THEN GO NAKED FOR ALL I CARE.
REMEMBER, YOU HAVE SEVEN MORE DAYS HERE. GOT IT?
OKAY, I'VE PUT IT ON, EVA-CHAN.
HUH? EVA-CHAN?
HELLO!? EVA-CHAN!?
HMM...
BWHOOOOO
ビュオオオオ

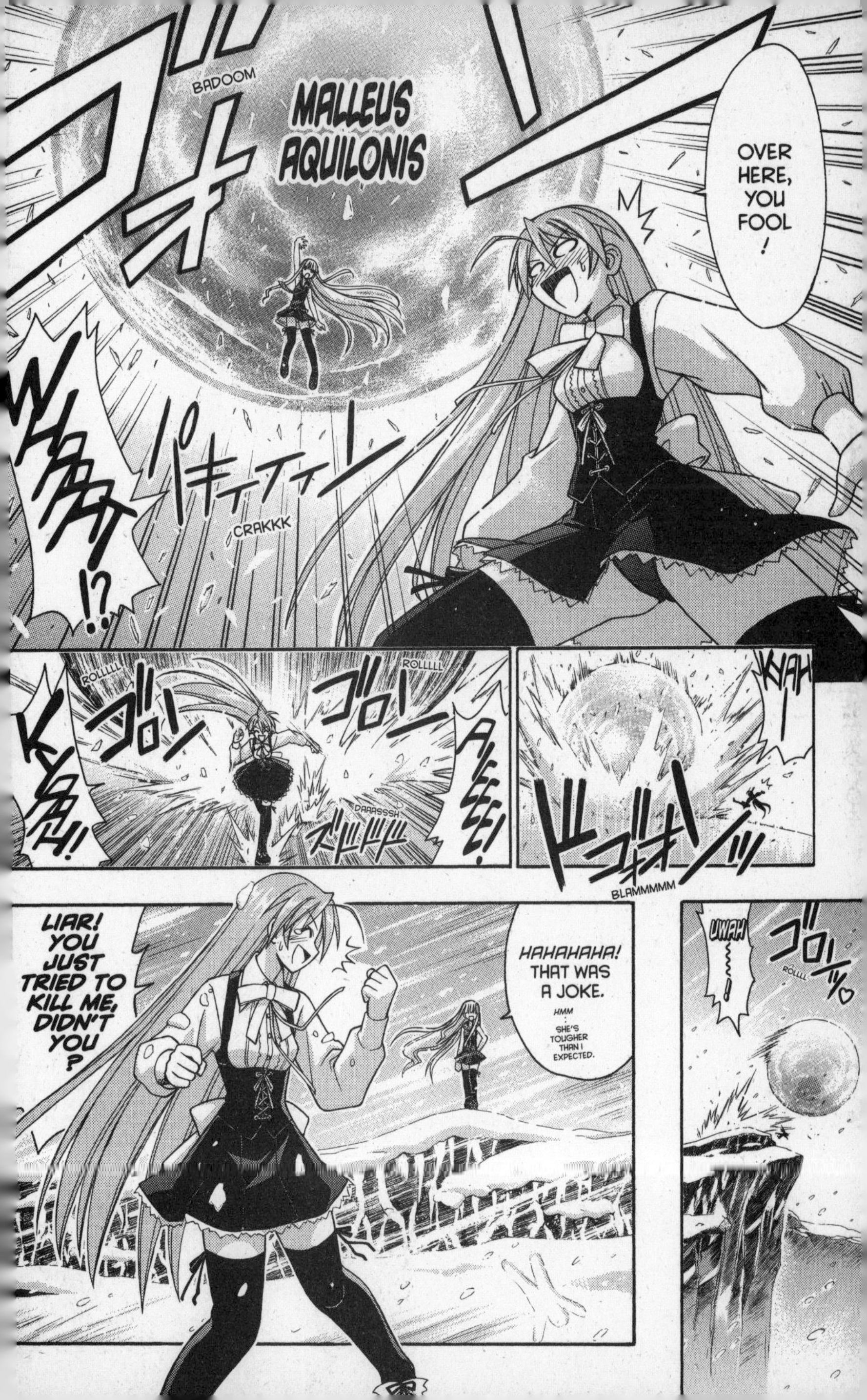
OVER HERE, YOU FOOL!
BADOOM
MALLEUS AQUILONIS
CRAKKK
WHAAT!?
KYAH!
BLAMMMMM
ROLLLLL
AIEEEE!
DARASSSH
ROLLLLL
KYAAAH!
UWAH~~~!
ROLLL
HAHAHAHA! THAT WAS A JOKE.
HMM... SHE'S TOUGHER THAN I EXPECTED.
LIAR! YOU JUST TRIED TO KILL ME, DIDN'T YOU?

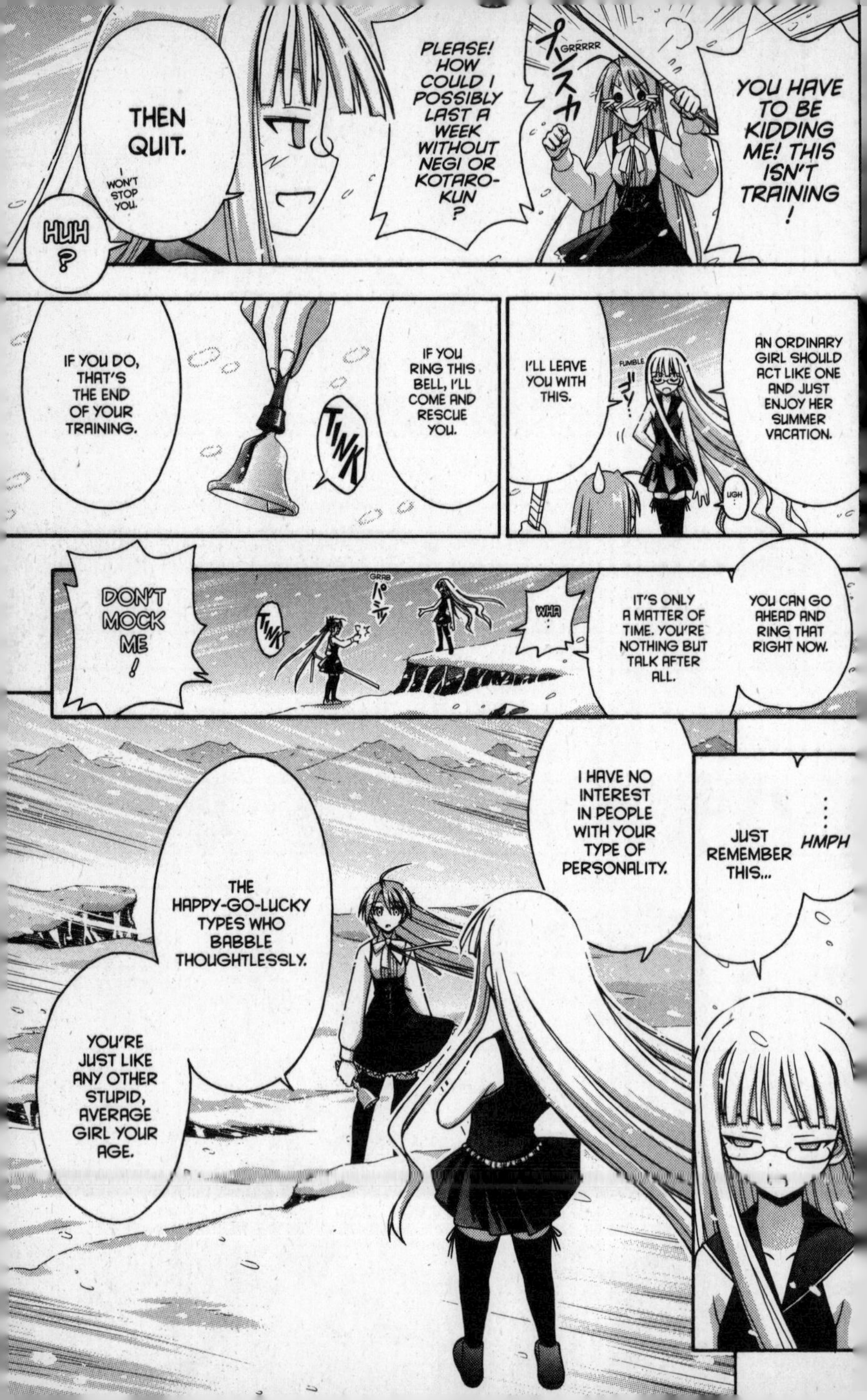
YOU HAVE TO BE KIDDING ME! THIS ISN'T TRAINING!
GRRRRR
PLEASE! HOW COULD I POSSIBLY LAST A WEEK WITHOUT NEGI OR KOTARO-KUN?
THEN QUIT.
I WON'T STOP YOU.
HUH?
AN ORDINARY GIRL SHOULD ACT LIKE ONE AND JUST ENJOY HER SUMMER VACATION.
FUMBLE
UGH...
I'LL LEAVE YOU WITH THIS.
IF YOU RING THIS BELL, I'LL COME AND RESCUE YOU.
TINK
IF YOU DO, THAT'S THE END OF YOUR TRAINING.
YOU CAN GO AHEAD AND RING THAT RIGHT NOW.
IT'S ONLY A MATTER OF TIME. YOU'RE NOTHING BUT TALK AFTER ALL.
WHA...
GRAB
TINK
DON'T MOCK ME!
...HMPH
JUST REMEMBER THIS...
I HAVE NO INTEREST IN PEOPLE WITH YOUR TYPE OF PERSONALITY.
THE HAPPY-GO-LUCKY TYPES WHO BABBLE THOUGHTLESSLY.
YOU'RE JUST LIKE ANY OTHER STUPID, AVERAGE GIRL YOUR AGE.

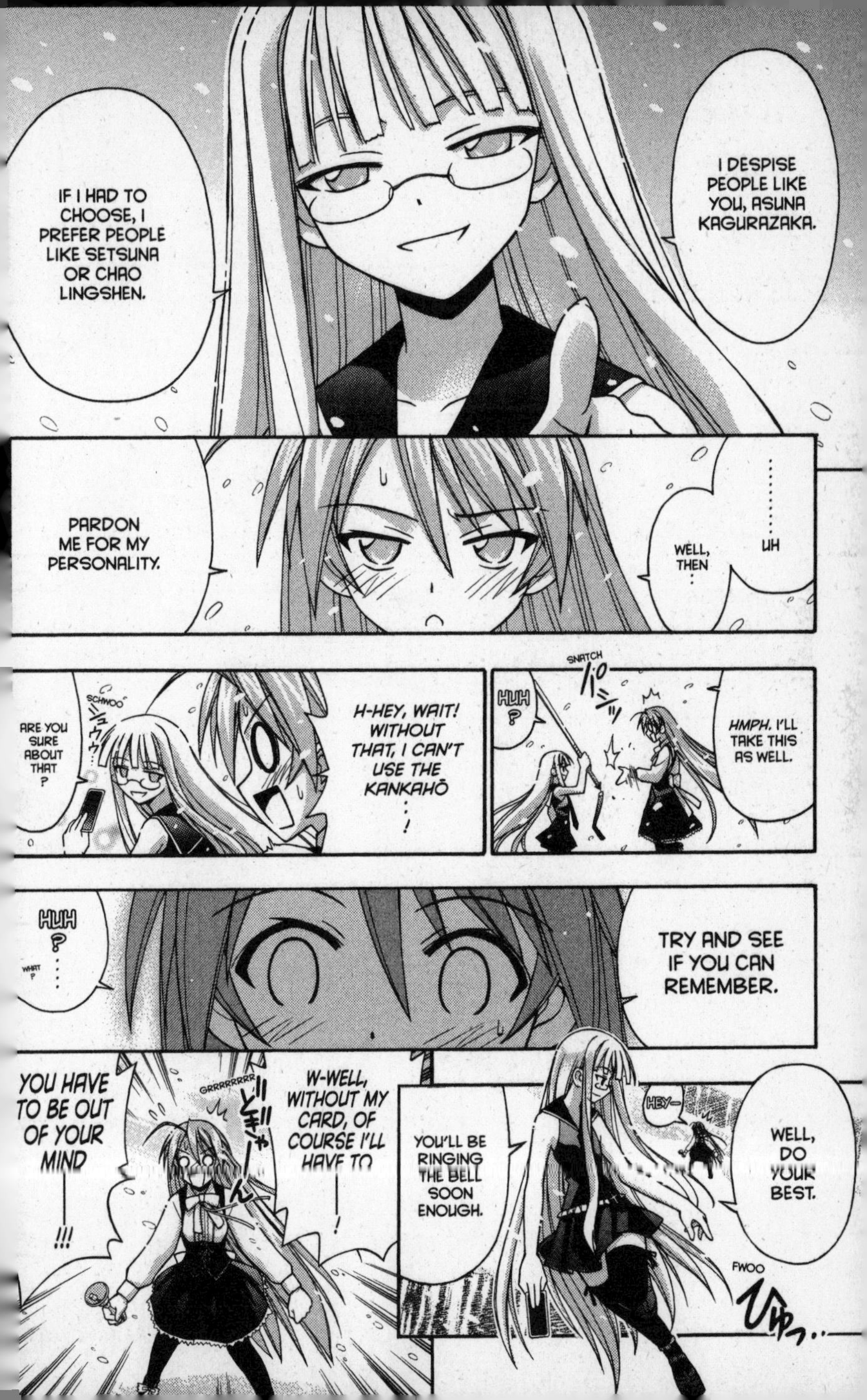
I DESPISE PEOPLE LIKE YOU, ASUNA KAGURAZAKA.
IF I HAD TO CHOOSE, I PREFER PEOPLE LIKE SETSUNA OR CHAO LINGSHEN.
......UH
WELL, THEN...
PARDON ME FOR MY PERSONALITY.
HMPH. I'LL TAKE THIS AS WELL.
SNATCH
HUH?
H-HEY, WAIT! WITHOUT THAT, I CAN'T USE THE KANKAHŌ...!
SCHWOO
ARE YOU SURE ABOUT THAT?
TRY AND SEE IF YOU CAN REMEMBER.
HUH? WHAT? ....
WELL, DO YOUR BEST.
HEY—
FWOO
YOU'LL BE RINGING THE BELL SOON ENOUGH.
W-WELL, WITHOUT MY CARD, OF COURSE I'LL HAVE TO—!
GRRRRRRRR
YOU HAVE TO BE OUT OF YOUR MIND—!!!

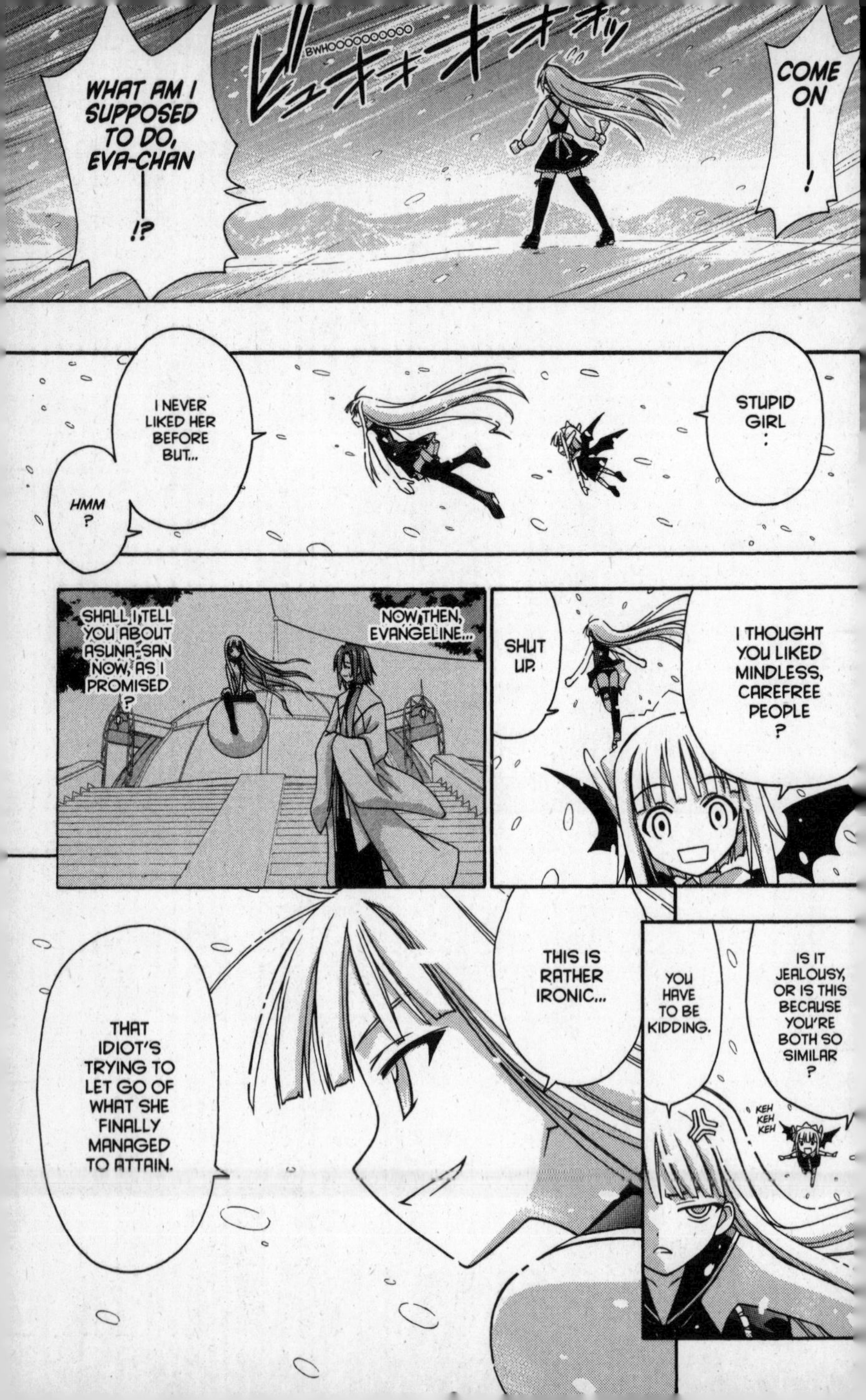
COME ON—!
BWHOOOOOOOOOOO
WHAT AM I SUPPOSED TO DO, EVA-CHAN—!?
STUPID GIRL...
I NEVER LIKED HER BEFORE BUT...
HMM?
I THOUGHT YOU LIKED MINDLESS, CAREFREE PEOPLE?
SHUT UP.
NOW, THEN, EVANGELINE...
SHALL I TELL YOU ABOUT ASUNA-SAN NOW, AS I PROMISED?
IS IT JEALOUSY, OR IS THIS BECAUSE YOU'RE BOTH SO SIMILAR?
KEH KEH KEH
YOU HAVE TO BE KIDDING.
THIS IS RATHER IRONIC...
THAT IDIOT'S TRYING TO LET GO OF WHAT SHE FINALLY MANAGED TO ATTAIN.

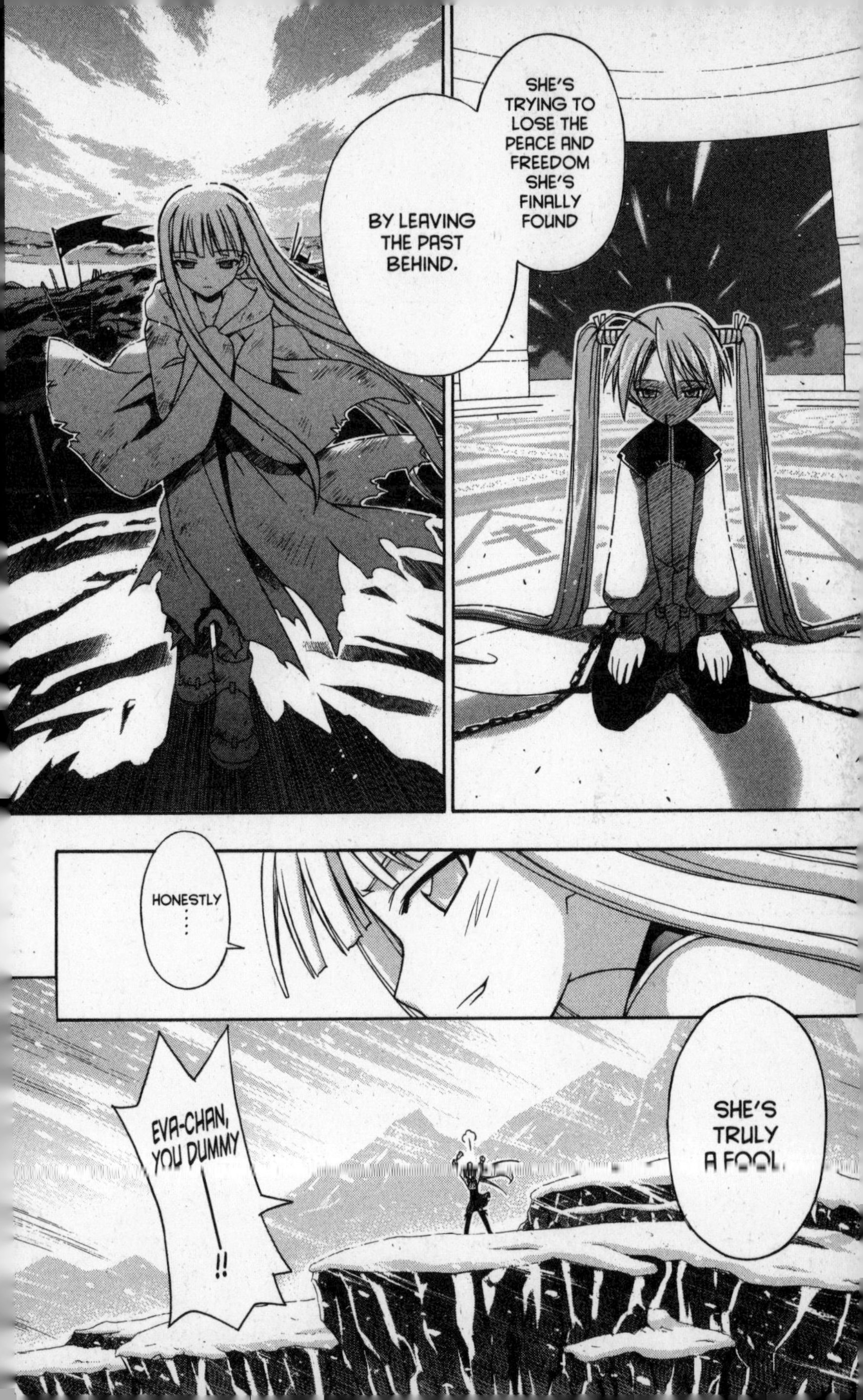
SHE'S TRYING TO LOSE THE PEACE AND FREEDOM SHE'S FINALLY FOUND
BY LEAVING THE PAST BEHIND.
HONESTLY......
SHE'S TRULY A FOOL.
EVA-CHAN, YOU DUMMY!!

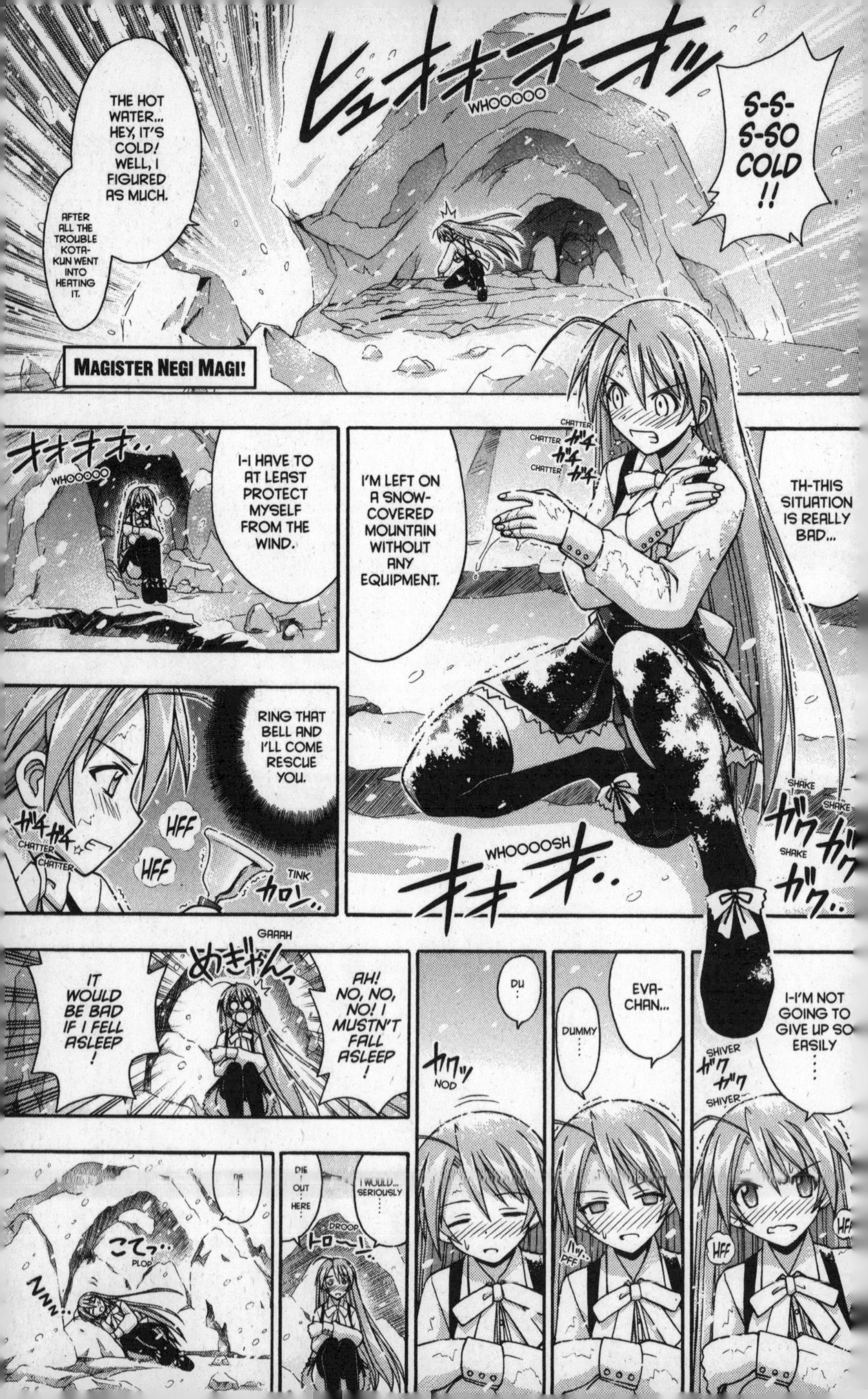
S-S-S-SO COLD!!
ヒュオォオオオッ
WHOOOOO
THE HOT WATER... HEY, IT'S COLD! WELL, I FIGURED AS MUCH.
AFTER ALL THE TROUBLE KOTA-KUN WENT INTO HEATING IT.
MAGISTER NEGI MAGI!
TH-THIS SITUATION IS REALLY BAD...
ガチ ガチ ガチ
CHATTER CHATTER CHATTER
I'M LEFT ON A SNOW-COVERED MOUNTAIN WITHOUT ANY EQUIPMENT.
ガク ガク ガク...
SHAKE SHAKE SHAKE
オォォ...
WHOOOOSH
オオオオ...
WHOOOOO
I-I HAVE TO AT LEAST PROTECT MYSELF FROM THE WIND.
RING THAT BELL AND I'LL COME RESCUE YOU.
HFF
HFF
ガチガチ
CHATTER CHATTER
カロン...
TINK
I-I'M NOT GOING TO GIVE UP SO EASILY......
ガク ガク
SHIVER SHIVER
HFF
HFF
EVA-CHAN...
DUMMY......
DU...
ハッ
PFF
カクッ
NOD
AH! NO, NO, NO! I MUSTN'T FALL ASLEEP!
めぎゃんっ
GAAAH
IT WOULD BE BAD IF I FELL ASLEEP!
I WOULD... SERIOUSLY......
DIE OUT HERE
トロ～ン
DROOP
こてっ...
PLOP
NNN...

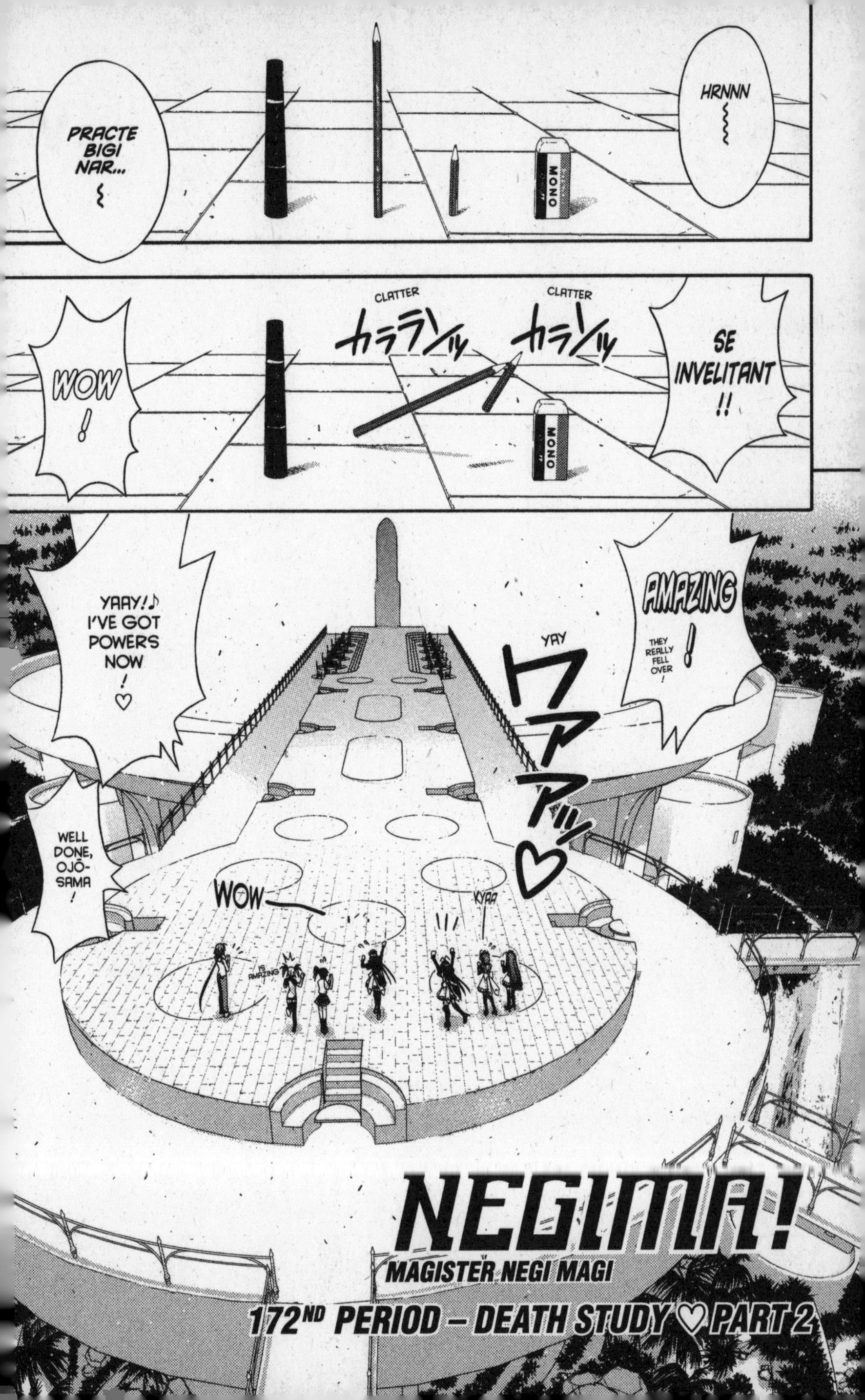
HRNNN ~
PRACTE BIGI NAR... ~
SE INVELITANT!!
CLATTER
カララン ッ
CLATTER
カラン ッ
WOW!
AMAZING!
THEY REALLY FELL OVER!
YAY
ワアアッ♡
KYAA
YAAY!♪ I'VE GOT POWERS NOW!♡
WOW—
IS AMAZING
WELL DONE, OJŌ-SAMA!
NEGIMA!
MAGISTER NEGI MAGI
172ND PERIOD – DEATH STUDY ♡ PART 2

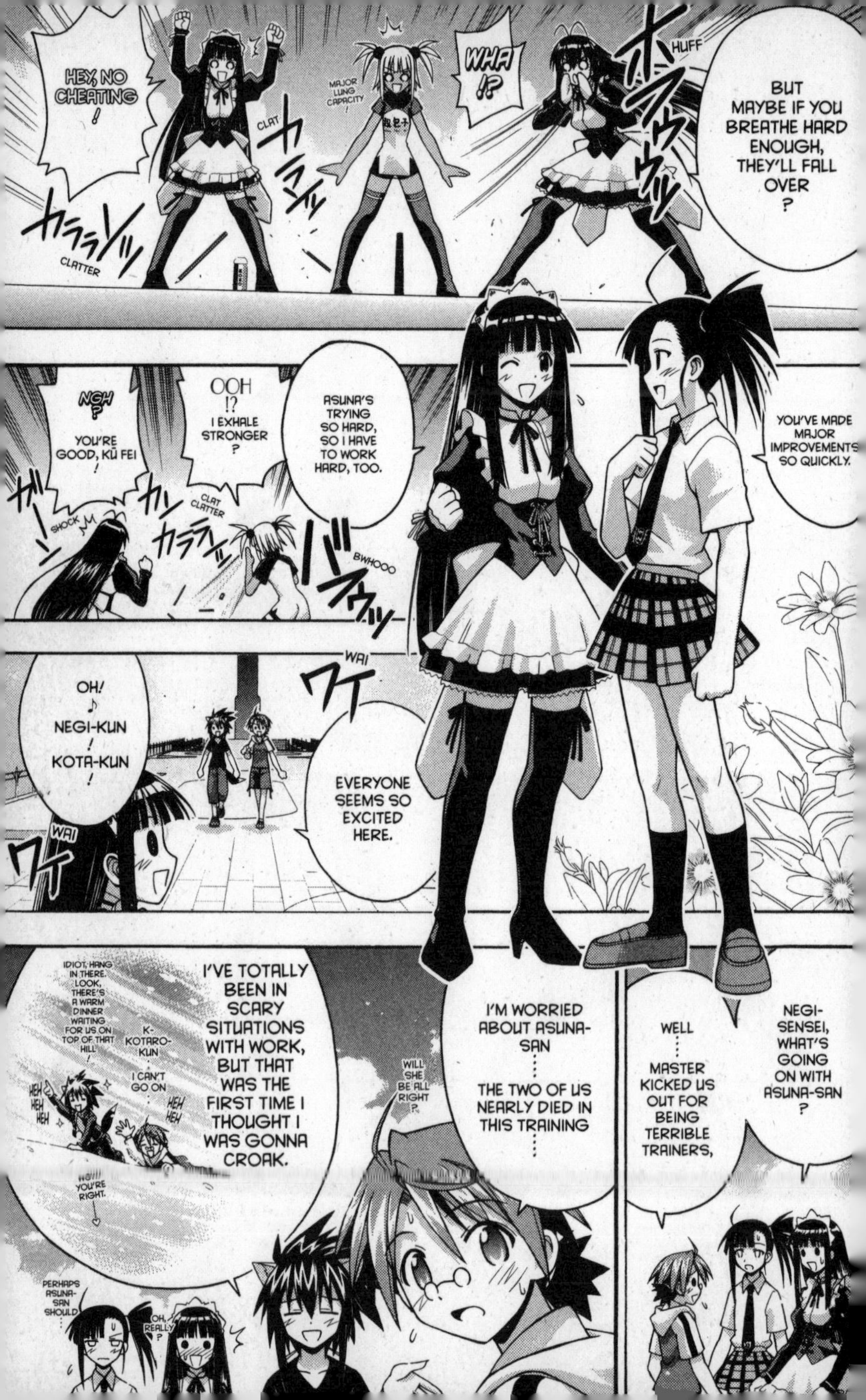
BUT MAYBE IF YOU BREATHE HARD ENOUGH, THEY'LL FALL OVER?
HUFF
WHA!?
MAJOR LUNG CAPACITY
CLAT
HEY, NO CHEATING!
CLATTER
YOU'VE MADE MAJOR IMPROVEMENTS SO QUICKLY.
ASUNA'S TRYING SO HARD, SO I HAVE TO WORK HARD, TOO.
BWHOOO
OOH!? I EXHALE STRONGER?
CLAT CLATTER
NGH? YOU'RE GOOD, KŪ FEI!
SHOCK
WAI
OH! ♪ NEGI-KUN! KOTA-KUN!
WAI
EVERYONE SEEMS SO EXCITED HERE.
NEGI-SENSEI, WHAT'S GOING ON WITH ASUNA-SAN?
WELL... MASTER KICKED US OUT FOR BEING TERRIBLE TRAINERS,
I'M WORRIED ABOUT ASUNA-SAN... THE TWO OF US NEARLY DIED IN THIS TRAINING...
WILL SHE BE ALL RIGHT?
I'VE TOTALLY BEEN IN SCARY SITUATIONS WITH WORK, BUT THAT WAS THE FIRST TIME I THOUGHT I WAS GONNA CROAK.
IDIOT, HANG IN THERE. LOOK, THERE'S A WARM DINNER WAITING FOR US ON TOP OF THAT HILL!
K-KOTARO-KUN
I CAN'T GO ON...
HEH HEH HEH
HEH HEH
YOU'RE RIGHT.
OH, REALLY?
PERHAPS ASUNA-SAN SHOULD...

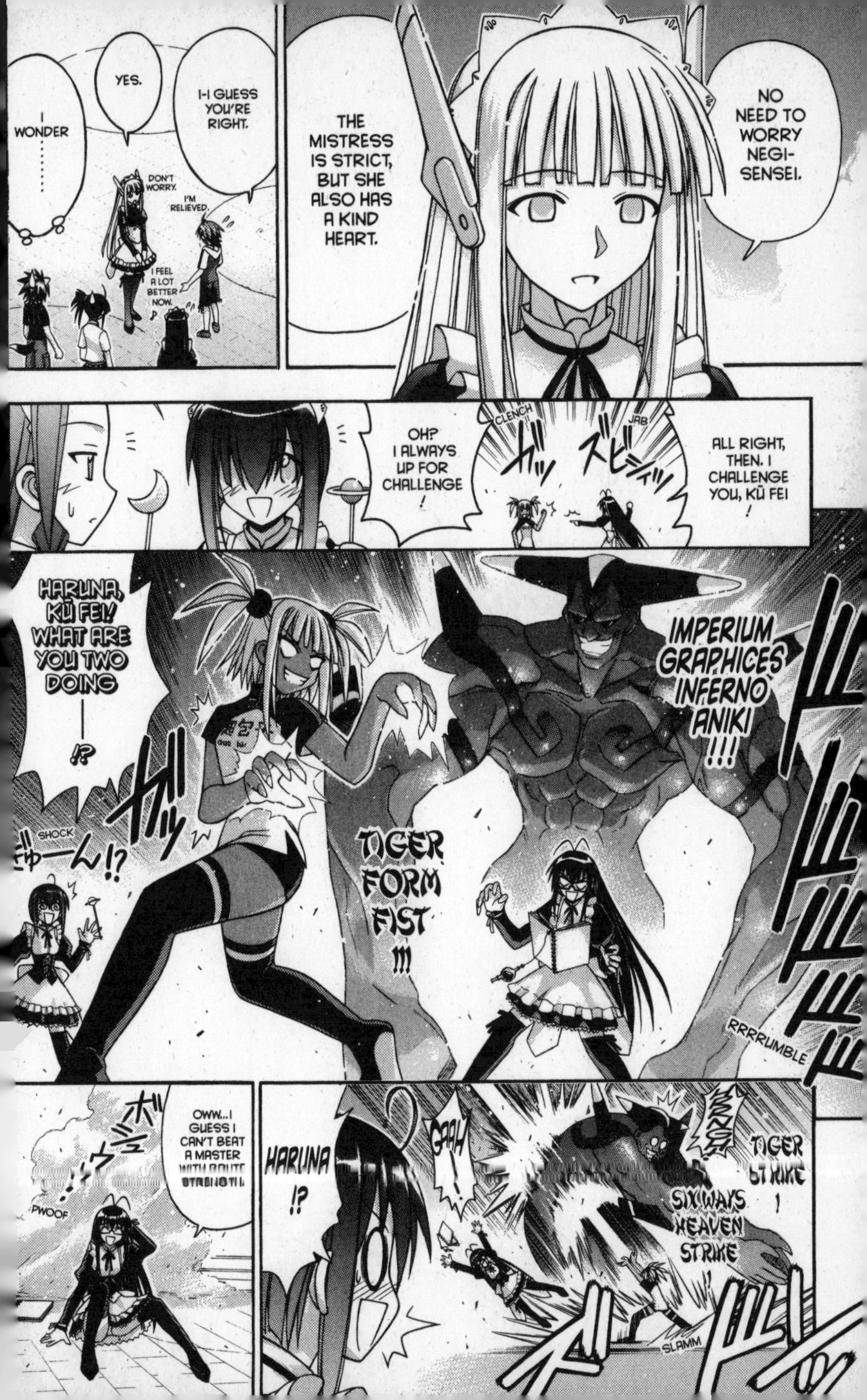
NO NEED TO WORRY NEGI-SENSEI.
THE MISTRESS IS STRICT, BUT SHE ALSO HAS A KIND HEART.
I-I GUESS YOU'RE RIGHT.
YES.
I WONDER ......
DON'T WORRY.
I'M RELIEVED.
I FEEL A LOT BETTER NOW.
ALL RIGHT, THEN. I CHALLENGE YOU, KŪ FEI!
JAB
CLENCH
OH? I ALWAYS UP FOR CHALLENGE!
IMPERIUM GRAPHICES INFERNO ANIKI!!!
RRRRUMBLE
TIGER FORM FIST!!!
HARUNA, KŪ FEI! WHAT ARE YOU TWO DOING—!?
SHOCK
TIGER STRIKE!
SIX WAYS HEAVEN STRIKE!
GAAH!
HARUNA!?
SLAMM
OWW... I GUESS I CAN'T BEAT A MASTER WITH BRUTE STRENGTH.
PWOOF

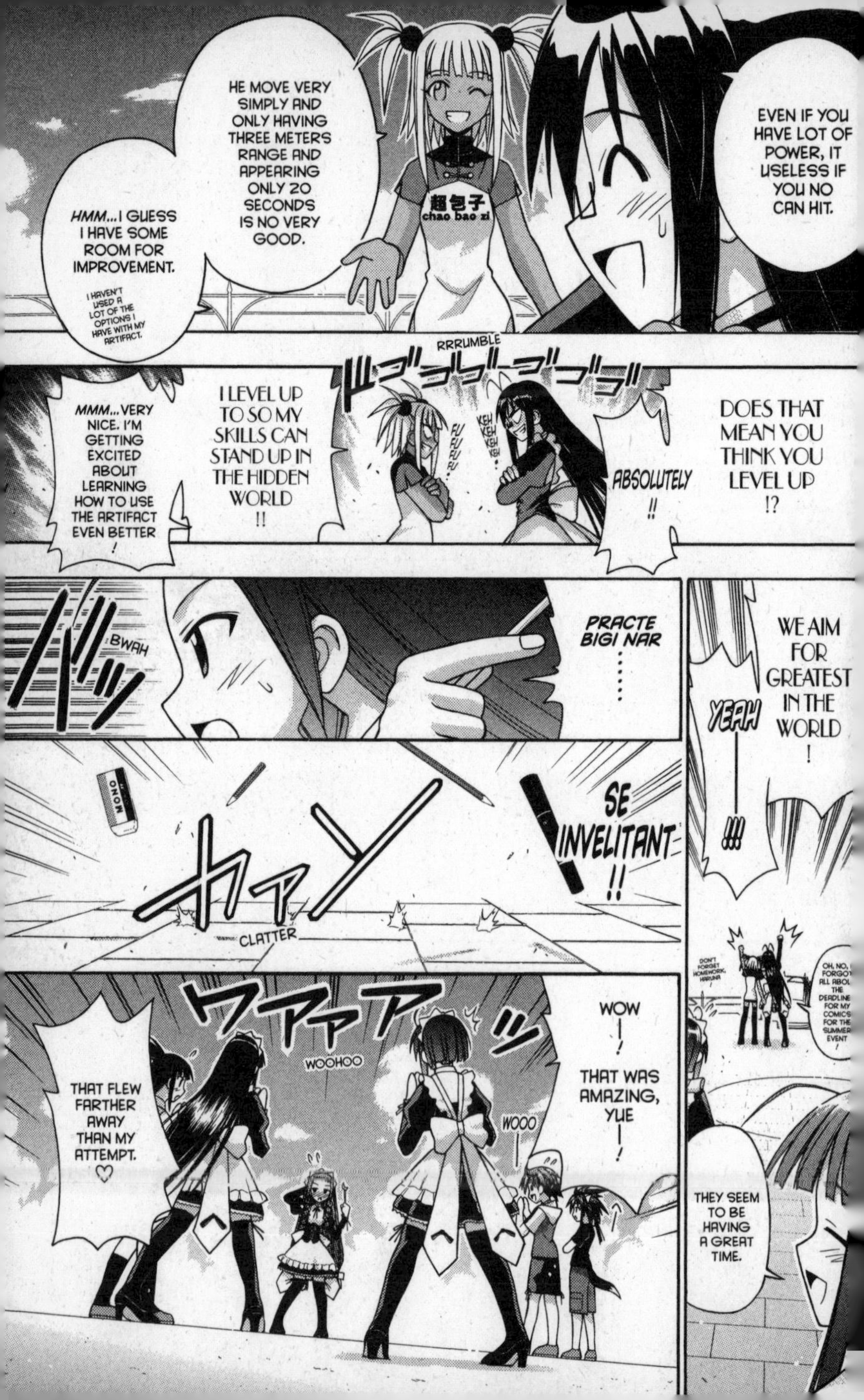
EVEN IF YOU HAVE LOT OF POWER, IT USELESS IF YOU NO CAN HIT.
HE MOVE VERY SIMPLY AND ONLY HAVING THREE METERS RANGE AND APPEARING ONLY 20 SECONDS IS NO VERY GOOD.
超包子 chao bao zi
HMM...I GUESS I HAVE SOME ROOM FOR IMPROVEMENT.
I HAVEN'T USED A LOT OF THE OPTIONS I HAVE WITH MY ARTIFACT.
RRRUMBLE
DOES THAT MEAN YOU THINK YOU LEVEL UP !?
ABSOLUTELY !!
KEH KEH KEH KEH
FU FU FU FU
I LEVEL UP TO SO MY SKILLS CAN STAND UP IN THE HIDDEN WORLD !!
MMM...VERY NICE. I'M GETTING EXCITED ABOUT LEARNING HOW TO USE THE ARTIFACT EVEN BETTER !
WE AIM FOR GREATEST IN THE WORLD !
YEAH !!!
DON'T FORGET HOMEWORK, HARUNA!
THEY SEEM TO BE HAVING A GREAT TIME.
BWAH
PRACTE BIGI NAR ......
MONO
SE INVELITANT !!
CLATTER
WOW ! THAT WAS AMAZING, YUE !
WOOO !
WOOHOO
THAT FLEW FARTHER AWAY THAN MY ATTEMPT. ♡

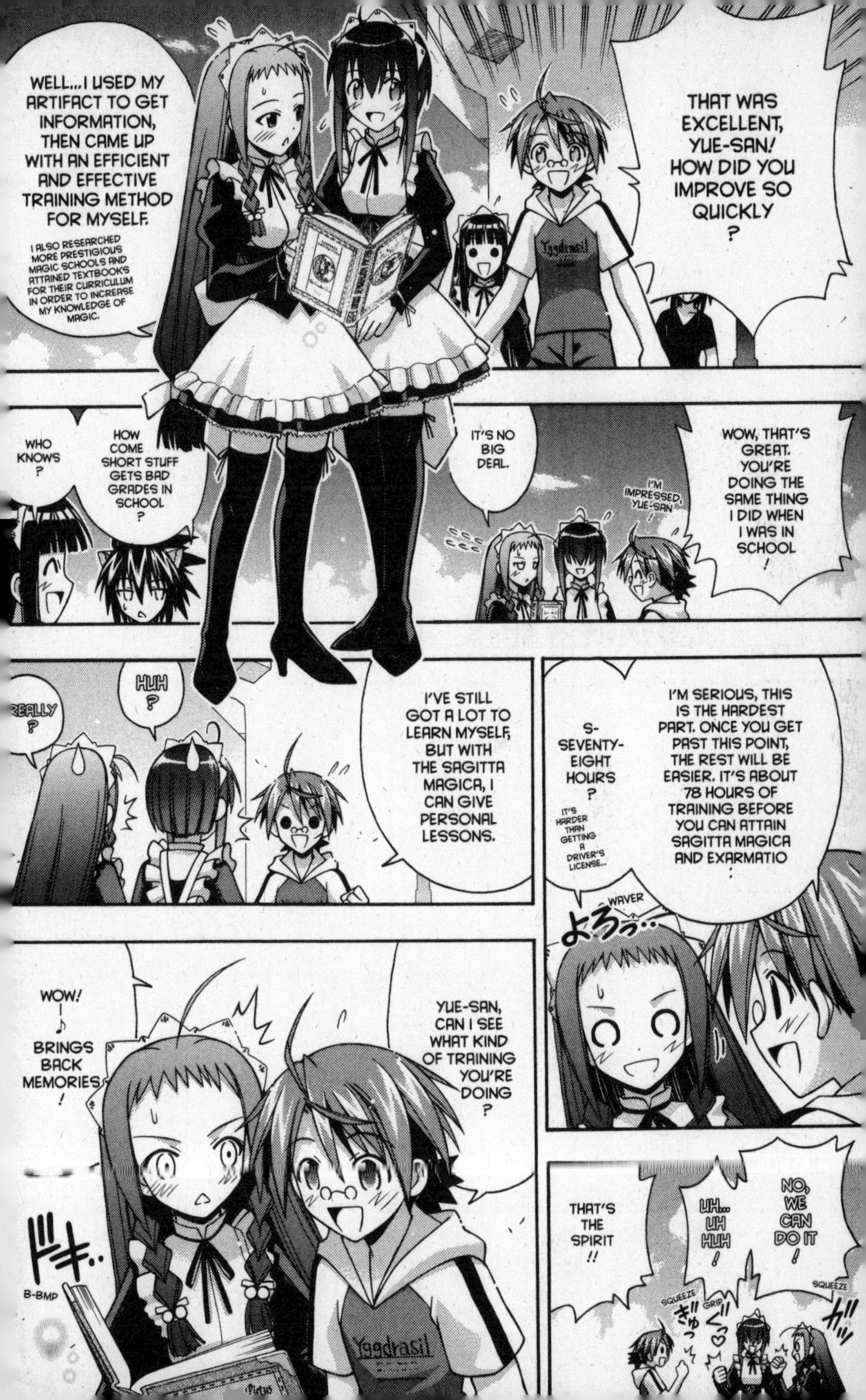
THAT WAS EXCELLENT, YUE-SAN! HOW DID YOU IMPROVE SO QUICKLY?
WELL...I USED MY ARTIFACT TO GET INFORMATION, THEN CAME UP WITH AN EFFICIENT AND EFFECTIVE TRAINING METHOD FOR MYSELF.
I ALSO RESEARCHED MORE PRESTIGIOUS MAGIC SCHOOLS AND ATTAINED TEXTBOOKS FOR THEIR CURRICULUM IN ORDER TO INCREASE MY KNOWLEDGE OF MAGIC.
WOW, THAT'S GREAT. YOU'RE DOING THE SAME THING I DID WHEN I WAS IN SCHOOL!
I'M IMPRESSED, YUE-SAN!
IT'S NO BIG DEAL.
HOW COME SHORT STUFF GETS BAD GRADES IN SCHOOL?
WHO KNOWS?
I'M SERIOUS, THIS IS THE HARDEST PART. ONCE YOU GET PAST THIS POINT, THE REST WILL BE EASIER. IT'S ABOUT 78 HOURS OF TRAINING BEFORE YOU CAN ATTAIN SAGITTA MAGICA AND EXARMATIO:
S-SEVENTY-EIGHT HOURS?
IT'S HARDER THAN GETTING A DRIVER'S LICENSE...
I'VE STILL GOT A LOT TO LEARN MYSELF, BUT WITH THE SAGITTA MAGICA, I CAN GIVE PERSONAL LESSONS.
HUH?
REALLY?
よろっ…
WAVER
NO, WE CAN DO IT!
UH... UH HUH!
THAT'S THE SPIRIT!!
SQUEEZE
きゅっ
SQUEEZE
GRIP
ぐっ
ガッ
YUE-SAN, CAN I SEE WHAT KIND OF TRAINING YOU'RE DOING?
WOW! ♪ BRINGS BACK MEMORIES!
ドキ…
B-BMP

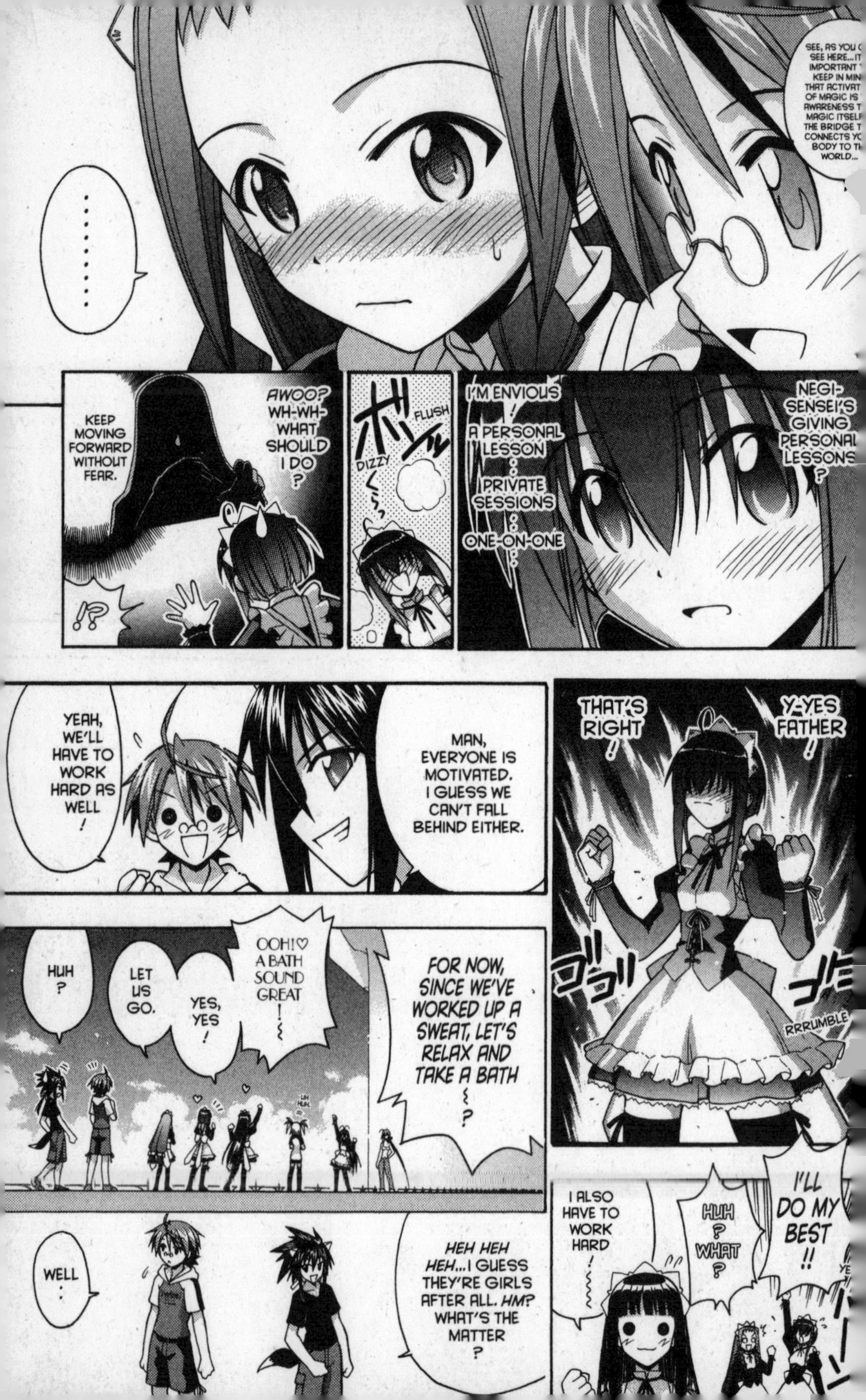
SEE, AS YOU C SEE HERE... IT IMPORTANT KEEP IN MIN THAT ACTIVAT OF MAGIC IS AWARENESS T MAGIC ITSELF THE BRIDGE T CONNECTS YO BODY TO T WORLD...
......
NEGI-SENSEI'S GIVING PERSONAL LESSONS?
I'M ENVIOUS! A PERSONAL LESSON... PRIVATE SESSIONS... ONE-ON-ONE...
FLUSH
DIZZY
AWOO? WH-WH-WHAT SHOULD I DO?
KEEP MOVING FORWARD WITHOUT FEAR.
!?
Y-YES FATHER!
THAT'S RIGHT!
RRRUMBLE
MAN, EVERYONE IS MOTIVATED. I GUESS WE CAN'T FALL BEHIND EITHER.
YEAH, WE'LL HAVE TO WORK HARD AS WELL!
FOR NOW, SINCE WE'VE WORKED UP A SWEAT, LET'S RELAX AND TAKE A BATH~?
OOH!♡ A BATH SOUND GREAT!~
YES, YES!
LET US GO.
HUH?
I'LL DO MY BEST!!
HUH? WHAT?
I ALSO HAVE TO WORK HARD!~~
HEH HEH HEH... I GUESS THEY'RE GIRLS AFTER ALL. HM? WHAT'S THE MATTER?
WELL...

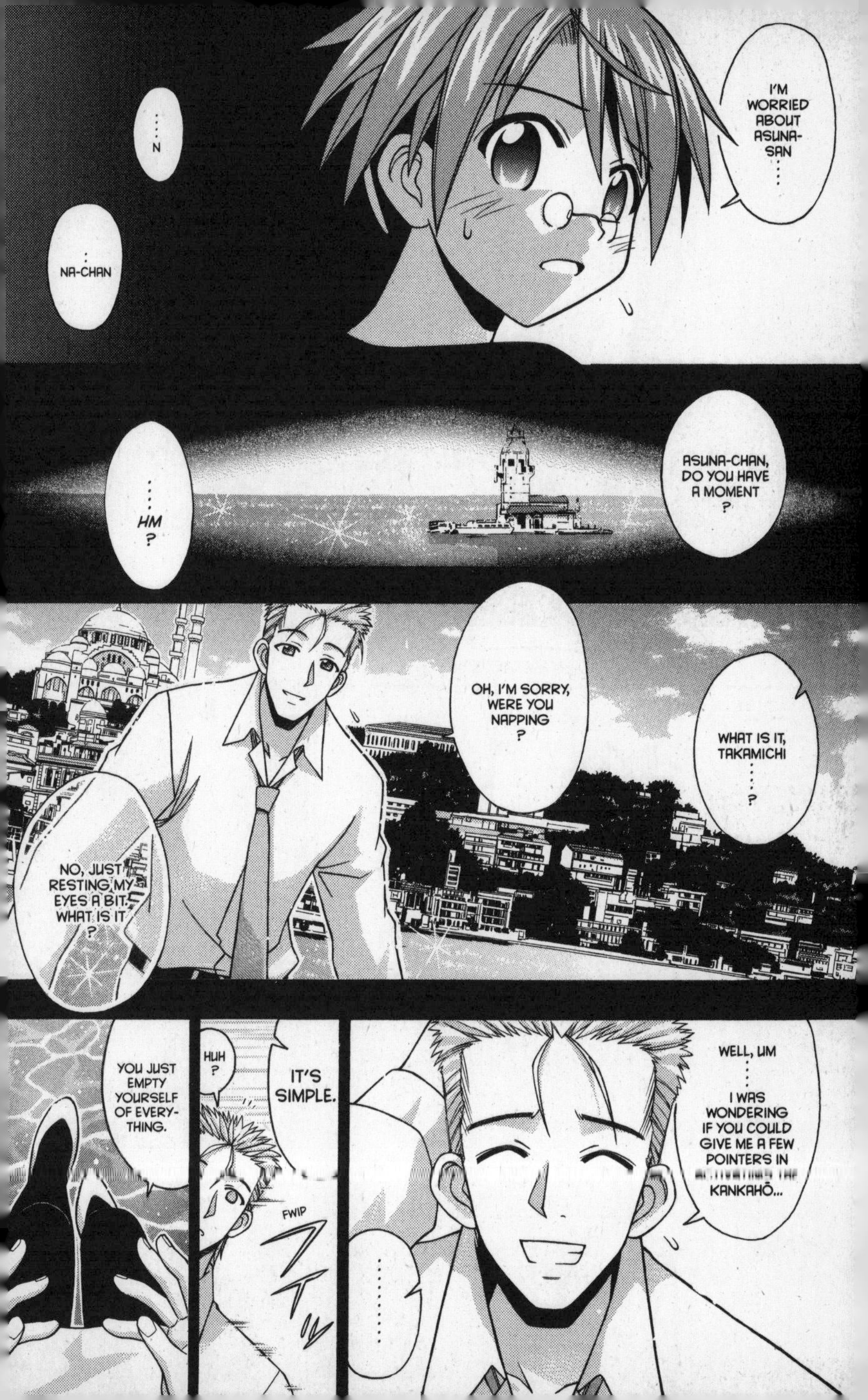
I'M WORRIED ABOUT ASUNA-SAN ....
....N
..NA-CHAN
ASUNA-CHAN, DO YOU HAVE A MOMENT ?
....HM ?
WHAT IS IT, TAKAMICHI ....?
OH, I'M SORRY, WERE YOU NAPPING ?
NO, JUST RESTING MY EYES A BIT. WHAT IS IT ?
WELL, UM .... I WAS WONDERING IF YOU COULD GIVE ME A FEW POINTERS IN
KANKAHŌ...
......
HUH ?
IT'S SIMPLE.
FWIP
YOU JUST EMPTY YOURSELF OF EVERY-THING.

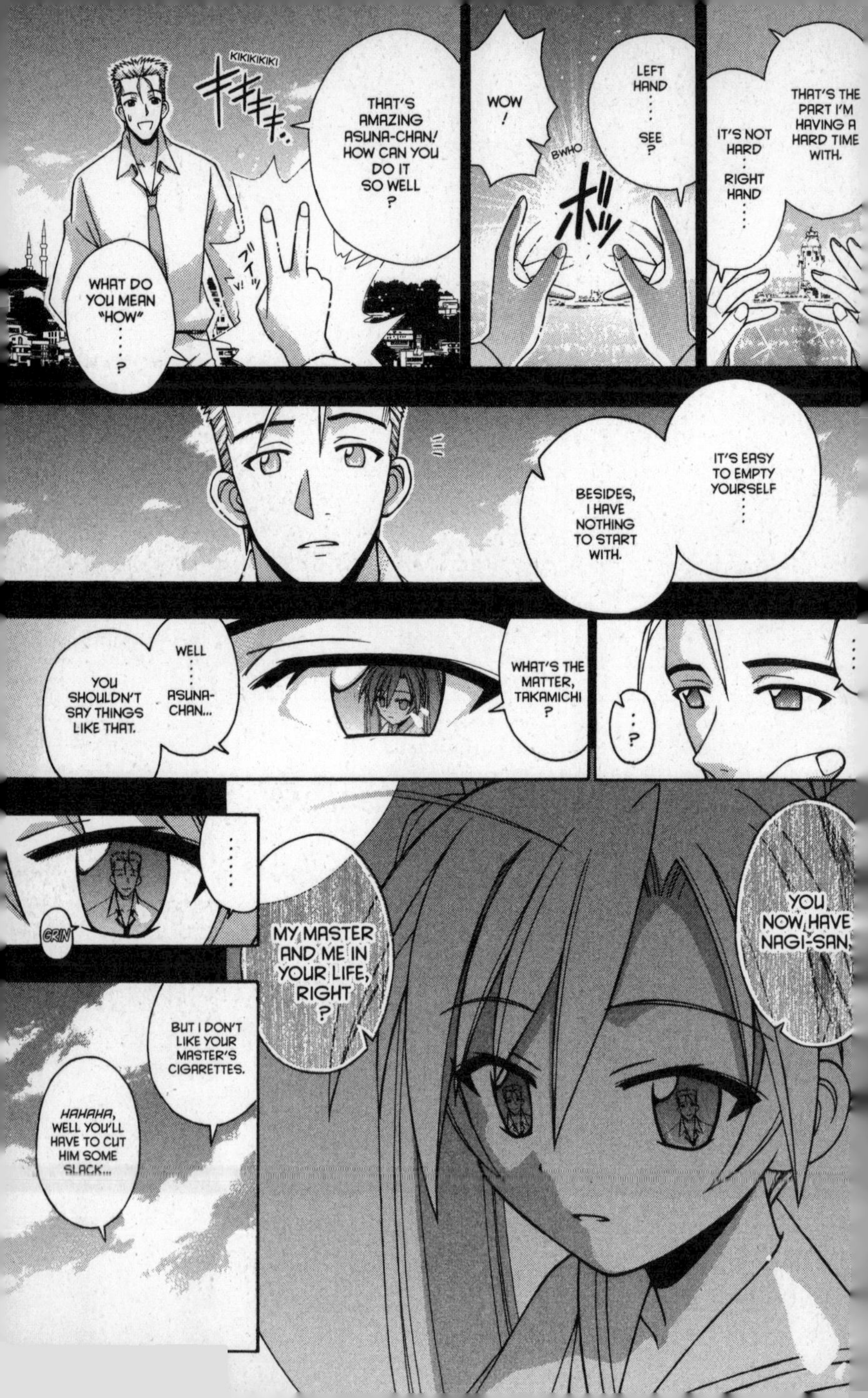
THAT'S THE PART I'M HAVING A HARD TIME WITH.
IT'S NOT HARD... RIGHT HAND...
LEFT HAND... SEE?
BWHO
WOW!
THAT'S AMAZING ASUNA-CHAN! HOW CAN YOU DO IT SO WELL?
KIKIKIKIKI
V!
WHAT DO YOU MEAN "HOW"...?
IT'S EASY TO EMPTY YOURSELF...
BESIDES, I HAVE NOTHING TO START WITH.
...
...?
WHAT'S THE MATTER, TAKAMICHI?
WELL... ASUNA-CHAN...
YOU SHOULDN'T SAY THINGS LIKE THAT.
YOU NOW HAVE NAGI-SAN,
MY MASTER AND ME IN YOUR LIFE, RIGHT?
......
GRIN
BUT I DON'T LIKE YOUR MASTER'S CIGARETTES.
HAHAHA, WELL YOU'LL HAVE TO CUT HIM SOME SLACK...

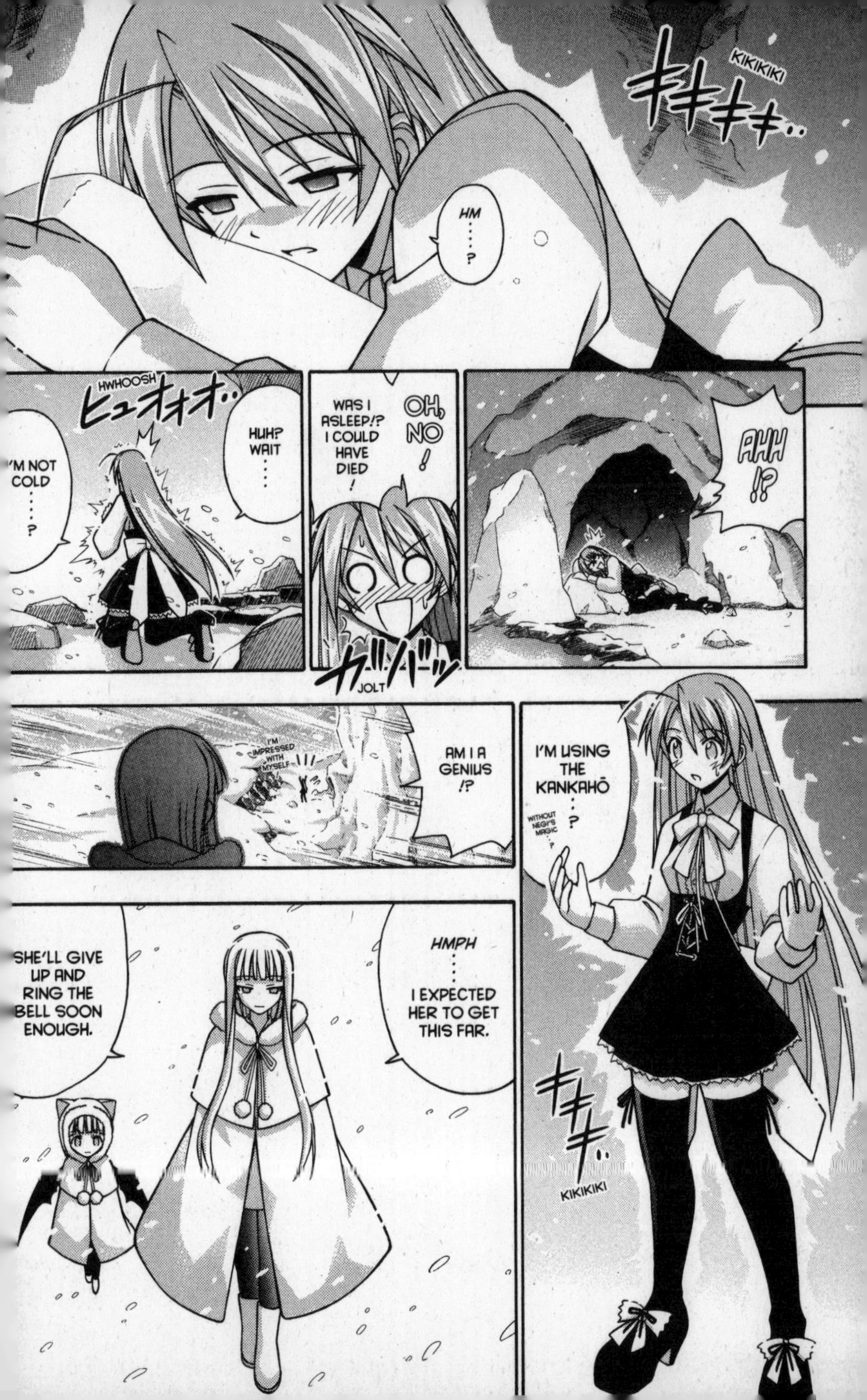
キキキキ
KIKIKIKI
HM....?
AHH!?
OH, NO!
WAS I ASLEEP!? I COULD HAVE DIED!
ガバッ
JOLT
ヒュオオオ
HWHOOSH
HUH? WAIT....
I'M NOT COLD....?
I'M USING THE KANKAHŌ...?
WITHOUT NEGI'S MAGIC...?
キキキ
KIKIKIKI
AM I A GENIUS!?
I'M IMPRESSED WITH MYSELF
HMPH.... I EXPECTED HER TO GET THIS FAR.
SHE'LL GIVE UP AND RING THE BELL SOON ENOUGH.

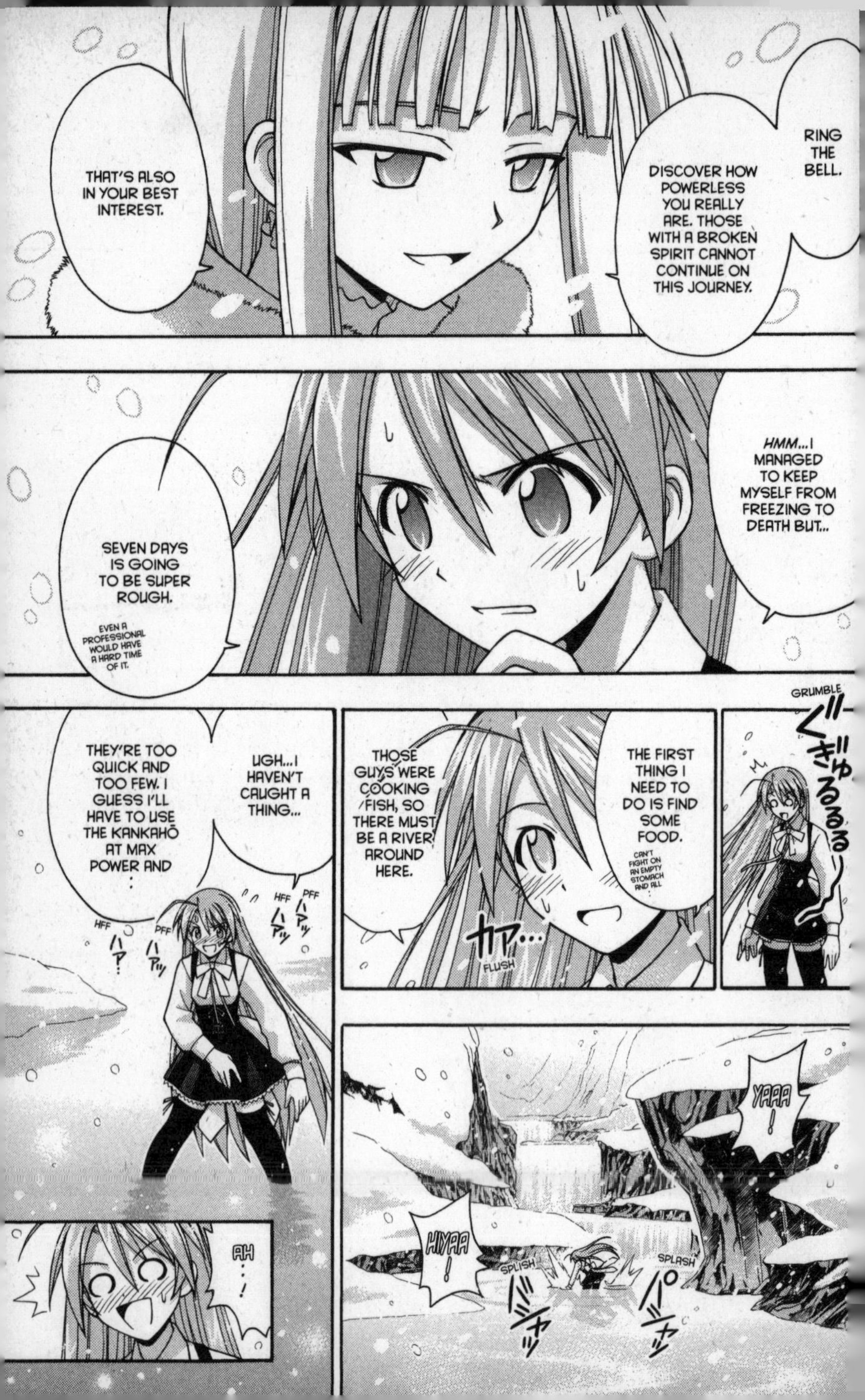
RING THE BELL.
DISCOVER HOW POWERLESS YOU REALLY ARE. THOSE WITH A BROKEN SPIRIT CANNOT CONTINUE ON THIS JOURNEY.
THAT'S ALSO IN YOUR BEST INTEREST.
HMM...I MANAGED TO KEEP MYSELF FROM FREEZING TO DEATH BUT...
SEVEN DAYS IS GOING TO BE SUPER ROUGH.
EVEN A PROFESSIONAL WOULD HAVE A HARD TIME OF IT.
GRUMBLE
ぐぎゅるるるる
THE FIRST THING I NEED TO DO IS FIND SOME FOOD.
CAN'T FIGHT ON AN EMPTY STOMACH AND ALL
THOSE GUYS WERE COOKING FISH, SO THERE MUST BE A RIVER AROUND HERE.
カア...
FLUSH
YAAA!
HIYAA!
SPLASH
パシャッ
SPLASH
バシャッ
UGH...I HAVEN'T CAUGHT A THING...
THEY'RE TOO QUICK AND TOO FEW. I GUESS I'LL HAVE TO USE THE KANKAHŌ AT MAX POWER AND
PFF
ハアッ
HFF
ハアッ
PFF
ハアッ
HFF
ハア
AH...!

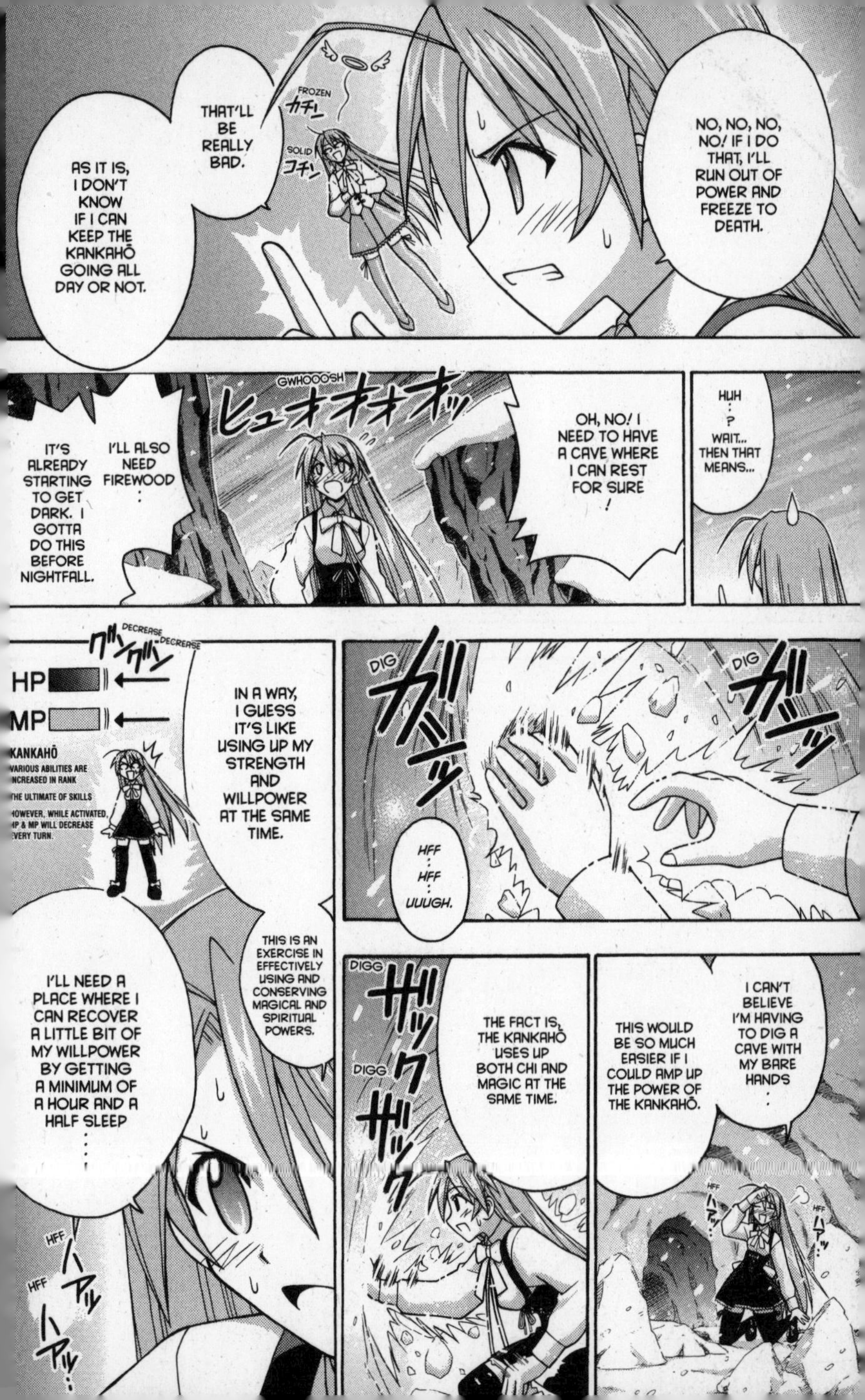
NO, NO, NO, NO! IF I DO THAT, I'LL RUN OUT OF POWER AND FREEZE TO DEATH.
FROZEN
SOLID
THAT'LL BE REALLY BAD.
AS IT IS, I DON'T KNOW IF I CAN KEEP THE KANKAHŌ GOING ALL DAY OR NOT.
HUH...? WAIT... THEN THAT MEANS...
GWHOOOSH
OH, NO! I NEED TO HAVE A CAVE WHERE I CAN REST FOR SURE!
I'LL ALSO NEED FIREWOOD...
IT'S ALREADY STARTING TO GET DARK. I GOTTA DO THIS BEFORE NIGHTFALL.
DIG
DIG
HFF... HFF... UUUGH.
DECREASE DECREASE
HP
MP
KANKAHŌ
VARIOUS ABILITIES ARE INCREASED IN RANK
THE ULTIMATE OF SKILLS
HOWEVER, WHILE ACTIVATED, HP & MP WILL DECREASE EVERY TURN.
IN A WAY, I GUESS IT'S LIKE USING UP MY STRENGTH AND WILLPOWER AT THE SAME TIME.
I CAN'T BELIEVE I'M HAVING TO DIG A CAVE WITH MY BARE HANDS...
THIS WOULD BE SO MUCH EASIER IF I COULD AMP UP THE POWER OF THE KANKAHŌ.
HFF
HFF
DIGG
DIGG
THE FACT IS, THE KANKAHŌ USES UP BOTH CHI AND MAGIC AT THE SAME TIME.
THIS IS AN EXERCISE IN EFFECTIVELY USING AND CONSERVING MAGICAL AND SPIRITUAL POWERS.
I'LL NEED A PLACE WHERE I CAN RECOVER A LITTLE BIT OF MY WILLPOWER BY GETTING A MINIMUM OF A HOUR AND A HALF SLEEP...
HFF
HFF

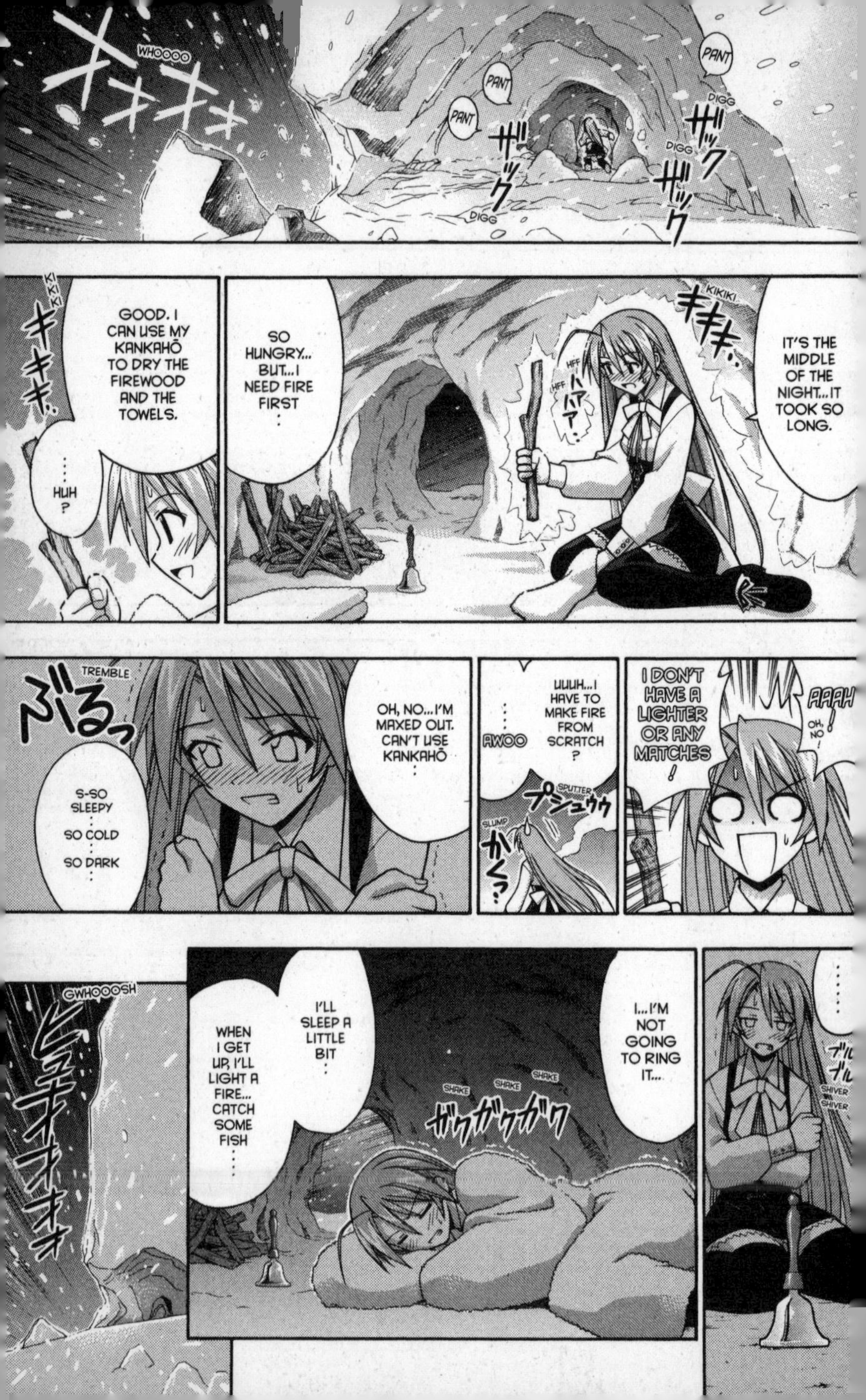
PANT
DIGG
DIGG
PANT
PANT
DIGG
WHOOOO
IT'S THE MIDDLE OF THE NIGHT...IT TOOK SO LONG.
KIKIKI
HFF
HFF
SO HUNGRY... BUT...I NEED FIRE FIRST...
GOOD. I CAN USE MY KANKAHŌ TO DRY THE FIREWOOD AND THE TOWELS.
KIKIKI
....HUH?
AAAH!
OH, NO!
I DON'T HAVE A LIGHTER OR ANY MATCHES!
UUUH...I HAVE TO MAKE FIRE FROM SCRATCH?
...AWOO
SPUTTER
SLUMP
OH, NO...I'M MAXED OUT. CAN'T USE KANKAHŌ...
TREMBLE
S-SO SLEEPY... SO COLD... SO DARK...
.....
SHIVER
SHIVER
I...I'M NOT GOING TO RING IT...
SHAKE
SHAKE
SHAKE
I'LL SLEEP A LITTLE BIT...
WHEN I GET UP, I'LL LIGHT A FIRE... CATCH SOME FISH.....
GWHOOOSH

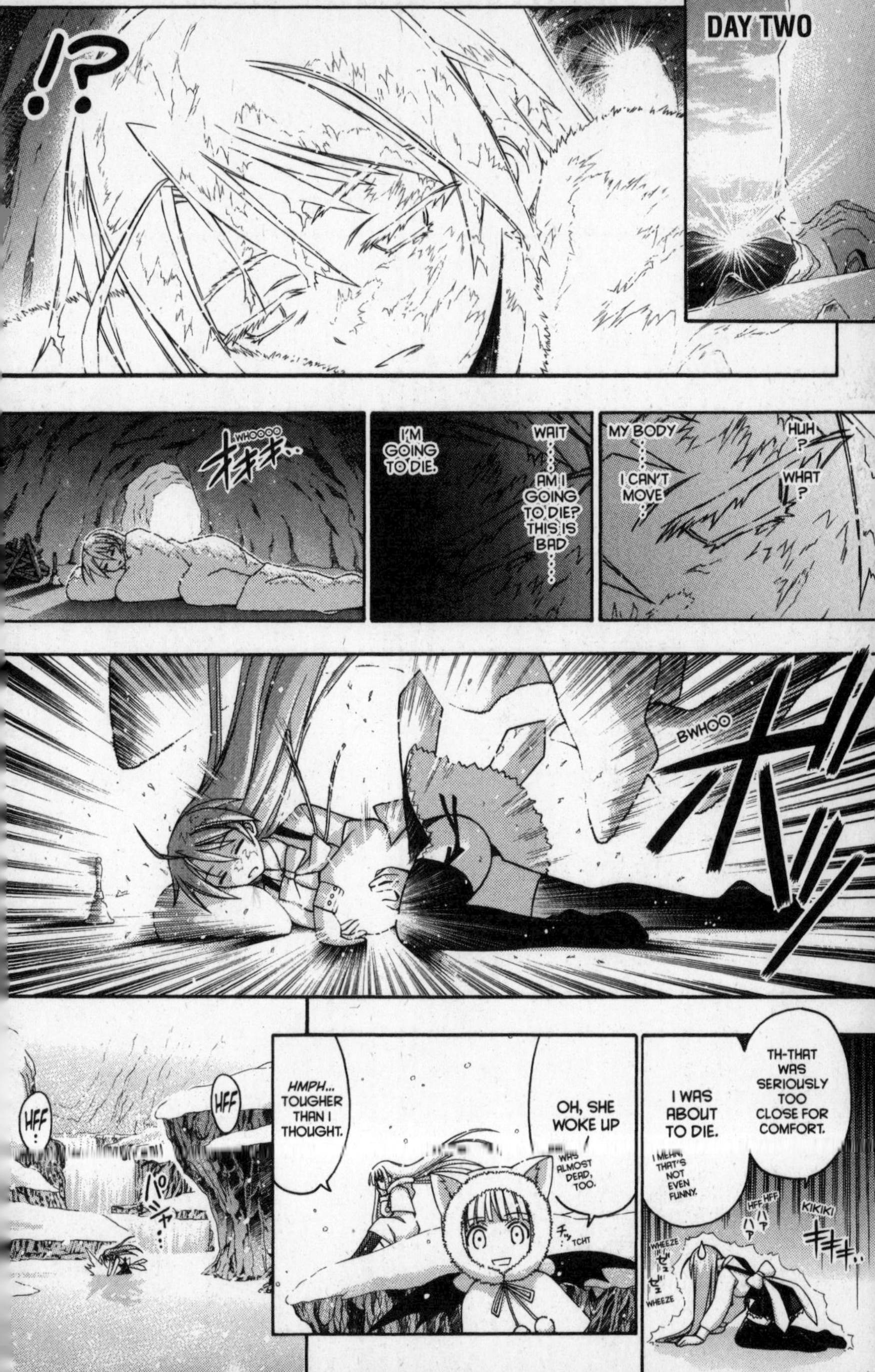
DAY TWO
!?
HUH?
WHAT?
MY BODY......
I CAN'T MOVE...
WAIT...... AM I GOING TO DIE? THIS IS BAD......
I'M GOING TO DIE.
WHOOOO
BWHOO
TH-THAT WAS SERIOUSLY TOO CLOSE FOR COMFORT.
I WAS ABOUT TO DIE.
I MEAN, THAT'S NOT EVEN FUNNY.
HFF HFF
KIKIKI
WHEEZE
WHEEZE
OH, SHE WOKE UP!
WAS ALMOST DEAD, TOO.
HMPH... TOUGHER THAN I THOUGHT.
TCHT
HFF
HFF

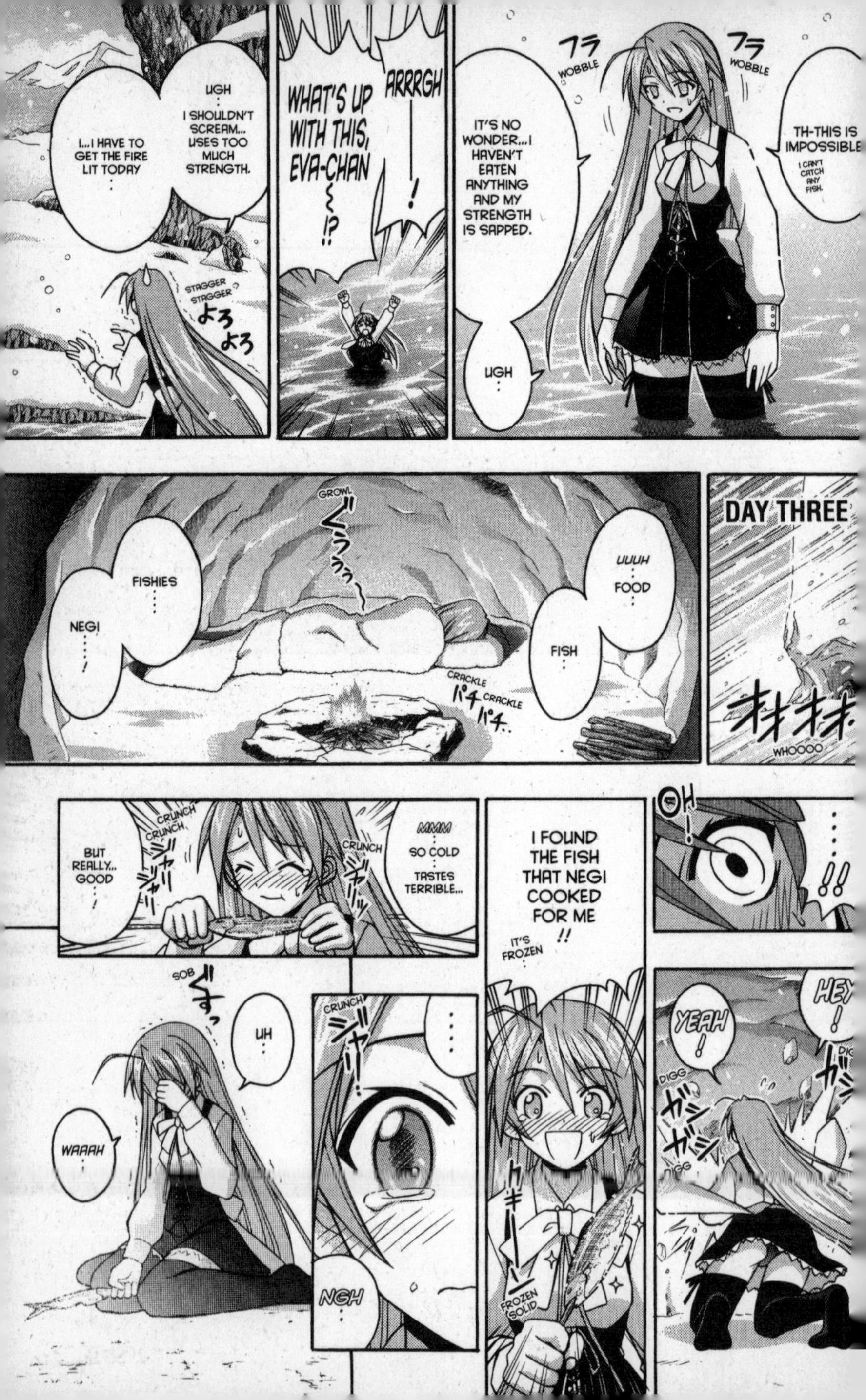
TH-THIS IS IMPOSSIBLE
I CAN'T CATCH ANY FISH.
フラ WOBBLE
フラ WOBBLE
IT'S NO WONDER...I HAVEN'T EATEN ANYTHING AND MY STRENGTH IS SAPPED.
UGH...
ARRRGH—!
WHAT'S UP WITH THIS, EVA-CHAN~~!?
UGH... I SHOULDN'T SCREAM... USES TOO MUCH STRENGTH.
I...I HAVE TO GET THE FIRE LIT TODAY...
STAGGER STAGGER
よろよろ
DAY THREE
オオオオ
WHOOOO
UUUH... FOOD...
FISH...
GROWL
ぐうううう~
CRACKLE パチ CRACKLE パチ
FISHIES...
NEGI...!
OH...!
...!!
HEY!
YEAH!
DIGG ガシ DIGG ガシ ガシ
I FOUND THE FISH THAT NEGI COOKED FOR ME!!
IT'S FROZEN...
FROZEN SOLID
MMM... SO COLD... TASTES TERRIBLE...
CRUNCH ジャリッ
CRUNCH CRUNCH ジャリ ジャリ
BUT REALLY.. GOOD...!
....
CRUNCH ジャー
NGH...
SOB ぐすっ
UH...
WAAAH...

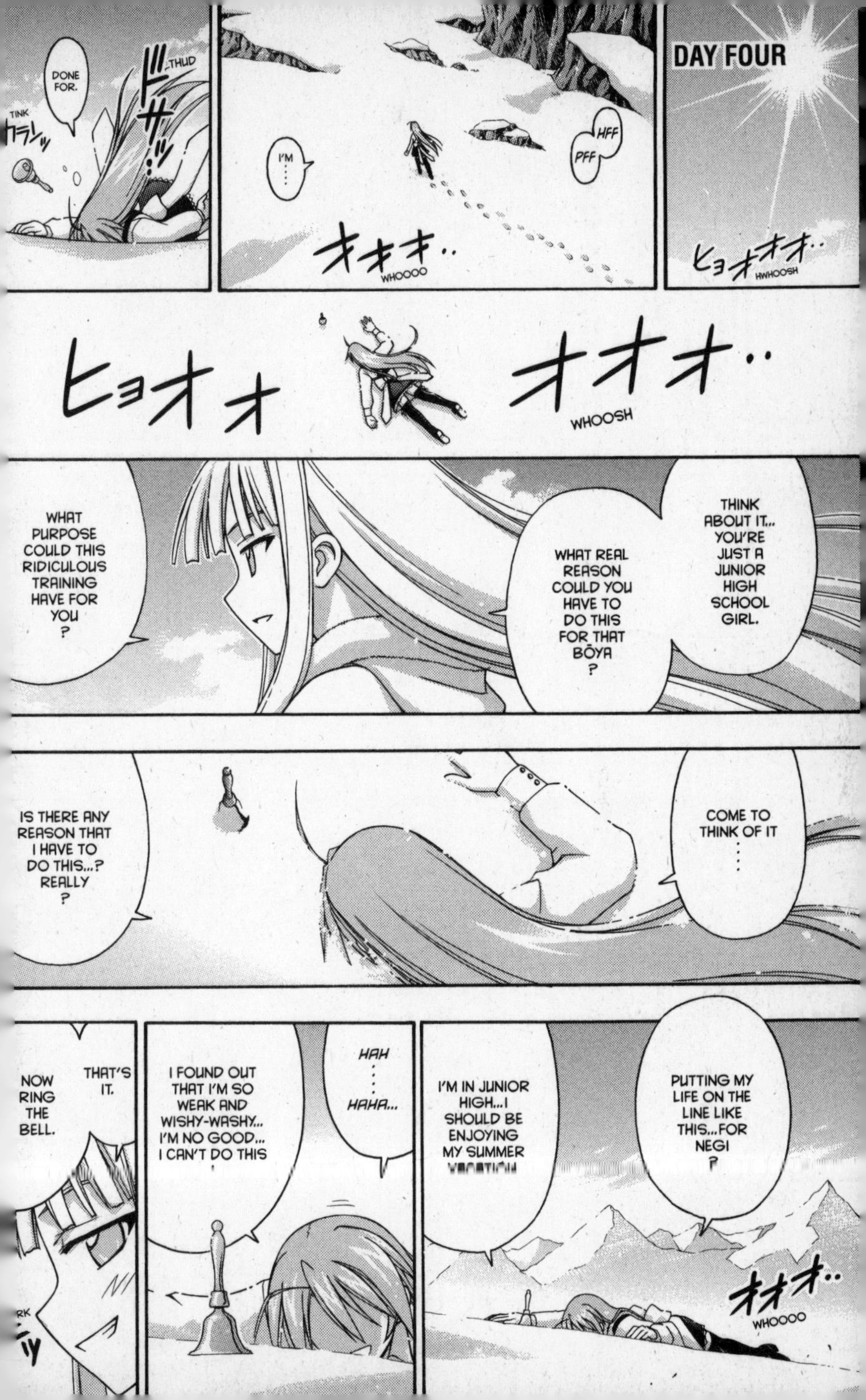

DAY FOUR
ヒョオオオ‥
HWHOOSH
HFF
PFF
I'M ......
オォォ‥
WHOOOO
DONE FOR.
ドサッ
THUD
カランッ
TINK
ヒョオオオオオオ‥
WHOOSH
THINK ABOUT IT... YOU'RE JUST A JUNIOR HIGH SCHOOL GIRL.
WHAT REAL REASON COULD YOU HAVE TO DO THIS FOR THAT BŌYA ?
WHAT PURPOSE COULD THIS RIDICULOUS TRAINING HAVE FOR YOU ?
COME TO THINK OF IT ....
IS THERE ANY REASON THAT I HAVE TO DO THIS...? REALLY ?
PUTTING MY LIFE ON THE LINE LIKE THIS...FOR NEGI ?
I'M IN JUNIOR HIGH...I SHOULD BE ENJOYING MY SUMMER
オオオ‥
WHOOOO
HAH ... HAHA...
I FOUND OUT THAT I'M SO WEAK AND WISHY-WASHY... I'M NO GOOD... I CAN'T DO THIS
THAT'S IT.
NOW RING THE BELL.

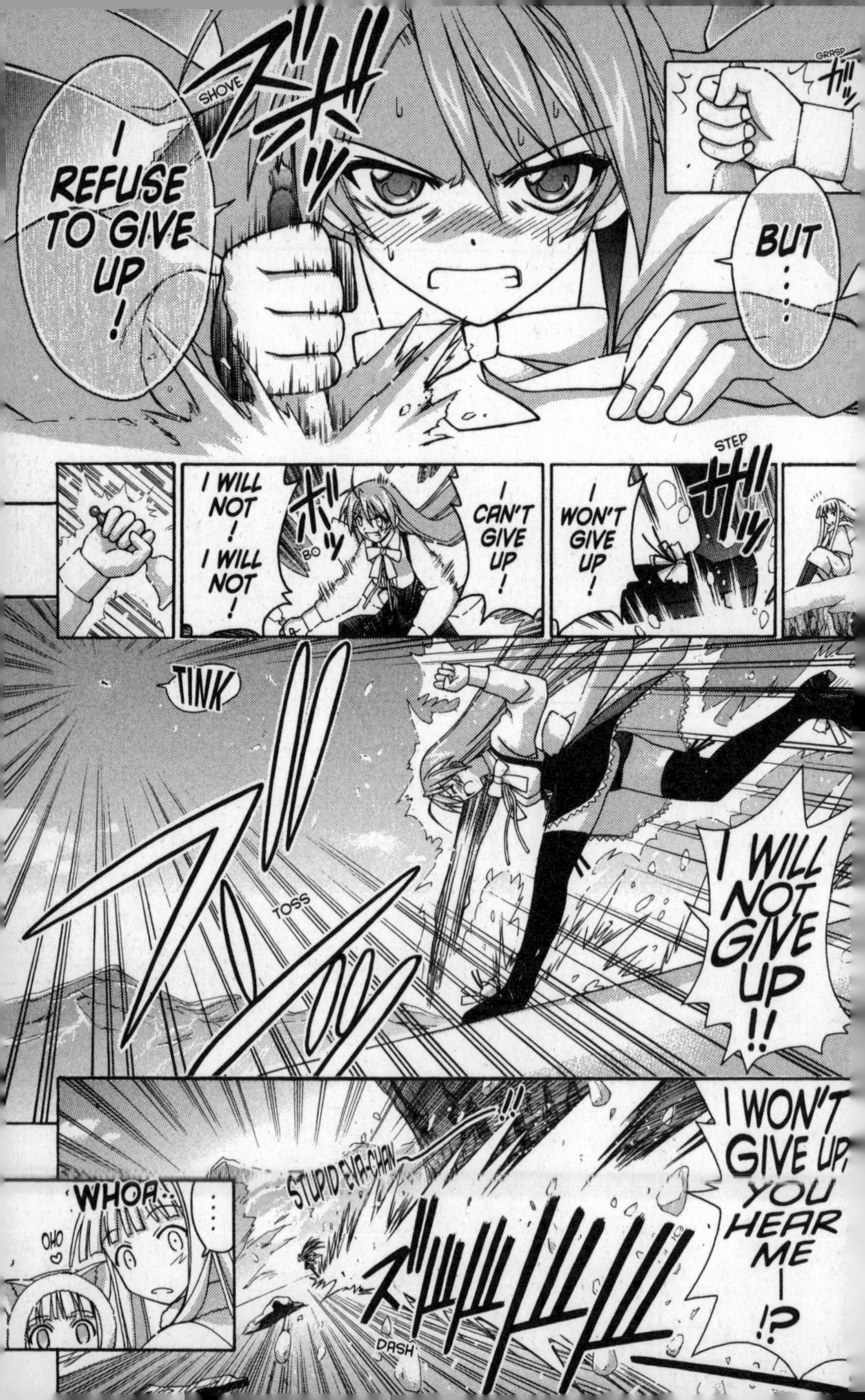
GRRSP
BUT....
SHOVE
I REFUSE TO GIVE UP!
STEP
I WON'T GIVE UP!
I CAN'T GIVE UP!
I WILL NOT! I WILL NOT!
BO
I WILL NOT GIVE UP!!
TOSS
TINK
I WON'T GIVE UP, YOU HEAR ME!?
STUPID EVA-CHAN
DASH
....
WHOA...
OHO

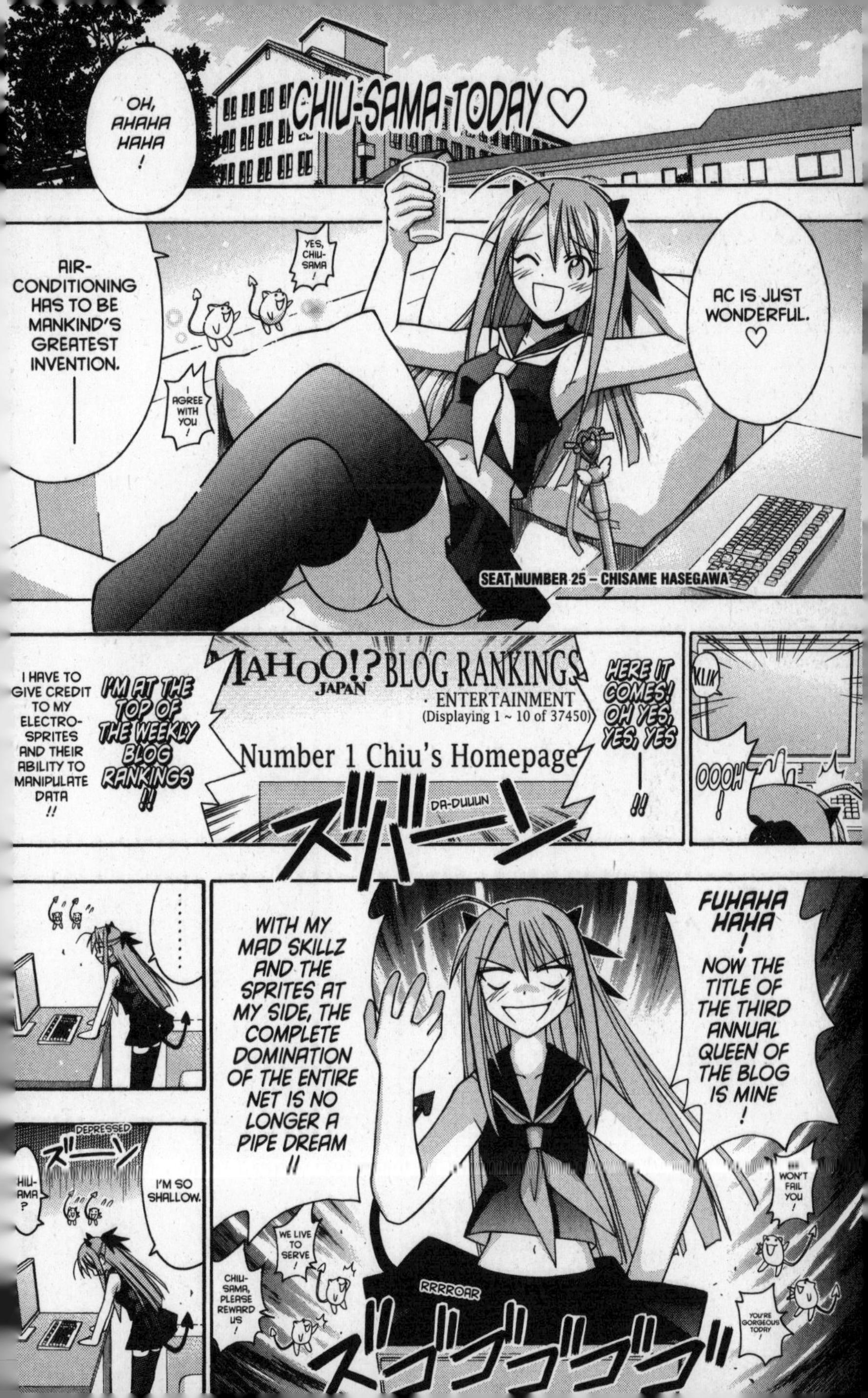
CHIU-SAMA TODAY ♡
OH, AHAHA HAHA!
AC IS JUST WONDERFUL. ♡
YES, CHIU-SAMA!
AIR-CONDITIONING HAS TO BE MANKIND'S GREATEST INVENTION.
I AGREE WITH YOU!
SEAT NUMBER 25 – CHISAME HASEGAWA
KLIK
OOOH!
HERE IT COMES! OH YES, YES, YES!!
MAHOO!? JAPAN BLOG RANKINGS
· ENTERTAINMENT
(Displaying 1 ~ 10 of 37450)
Number 1 Chiu's Homepage
I'M AT THE TOP OF THE WEEKLY BLOG RANKINGS!!
I HAVE TO GIVE CREDIT TO MY ELECTRO-SPRITES AND THEIR ABILITY TO MANIPULATE DATA!!
DA-DUUUN
FUHAHA HAHA! NOW THE TITLE OF THE THIRD ANNUAL QUEEN OF THE BLOG IS MINE!
WITH MY MAD SKILLZ AND THE SPRITES AT MY SIDE, THE COMPLETE DOMINATION OF THE ENTIRE NET IS NO LONGER A PIPE DREAM!!
WON'T FAIL YOU!
WE LIVE TO SERVE!
CHIU-SAMA, PLEASE REWARD US
YOU'RE GORGEOUS TODAY!
RRRROAR
......
DEPRESSED
I'M SO SHALLOW.
HIU-SAMA?

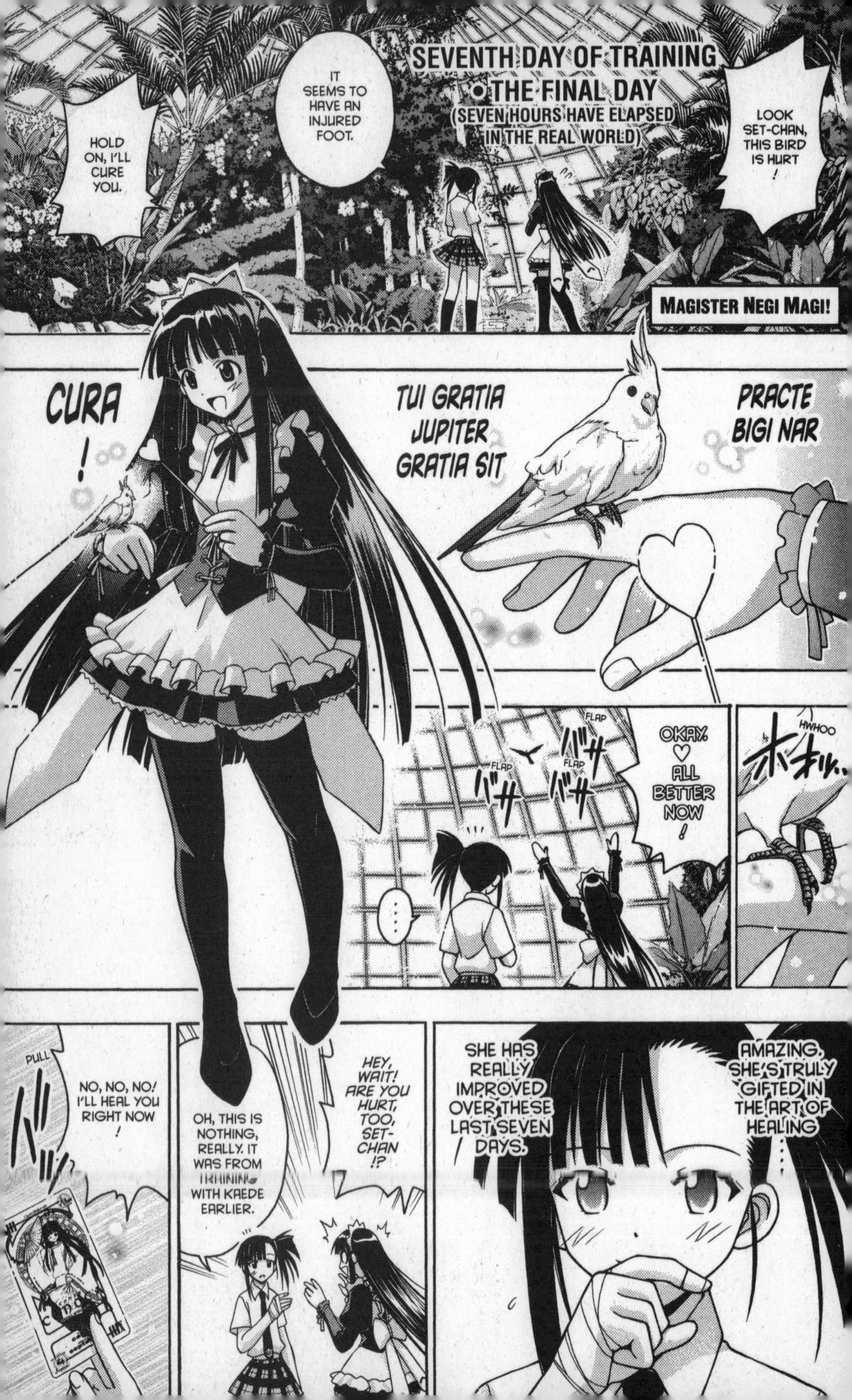
LOOK SET-CHAN, THIS BIRD IS HURT!
SEVENTH DAY OF TRAINING
THE FINAL DAY
(SEVEN HOURS HAVE ELAPSED IN THE REAL WORLD)
IT SEEMS TO HAVE AN INJURED FOOT.
HOLD ON, I'LL CURE YOU.
MAGISTER NEGI MAGI!
PRACTE BIGI NAR
TUI GRATIA JUPITER GRATIA SIT
CURA!
HWHOO
OKAY. ♥ ALL BETTER NOW!
FLAP
FLAP
FLAP
...
AMAZING, SHE'S TRULY GIFTED IN THE ART OF HEALING
SHE HAS REALLY IMPROVED OVER THESE LAST SEVEN DAYS!
HEY, WAIT! ARE YOU HURT, TOO, SET-CHAN!?
OH, THIS IS NOTHING, REALLY. IT WAS FROM TRAINING WITH KAEDE EARLIER.
NO, NO, NO! I'LL HEAL YOU RIGHT NOW!
PULL

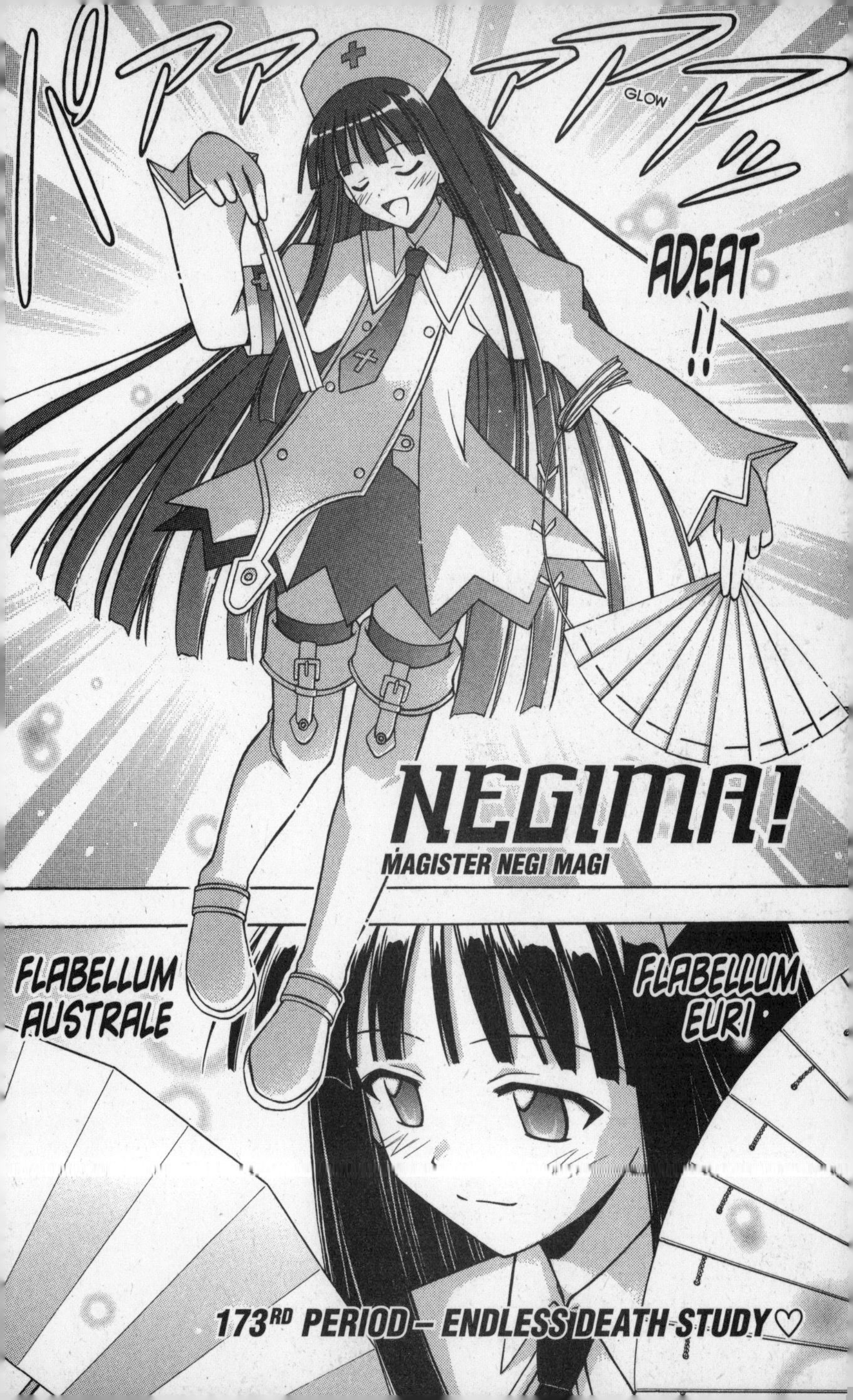
GLOW
ADEAT !!
NEGIMA!
MAGISTER NEGI MAGI
FLABELLUM EURI
FLABELLUM AUSTRALE
173RD PERIOD – ENDLESS DEATH STUDY♡

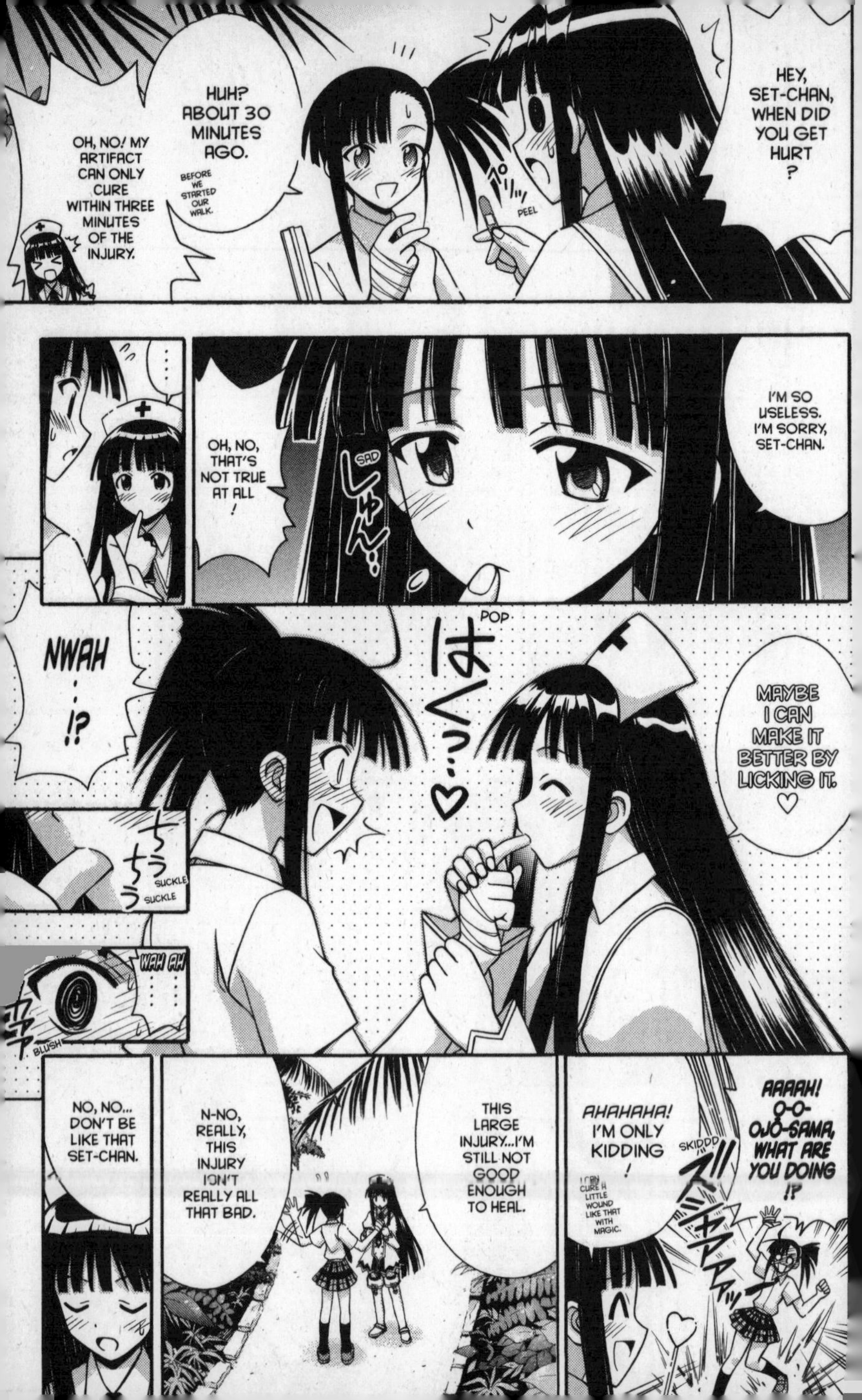
HEY, SET-CHAN, WHEN DID YOU GET HURT?
PEEL
HUH? ABOUT 30 MINUTES AGO.
BEFORE WE STARTED OUR WALK.
OH, NO! MY ARTIFACT CAN ONLY CURE WITHIN THREE MINUTES OF THE INJURY.
I'M SO USELESS. I'M SORRY, SET-CHAN.
SAD
しゅん…
OH, NO, THAT'S NOT TRUE AT ALL!
...
MAYBE I CAN MAKE IT BETTER BY LICKING IT. ♡
POP
はくっ…♡
NWAH...!?
ちう ちう
SUCKLE SUCKLE
WAH AH
BLUSH
AAAAH! O-O-OJO-SAMA, WHAT ARE YOU DOING!?
SKIDDD
AHAHAHA! I'M ONLY KIDDING!
I CAN CURE A LITTLE WOUND LIKE THAT WITH MAGIC.
THIS LARGE INJURY...I'M STILL NOT GOOD ENOUGH TO HEAL.
N-NO, REALLY, THIS INJURY ISN'T REALLY ALL THAT BAD.
NO, NO... DON'T BE LIKE THAT SET-CHAN.

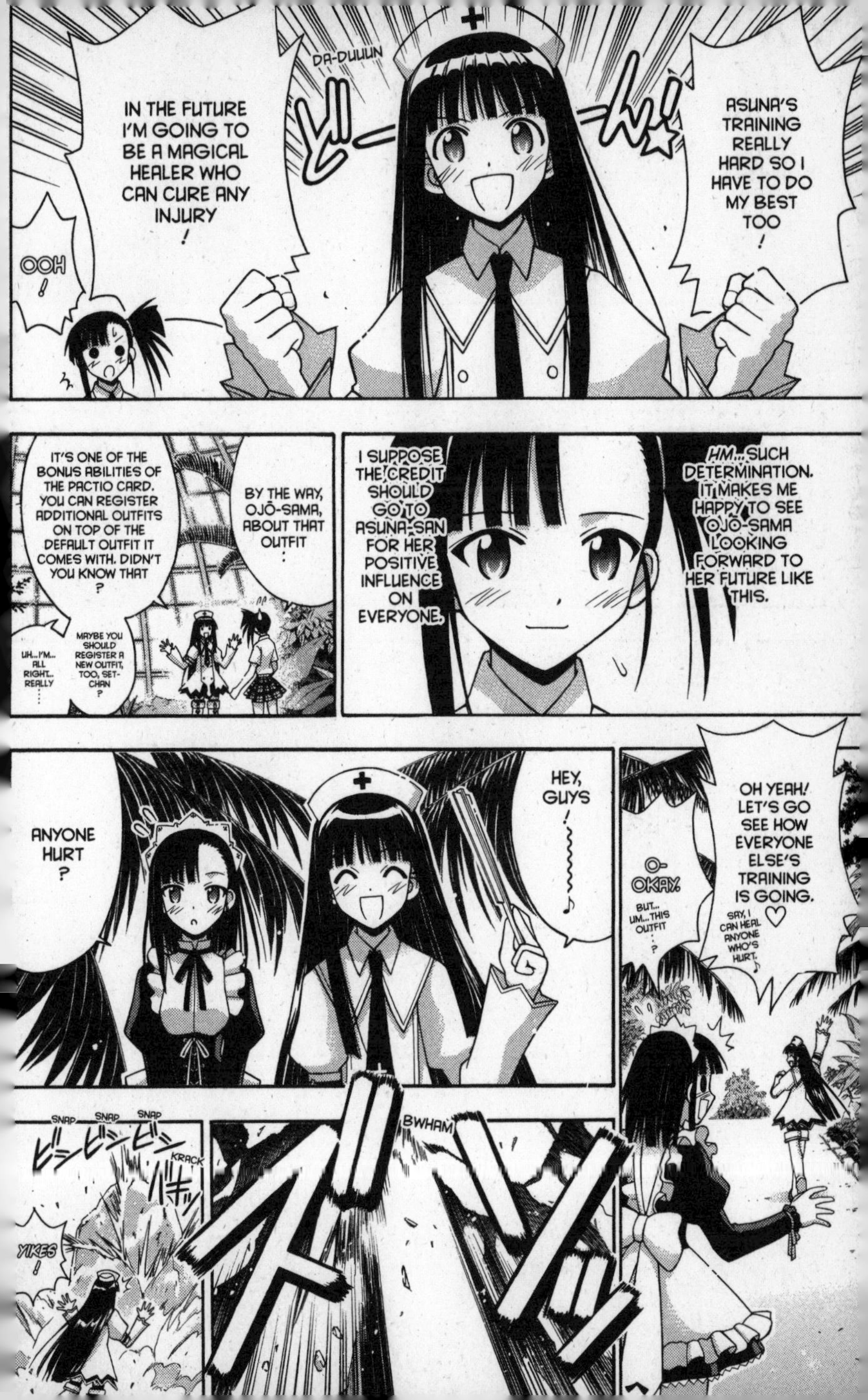

ASUNA'S TRAINING REALLY HARD SO I HAVE TO DO MY BEST TOO!
DA-DUUUN
IN THE FUTURE I'M GOING TO BE A MAGICAL HEALER WHO CAN CURE ANY INJURY!
OOH!
HM... SUCH DETERMINATION. IT MAKES ME HAPPY TO SEE OJŌ-SAMA LOOKING FORWARD TO HER FUTURE LIKE THIS.
I SUPPOSE THE CREDIT SHOULD GO TO ASUNA-SAN FOR HER POSITIVE INFLUENCE ON EVERYONE.
BY THE WAY, OJŌ-SAMA, ABOUT THAT OUTFIT...
IT'S ONE OF THE BONUS ABILITIES OF THE PACTIO CARD. YOU CAN REGISTER ADDITIONAL OUTFITS ON TOP OF THE DEFAULT OUTFIT IT COMES WITH. DIDN'T YOU KNOW THAT?
MAYBE YOU SHOULD REGISTER A NEW OUTFIT, TOO, SET-CHAN?
UH... I'M... ALL RIGHT... REALLY...
OH YEAH! LET'S GO SEE HOW EVERYONE ELSE'S TRAINING IS GOING.
SAY, I CAN HEAL ANYONE WHO'S HURT. ♪
O-OKAY.
BUT... UM... THIS OUTFIT...?
HEY, GUYS!~♪
ANYONE HURT?
BWHAM
SNAP SNAP SNAP
KRACK
YIKES!

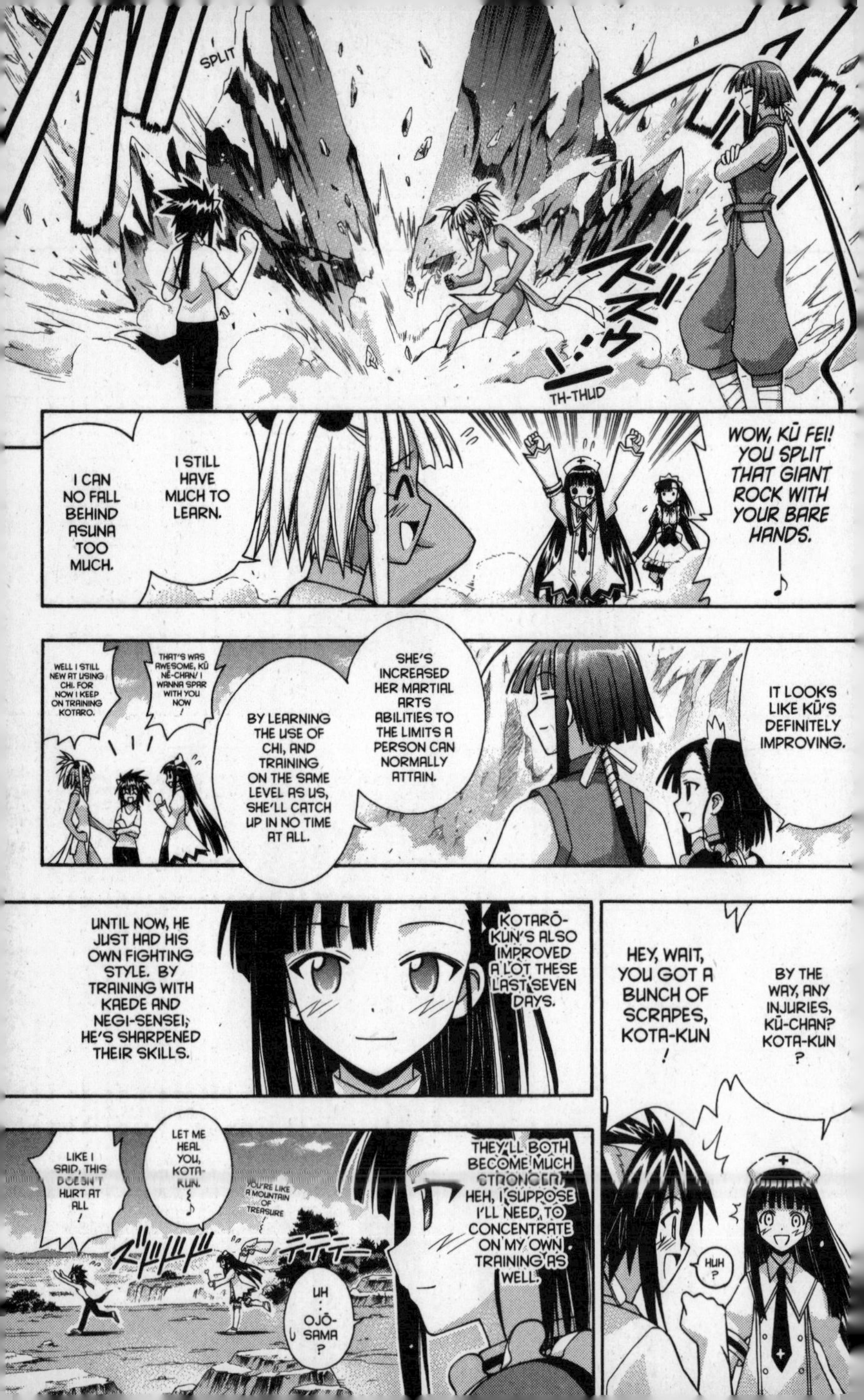
SPLIT
TH-THUD
WOW, KŪ FEI! YOU SPLIT THAT GIANT ROCK WITH YOUR BARE HANDS. ♪
I STILL HAVE MUCH TO LEARN.
I CAN NO FALL BEHIND ASUNA TOO MUCH.
IT LOOKS LIKE KŪ'S DEFINITELY IMPROVING.
SHE'S INCREASED HER MARTIAL ARTS ABILITIES TO THE LIMITS A PERSON CAN NORMALLY ATTAIN.
BY LEARNING THE USE OF CHI, AND TRAINING ON THE SAME LEVEL AS US, SHE'LL CATCH UP IN NO TIME AT ALL.
THAT'S WAS AWESOME, KŪ NĒ-CHAN! I WANNA SPAR WITH YOU NOW!
WELL I STILL NEW AT USING CHI. FOR NOW I KEEP ON TRAINING KOTARO.
BY THE WAY, ANY INJURIES, KŪ-CHAN? KOTA-KUN?
HEY, WAIT, YOU GOT A BUNCH OF SCRAPES, KOTA-KUN!
HUH?
KOTARŌ-KUN'S ALSO IMPROVED A LOT THESE LAST SEVEN DAYS.
UNTIL NOW, HE JUST HAD HIS OWN FIGHTING STYLE. BY TRAINING WITH KAEDE AND NEGI-SENSEI, HE'S SHARPENED THEIR SKILLS.
THEY'LL BOTH BECOME MUCH STRONGER. HEH, I SUPPOSE I'LL NEED TO CONCENTRATE ON MY OWN TRAINING AS WELL.
UH... OJŌ-SAMA?
LET ME HEAL YOU, KOTA-KUN. ♪
YOU'RE LIKE A MOUNTAIN OF TREASURE
LIKE I SAID, THIS DOESN'T HURT AT ALL!

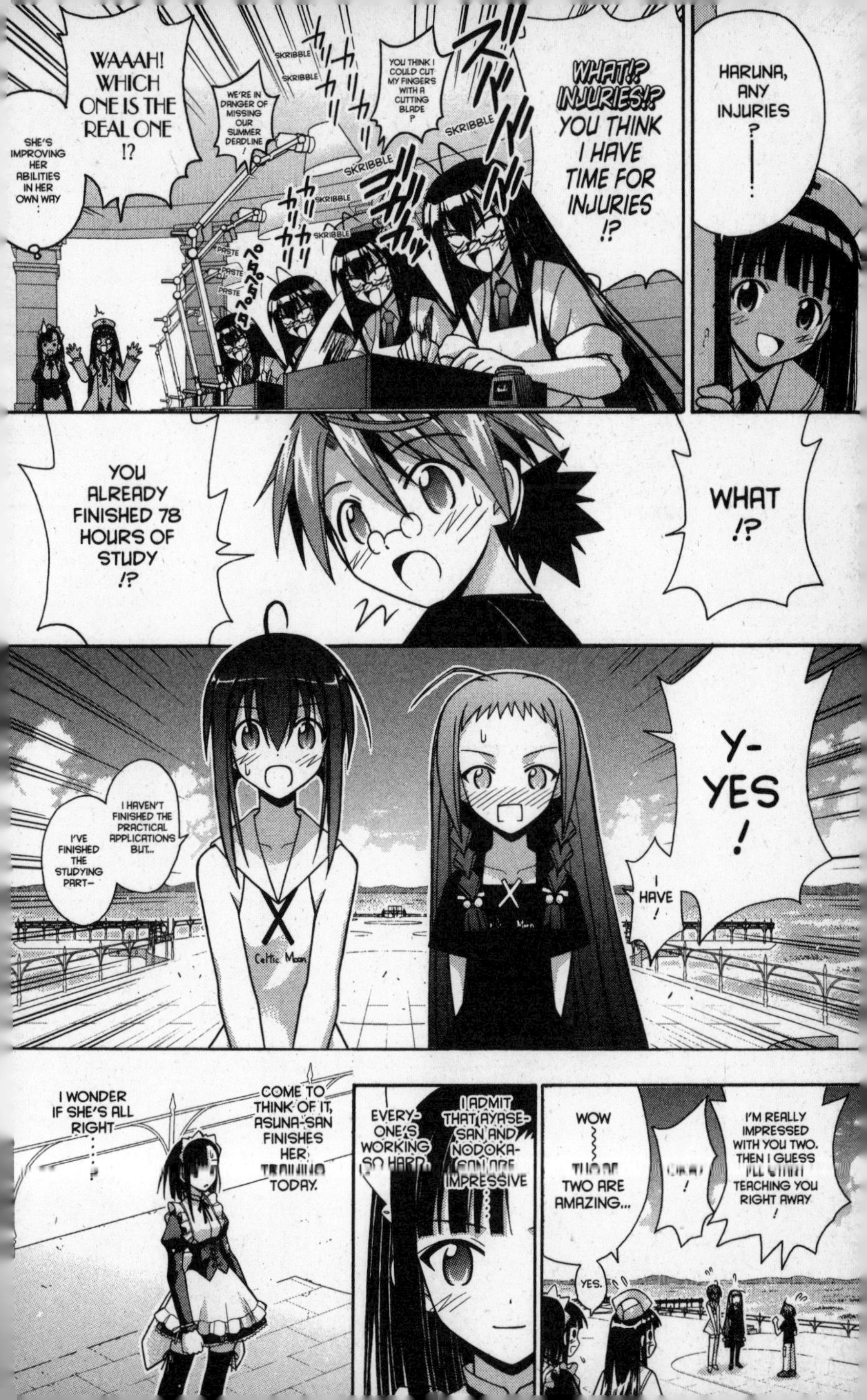

HARUNA, ANY INJURIES?
WHAT!? INJURIES!? YOU THINK I HAVE TIME FOR INJURIES!?
YOU THINK I COULD CUT MY FINGERS WITH A CUTTING BLADE?
SKRIBBLE
SKRIBBLE
SKRIBBLE
WE'RE IN DANGER OF MISSING OUR SUMMER DEADLINE!
SKRIBBLE
SKRIBBLE
SKRIBBLE
WAAAH! WHICH ONE IS THE REAL ONE!?
PASTE
PASTE
PASTE
SHE'S IMPROVING HER ABILITIES IN HER OWN WAY...
WHAT!?
YOU ALREADY FINISHED 78 HOURS OF STUDY!?
Y-YES!
I HAVE!
I HAVEN'T FINISHED THE PRACTICAL APPLICATIONS BUT...
I'VE FINISHED THE STUDYING PART—
Celtic Moon
I'M REALLY IMPRESSED WITH YOU TWO. THEN I GUESS
TEACHING YOU RIGHT AWAY!
!
WOW...
TWO ARE AMAZING...
YES.
I ADMIT THAT AYASE-SAN AND NODOKA-
IMPRESSIVE
EVERY-ONE'S WORKING SO HARD
COME TO THINK OF IT, ASUNA-SAN FINISHES HER
TODAY.
I WONDER IF SHE'S ALL RIGHT...

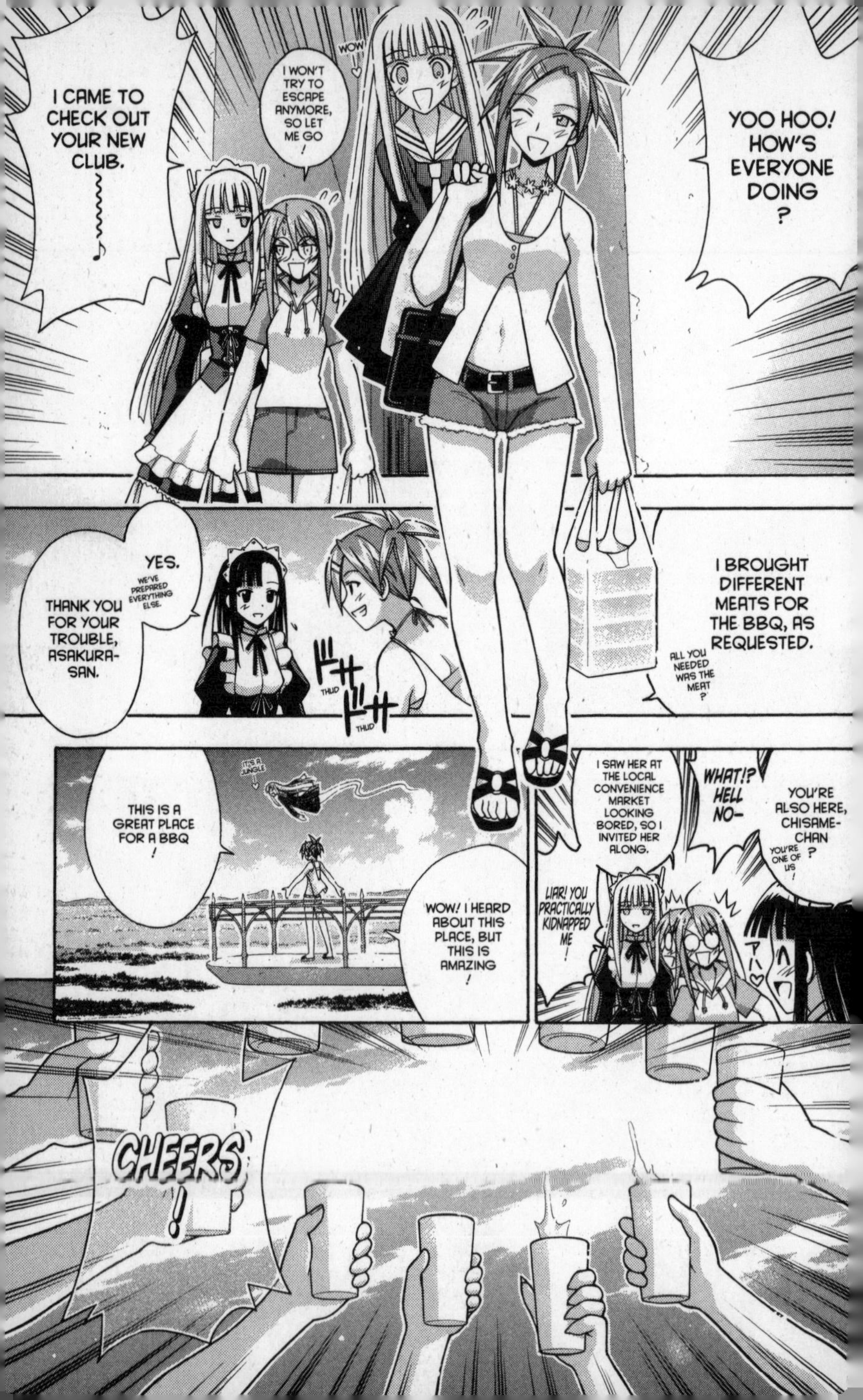
YOO HOO! HOW'S EVERYONE DOING?
WOW ♡
I WON'T TRY TO ESCAPE ANYMORE, SO LET ME GO!
I CAME TO CHECK OUT YOUR NEW CLUB. ♪
I BROUGHT DIFFERENT MEATS FOR THE BBQ, AS REQUESTED.
ALL YOU NEEDED WAS THE MEAT?
THUD
THUD
YES.
WE'VE PREPARED EVERYTHING ELSE.
THANK YOU FOR YOUR TROUBLE, ASAKURA-SAN.
YOU'RE ALSO HERE, CHISAME-CHAN?
YOU'RE ONE OF US!
WHAT!? HELL NO-
I SAW HER AT THE LOCAL CONVENIENCE MARKET LOOKING BORED, SO I INVITED HER ALONG.
LIAR! YOU PRACTICALLY KIDNAPPED ME!
WOW! I HEARD ABOUT THIS PLACE, BUT THIS IS AMAZING!
THIS IS A GREAT PLACE FOR A BBQ!
IT'S A JUNGLE ♡
CHEERS!

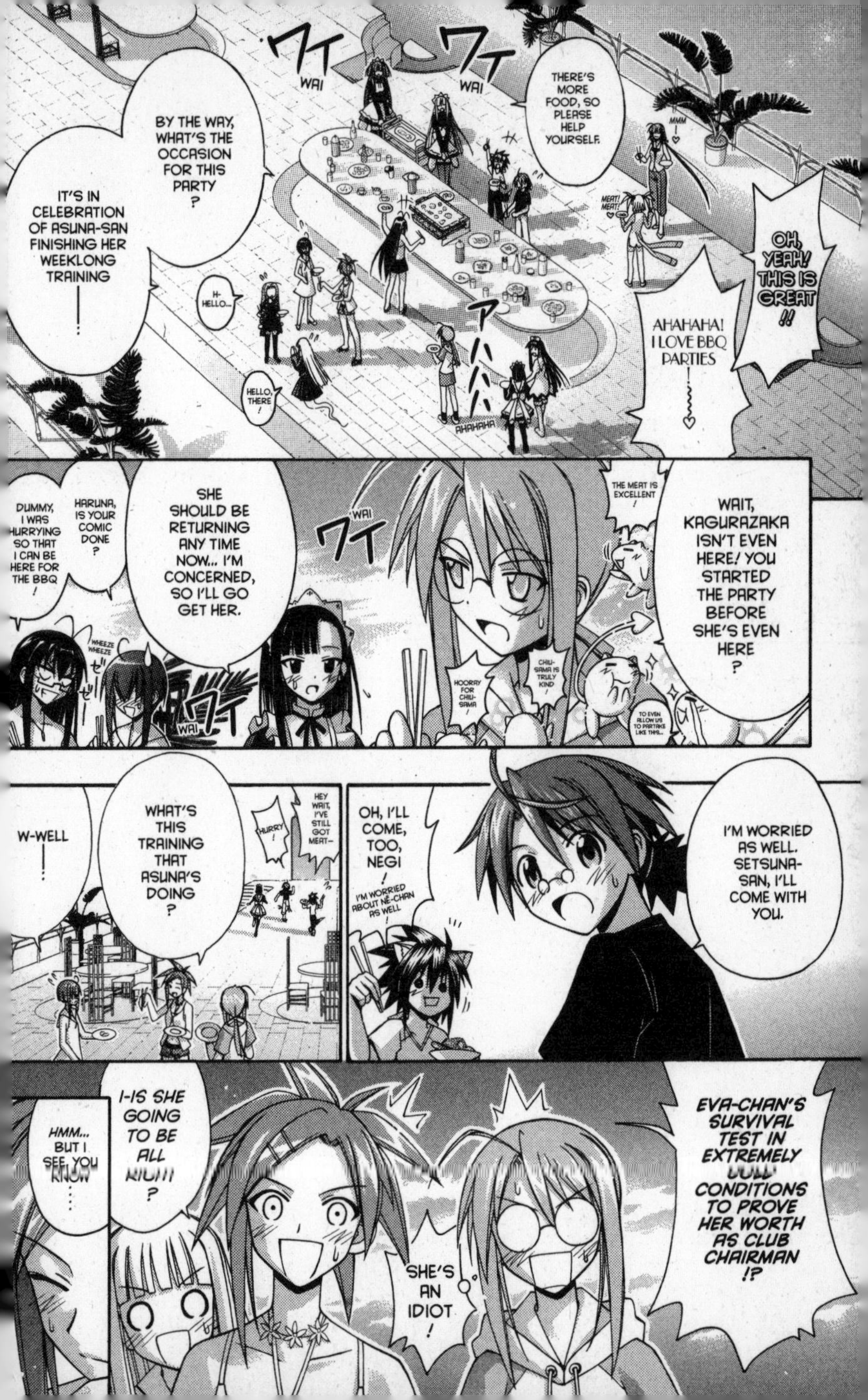
OH, YEAH! THIS IS GREAT!!
AHAHAHA! I LOVE BBQ PARTIES!
MMM
MEAT! MEAT!
THERE'S MORE FOOD, SO PLEASE HELP YOURSELF.
WAI
WAI
BY THE WAY, WHAT'S THE OCCASION FOR THIS PARTY?
IT'S IN CELEBRATION OF ASUNA-SAN FINISHING HER WEEKLONG TRAINING!
H-HELLO...
HELLO, THERE!
AHAHAHA
WAIT, KAGURAZAKA ISN'T EVEN HERE! YOU STARTED THE PARTY BEFORE SHE'S EVEN HERE?
THE MEAT IS EXCELLENT!
CHIU-SAMA IS TRULY KIND!
TO EVEN ALLOW US TO PARTAKE LIKE THIS...
HOORRY FOR CHIU-SAMA!
WAI
SHE SHOULD BE RETURNING ANY TIME NOW... I'M CONCERNED, SO I'LL GO GET HER.
HARUNA, IS YOUR COMIC DONE?
DUMMY, I WAS HURRYING SO THAT I CAN BE HERE FOR THE BBQ!
WHEEZE WHEEZE
WAI
I'M WORRIED AS WELL. SETSUNA-SAN, I'LL COME WITH YOU.
OH, I'LL COME, TOO, NEGI!
I'M WORRIED ABOUT NE-CHAN AS WELL!
HEY WAIT, I'VE STILL GOT MEAT—
HURRY!
WHAT'S THIS TRAINING THAT ASUNA'S DOING?
W-WELL...!
EVA-CHAN'S SURVIVAL TEST IN EXTREMELY CONDITIONS TO PROVE HER WORTH AS CLUB CHAIRMAN!?
SHE'S AN IDIOT!
I-IS SHE GOING TO BE ALL ?
HMM... BUT I
....

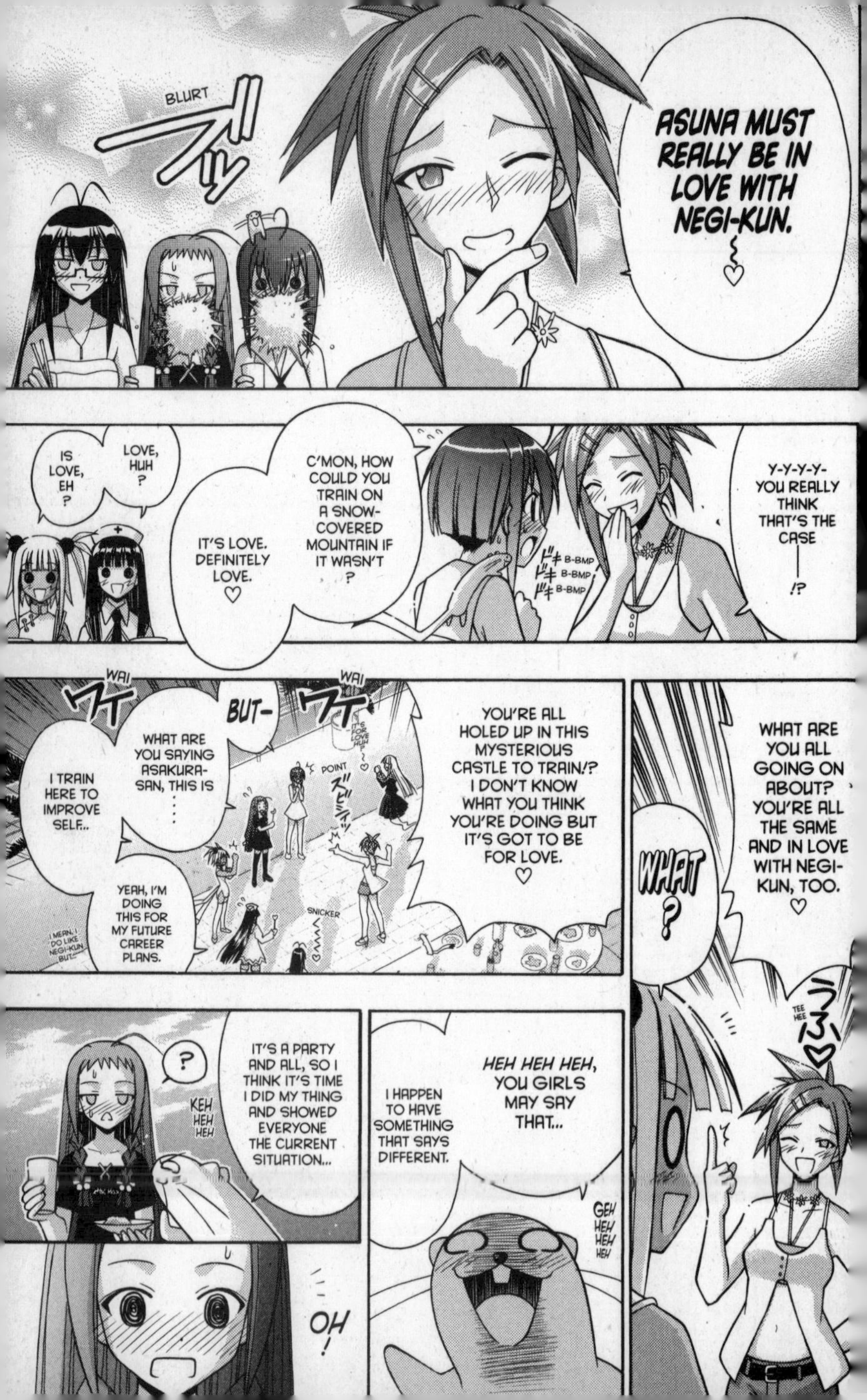
ASUNA MUST REALLY BE IN LOVE WITH NEGI-KUN.
BLURT
Y-Y-Y-Y- YOU REALLY THINK THAT'S THE CASE —— !?
B-BMP B-BMP B-BMP
C'MON, HOW COULD YOU TRAIN ON A SNOW-COVERED MOUNTAIN IF IT WASN'T?
IT'S LOVE. DEFINITELY LOVE. ♡
LOVE, HUH?
IS LOVE, EH?
WHAT ARE YOU ALL GOING ON ABOUT? YOU'RE ALL THE SAME AND IN LOVE WITH NEGI-KUN, TOO. ♡
WHAT?
TEE HEE
YOU'RE ALL HOLED UP IN THIS MYSTERIOUS CASTLE TO TRAIN!? I DON'T KNOW WHAT YOU THINK YOU'RE DOING BUT IT'S GOT TO BE FOR LOVE. ♡
WAI
BUT-
IT'S FOR LOVE HUH?
POINT
WAI
WHAT ARE YOU SAYING ASAKURA-SAN, THIS IS...
I TRAIN HERE TO IMPROVE SELF...
YEAH, I'M DOING THIS FOR MY FUTURE CAREER PLANS.
SNICKER
I MEAN, I DO LIKE NEGI-KUN BUT...
HEH HEH HEH, YOU GIRLS MAY SAY THAT...
I HAPPEN TO HAVE SOMETHING THAT SAYS DIFFERENT.
GEH HEH HEH HEH
IT'S A PARTY AND ALL, SO I THINK IT'S TIME I DID MY THING AND SHOWED EVERYONE THE CURRENT SITUATION...
?
KEH HEH HEH
OH!

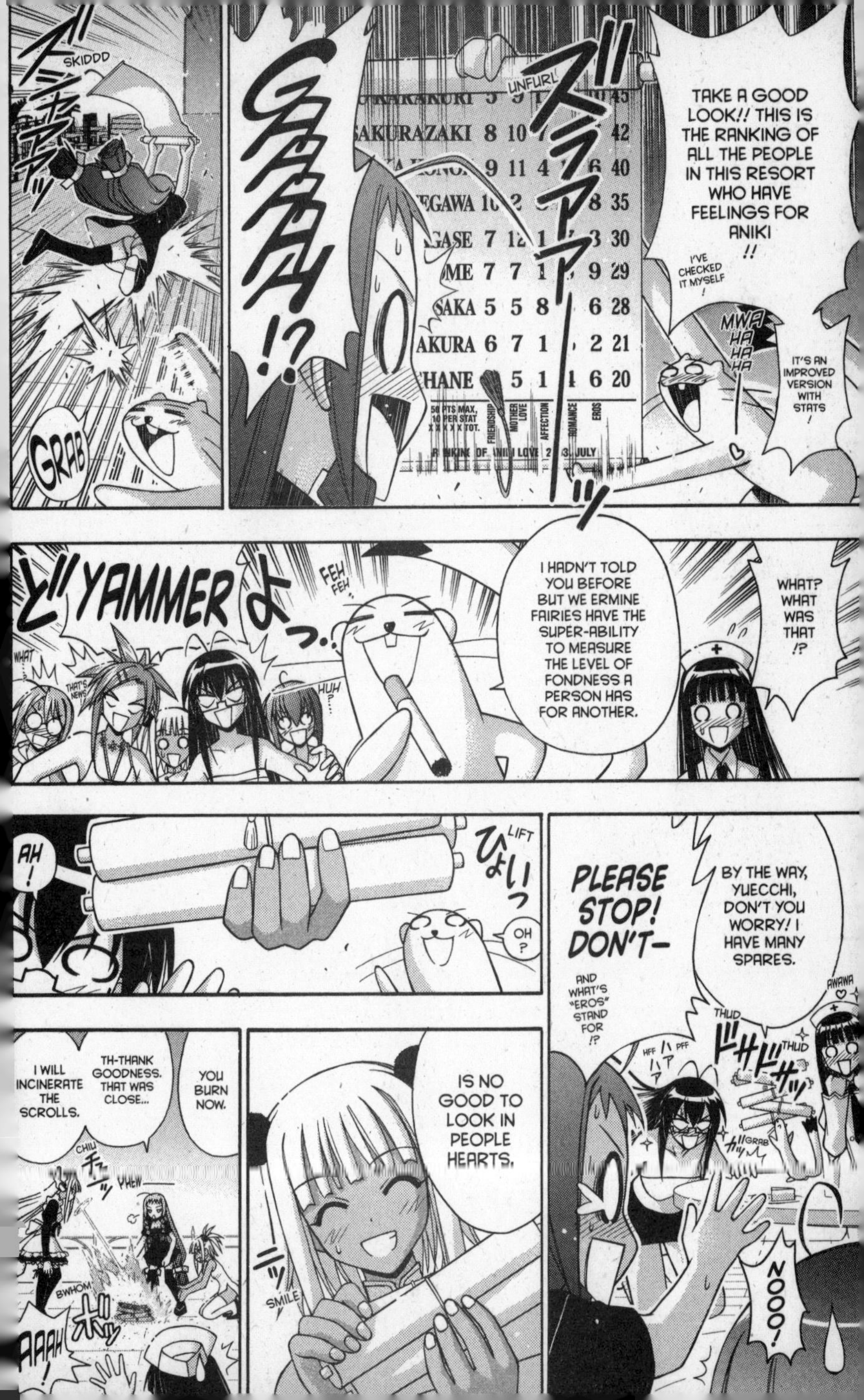
TAKE A GOOD LOOK!! THIS IS THE RANKING OF ALL THE PEOPLE IN THIS RESORT WHO HAVE FEELINGS FOR ANIKI!!
I'VE CHECKED IT MYSELF!
MWA HA HA HA
IT'S AN IMPROVED VERSION WITH STATS!
UNFURL
SAKURAZAKI 8 10 42
EGAWA 35
GASE 7 12 1 3 30
ME 7 7 1 9 29
SAKA 5 5 8 6 28
AKURA 6 7 1 2 21
HANE 5 1 6 20
50 PTS MAX, 10 PER STAT
FRIENDSHIP
MOTHER LOVE
AFFECTION
ROMANCE
EROS
JULY
!?
SKIDDD
GRAB
WHAT? WHAT WAS THAT!?
I HADN'T TOLD YOU BEFORE BUT WE ERMINE FAIRIES HAVE THE SUPER-ABILITY TO MEASURE THE LEVEL OF FONDNESS A PERSON HAS FOR ANOTHER.
FEH FEH
YAMMER
WHAT
THAT'S NEWS
HUH?
BY THE WAY, YUECCHI, DON'T YOU WORRY! I HAVE MANY SPARES.
PLEASE STOP! DON'T-
AND WHAT'S "EROS" STAND FOR!?
AWAWA
THUD
THUD
HFF
PFF
GRAB
NOOO!
LIFT
OH?
AH!
IS NO GOOD TO LOOK IN PEOPLE HEARTS.
SMILE
YOU BURN NOW.
TH-THANK GOODNESS. THAT WAS CLOSE...
I WILL INCINERATE THE SCROLLS.
CHIU
PHEW
BWHOM
AAAH

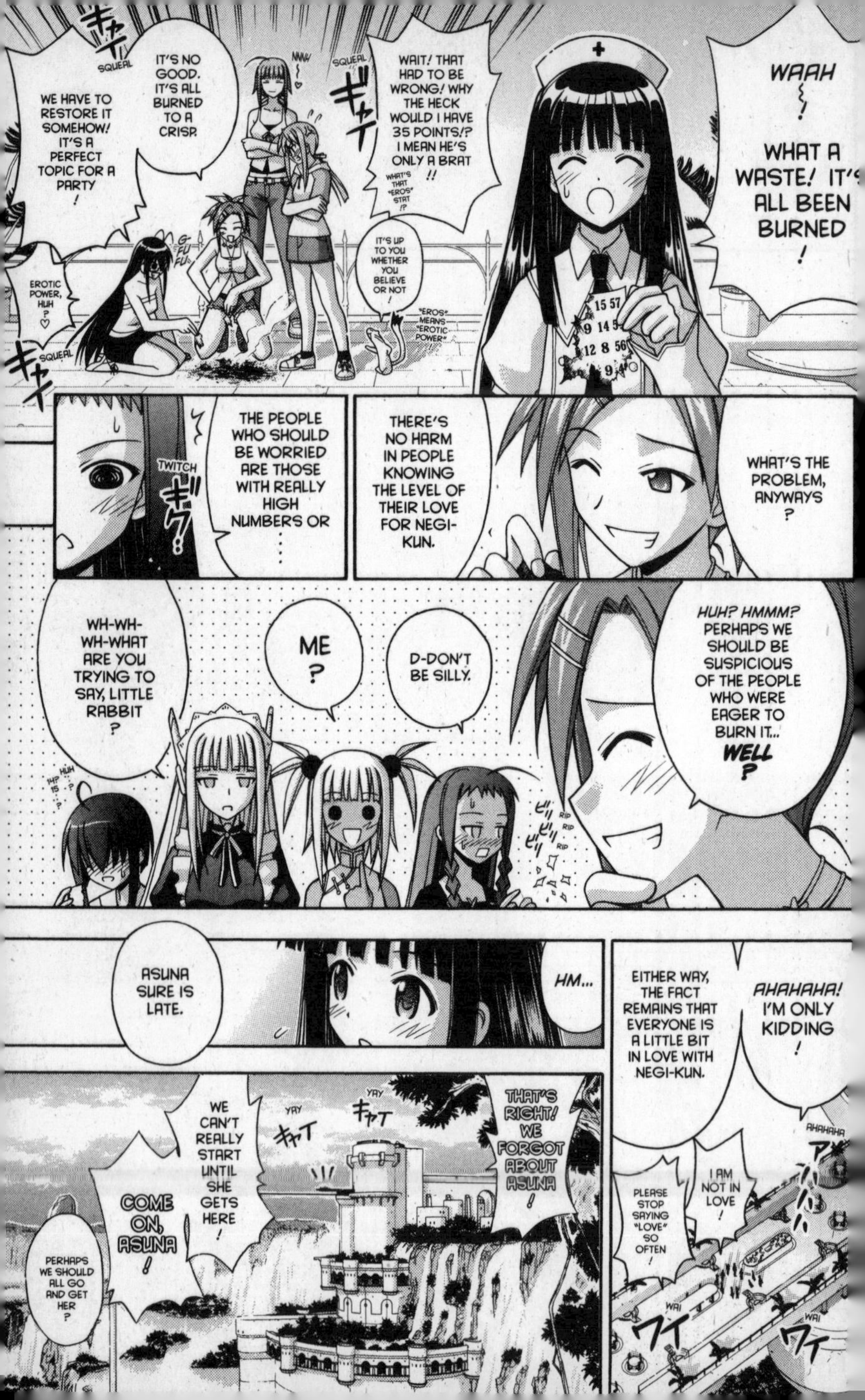
WAAH~! WHAT A WASTE! IT'S ALL BEEN BURNED!
SQUEAL
WAIT! THAT HAD TO BE WRONG! WHY THE HECK WOULD I HAVE 35 POINTS!? I MEAN HE'S ONLY A BRAT!!
NNH~♡
IT'S NO GOOD. IT'S ALL BURNED TO A CRISP.
SQUEAL
WE HAVE TO RESTORE IT SOMEHOW! IT'S A PERFECT TOPIC FOR A PARTY!
WHAT'S THAT "EROS" STAT!?
IT'S UP TO YOU WHETHER YOU BELIEVE OR NOT!
G-FU-FU
EROTIC POWER, HUH?♡
*"EROS" MEANS "EROTIC POWER"
SQUEAL
15 57
9 14 5
12 8 56
9
WHAT'S THE PROBLEM, ANYWAYS?
THERE'S NO HARM IN PEOPLE KNOWING THE LEVEL OF THEIR LOVE FOR NEGI-KUN.
THE PEOPLE WHO SHOULD BE WORRIED ARE THOSE WITH REALLY HIGH NUMBERS OR.....
TWITCH
HUH? HMMM? PERHAPS WE SHOULD BE SUSPICIOUS OF THE PEOPLE WHO WERE EAGER TO BURN IT... WELL?
RIP
RIP
RIP
D-DON'T BE SILLY.
ME?
WH-WH-WH-WHAT ARE YOU TRYING TO SAY, LITTLE RABBIT?
AHAHAHA! I'M ONLY KIDDING!
EITHER WAY, THE FACT REMAINS THAT EVERYONE IS A LITTLE BIT IN LOVE WITH NEGI-KUN.
AHAHAHA
I AM NOT IN LOVE!
PLEASE STOP SAYING "LOVE" SO OFTEN!
WAI
WAI
HM...
ASUNA SURE IS LATE.
THAT'S RIGHT! WE FORGOT ABOUT ASUNA!
YAY
YAY
WE CAN'T REALLY START UNTIL SHE GETS HERE
COME ON, ASUNA!
PERHAPS WE SHOULD ALL GO AND GET HER?

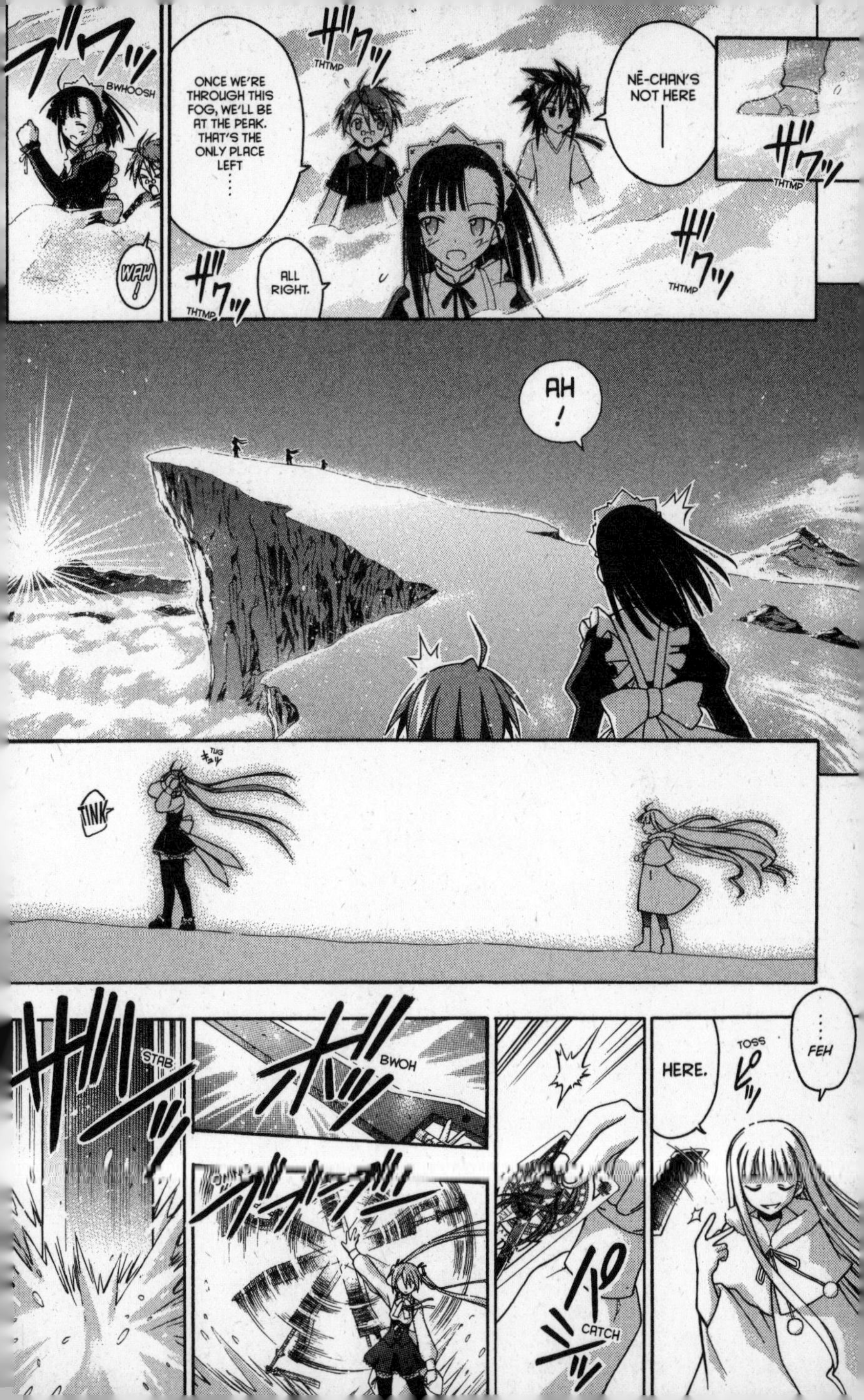
THTMP
NĒ-CHAN'S NOT HERE —
THTMP
ONCE WE'RE THROUGH THIS FOG, WE'LL BE AT THE PEAK. THAT'S THE ONLY PLACE LEFT ...
ALL RIGHT.
THTMP
THTMP
BWHOOSH
WAH!
AH!
TUG
TINK
... FEH
TOSS
HERE.
CATCH
BWOH
STAB.

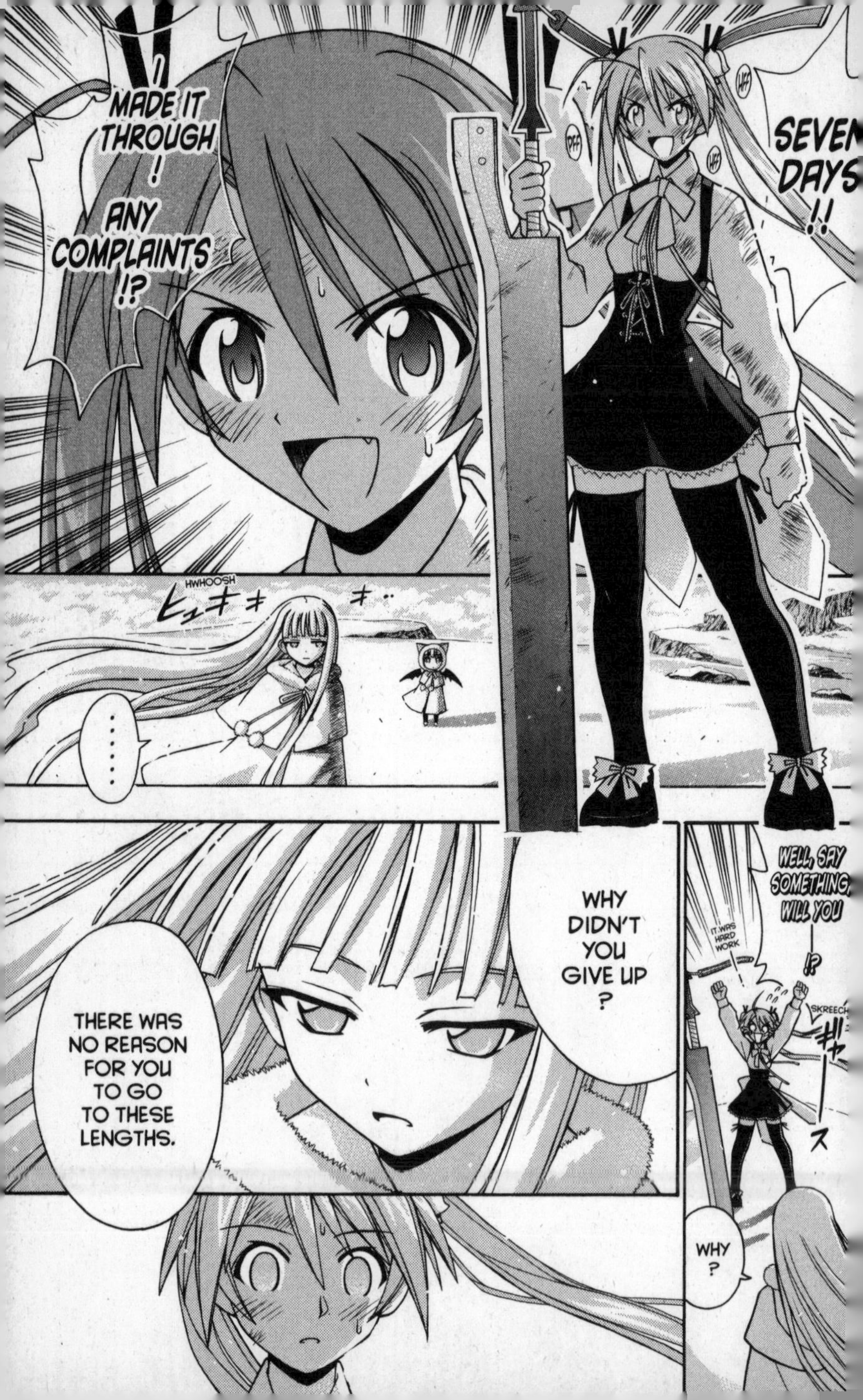
HFF
PFF
HFF
SEVEN DAYS!!
I MADE IT THROUGH!
ANY COMPLAINTS!?
HWHOOSH
......
WELL, SAY SOMETHING, WILL YOU!?
IT WAS HARD WORK
SKREECH
WHY DIDN'T YOU GIVE UP?
THERE WAS NO REASON FOR YOU TO GO TO THESE LENGTHS.
WHY?

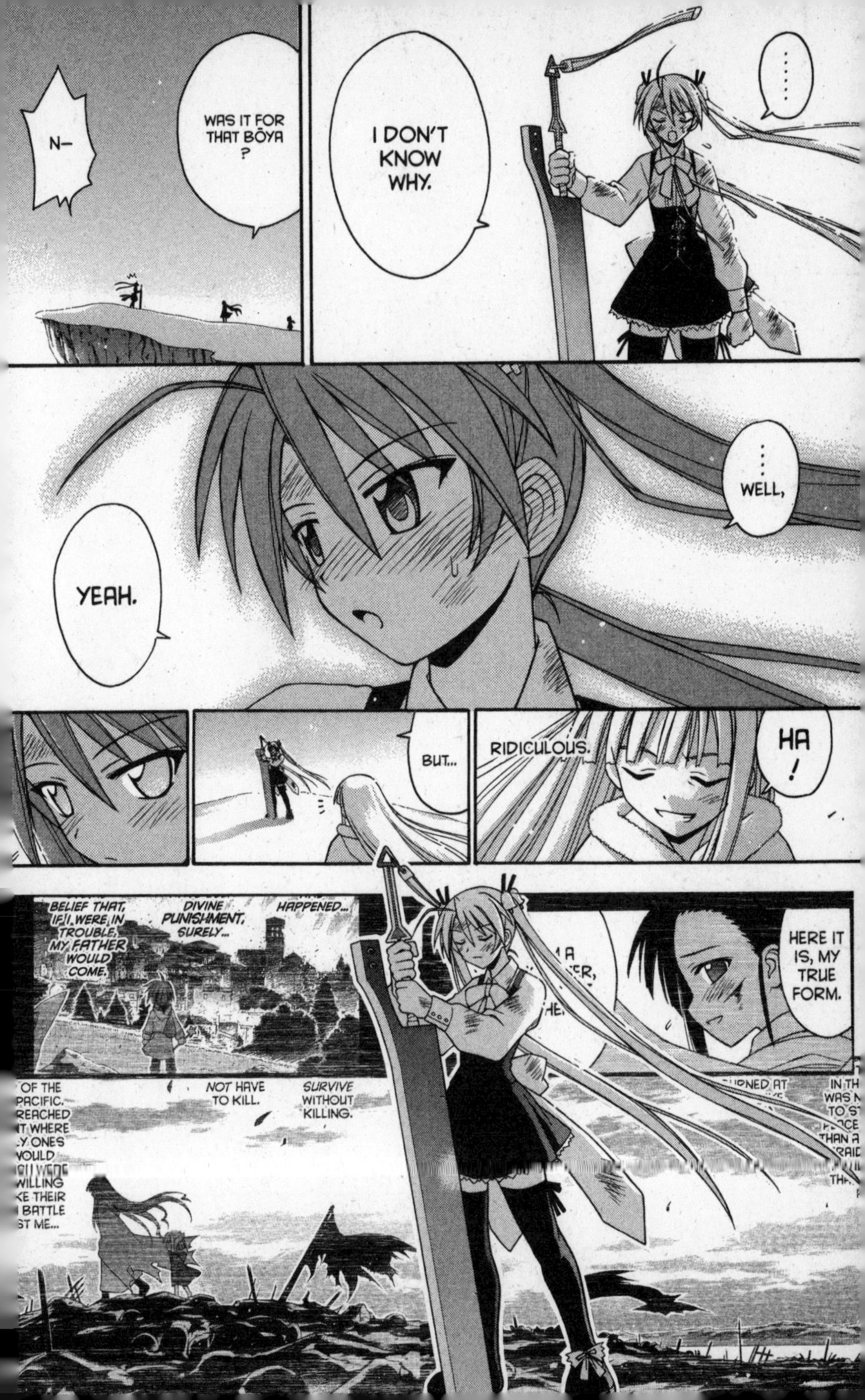
……
I DON'T KNOW WHY.
WAS IT FOR THAT BŌYA ?
N—
… WELL,
YEAH.
HA !
RIDICULOUS.
BUT…
HERE IT IS, MY TRUE FORM.
HAPPENED…
DIVINE PUNISHMENT, SURELY…
BELIEF THAT, IF I WERE IN TROUBLE, MY FATHER WOULD COME.
SURVIVE WITHOUT KILLING.
NOT HAVE TO KILL.
OF THE PACIFIC.

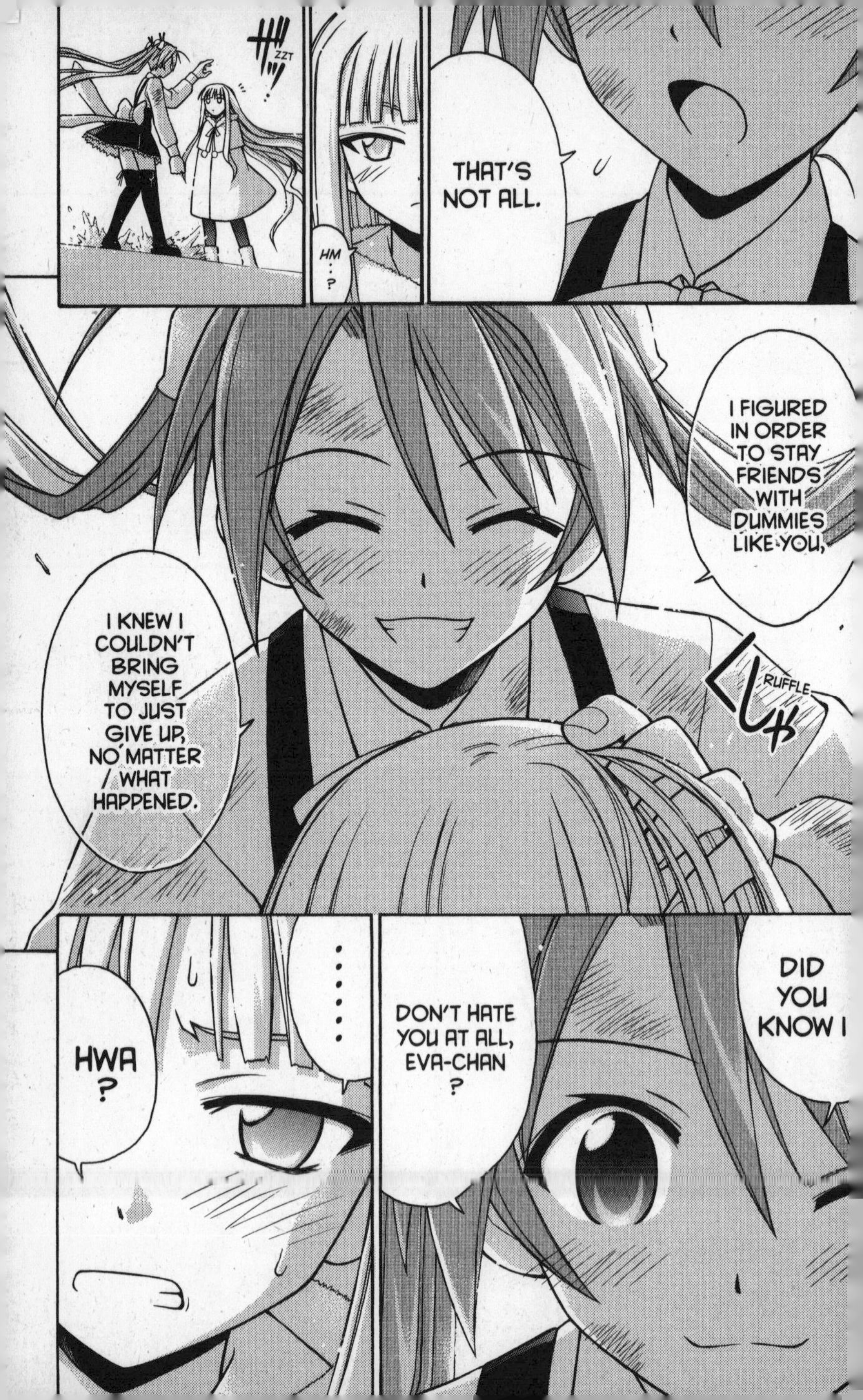
THAT'S NOT ALL.
HM..?
ZZT
I FIGURED IN ORDER TO STAY FRIENDS WITH DUMMIES LIKE YOU,
RUFFLE
I KNEW I COULDN'T BRING MYSELF TO JUST GIVE UP, NO MATTER WHAT HAPPENED.
DID YOU KNOW I
DON'T HATE YOU AT ALL, EVA-CHAN?
......
HWA?

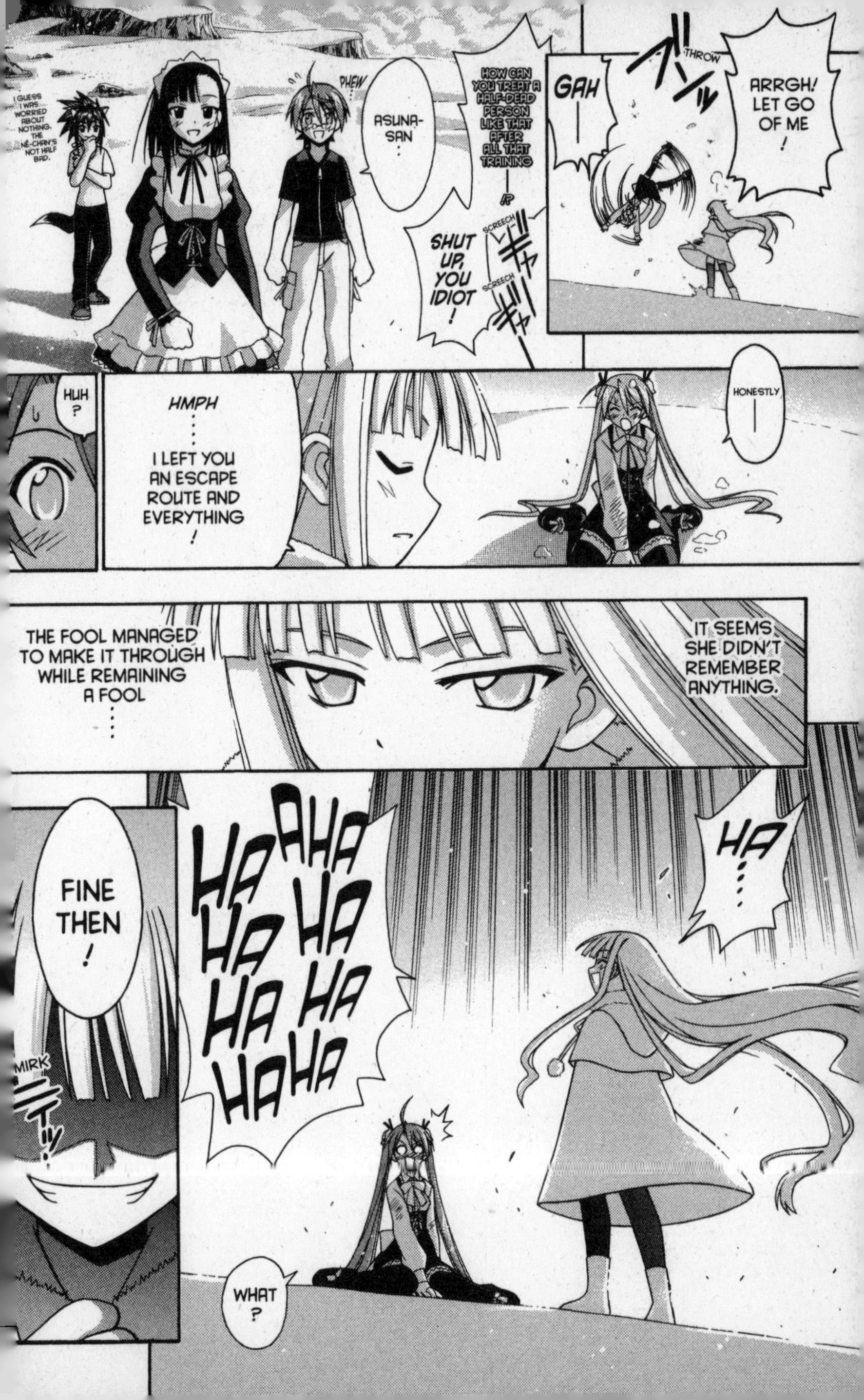
THROW
ARRGH! LET GO OF ME!
GAH—
HOW CAN YOU TREAT A HALF-DEAD PERSON LIKE THAT AFTER ALL THAT TRAINING—!?
SHUT UP, YOU IDIOT!
SCREECH
SCREECH
ASUNA-SAN...
PHEW
I GUESS I WAS... WORRIED ABOUT NOTHING. THE NE-CHAN'S NOT HALF BAD.
HONESTLY—
HMPH... I LEFT YOU AN ESCAPE ROUTE AND EVERYTHING!
HUH?
IT SEEMS SHE DIDN'T REMEMBER ANYTHING.
THE FOOL MANAGED TO MAKE IT THROUGH WHILE REMAINING A FOOL...
HA...
HAHAHA HA HA HA HA HA HA HAHA
WHAT?
FINE THEN!
SMIRK

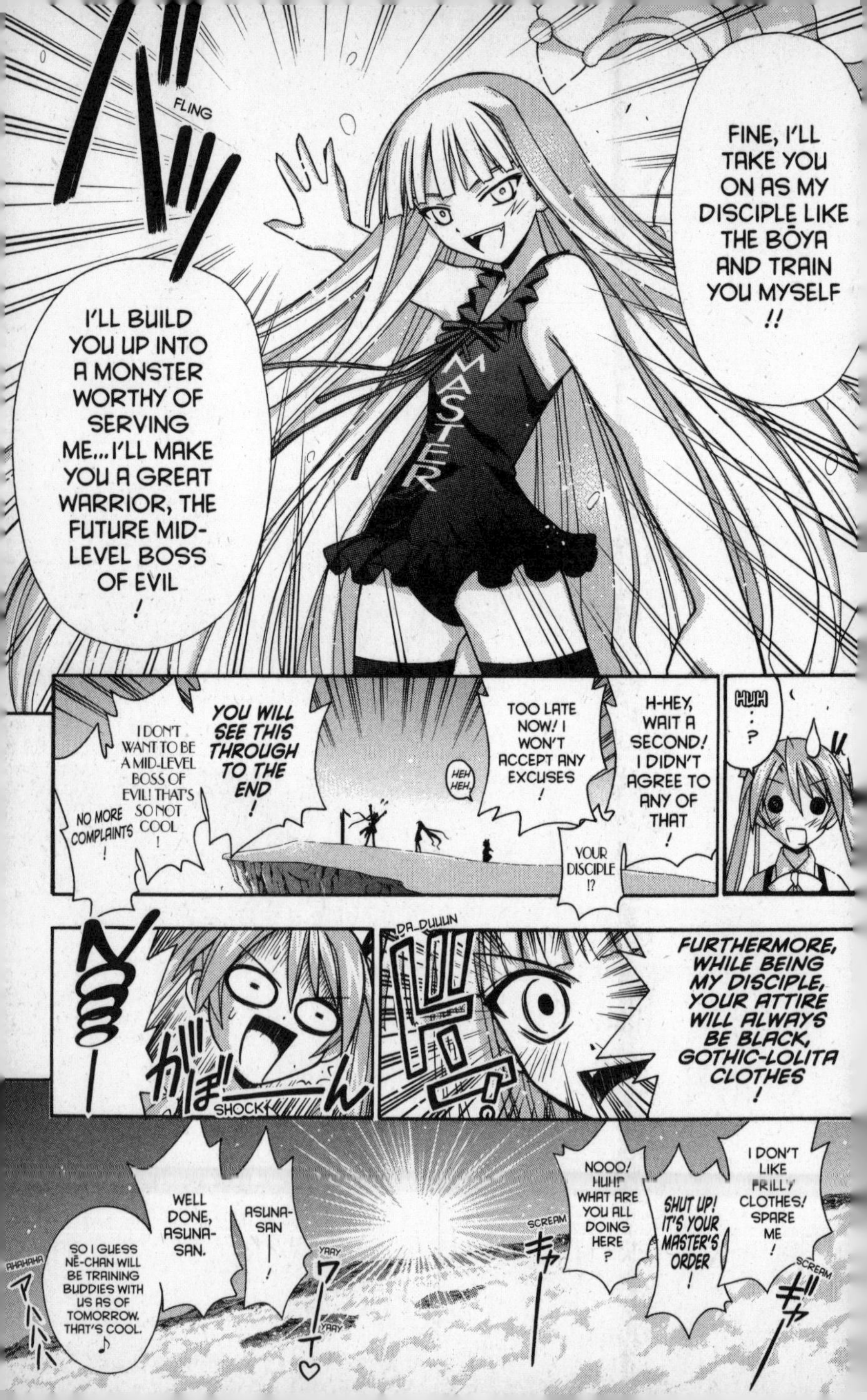
FLING
FINE, I'LL TAKE YOU ON AS MY DISCIPLE LIKE THE BŌYA AND TRAIN YOU MYSELF !!
I'LL BUILD YOU UP INTO A MONSTER WORTHY OF SERVING ME...I'LL MAKE YOU A GREAT WARRIOR, THE FUTURE MID-LEVEL BOSS OF EVIL !
HUH . . ?
H-HEY, WAIT A SECOND! I DIDN'T AGREE TO ANY OF THAT !
YOUR DISCIPLE !?
TOO LATE NOW! I WON'T ACCEPT ANY EXCUSES !
HEH HEH
YOU WILL SEE THIS THROUGH TO THE END !
I DON'T WANT TO BE A MID-LEVEL BOSS OF EVIL! THAT'S SO NOT COOL !
NO MORE COMPLAINTS !
FURTHERMORE, WHILE BEING MY DISCIPLE, YOUR ATTIRE WILL ALWAYS BE BLACK, GOTHIC-LOLITA CLOTHES !
DA-DUUUN
SHOCK
I DON'T LIKE FRILLY CLOTHES! SPARE ME !
SCREAM
SHUT UP! IT'S YOUR MASTER'S ORDER !
NOOO! HUH!? WHAT ARE YOU ALL DOING HERE ?
SCREAM
ASUNA-SAN !
YAAY
YAAY
WELL DONE, ASUNA-SAN.
SO I GUESS NĒ-CHAN WILL BE TRAINING BUDDIES WITH US AS OF TOMORROW. THAT'S COOL. ♪
AHAHAHA

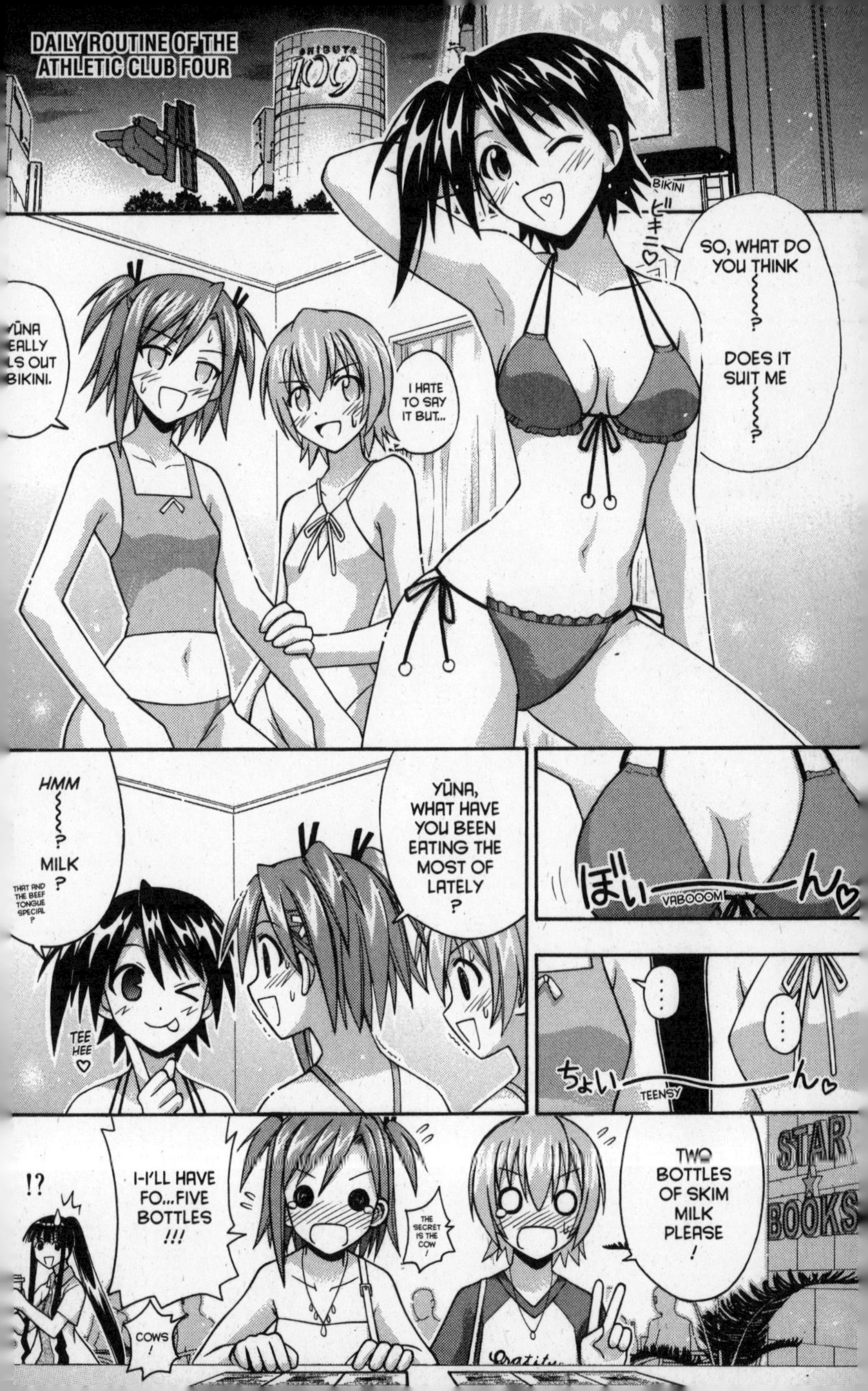
DAILY ROUTINE OF THE ATHLETIC CLUB FOUR
SHIBUYA 109
BIKINI ビキニ♡
SO, WHAT DO YOU THINK~? DOES IT SUIT ME~?
I HATE TO SAY IT BUT...
YŪNA EALLY LS OUT BIKINI.
ぼい〜ん♡ VABOOOM
....
....
ちょい〜ん♡ TEENSY
YŪNA, WHAT HAVE YOU BEEN EATING THE MOST OF LATELY?
HMM~? MILK?
THAT AND THE BEEF TONGUE SPECIAL?
TEE HEE ♡
STAR BOOKS
TWO BOTTLES OF SKIM MILK PLEASE!
THE SECRET IS THE COW!
I-I'LL HAVE FO...FIVE BOTTLES!!!
!?
COWS!

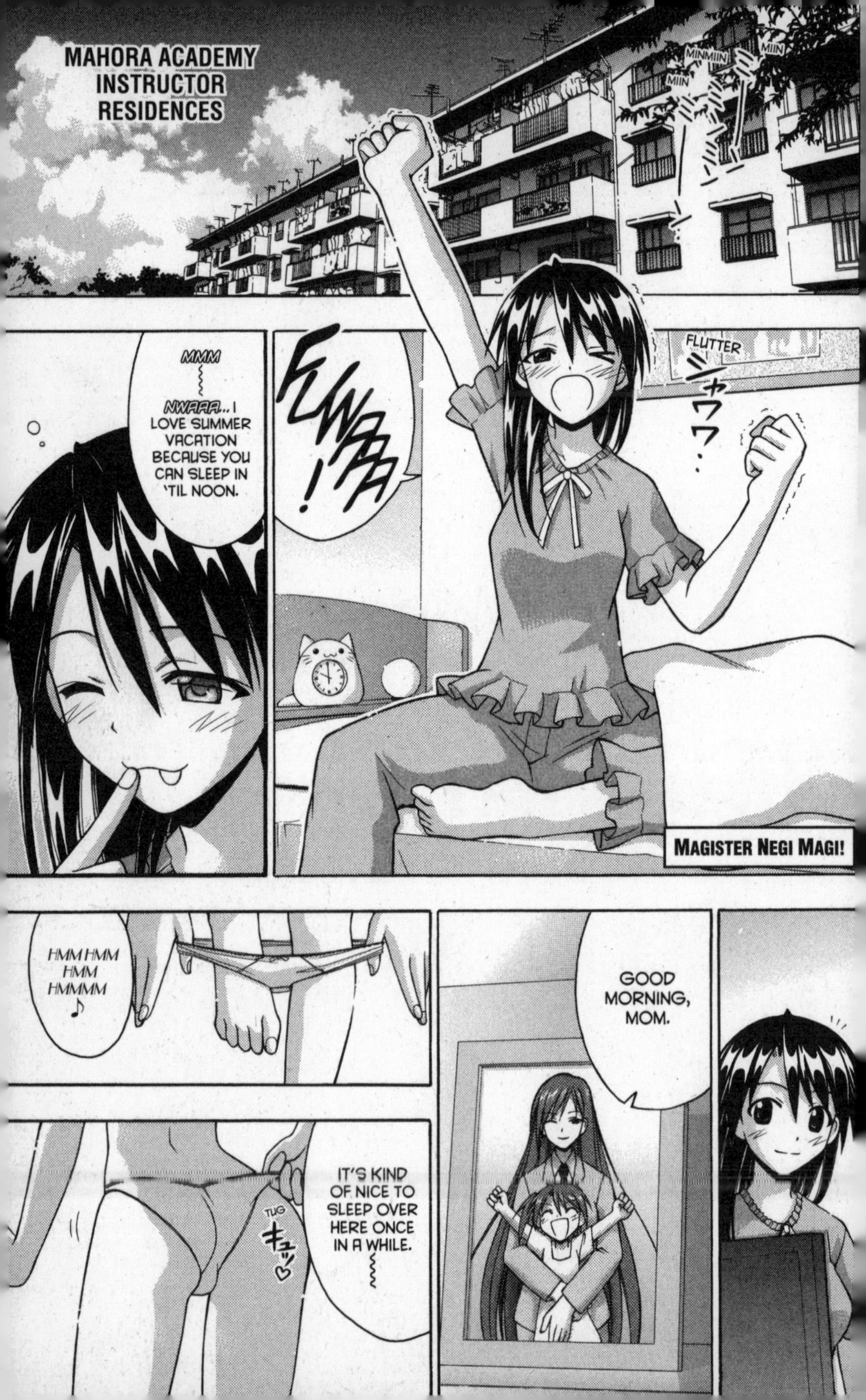
MAHORA ACADEMY INSTRUCTOR RESIDENCES
MIINMIIN
MIIN
MIIN
FLUTTER
シャワワ・・
FUWAAA!
MAGISTER NEGI MAGI!
MMM~ NWAAAA... I LOVE SUMMER VACATION BECAUSE YOU CAN SLEEP IN 'TIL NOON.
GOOD MORNING, MOM.
HMM HMM HMM HMMM ♪
IT'S KIND OF NICE TO SLEEP OVER HERE ONCE IN A WHILE.
TUG
キュッ♡

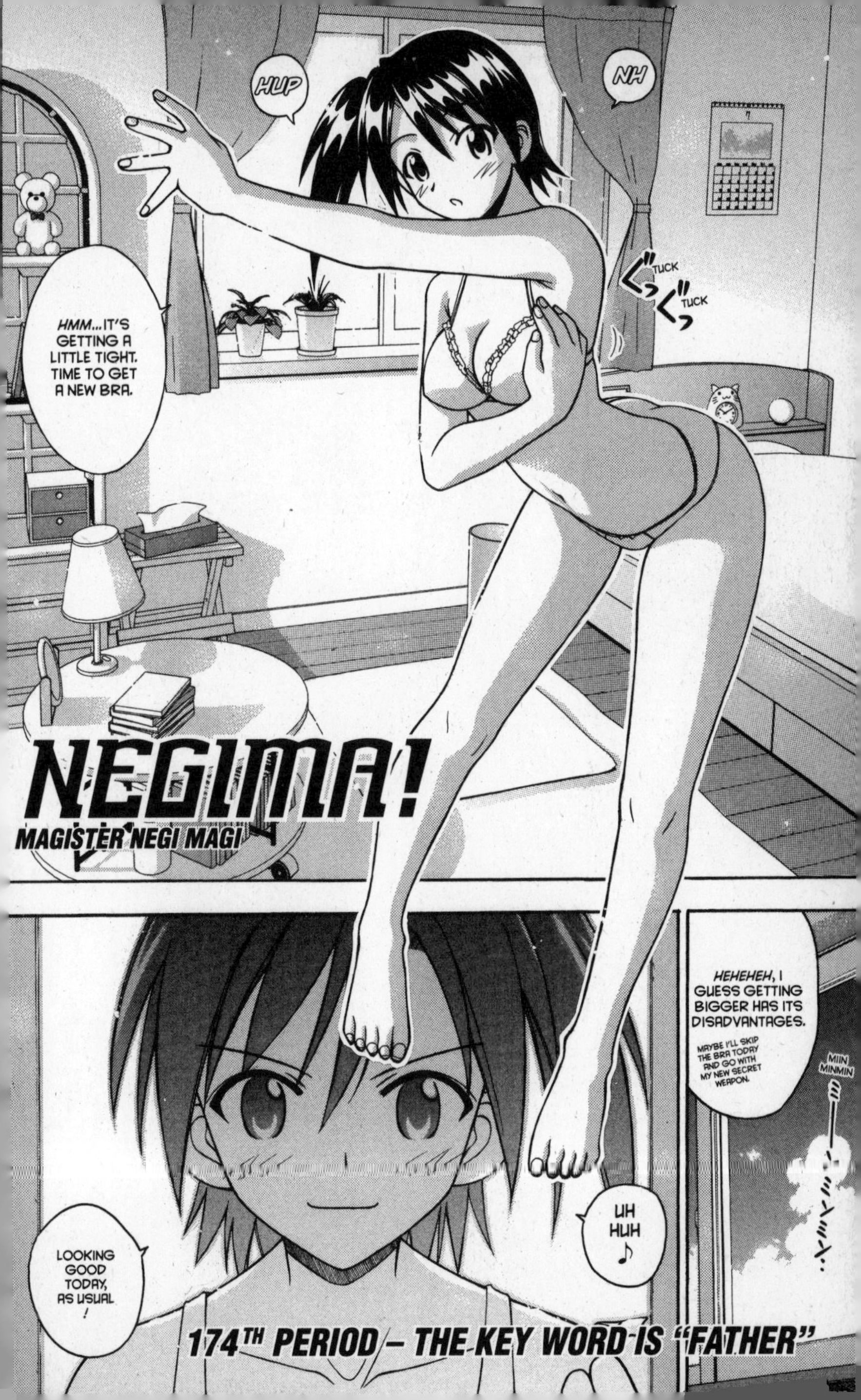
NH
HUP
TUCK
TUCK
HMM...IT'S GETTING A LITTLE TIGHT. TIME TO GET A NEW BRA.
NEGIMA!
MAGISTER NEGI MAGI
HEHEHEH, I GUESS GETTING BIGGER HAS ITS DISADVANTAGES.
MAYBE I'LL SKIP THE BRA TODAY AND GO WITH MY NEW SECRET WEAPON.
MIIN MINMIN
UH HUH ♪
LOOKING GOOD TODAY, AS USUAL!
174TH PERIOD – THE KEY WORD IS "FATHER"

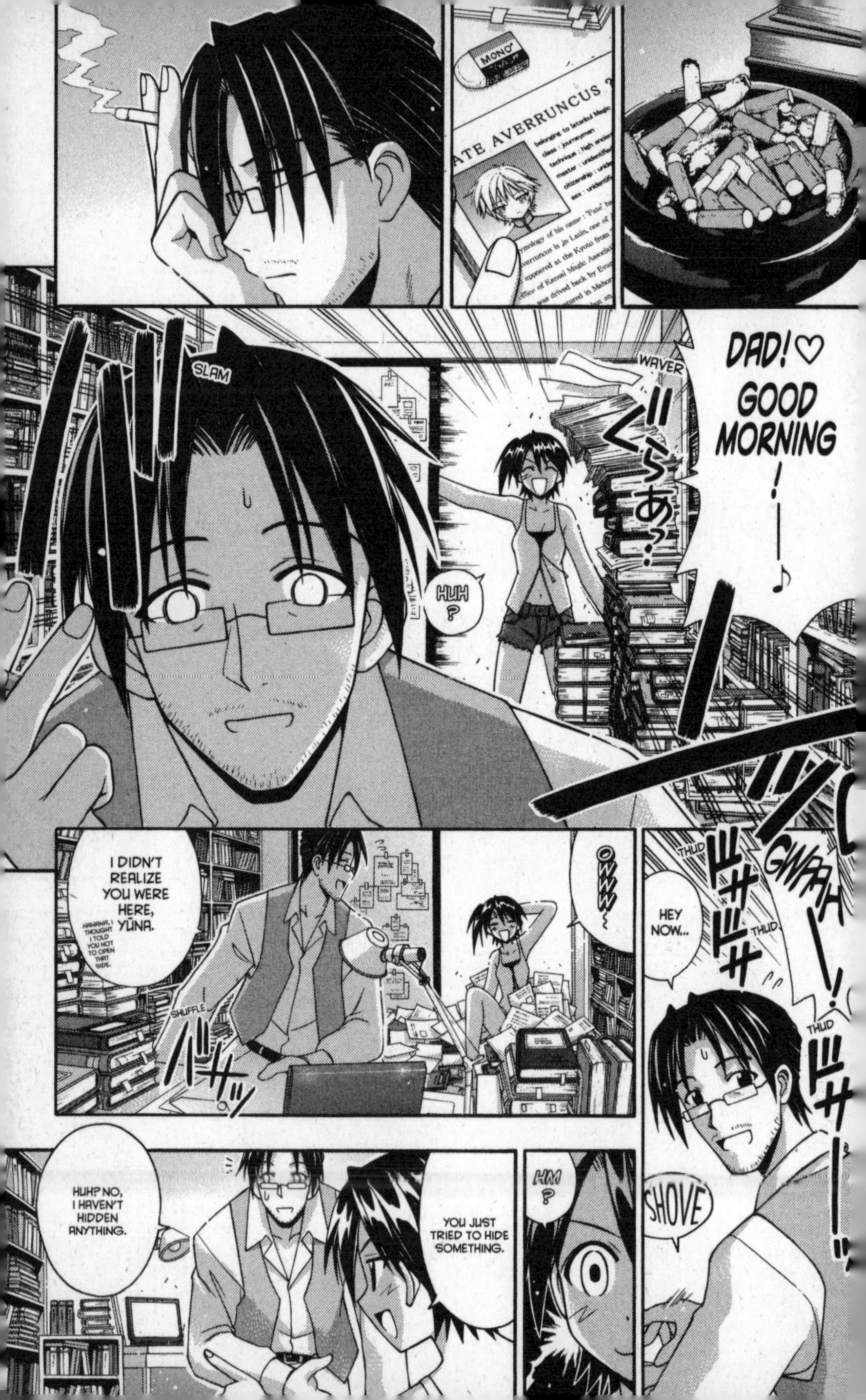
MONO
ATE AVERRUNCUS
DAD! ♡ GOOD MORNING!―♪
WAVER
SLAM
HUH?
GWRAAH―!
THUD
THUD
THUD
HEY NOW...
SHOVE
OWWW~
I DIDN'T REALIZE YOU WERE HERE, YŪNA.
HAHAHA, I THOUGHT I TOLD YOU NOT TO OPEN THAT SIDE.
SHUFFLE
HM?
YOU JUST TRIED TO HIDE SOMETHING.
HUH? NO, I HAVEN'T HIDDEN ANYTHING.

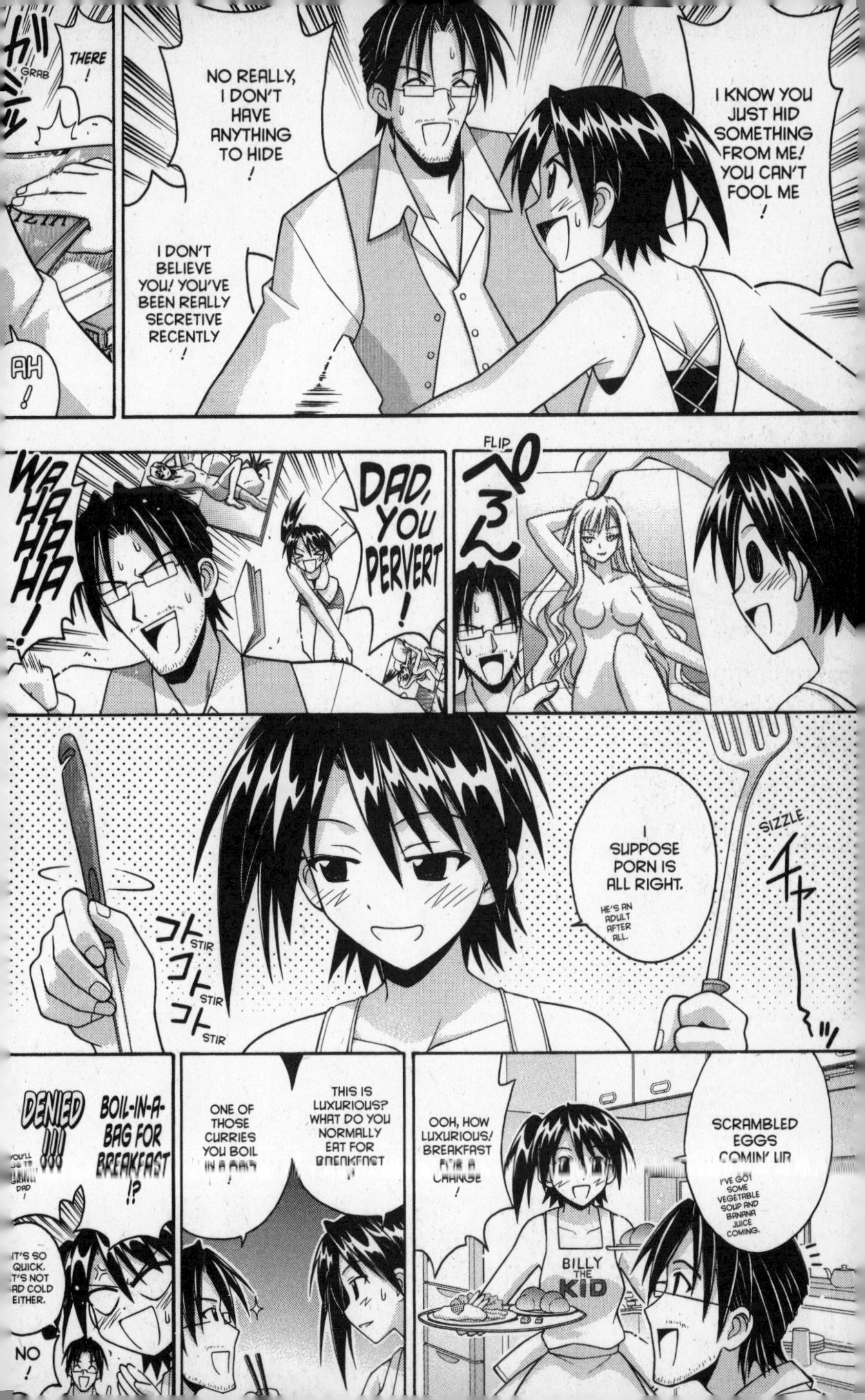
I KNOW YOU JUST HID SOMETHING FROM ME! YOU CAN'T FOOL ME!
NO REALLY, I DON'T HAVE ANYTHING TO HIDE!
I DON'T BELIEVE YOU! YOU'VE BEEN REALLY SECRETIVE RECENTLY!
GRAB
THERE!
AH!
FLIP
DAD, YOU PERVERT!
WAHAHAHA!
SIZZLE
I SUPPOSE PORN IS ALL RIGHT.
HE'S AN ADULT AFTER ALL.
STIR
STIR
STIR
SCRAMBLED EGGS COMIN' UP
I'VE GOT SOME VEGETABLE SOUP AND BANANA JUICE COMING.
OOH, HOW LUXURIOUS! BREAKFAST FOR A CHANGE!
THIS IS LUXURIOUS? WHAT DO YOU NORMALLY EAT FOR BREAKFAST?
ONE OF THOSE CURRIES YOU BOIL IN A BAG!
BOIL-IN-A-BAG FOR BREAKFAST!?
DENIED!!!
IT'S SO QUICK. IT'S NOT BAD COLD EITHER.
NO!
BILLY THE KID

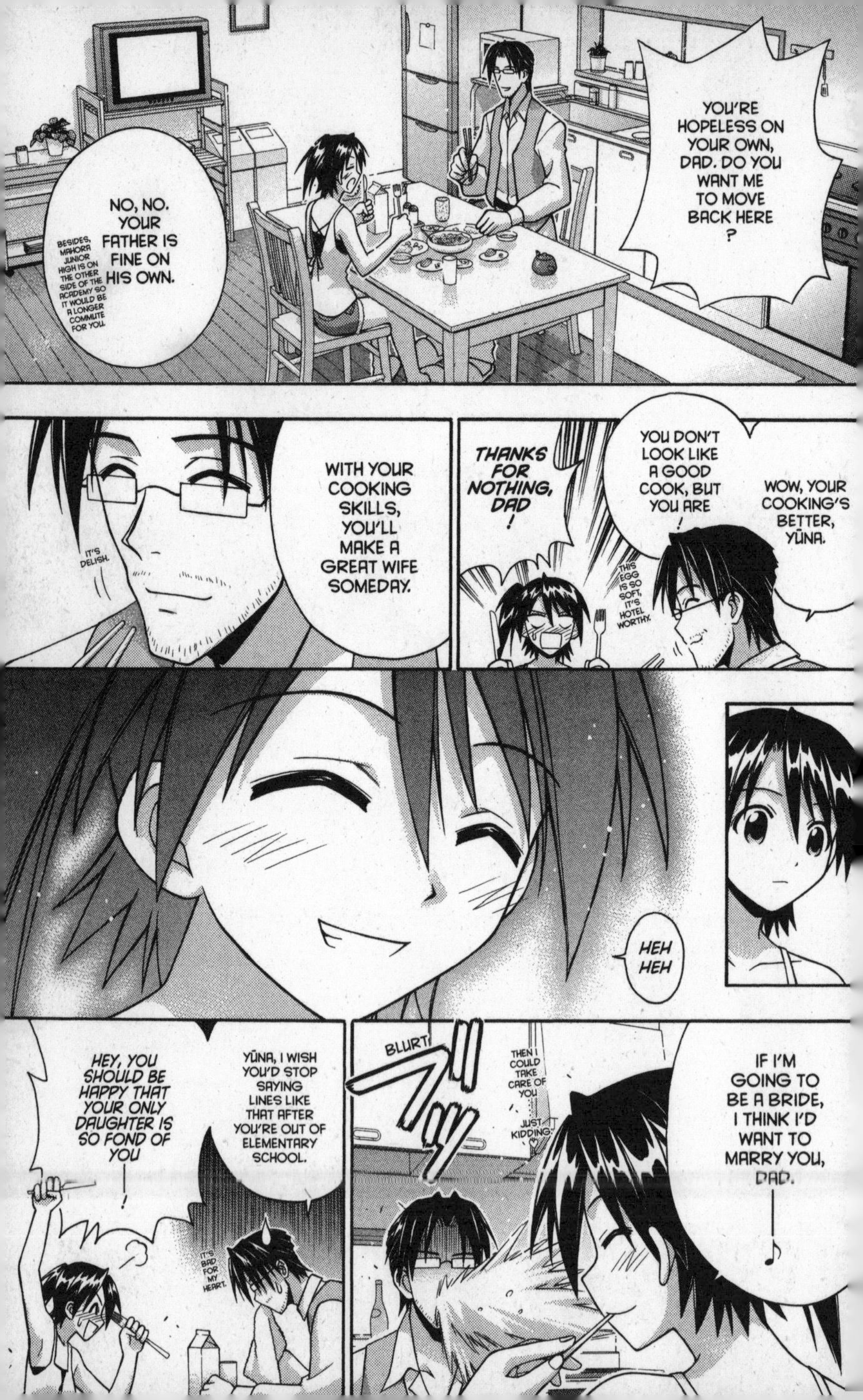
YOU'RE HOPELESS ON YOUR OWN, DAD. DO YOU WANT ME TO MOVE BACK HERE?
NO, NO. YOUR FATHER IS FINE ON HIS OWN.
BESIDES, MAHORA JUNIOR HIGH IS ON THE OTHER SIDE OF THE ACADEMY SO IT WOULD BE A LONGER COMMUTE FOR YOU.
WOW, YOUR COOKING'S BETTER, YŪNA.
YOU DON'T LOOK LIKE A GOOD COOK, BUT YOU ARE!
THIS EGG IS SO SOFT, IT'S HOTEL WORTHY.
THANKS FOR NOTHING, DAD!
WITH YOUR COOKING SKILLS, YOU'LL MAKE A GREAT WIFE SOMEDAY.
IT'S DELISH.
HEH HEH
IF I'M GOING TO BE A BRIDE, I THINK I'D WANT TO MARRY YOU, DAD. ♪
THEN I COULD TAKE CARE OF YOU
JUST KIDDING.
BLURT
YŪNA, I WISH YOU'D STOP SAYING LINES LIKE THAT AFTER YOU'RE OUT OF ELEMENTARY SCHOOL.
IT'S BAD FOR MY HEART.
HEY, YOU SHOULD BE HAPPY THAT YOUR ONLY DAUGHTER IS SO FOND OF YOU!

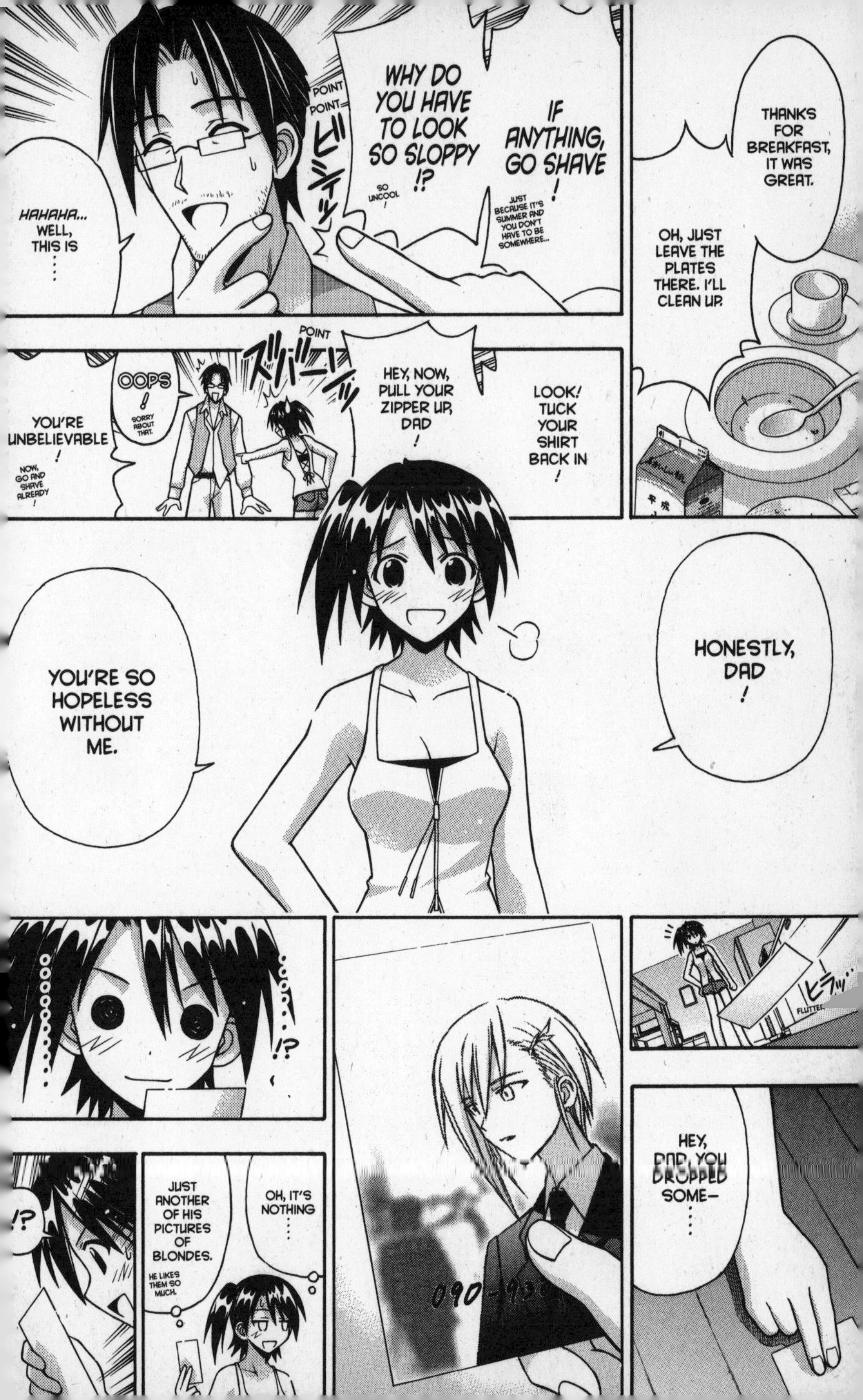
THANKS FOR BREAKFAST, IT WAS GREAT.
OH, JUST LEAVE THE PLATES THERE. I'LL CLEAN UP.
IF ANYTHING, GO SHAVE!
JUST BECAUSE IT'S SUMMER AND YOU DON'T HAVE TO BE SOMEWHERE...
WHY DO YOU HAVE TO LOOK SO SLOPPY!?
SO UNCOOL!
POINT POINT
HAHAHA... WELL, THIS IS ....
LOOK! TUCK YOUR SHIRT BACK IN!
HEY, NOW, PULL YOUR ZIPPER UP, DAD!
POINT
OOPS! SORRY ABOUT THAT.
YOU'RE UNBELIEVABLE!
NOW, GO AND SHAVE ALREADY!
HONESTLY, DAD!
YOU'RE SO HOPELESS WITHOUT ME.
FLUTTER
HEY, DAD, YOU DROPPED SOME—....
!?
OH, IT'S NOTHING....
JUST ANOTHER OF HIS PICTURES OF BLONDES.
HE LIKES THEM SO MUCH.
!?

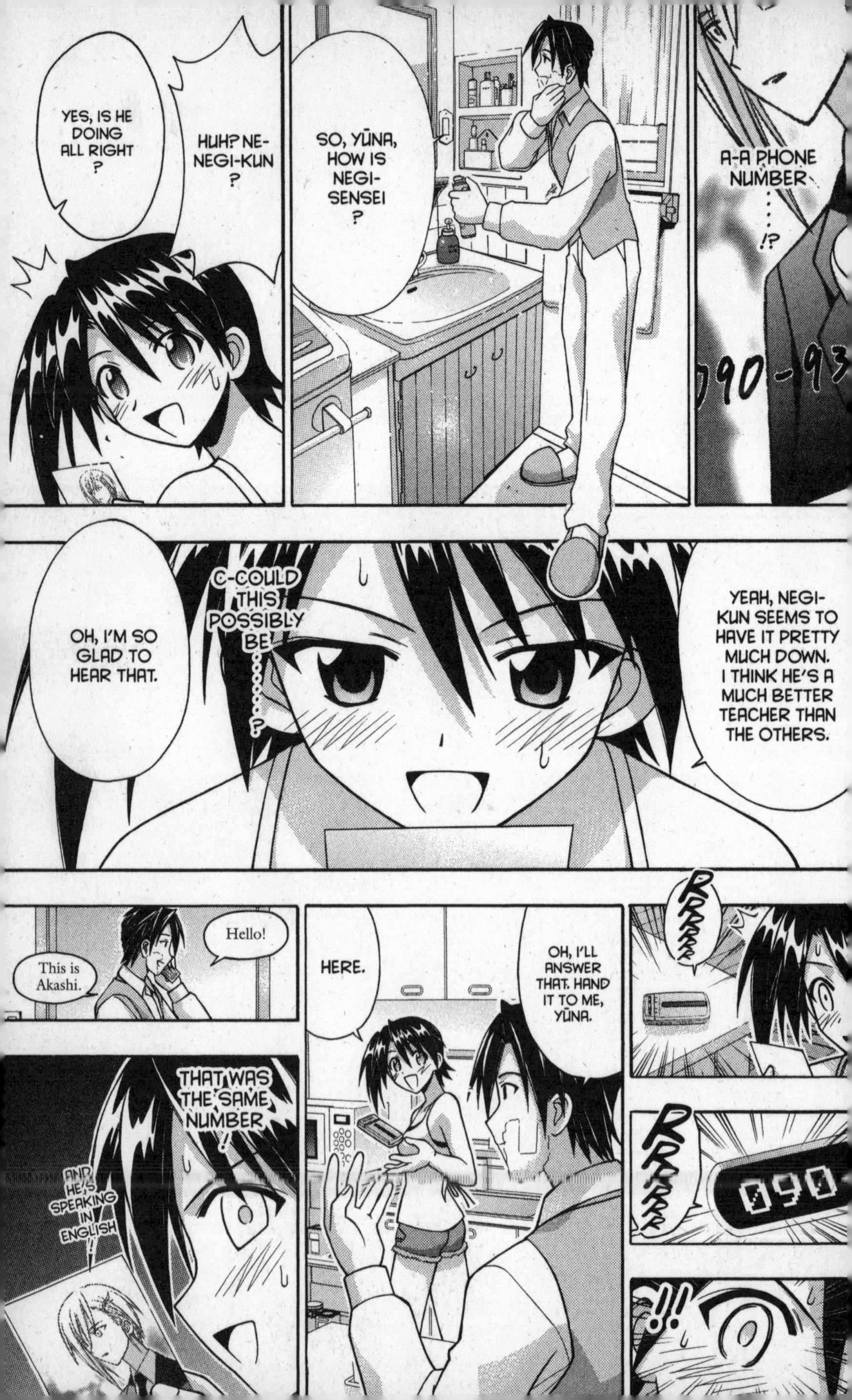
A-A PHONE NUMBER......!?
090-93
SO, YŪNA, HOW IS NEGI-SENSEI?
HUH? NE-NEGI-KUN?
YES, IS HE DOING ALL RIGHT?
YEAH, NEGI-KUN SEEMS TO HAVE IT PRETTY MUCH DOWN. I THINK HE'S A MUCH BETTER TEACHER THAN THE OTHERS.
C-COULD THIS POSSIBLY BE......?
OH, I'M SO GLAD TO HEAR THAT.
RRRRRR
RRRRRR
090
!!
OH, I'LL ANSWER THAT. HAND IT TO ME, YŪNA.
HERE.
Hello!
This is Akashi.
THAT WAS THE SAME NUMBER!
AND HE'S SPEAKING IN ENGLISH!!

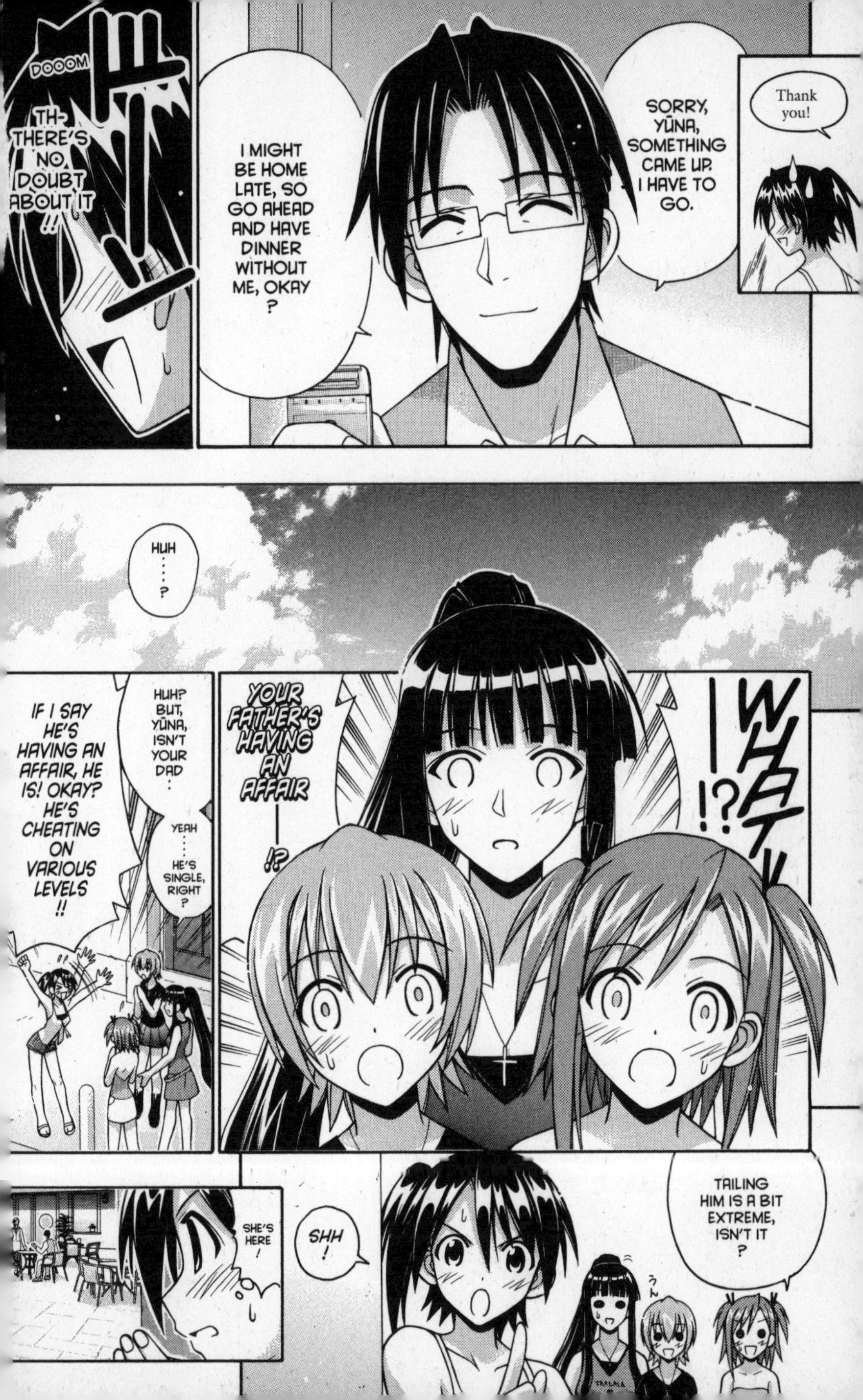
Thank you!
SORRY, YŪNA, SOMETHING CAME UP. I HAVE TO GO.
I MIGHT BE HOME LATE, SO GO AHEAD AND HAVE DINNER WITHOUT ME, OKAY?
DOOOM
TH-THERE'S NO DOUBT ABOUT IT!!
HUH.....?
WHAT!?
YOUR FATHER'S HAVING AN AFFAIR—!?
HUH? BUT, YŪNA, ISN'T YOUR DAD...
YEAH... HE'S SINGLE, RIGHT?
IF I SAY HE'S HAVING AN AFFAIR, HE IS! OKAY? HE'S CHEATING ON VARIOUS LEVELS!!
TAILING HIM IS A BIT EXTREME, ISN'T IT?
SHH!
SHE'S HERE!

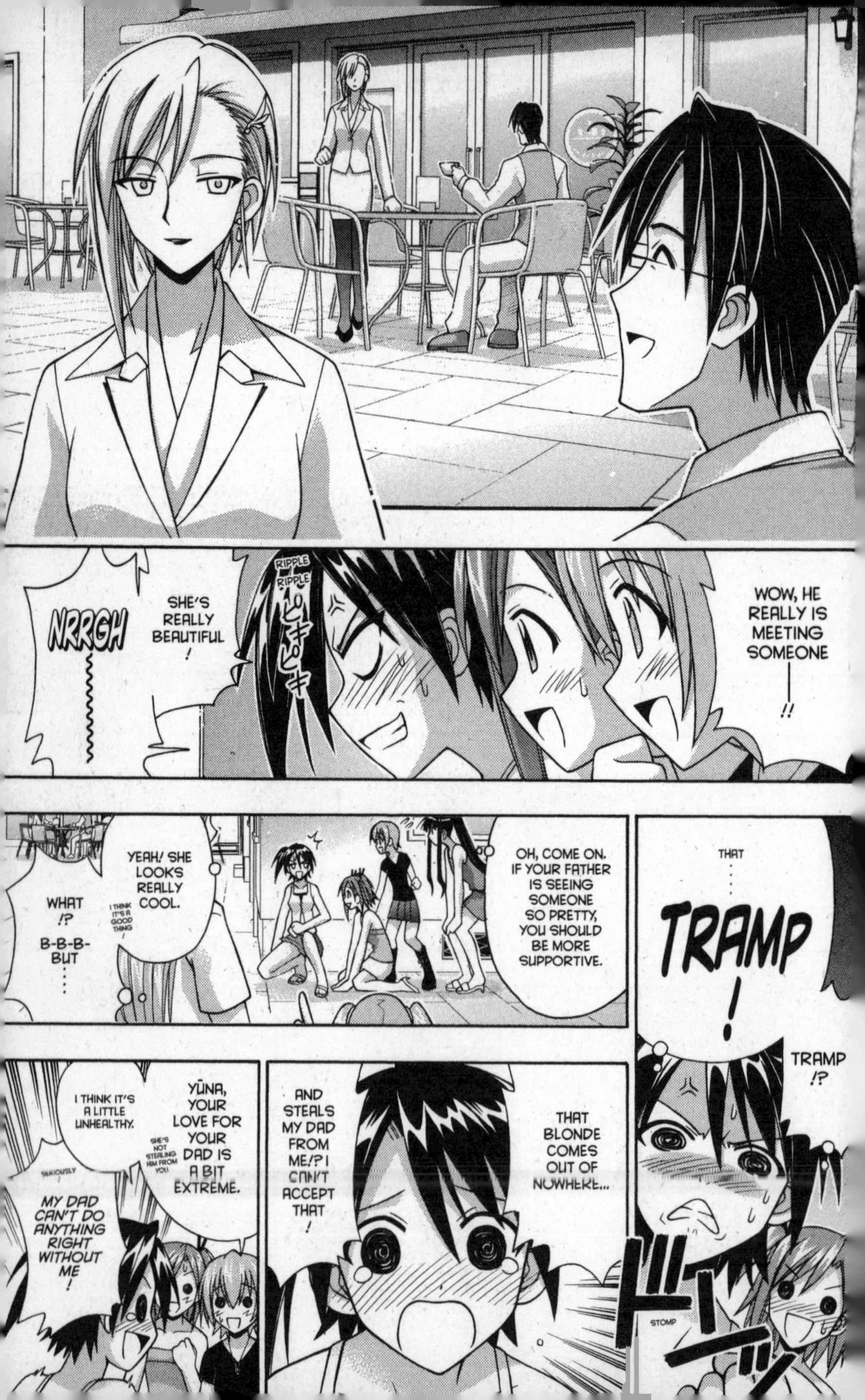
WOW, HE REALLY IS MEETING SOMEONE—!!
RIPPLE RIPPLE
ピキピキ
SHE'S REALLY BEAUTIFUL!
NRRGH
THAT...... TRAMP!
TRAMP!?
STOMP
ドドッ
OH, COME ON. IF YOUR FATHER IS SEEING SOMEONE SO PRETTY, YOU SHOULD BE MORE SUPPORTIVE.
YEAH! SHE LOOKS REALLY COOL.
I THINK IT'S A GOOD THING!
WHAT!? B-B-B-BUT......
THAT BLONDE COMES OUT OF NOWHERE...
AND STEALS MY DAD FROM ME!? I CAN'T ACCEPT THAT!
YŪNA, YOUR LOVE FOR YOUR DAD IS A BIT EXTREME.
SHE'S NOT STEALING HIM FROM YOU!
I THINK IT'S A LITTLE UNHEALTHY.
SERIOUSLY!
MY DAD CAN'T DO ANYTHING RIGHT WITHOUT ME!

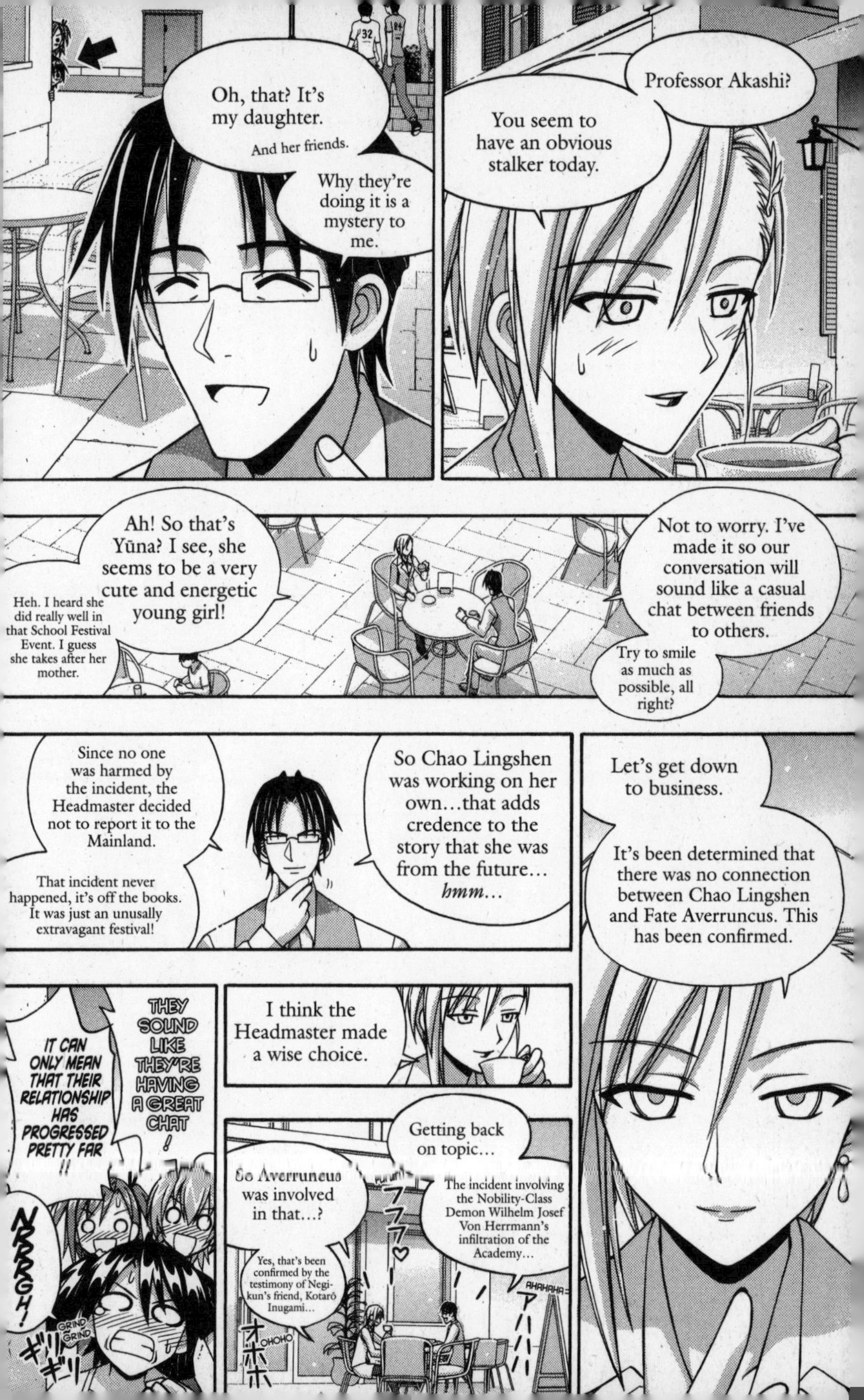

Professor Akashi?
You seem to have an obvious stalker today.
Oh, that? It's my daughter.
And her friends.
Why they're doing it is a mystery to me.
Not to worry. I've made it so our conversation will sound like a casual chat between friends to others.
Try to smile as much as possible, all right?
Ah! So that's Yūna? I see, she seems to be a very cute and energetic young girl!
Heh. I heard she did really well in that School Festival Event. I guess she takes after her mother.
Let's get down to business.
It's been determined that there was no connection between Chao Lingshen and Fate Averruncus. This has been confirmed.
So Chao Lingshen was working on her own…that adds credence to the story that she was from the future… *hmm*…
Since no one was harmed by the incident, the Headmaster decided not to report it to the Mainland.
That incident never happened, it's off the books. It was just an unusally extravagant festival!
I think the Headmaster made a wise choice.
Getting back on topic…
The incident involving the Nobility-Class Demon Wilhelm Josef Von Herrmann's infiltration of the Academy…
AHAHAHA
So Averruncus was involved in that…?
Yes, that's been confirmed by the testimony of Negi-kun's friend, Kotarō Inugami…
OHOHO
THEY SOUND LIKE THEY'RE HAVING A GREAT CHAT!
IT CAN ONLY MEAN THAT THEIR RELATIONSHIP HAS PROGRESSED PRETTY FAR!!
NRRRGH!
GRIND GRIND

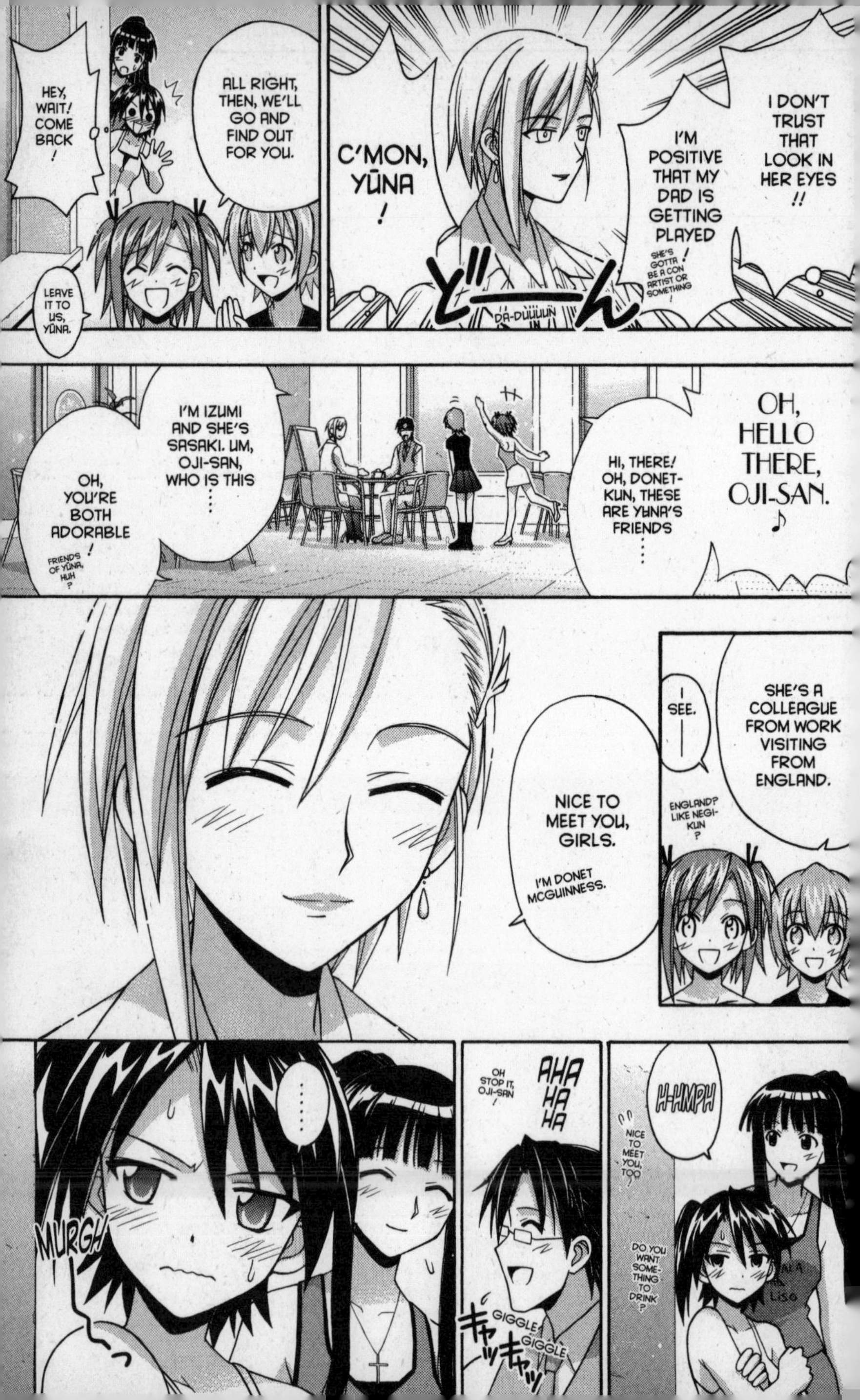
I DON'T TRUST THAT LOOK IN HER EYES!!
I'M POSITIVE THAT MY DAD IS GETTING PLAYED!
SHE'S GOTTA BE A CON ARTIST OR SOMETHING!
C'MON, YŪNA!
どーん
DA-DUUUUN
ALL RIGHT, THEN, WE'LL GO AND FIND OUT FOR YOU.
HEY, WAIT! COME BACK!
LEAVE IT TO US, YŪNA.
OH, HELLO THERE, OJI-SAN. ♪
HI, THERE! OH, DONET-KUN, THESE ARE YUNA'S FRIENDS...
I'M IZUMI AND SHE'S SASAKI. UM, OJI-SAN, WHO IS THIS...
OH, YOU'RE BOTH ADORABLE!
FRIENDS OF YŪNA, HUH?
SHE'S A COLLEAGUE FROM WORK VISITING FROM ENGLAND.
I SEE.
ENGLAND? LIKE NEGI-KUN?
NICE TO MEET YOU, GIRLS.
I'M DONET MCGUINNESS.
H-HMPH
NICE TO MEET YOU, TOO?
DO YOU WANT SOMETHING TO DRINK?
AHA HA HA
OH STOP IT, OJI-SAN!
GIGGLE GIGGLE
......
MURGH

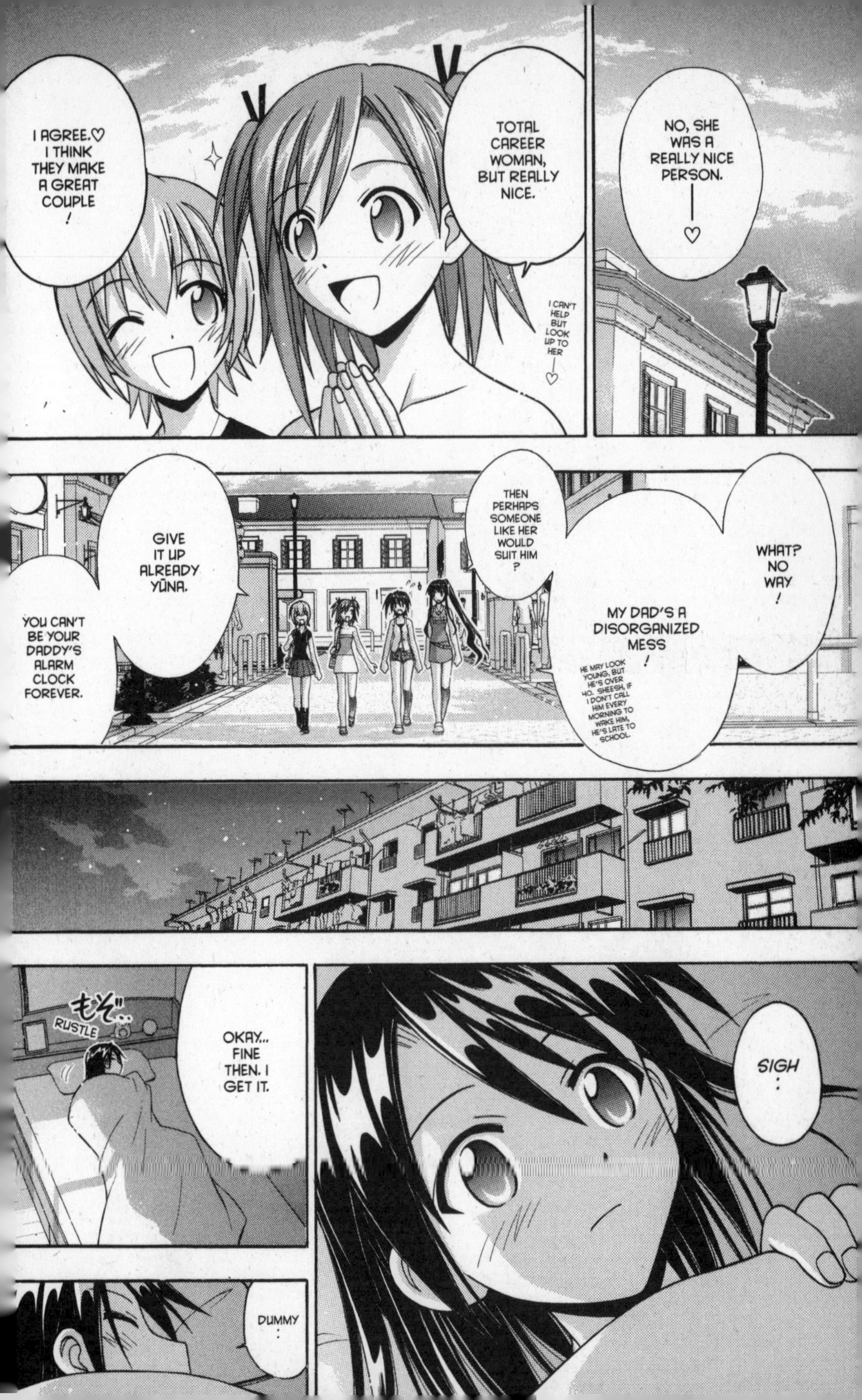
NO, SHE WAS A REALLY NICE PERSON. —♡
TOTAL CAREER WOMAN, BUT REALLY NICE.
I CAN'T HELP BUT LOOK UP TO HER —♡
I AGREE.♡ I THINK THEY MAKE A GREAT COUPLE!
WHAT? NO WAY!
MY DAD'S A DISORGANIZED MESS!
HE MAY LOOK YOUNG, BUT HE'S OVER 40. SHEESH, IF I DON'T CALL HIM EVERY MORNING TO WAKE HIM, HE'S LATE TO SCHOOL.
THEN PERHAPS SOMEONE LIKE HER WOULD SUIT HIM?
GIVE IT UP ALREADY YŪNA.
YOU CAN'T BE YOUR DADDY'S ALARM CLOCK FOREVER.
SIGH...
もぞ... RUSTLE
OKAY... FINE THEN. I GET IT.
DUMMY...

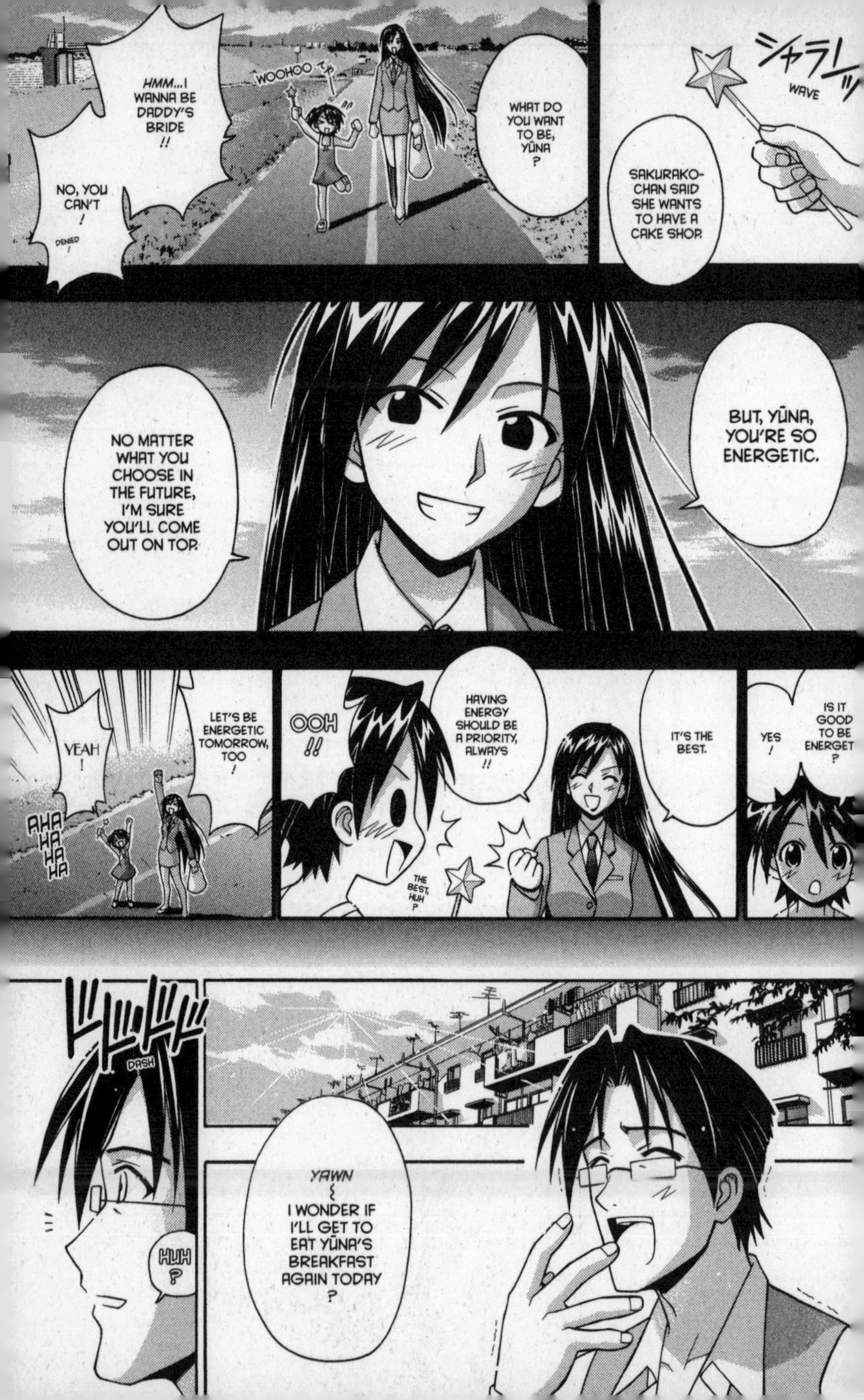
WAVE
SAKURAKO-CHAN SAID SHE WANTS TO HAVE A CAKE SHOP.
WHAT DO YOU WANT TO BE, YŪNA?
WOOHOO
HMM...I WANNA BE DADDY'S BRIDE!!
NO, YOU CAN'T!
DENIED!
BUT, YŪNA, YOU'RE SO ENERGETIC.
NO MATTER WHAT YOU CHOOSE IN THE FUTURE, I'M SURE YOU'LL COME OUT ON TOP.
IS IT GOOD TO BE ENERGET?
YES!
IT'S THE BEST.
HAVING ENERGY SHOULD BE A PRIORITY, ALWAYS!!
OOH!!
THE BEST, HUH?
LET'S BE ENERGETIC TOMORROW, TOO!
YEAH!
AHA HA HA HA
YAWN ~ I WONDER IF I'LL GET TO EAT YŪNA'S BREAKFAST AGAIN TODAY?
DASH
HUH?

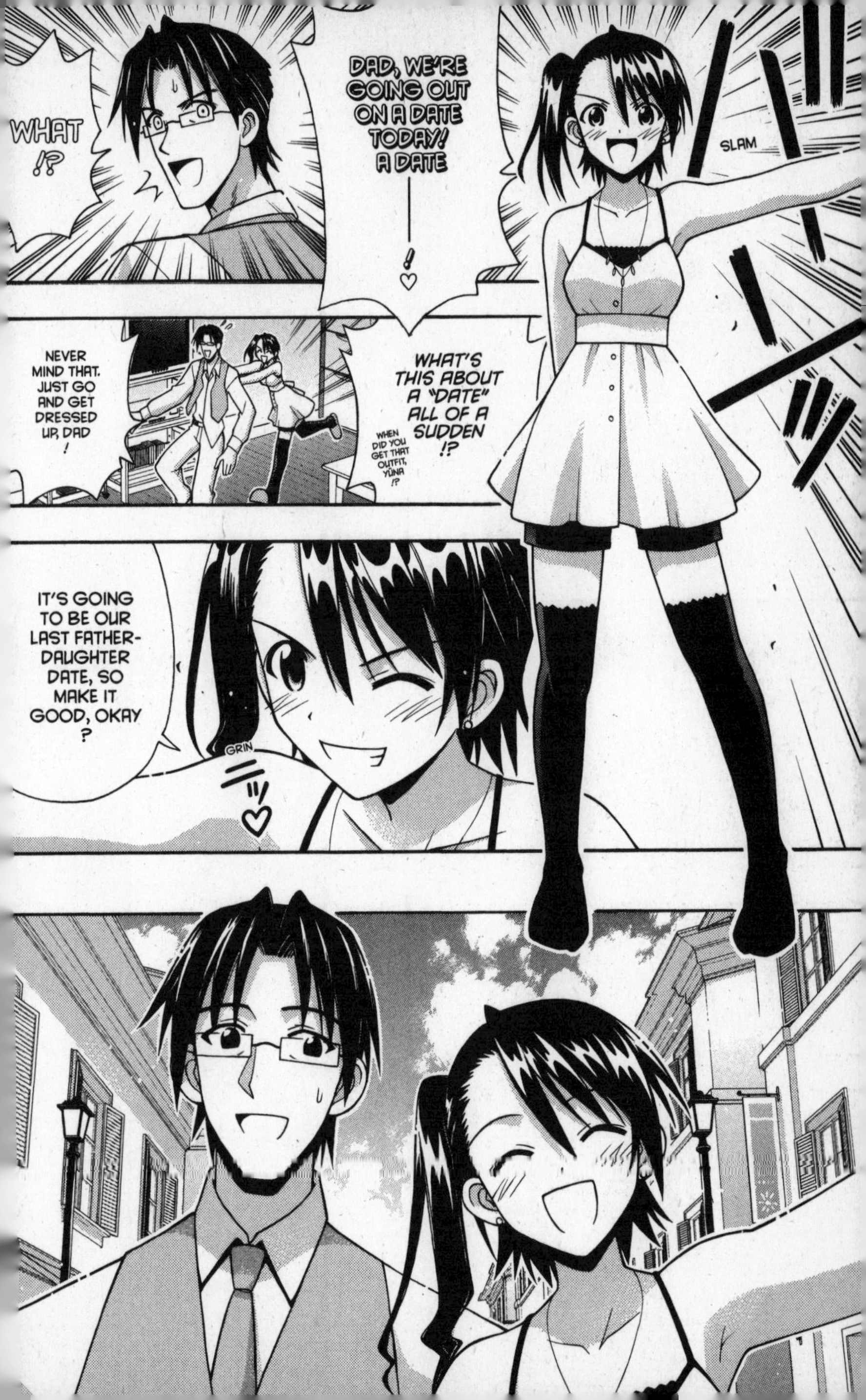
DAD, WE'RE GOING OUT ON A DATE TODAY! A DATE —!♡
SLAM
WHAT !?
WHAT'S THIS ABOUT A "DATE" ALL OF A SUDDEN !?
WHEN DID YOU GET THAT OUTFIT, YŪNA !?
NEVER MIND THAT. JUST GO AND GET DRESSED UP, DAD !
IT'S GOING TO BE OUR LAST FATHER-DAUGHTER DATE, SO MAKE IT GOOD, OKAY ?
GRIN

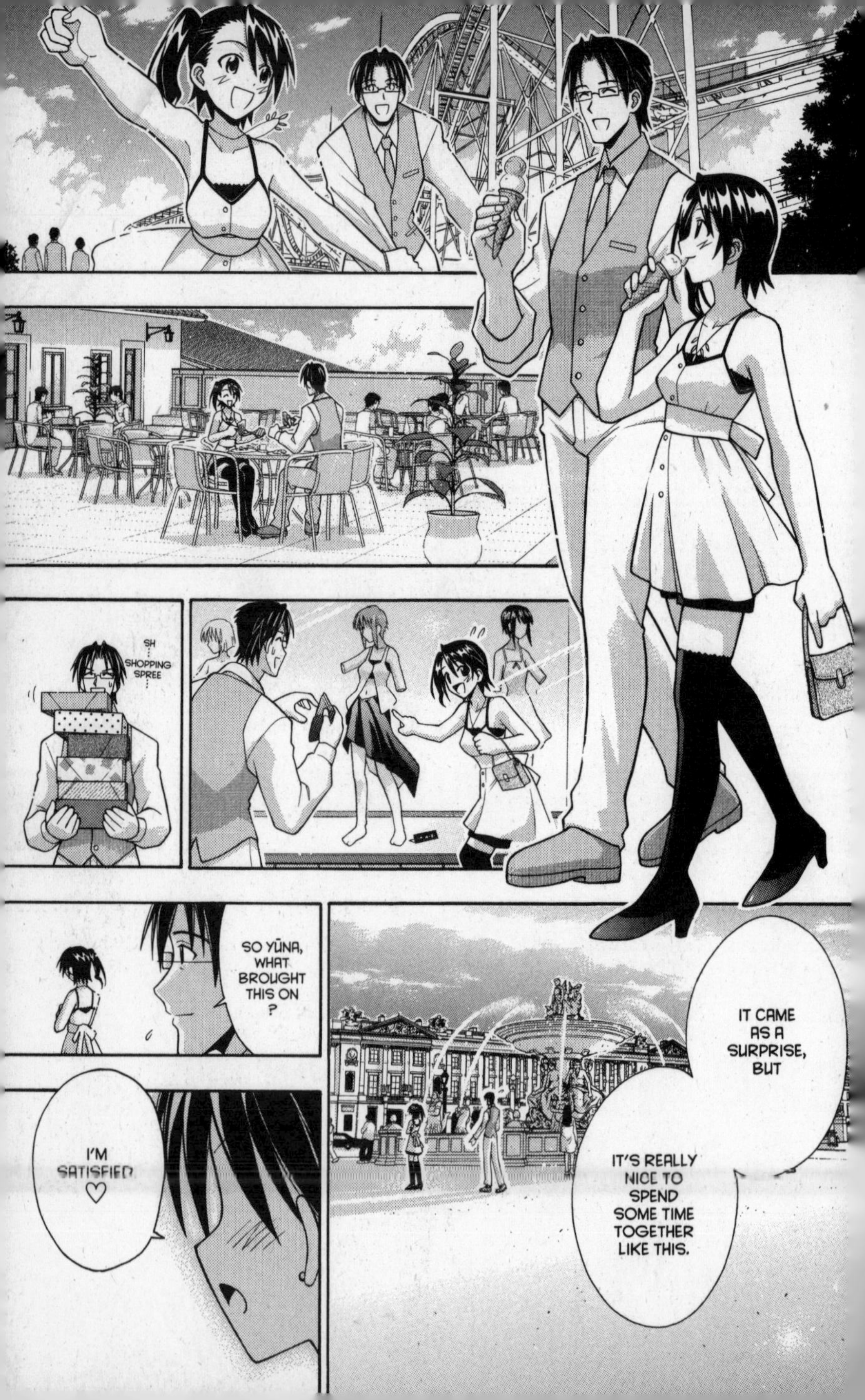
SH... SHOPPING SPREE...
IT CAME AS A SURPRISE, BUT
IT'S REALLY NICE TO SPEND SOME TIME TOGETHER LIKE THIS.
SO YŪNA, WHAT BROUGHT THIS ON ?
I'M SATISFIED ♡

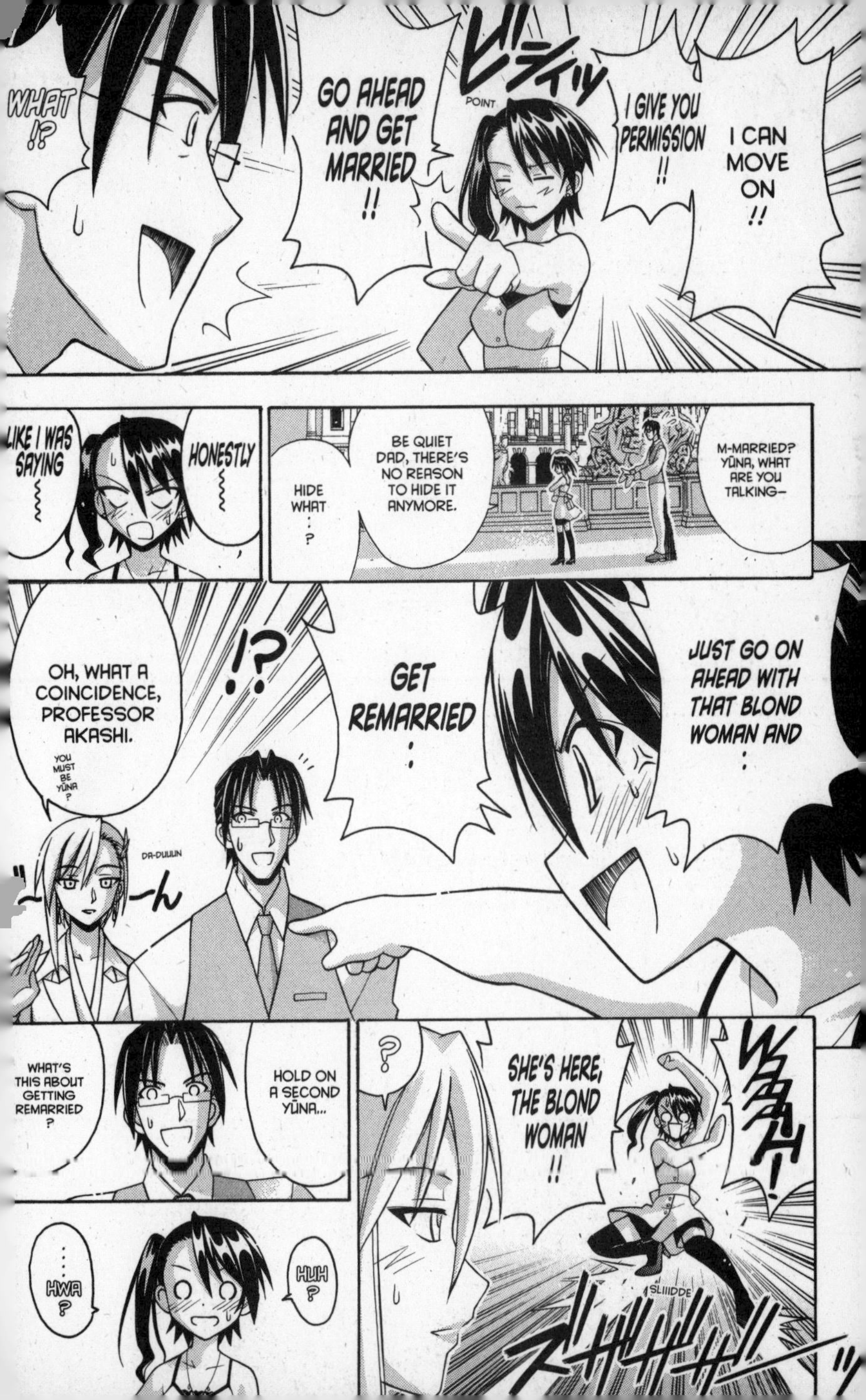
I CAN MOVE ON!!
I GIVE YOU PERMISSION!!
POINT
GO AHEAD AND GET MARRIED!!
WHAT!?
M-MARRIED? YŪNA, WHAT ARE YOU TALKING—
BE QUIET DAD, THERE'S NO REASON TO HIDE IT ANYMORE.
HIDE WHAT...?
HONESTLY...
LIKE I WAS SAYING...
JUST GO ON AHEAD WITH THAT BLOND WOMAN AND:
GET REMARRIED:
!?
OH, WHAT A COINCIDENCE, PROFESSOR AKASHI.
YOU MUST BE YŪNA?
DA-DUUUN
SHE'S HERE, THE BLOND WOMAN!!
?
SLIIIDDE
HOLD ON A SECOND YŪNA...
WHAT'S THIS ABOUT GETTING REMARRIED?
HUH?
...HWA?

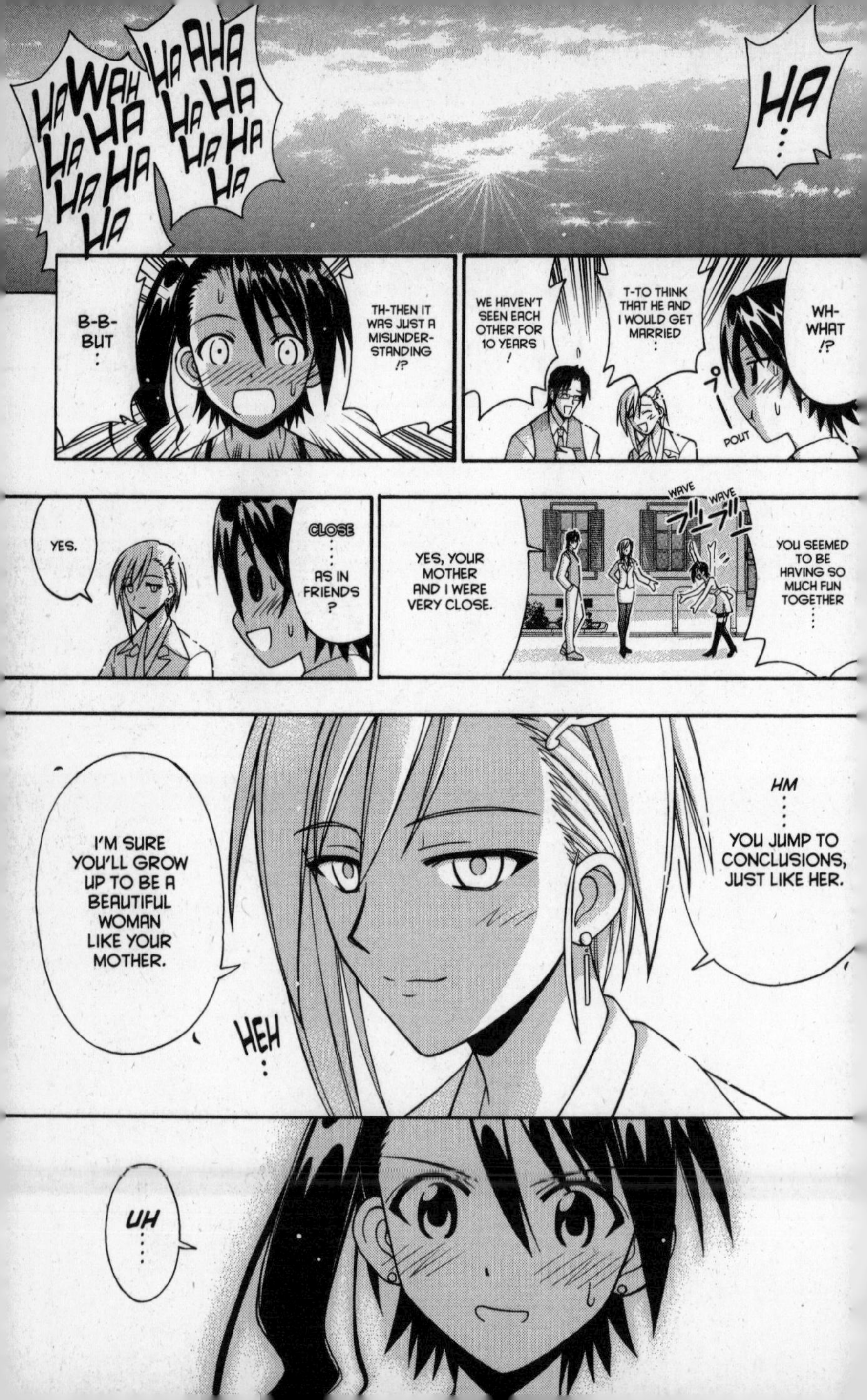
HA...
HA AHA HA HA HA HA HA
HA WAH HA HA HA HA HA HA HA
WH-WHAT!?
POUT
T-TO THINK THAT HE AND I WOULD GET MARRIED...
WE HAVEN'T SEEN EACH OTHER FOR 10 YEARS!
TH-THEN IT WAS JUST A MISUNDERSTANDING!?
B-B-BUT...
WAVE WAVE
YOU SEEMED TO BE HAVING SO MUCH FUN TOGETHER...
YES, YOUR MOTHER AND I WERE VERY CLOSE.
CLOSE... AS IN FRIENDS?
YES.
HM... YOU JUMP TO CONCLUSIONS, JUST LIKE HER.
I'M SURE YOU'LL GROW UP TO BE A BEAUTIFUL WOMAN LIKE YOUR MOTHER.
HEH...
UH...

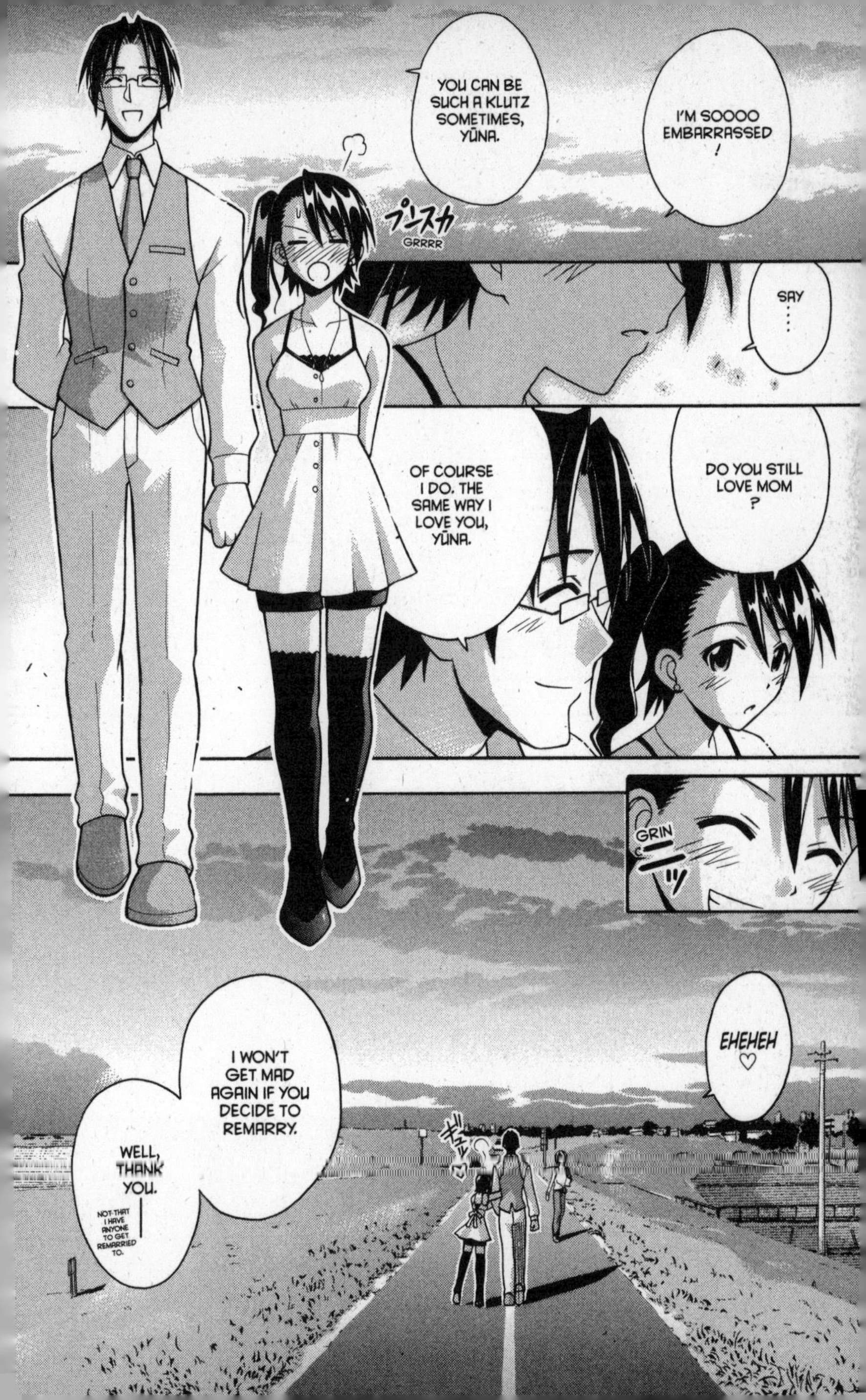
I'M SOOOO EMBARRASSED!
YOU CAN BE SUCH A KLUTZ SOMETIMES, YŪNA.
プンスカ
GRRRR
SAY....
DO YOU STILL LOVE MOM?
OF COURSE I DO. THE SAME WAY I LOVE YOU, YŪNA.
GRIN
EHEHEH ♡
I WON'T GET MAD AGAIN IF YOU DECIDE TO REMARRY.
WELL, THANK YOU.
NOT THAT I HAVE ANYONE TO GET REMARRIED TO.

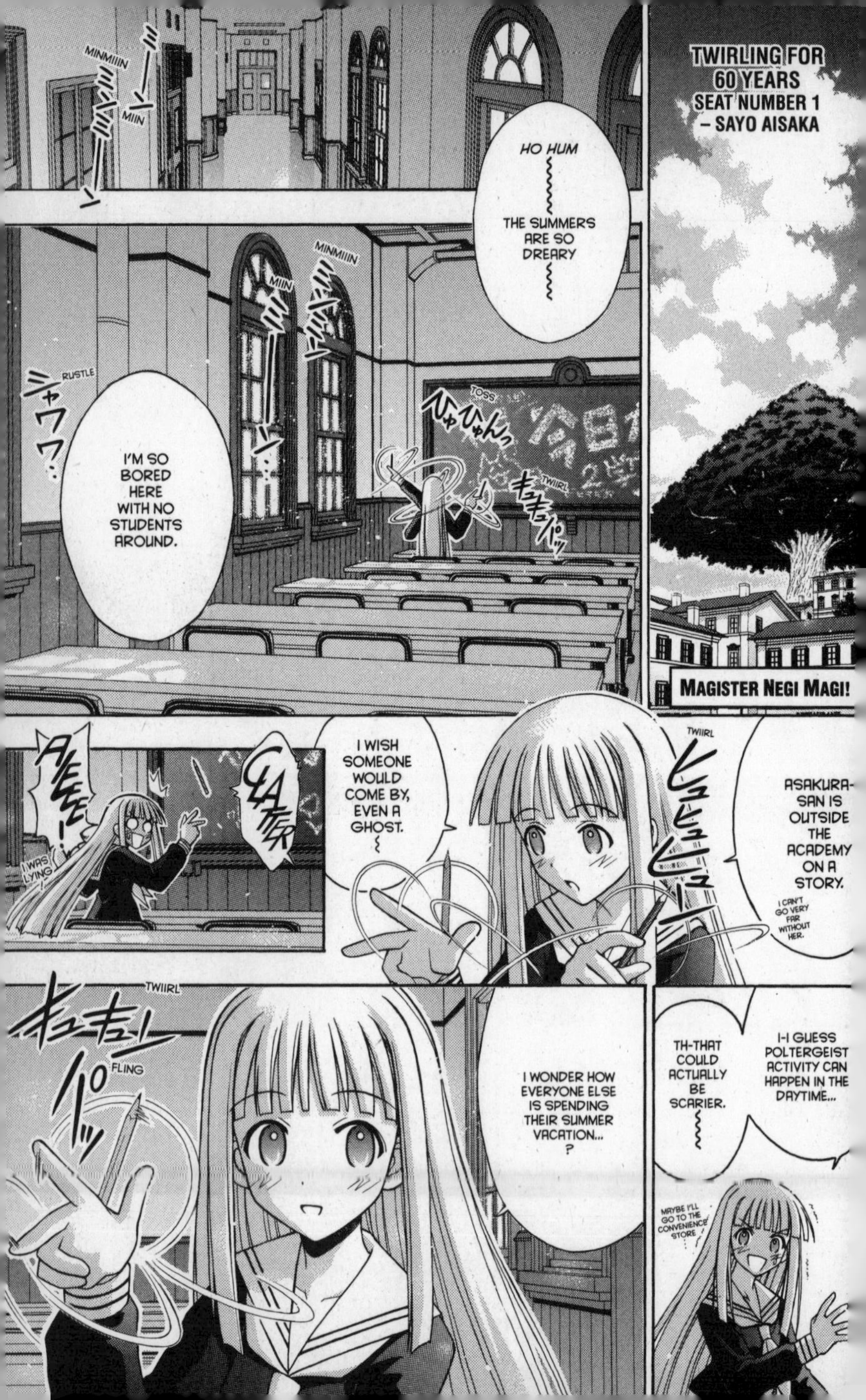
TWIRLING FOR 60 YEARS
SEAT NUMBER 1 – SAYO AISAKA
MAGISTER NEGI MAGI!
MINMIIIN
MIIN
HO HUM ~ THE SUMMERS ARE SO DREARY ~
MINMIIIN
MIIN
TOSS
TWIRL
I'M SO BORED HERE WITH NO STUDENTS AROUND.
RUSTLE
TWIIRL
ASAKURA-SAN IS OUTSIDE THE ACADEMY ON A STORY.
I CAN'T GO VERY FAR WITHOUT HER.
I WISH SOMEONE WOULD COME BY, EVEN A GHOST. ~
CLATTER
AIEEE!
I WAS LYING
I-I GUESS POLTERGEIST ACTIVITY CAN HAPPEN IN THE DAYTIME...
TH-THAT COULD ACTUALLY BE SCARIER. ~
MAYBE I'LL GO TO THE CONVENIENCE STORE
I WONDER HOW EVERYONE ELSE IS SPENDING THEIR SUMMER VACATION... ?
TWIIRL
FLING

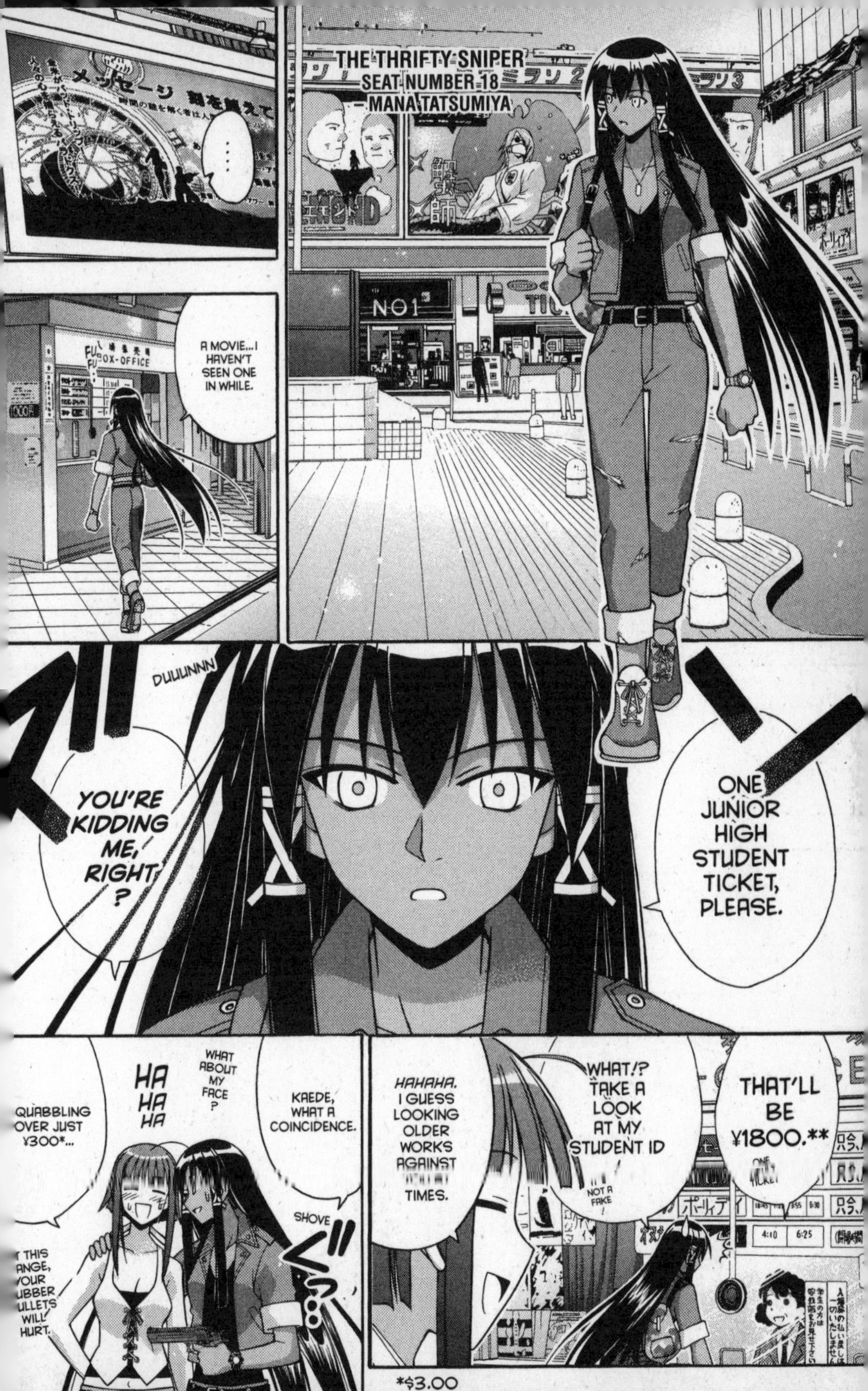
THE THRIFTY SNIPER
SEAT NUMBER 18
MANA TATSUMIYA
...
A MOVIE...I HAVEN'T SEEN ONE IN WHILE.
BOX-OFFICE
DUUUNNN
ONE JUNIOR HIGH STUDENT TICKET, PLEASE.
YOU'RE KIDDING ME, RIGHT?
THAT'LL BE ¥1800.**
ONE TICKET
WHAT!? TAKE A LOOK AT MY STUDENT ID
NOT A FAKE!
HAHAHA. I GUESS LOOKING OLDER WORKS AGAINST TIMES.
KAEDE, WHAT A COINCIDENCE.
WHAT ABOUT MY FACE?
HA HA HA
SHOVE
QUABBLING OVER JUST ¥300*...
T THIS ANGE, YOUR UBBER ULLETS WILL HURT.

*$3.00
**$18.00

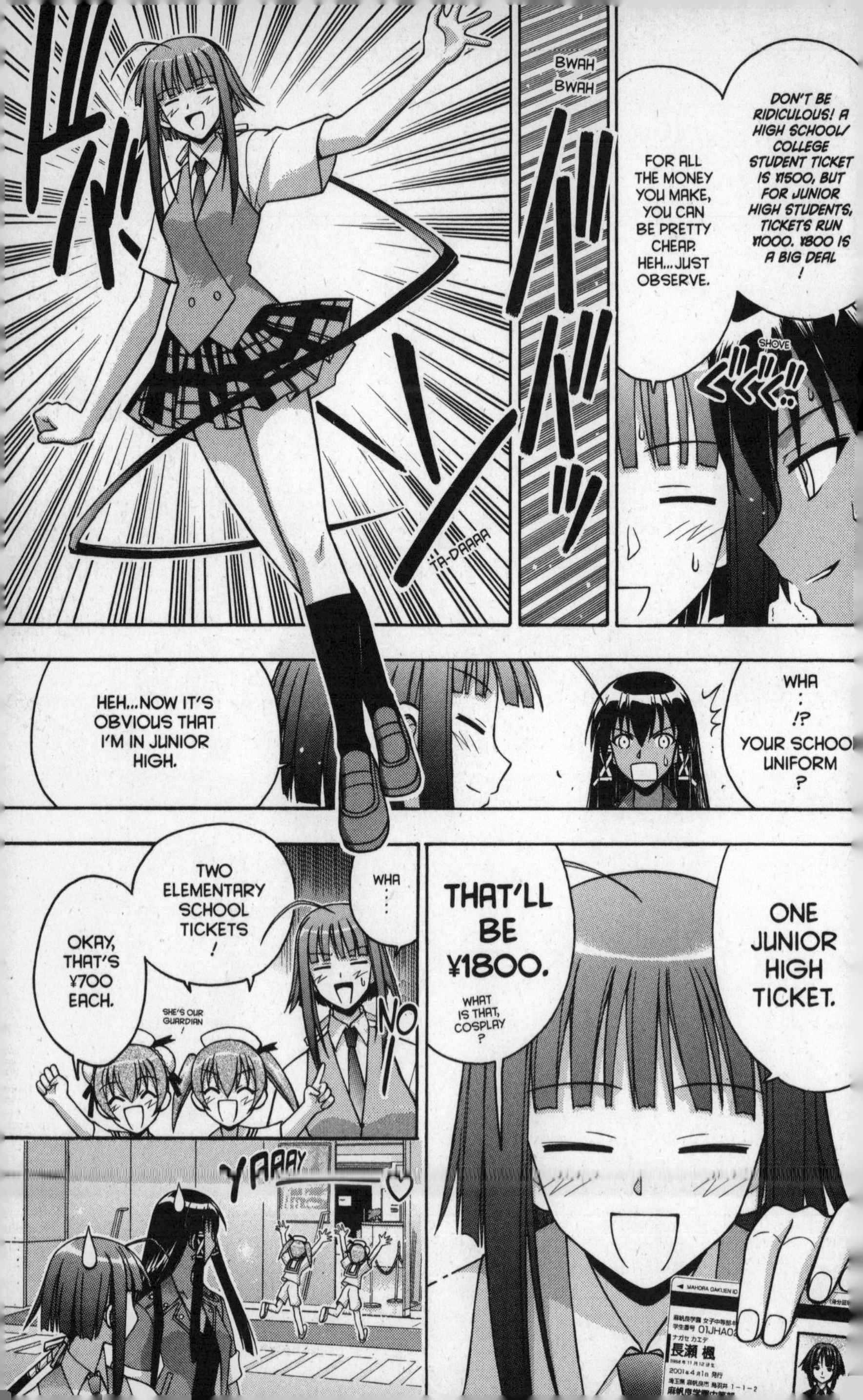
DON'T BE RIDICULOUS! A HIGH SCHOOL/ COLLEGE STUDENT TICKET IS ¥1500, BUT FOR JUNIOR HIGH STUDENTS, TICKETS RUN ¥1000. ¥800 IS A BIG DEAL!
SHOVE
FOR ALL THE MONEY YOU MAKE, YOU CAN BE PRETTY CHEAP. HEH... JUST OBSERVE.
BWAH BWAH
TA-DAAAA
WHA...!? YOUR SCHOOL UNIFORM?
HEH... NOW IT'S OBVIOUS THAT I'M IN JUNIOR HIGH.
ONE JUNIOR HIGH TICKET.
THAT'LL BE ¥1800.
WHAT IS THAT, COSPLAY?
WHA...
TWO ELEMENTARY SCHOOL TICKETS!
OKAY, THAT'S ¥700 EACH.
NO!
SHE'S OUR GUARDIAN!
YAAAY

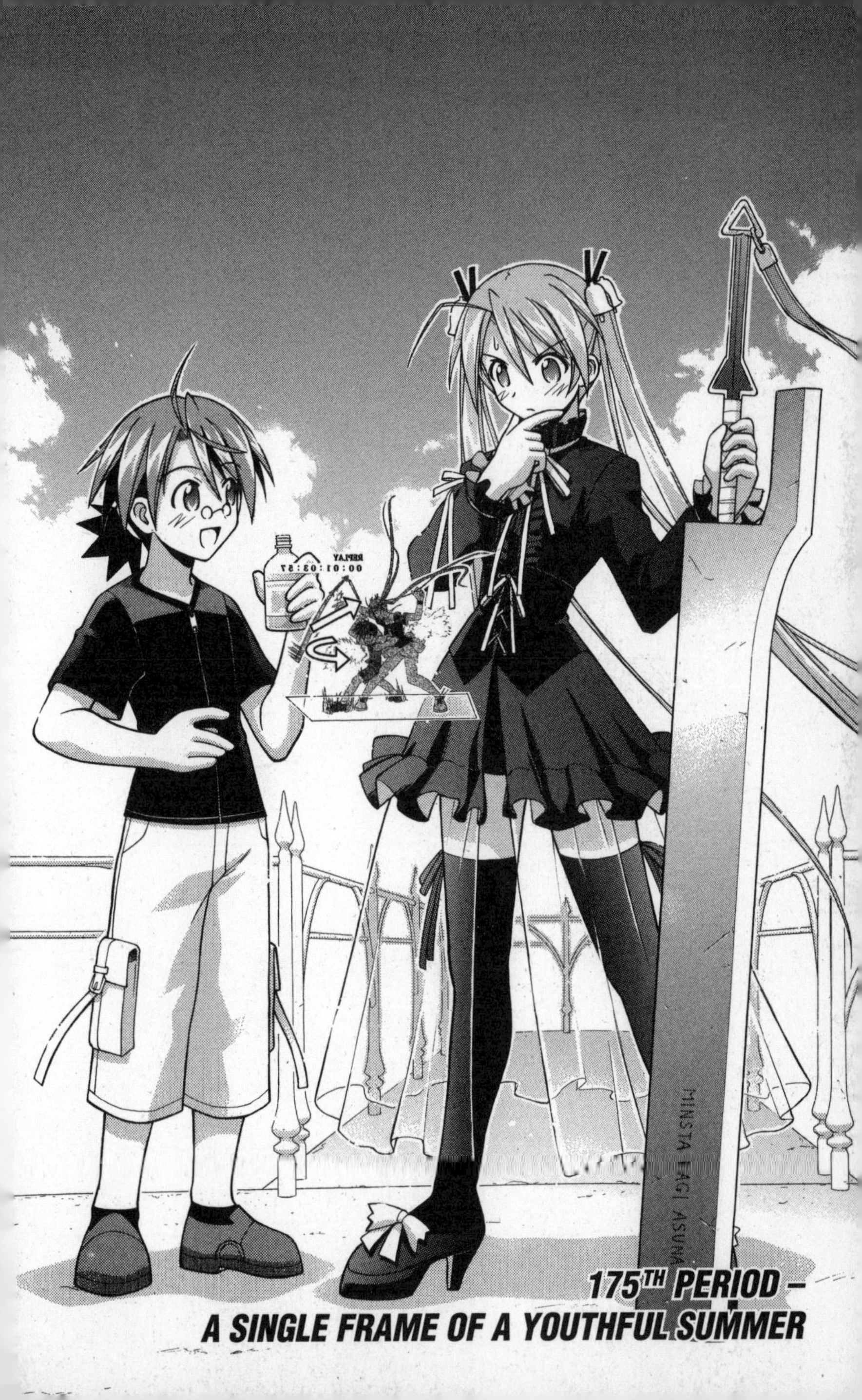

175TH PERIOD – A SINGLE FRAME OF A YOUTHFUL SUMMER

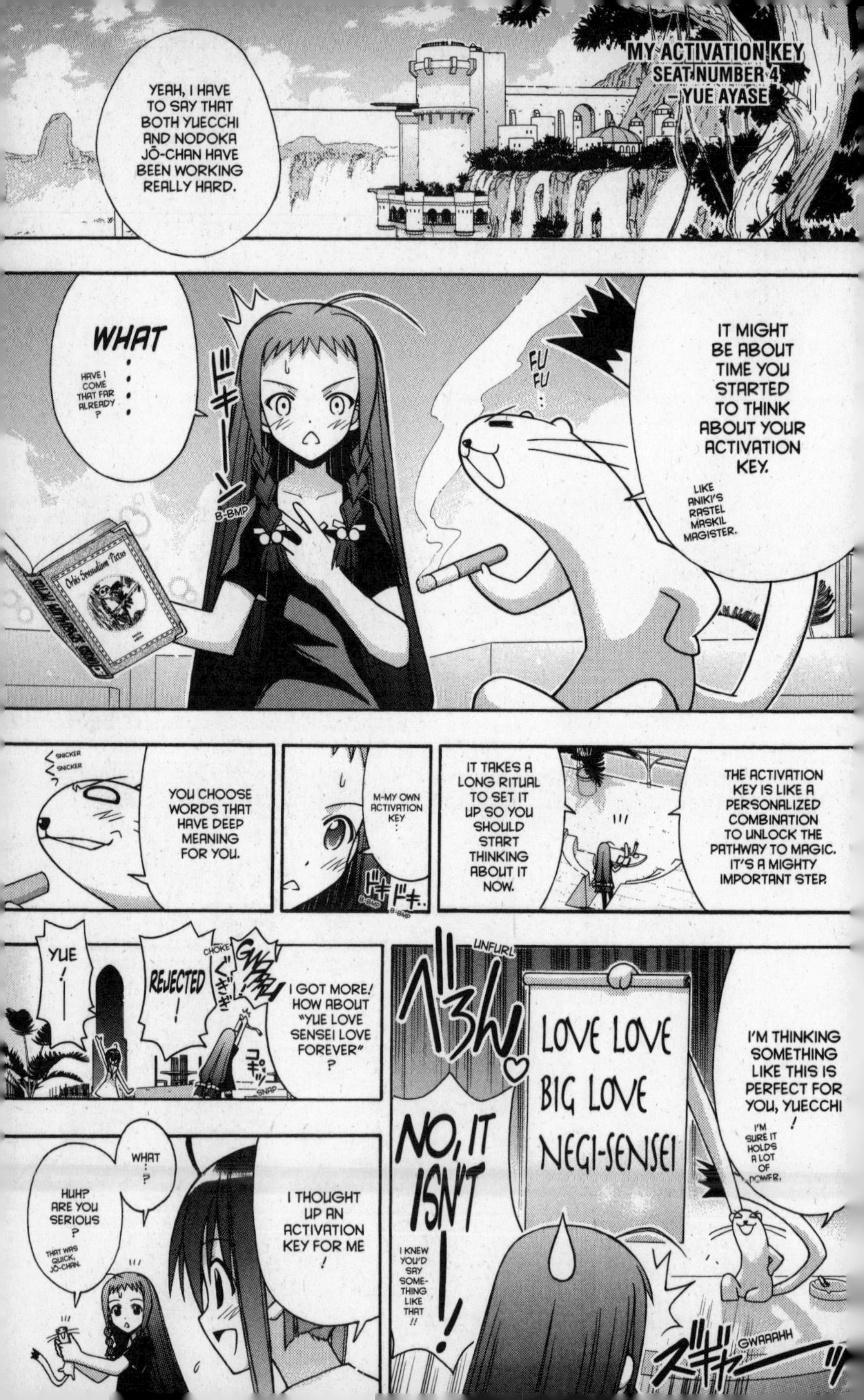

MY ACTIVATION KEY
SEAT NUMBER 4
– YUE AYASE
YEAH, I HAVE TO SAY THAT BOTH YUECCHI AND NODOKA JŌ-CHAN HAVE BEEN WORKING REALLY HARD.
IT MIGHT BE ABOUT TIME YOU STARTED TO THINK ABOUT YOUR ACTIVATION KEY.
LIKE ANIKI'S RASTEL MASKIL MAGISTER.
FU FU...
B-BMP
WHAT....
HAVE I COME THAT FAR ALREADY?
THE ACTIVATION KEY IS LIKE A PERSONALIZED COMBINATION TO UNLOCK THE PATHWAY TO MAGIC. IT'S A MIGHTY IMPORTANT STEP.
IT TAKES A LONG RITUAL TO SET IT UP SO YOU SHOULD START THINKING ABOUT IT NOW.
M-MY OWN ACTIVATION KEY...
B-BMP B-BMP
YOU CHOOSE WORDS THAT HAVE DEEP MEANING FOR YOU.
SNICKER SNICKER
I'M THINKING SOMETHING LIKE THIS IS PERFECT FOR YOU, YUECCHI!
I'M SURE IT HOLDS A LOT OF POWER.
UNFURL
LOVE LOVE BIG LOVE NEGI-SENSEI
NO, IT ISN'T!
I KNEW YOU'D SAY SOMETHING LIKE THAT!!
GWAAAHH
I GOT MORE! HOW ABOUT "YUE LOVE SENSEI LOVE FOREVER"?
CHOKE
SNAP
REJECTED!
YUE!
I THOUGHT UP AN ACTIVATION KEY FOR ME!
WHAT...?
HUH? ARE YOU SERIOUS?
THAT WAS QUICK, JŌ-CHAN.

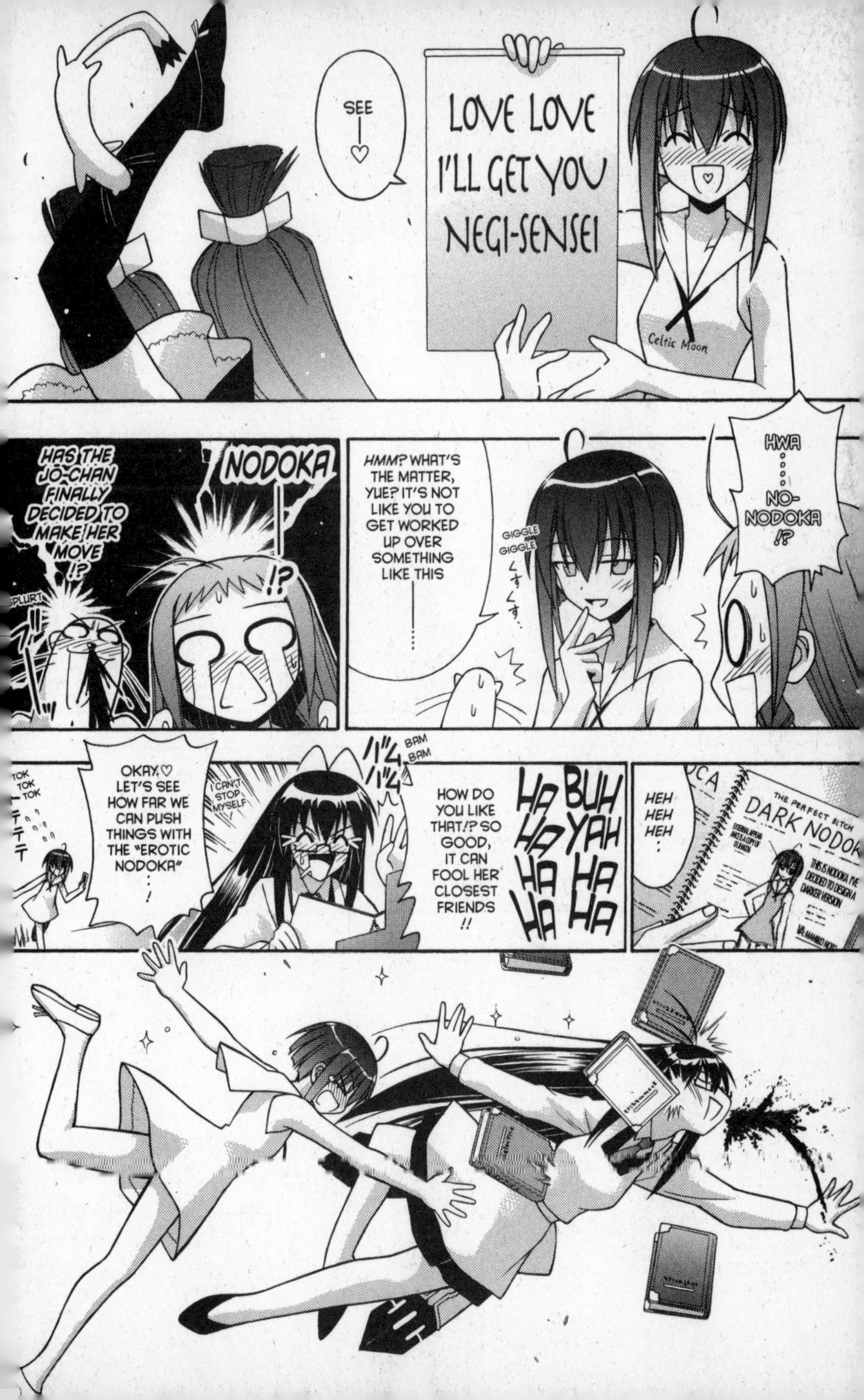

LOVE LOVE I'LL GET YOU NEGI-SENSEI
Celtic Moon
SEE —♡
HWA... NO-NODOKA !?
HMM? WHAT'S THE MATTER, YUE? IT'S NOT LIKE YOU TO GET WORKED UP OVER SOMETHING LIKE THIS —......
GIGGLE GIGGLE
くすくす...
NODOKA —!?
HAS THE JO-CHAN FINALLY DECIDED TO MAKE HER MOVE !?
SPLURT
THE PERFECT BITCH
DARK NODOKA
THIS IS NODOKA. I'VE DECIDED TO DESIGN A DARKER VERSION
HEH HEH HEH...
BUH YAH HA HA HA
HA HA HA HA
HOW DO YOU LIKE THAT!? SO GOOD, IT CAN FOOL HER CLOSEST FRIENDS !!
BAM BAM
I CAN'T STOP MYSELF
OKAY,♡ LET'S SEE HOW FAR WE CAN PUSH THINGS WITH THE "EROTIC NODOKA"...!
TOK TOK TOK

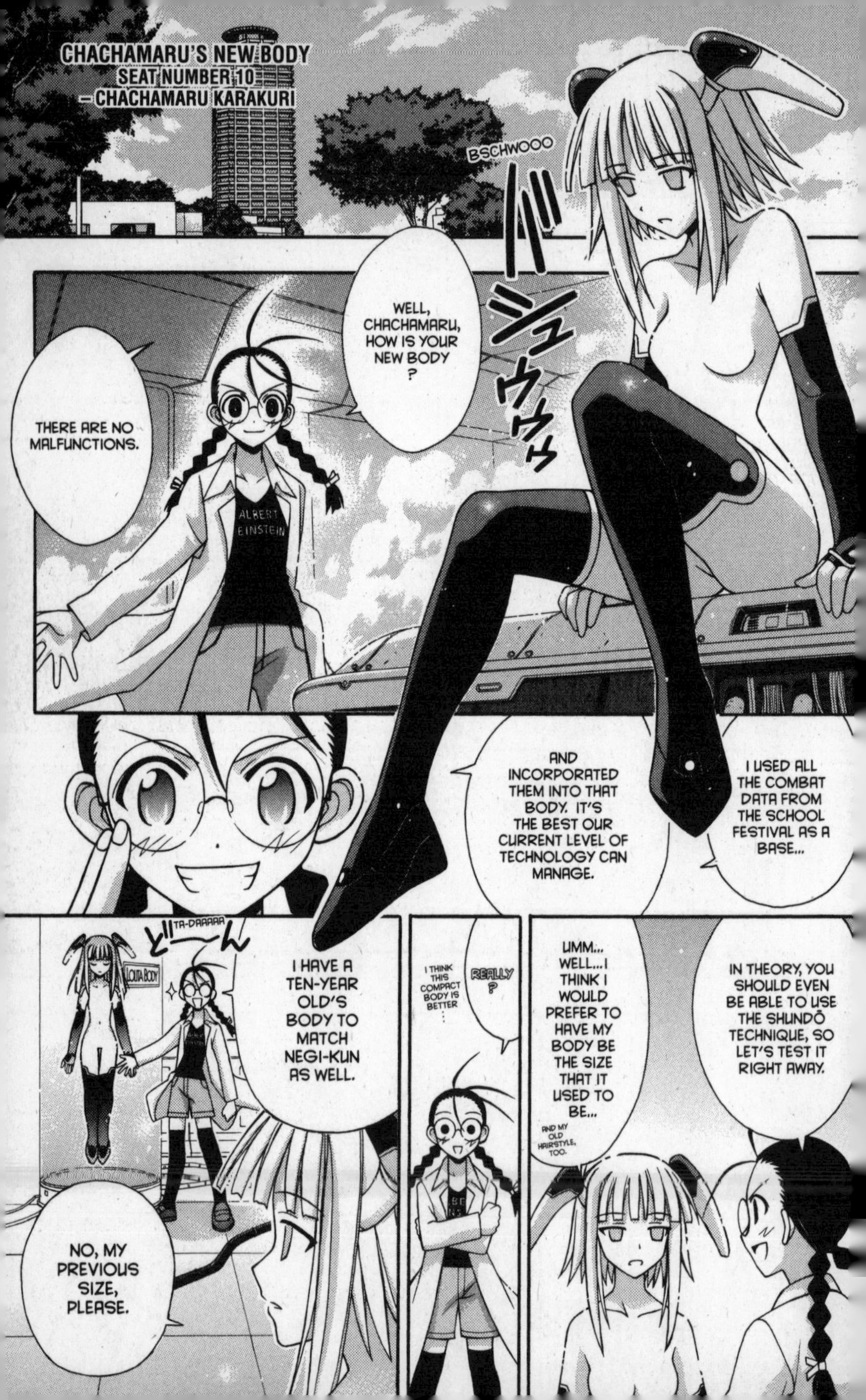
CHACHAMARU'S NEW BODY
SEAT NUMBER 10
– CHACHAMARU KARAKURI
BSCHWOOO
WELL, CHACHAMARU, HOW IS YOUR NEW BODY?
ALBERT EINSTEIN
THERE ARE NO MALFUNCTIONS.
I USED ALL THE COMBAT DATA FROM THE SCHOOL FESTIVAL AS A BASE...
AND INCORPORATED THEM INTO THAT BODY. IT'S THE BEST OUR CURRENT LEVEL OF TECHNOLOGY CAN MANAGE.
IN THEORY, YOU SHOULD EVEN BE ABLE TO USE THE SHUNDŌ TECHNIQUE, SO LET'S TEST IT RIGHT AWAY.
UMM... WELL... I THINK I WOULD PREFER TO HAVE MY BODY BE THE SIZE THAT IT USED TO BE...
AND MY OLD HAIRSTYLE, TOO.
REALLY?
I THINK THIS COMPACT BODY IS BETTER...
TA-DAAAAA
LOLITA BODY
I HAVE A TEN-YEAR OLD'S BODY TO MATCH NEGI-KUN AS WELL.
NO, MY PREVIOUS SIZE, PLEASE.

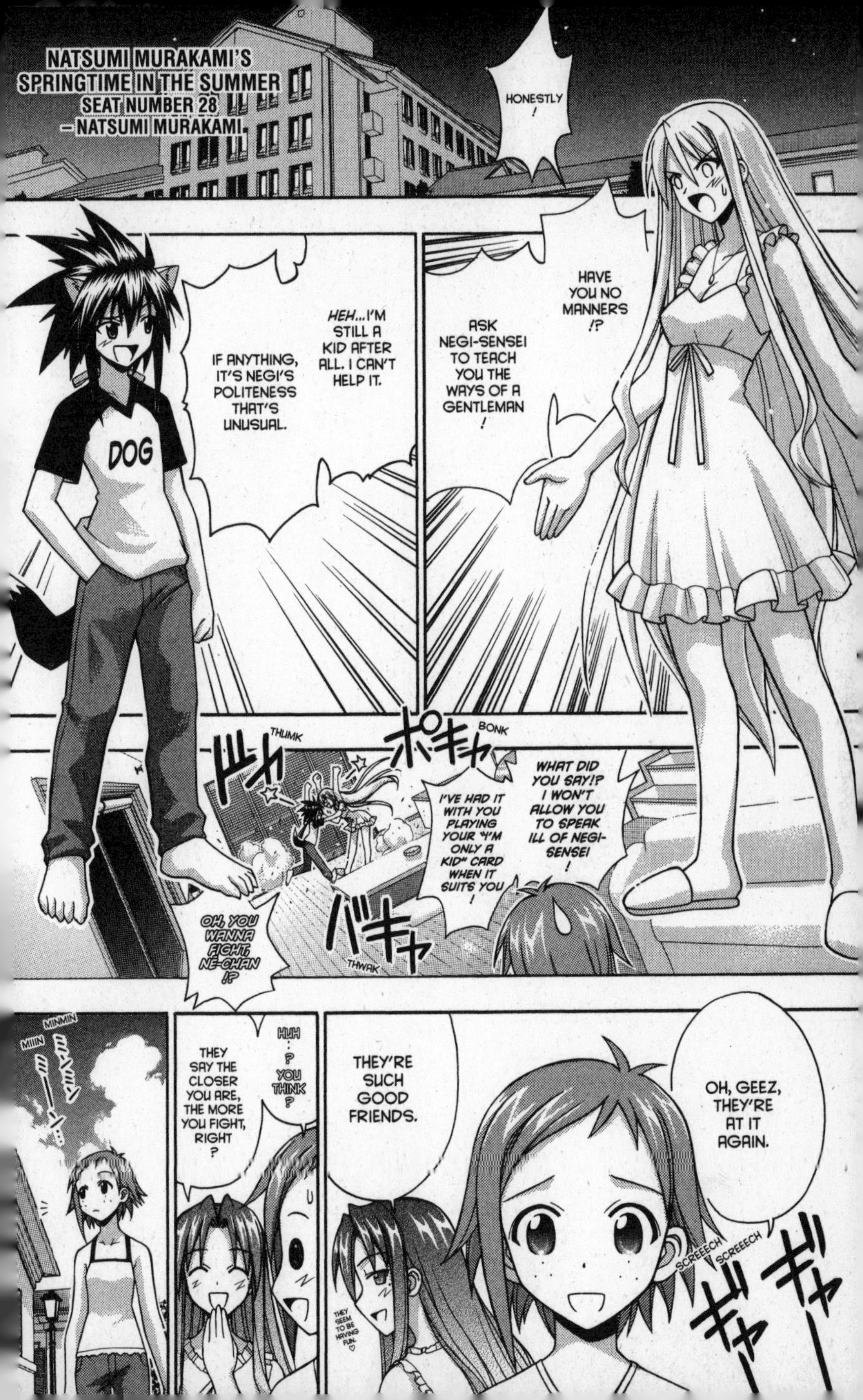
NATSUMI MURAKAMI'S SPRINGTIME IN THE SUMMER
SEAT NUMBER 28 – NATSUMI MURAKAMI
HONESTLY!
HAVE YOU NO MANNERS!?
ASK NEGI-SENSEI TO TEACH YOU THE WAYS OF A GENTLEMAN!
HEH...I'M STILL A KID AFTER ALL. I CAN'T HELP IT.
IF ANYTHING, IT'S NEGI'S POLITENESS THAT'S UNUSUAL.
BONK
WHAT DID YOU SAY!? I WON'T ALLOW YOU TO SPEAK ILL OF NEGI-SENSEI!
I'VE HAD IT WITH YOU PLAYING YOUR "I'M ONLY A KID" CARD WHEN IT SUITS YOU!
THUMK
OH, YOU WANNA FIGHT, NE-CHAN!?
THWAK
OH, GEEZ, THEY'RE AT IT AGAIN.
SCREEECH
SCREEECH
THEY'RE SUCH GOOD FRIENDS.
THEY SEEM TO BE HAVING FUN. ♡
HUH..? YOU THINK?
THEY SAY THE CLOSER YOU ARE, THE MORE YOU FIGHT, RIGHT?
MINMIN
MIIN

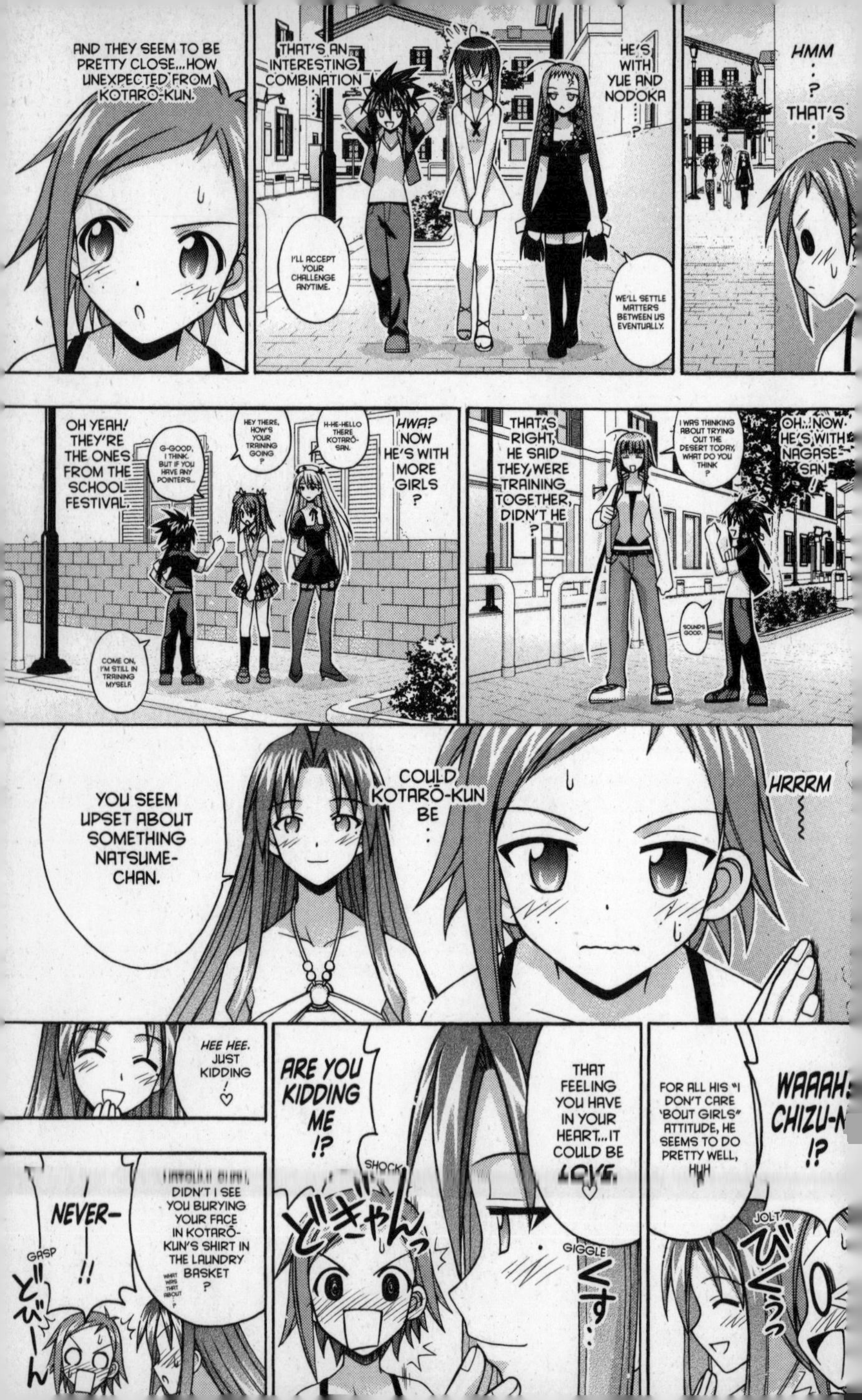
HMM...? THAT'S...
HE'S WITH YUE AND NODOKA...?
THAT'S AN INTERESTING COMBINATION
I'LL ACCEPT YOUR CHALLENGE ANYTIME.
WE'LL SETTLE MATTERS BETWEEN US EVENTUALLY.
AND THEY SEEM TO BE PRETTY CLOSE...HOW UNEXPECTED FROM KOTARO-KUN.
OH... NOW HE'S WITH NAGASE-SAN!
I WAS THINKING ABOUT TRYING OUT THE DESERT TODAY, WHAT DO YOU THINK?
SOUNDS GOOD.
THAT'S RIGHT, HE SAID THEY WERE TRAINING TOGETHER, DIDN'T HE?
HWA? NOW HE'S WITH MORE GIRLS?
H-HE-HELLO THERE KOTARŌ-SAN.
HEY THERE, HOW'S YOUR TRAINING GOING?
G-GOOD, I THINK. BUT IF YOU HAVE ANY POINTERS...
COME ON, I'M STILL IN TRAINING MYSELF.
OH YEAH! THEY'RE THE ONES FROM THE SCHOOL FESTIVAL.
HRRRM
COULD KOTARŌ-KUN BE...
YOU SEEM UPSET ABOUT SOMETHING NATSUME-CHAN.
WAAAH! CHIZU-N !?
JOLT
FOR ALL HIS "I DON'T CARE 'BOUT GIRLS" ATTITUDE, HE SEEMS TO DO PRETTY WELL, HUH
THAT FEELING YOU HAVE IN YOUR HEART...IT COULD BE LOVE. ♡
GIGGLE
ARE YOU KIDDING ME!?
SHOCK
HEE HEE. JUST KIDDING! ♡
DIDN'T I SEE YOU BURYING YOUR FACE IN KOTARŌ-KUN'S SHIRT IN THE LAUNDRY BASKET?
WHAT WAS THAT ABOUT?
NEVER—!!
GASP

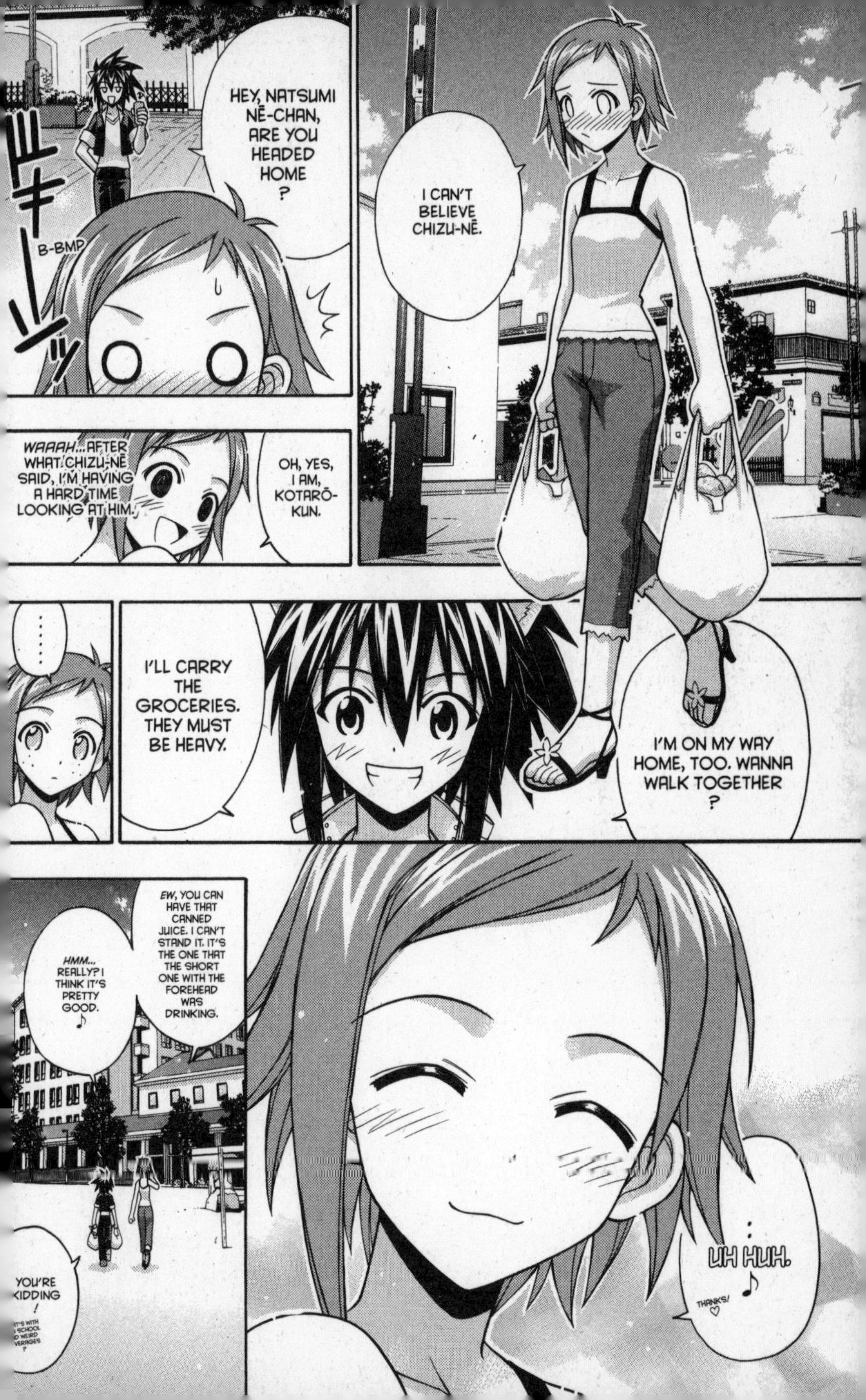
I CAN'T BELIEVE CHIZU-NĒ.
HEY, NATSUMI NĒ-CHAN, ARE YOU HEADED HOME?
B-BMP
OH, YES, I AM, KOTARŌ-KUN.
WAAAH... AFTER WHAT CHIZU-NĒ SAID, I'M HAVING A HARD TIME LOOKING AT HIM.
I'M ON MY WAY HOME, TOO. WANNA WALK TOGETHER?
I'LL CARRY THE GROCERIES. THEY MUST BE HEAVY.
......
UH HUH. ♪
THANKS! ♡
EW, YOU CAN HAVE THAT CANNED JUICE. I CAN'T STAND IT. IT'S THE ONE THAT THE SHORT ONE WITH THE FOREHEAD WAS DRINKING.
HMM... REALLY? I THINK IT'S PRETTY GOOD. ♪
YOU'RE KIDDING!

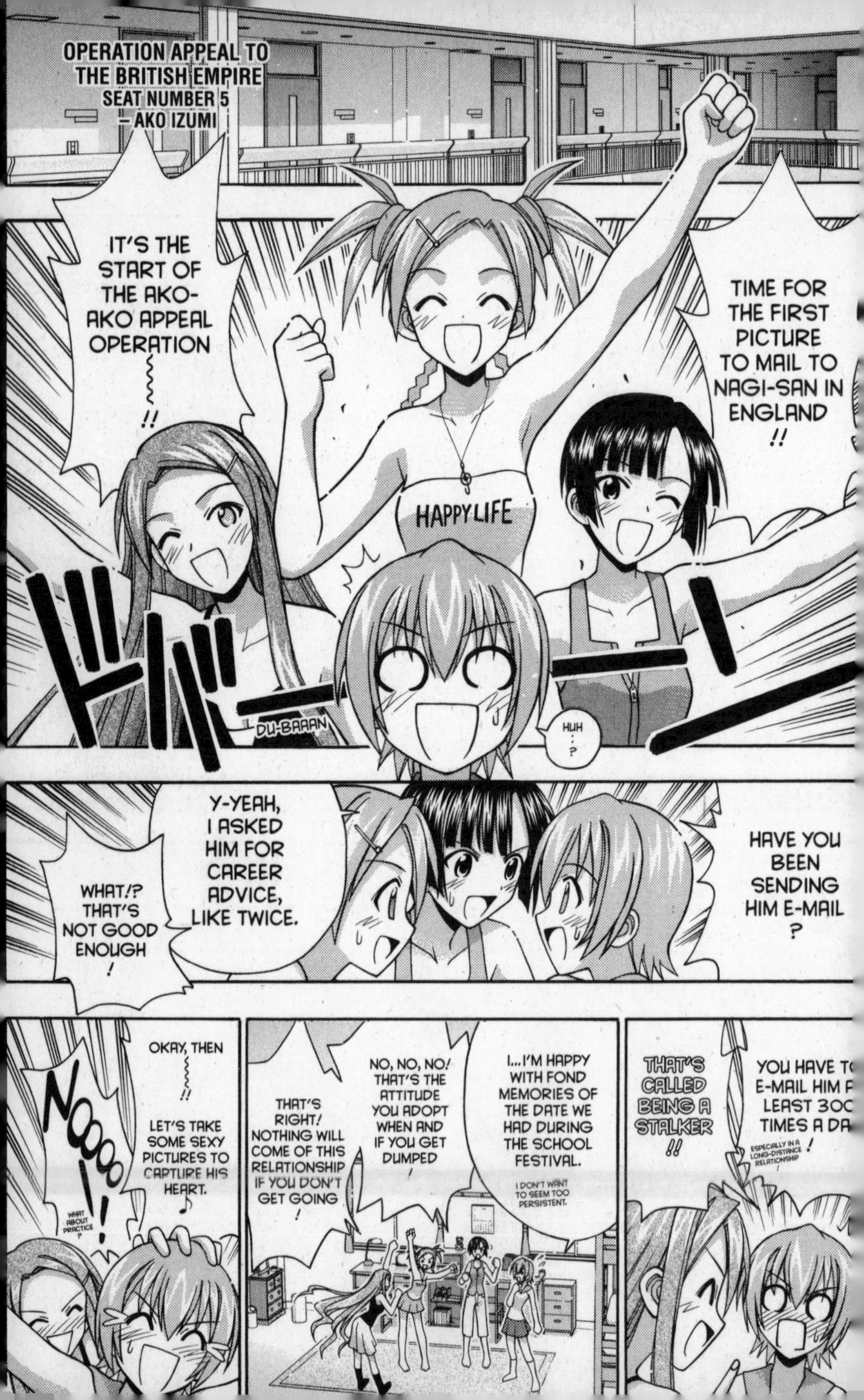
OPERATION APPEAL TO THE BRITISH EMPIRE SEAT NUMBER 5 – AKO IZUMI
IT'S THE START OF THE AKO-AKO APPEAL OPERATION ~!!
TIME FOR THE FIRST PICTURE TO MAIL TO NAGI-SAN IN ENGLAND!!
HAPPY LIFE
DU-BAAAN
HUH...?
HAVE YOU BEEN SENDING HIM E-MAIL?
Y-YEAH, I ASKED HIM FOR CAREER ADVICE, LIKE TWICE.
WHAT!? THAT'S NOT GOOD ENOUGH!
YOU HAVE TO E-MAIL HIM A LEAST 300 TIMES A DA!
ESPECIALLY IN A LONG-DISTANCE RELATIONSHIP!
THAT'S CALLED BEING A STALKER!!
I...I'M HAPPY WITH FOND MEMORIES OF THE DATE WE HAD DURING THE SCHOOL FESTIVAL.
I DON'T WANT TO SEEM TOO PERSISTENT.
NO, NO, NO! THAT'S THE ATTITUDE YOU ADOPT WHEN AND IF YOU GET DUMPED!
THAT'S RIGHT! NOTHING WILL COME OF THIS RELATIONSHIP IF YOU DON'T GET GOING!
OKAY, THEN ~!!
LET'S TAKE SOME SEXY PICTURES TO CAPTURE HIS HEART. ♪
NOOOO!!
WHAT ABOUT PRACTICE?

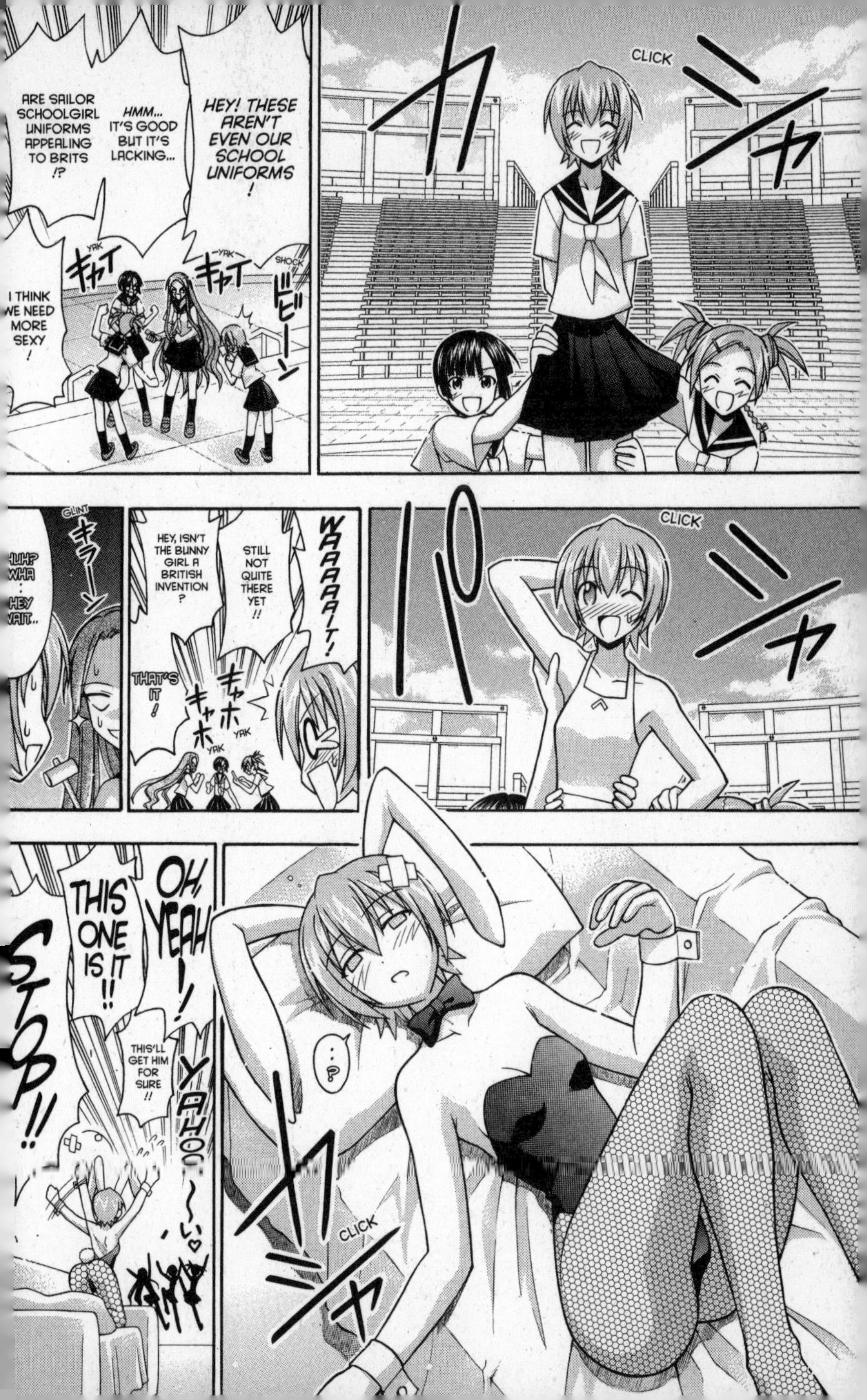

CLICK
カシャ
HEY! THESE AREN'T EVEN OUR SCHOOL UNIFORMS!
HMM... IT'S GOOD BUT IT'S LACKING...
ARE SAILOR SCHOOLGIRL UNIFORMS APPEALING TO BRITS!?
SHOCK
ドビーン
YAK
キャイ
YAK
キャイ
I THINK WE NEED MORE SEXY!
CLICK
パシャ
WAAAAAIT!
STILL NOT QUITE THERE YET!!
HEY, ISN'T THE BUNNY GIRL A BRITISH INVENTION?
THAT'S IT!
キャホ キャホ
YAK YAK
GLINT
キラーン
HUH? WHA : HEY WAIT..
CLICK
カシャ
..?
OH, YEAH!!
THIS ONE IS IT!!
STOP!!
THIS'LL GET HIM FOR SURE!!
YAHOO~い♡

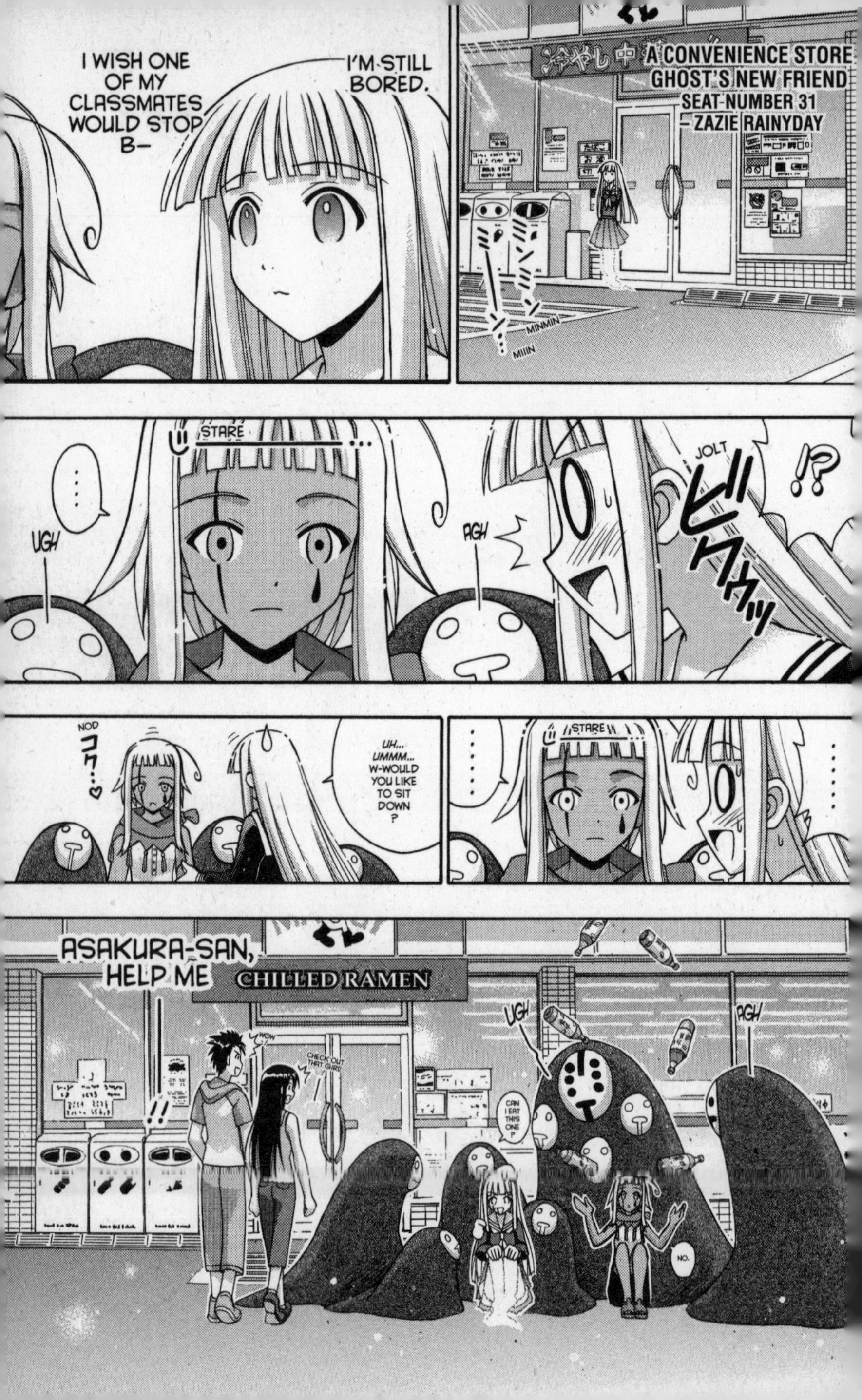
A CONVENIENCE STORE GHOST'S NEW FRIEND
SEAT NUMBER 31 – ZAZIE RAINYDAY
MINMIN
MIIN
I'M STILL BORED.
I WISH ONE OF MY CLASSMATES WOULD STOP B—
!?
JOLT
STARE
AGH
...
UGH
......
STARE
......
UH... UMMM... W-WOULD YOU LIKE TO SIT DOWN?
NOD
AGH
UGH
CAN I EAT THIS ONE?
CHECK OUT THAT GIRL!
WOW
CHILLED RAMEN
ASAKURA-SAN, HELP ME
!!
NO.

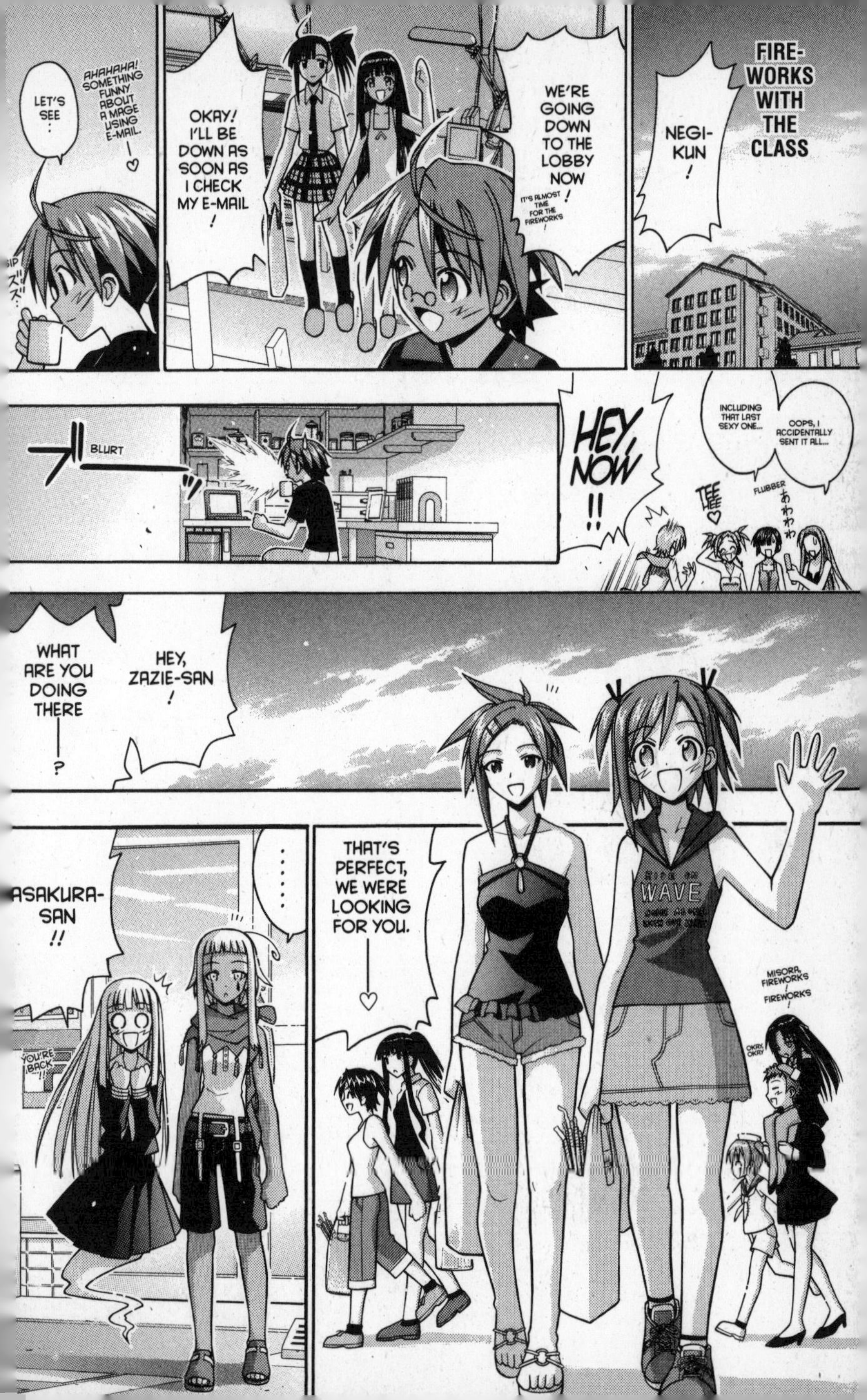

FIRE-WORKS WITH THE CLASS
NEGI-KUN!
WE'RE GOING DOWN TO THE LOBBY NOW!
IT'S ALMOST TIME FOR THE FIREWORKS!
OKAY! I'LL BE DOWN AS SOON AS I CHECK MY E-MAIL!
AHAHAHA! SOMETHING FUNNY ABOUT A MAGE USING E-MAIL. ♡
LET'S SEE...
SIP
HEY NOW!!
OOPS, I ACCIDENTALLY SENT IT ALL...
INCLUDING THAT LAST SEXY ONE...
TEE HEE ♡
FLUBBER
あわわわ
BLURT
HEY, ZAZIE-SAN!
WHAT ARE YOU DOING THERE?
THAT'S PERFECT, WE WERE LOOKING FOR YOU. ♡
MISORA, FIREWORKS! FIREWORKS!
OKAY OKAY
......
ASAKURA-SAN!!
YOU'RE BACK!!

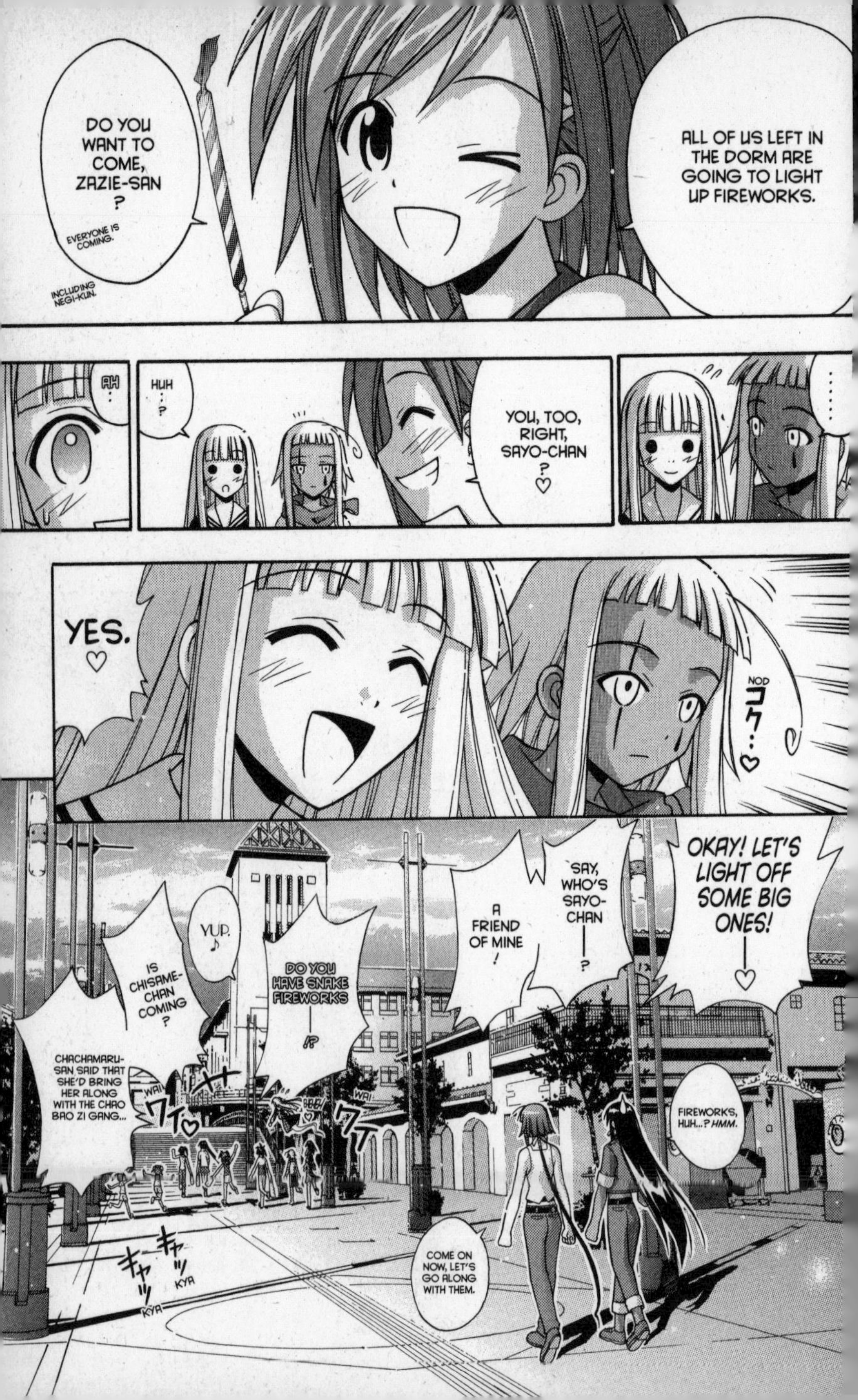
ALL OF US LEFT IN THE DORM ARE GOING TO LIGHT UP FIREWORKS.
DO YOU WANT TO COME, ZAZIE-SAN ?
EVERYONE IS COMING.
INCLUDING NEGI-KUN.
......
YOU, TOO, RIGHT, SAYO-CHAN ? ♡
HUH...?
AH...
NOD
YES. ♡
OKAY! LET'S LIGHT OFF SOME BIG ONES! ♡
SAY, WHO'S SAYO-CHAN ?
A FRIEND OF MINE!
DO YOU HAVE SNAKE FIREWORKS !?
YUP. ♪
IS CHISAME-CHAN COMING ?
CHACHAMARU-SAN SAID THAT SHE'D BRING HER ALONG WITH THE CHAO BAO ZI GANG...
WAI
WAI
FIREWORKS, HUH...? HMM.
COME ON NOW, LET'S GO ALONG WITH THEM.
KYA
KYA

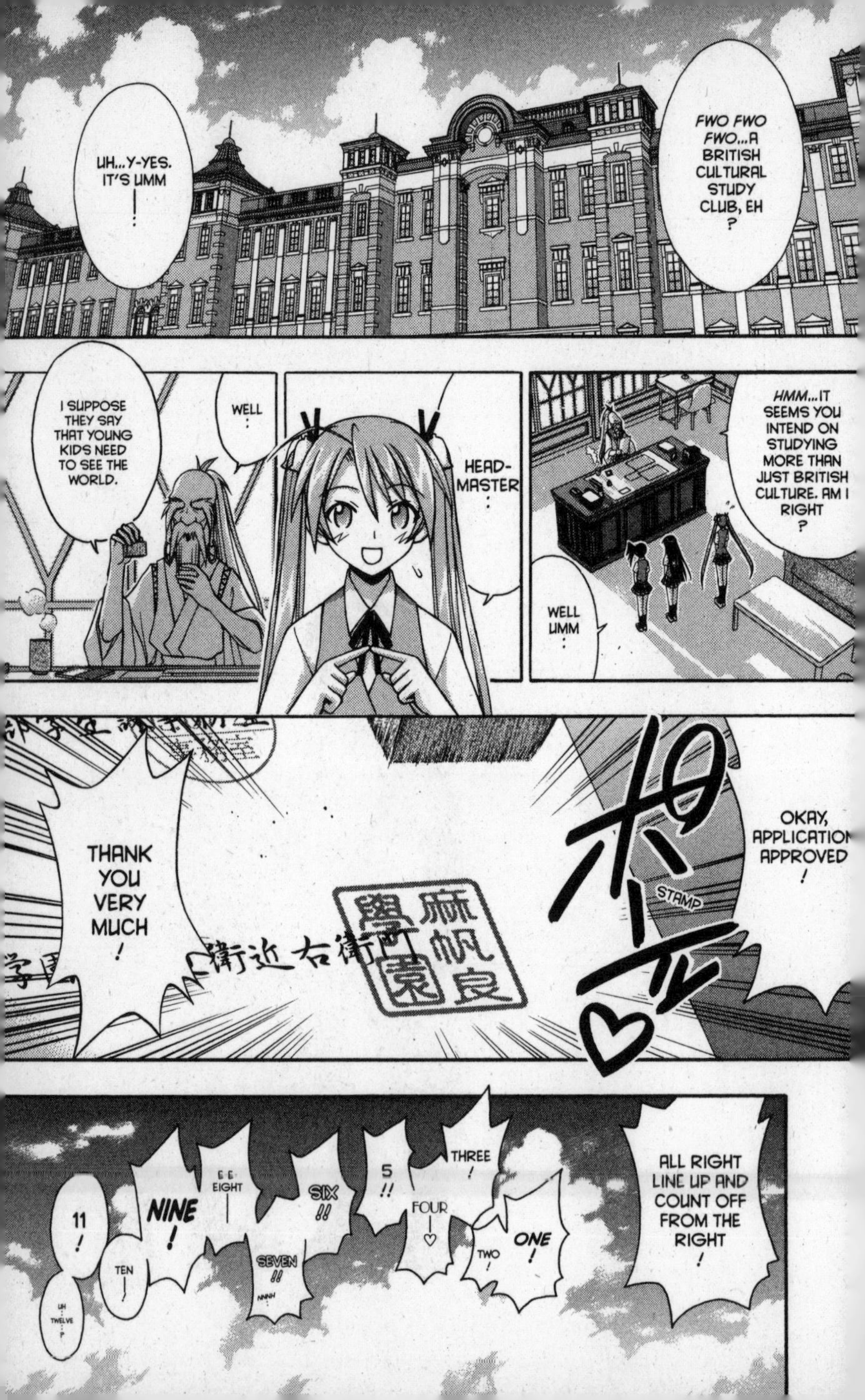

FWO FWO FWO...A BRITISH CULTURAL STUDY CLUB, EH?
UH...Y-YES. IT'S UMM—!
HMM...IT SEEMS YOU INTEND ON STUDYING MORE THAN JUST BRITISH CULTURE. AM I RIGHT?
WELL UMM...
HEAD-MASTER...
WELL...
I SUPPOSE THEY SAY THAT YOUNG KIDS NEED TO SEE THE WORLD.
OKAY, APPLICATION APPROVED!
STAMP
THANK YOU VERY MUCH!
ALL RIGHT LINE UP AND COUNT OFF FROM THE RIGHT!
ONE!
TWO!
THREE!
FOUR—♡
5!!
SIX!!
SEVEN!!
NNNH
EIGHT—
NINE!
TEN—
11!
UH... TWELVE...?

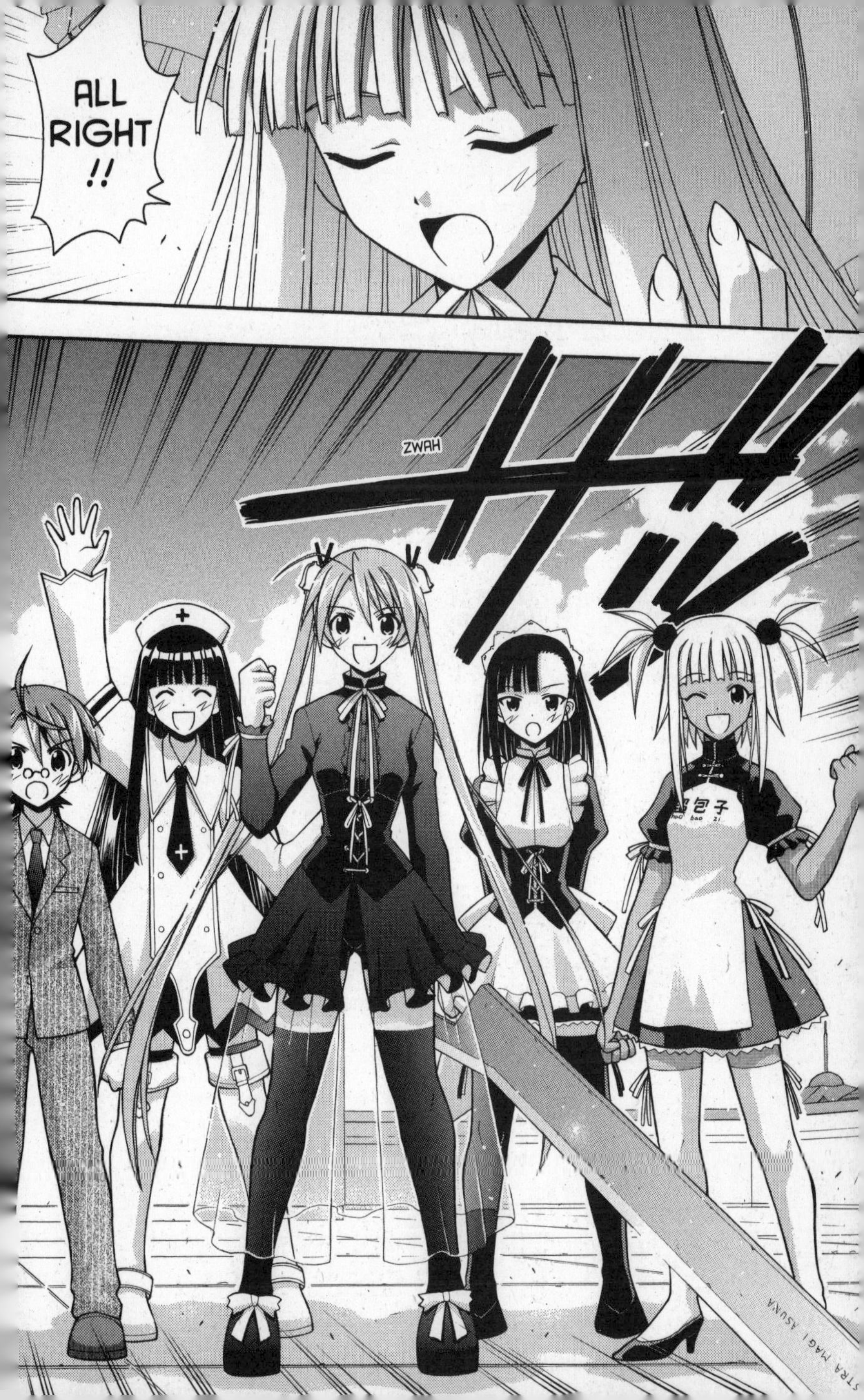
ALL RIGHT !!
ZWAH

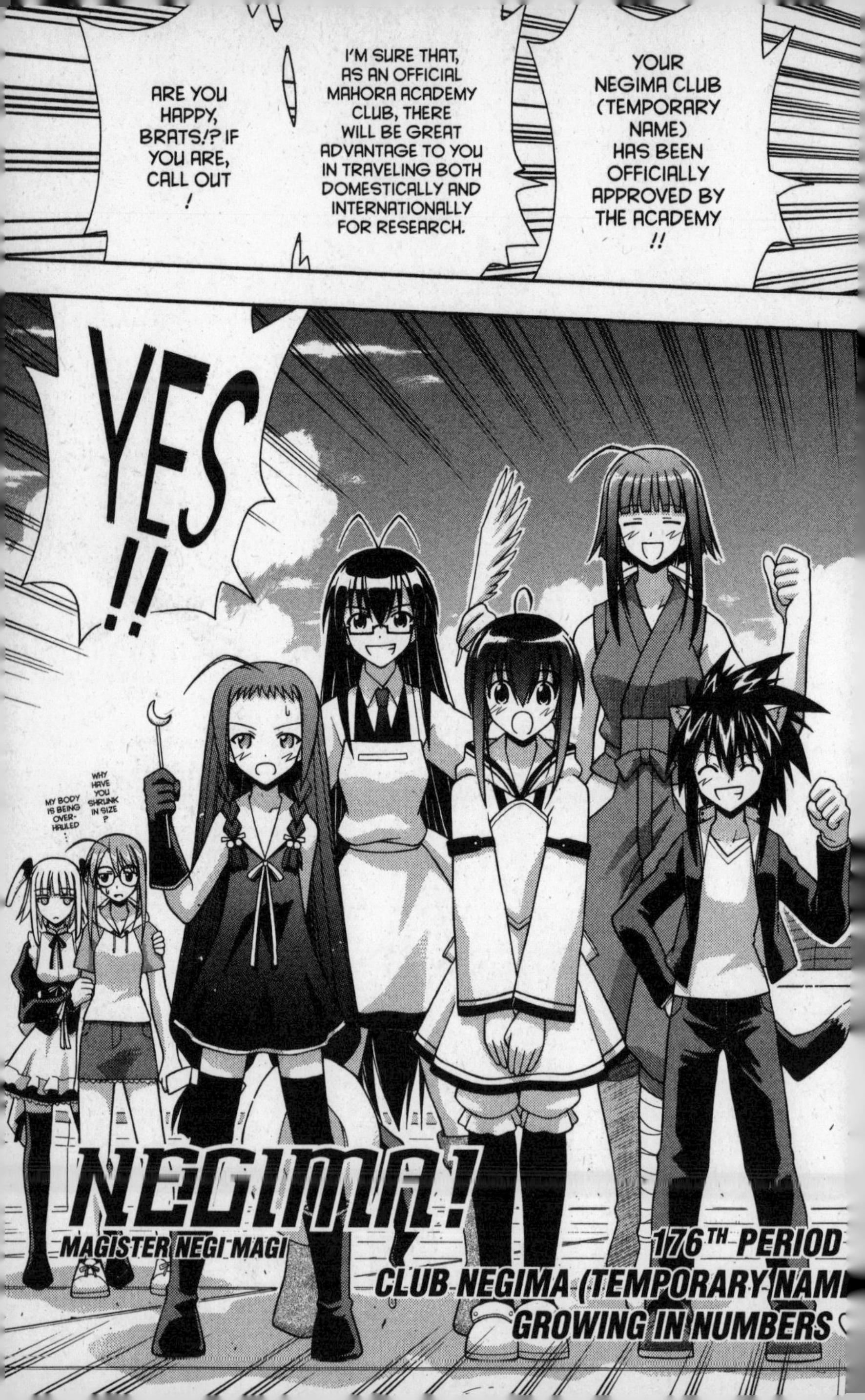
YOUR NEGIMA CLUB (TEMPORARY NAME) HAS BEEN OFFICIALLY APPROVED BY THE ACADEMY !!
I'M SURE THAT, AS AN OFFICIAL MAHORA ACADEMY CLUB, THERE WILL BE GREAT ADVANTAGE TO YOU IN TRAVELING BOTH DOMESTICALLY AND INTERNATIONALLY FOR RESEARCH.
ARE YOU HAPPY, BRATS!? IF YOU ARE, CALL OUT !
YES!!
WHY HAVE YOU SHRUNK IN SIZE ?
MY BODY IS BEING OVER-HAULED ...
NEGIMA!
MAGISTER NEGI MAGI
176TH PERIOD
CLUB NEGIMA (TEMPORARY NAM
GROWING IN NUMBERS

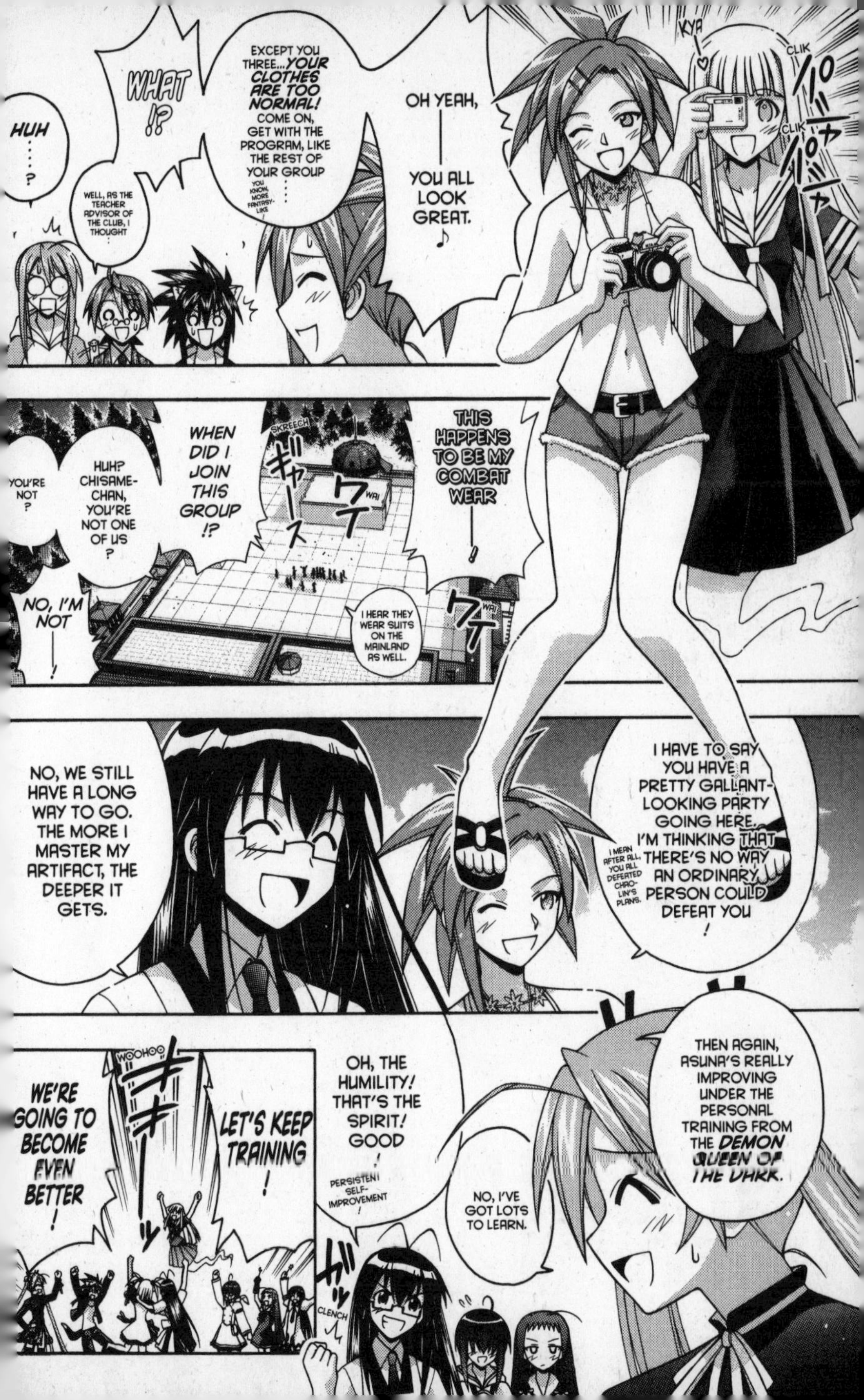
KYA ♡
CLIK
CLIK
OH YEAH, — YOU ALL LOOK GREAT. ♪
EXCEPT YOU THREE...YOUR CLOTHES ARE TOO NORMAL! COME ON, GET WITH THE PROGRAM, LIKE THE REST OF YOUR GROUP
YOU KNOW, MORE FANTASY-LIKE...
WHAT!?
HUH...?
WELL, AS THE TEACHER ADVISOR OF THE CLUB, I THOUGHT...
THIS HAPPENS TO BE MY COMBAT WEAR—!
WAI
I HEAR THEY WEAR SUITS ON THE MAINLAND AS WELL.
WAI
SKREECH
WHEN DID I JOIN THIS GROUP!?
HUH? CHISAME-CHAN, YOU'RE NOT ONE OF US?
YOU'RE NOT?
NO, I'M NOT—!
I HAVE TO SAY YOU HAVE A PRETTY GALLANT-LOOKING PARTY GOING HERE. I'M THINKING THAT THERE'S NO WAY AN ORDINARY PERSON COULD DEFEAT YOU!
I MEAN AFTER ALL, YOU ALL DEFEATED CHAO-LIN'S PLANS.
NO, WE STILL HAVE A LONG WAY TO GO. THE MORE I MASTER MY ARTIFACT, THE DEEPER IT GETS.
THEN AGAIN, ASUNA'S REALLY IMPROVING UNDER THE PERSONAL TRAINING FROM THE DEMON QUEEN OF THE DARK.
NO, I'VE GOT LOTS TO LEARN.
OH, THE HUMILITY! THAT'S THE SPIRIT! GOOD!
PERSISTENT SELF-IMPROVEMENT!
CLENCH
LET'S KEEP TRAINING!
WOOHOO
WE'RE GOING TO BECOME EVEN BETTER!

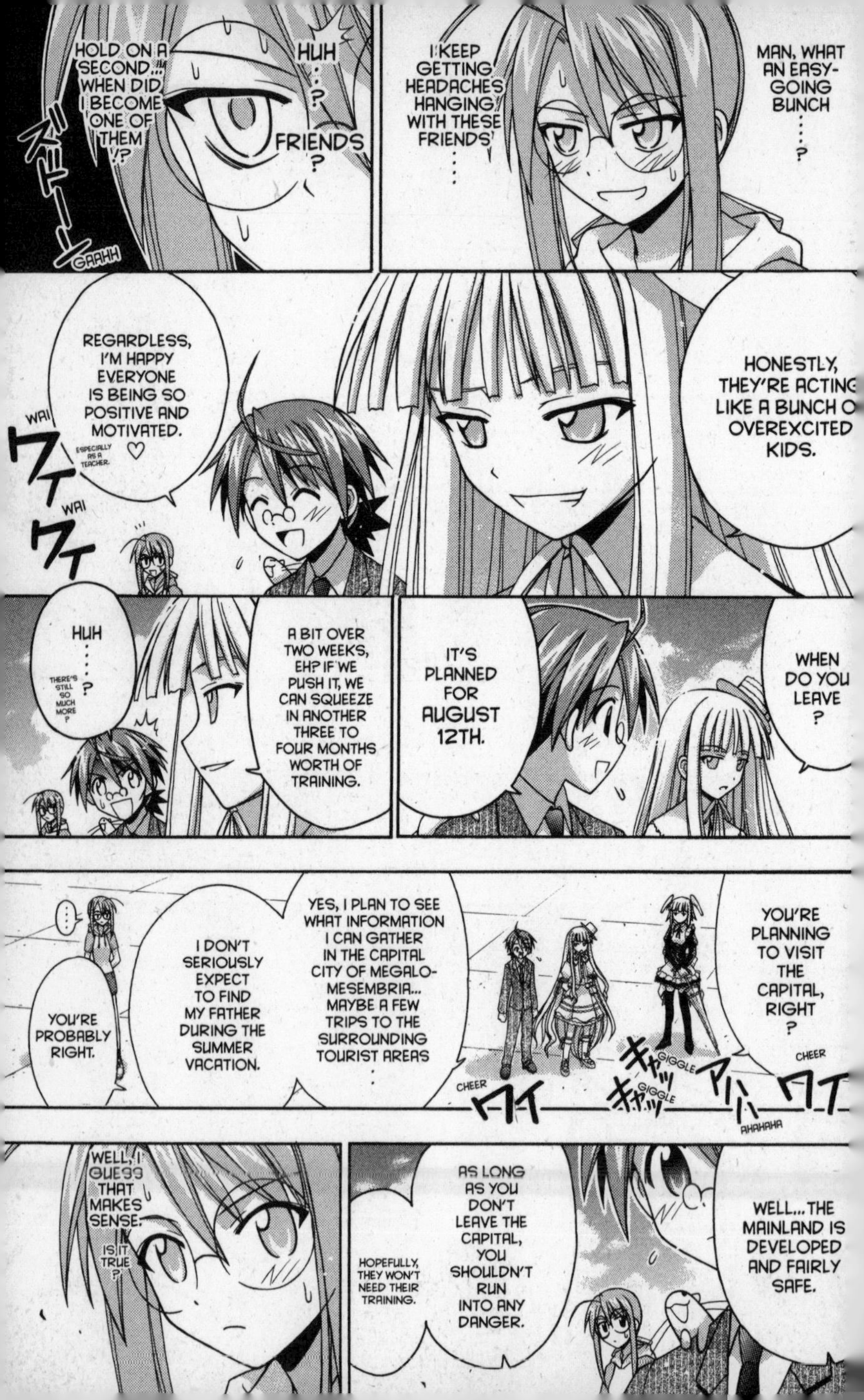
MAN, WHAT AN EASY-GOING BUNCH ...?
I KEEP GETTING HEADACHES HANGING WITH THESE FRIENDS' ...
HUH ...?
FRIENDS ?
HOLD ON A SECOND... WHEN DID I BECOME ONE OF THEM!?
GAAHH
HONESTLY, THEY'RE ACTING LIKE A BUNCH O OVEREXCITED KIDS.
REGARDLESS, I'M HAPPY EVERYONE IS BEING SO POSITIVE AND MOTIVATED. ♡
ESPECIALLY AS A TEACHER.
WAI
WAI
WHEN DO YOU LEAVE ?
IT'S PLANNED FOR AUGUST 12TH.
A BIT OVER TWO WEEKS, EH? IF WE PUSH IT, WE CAN SQUEEZE IN ANOTHER THREE TO FOUR MONTHS WORTH OF TRAINING.
HUH ...?
THERE'S STILL SO MUCH MORE ?
YOU'RE PLANNING TO VISIT THE CAPITAL, RIGHT ?
CHEER
AHAHAHA
GIGGLE
GIGGLE
CHEER
YES, I PLAN TO SEE WHAT INFORMATION I CAN GATHER IN THE CAPITAL CITY OF MEGALO-MESEMBRIA... MAYBE A FEW TRIPS TO THE SURROUNDING TOURIST AREAS ...
I DON'T SERIOUSLY EXPECT TO FIND MY FATHER DURING THE SUMMER VACATION.
...
YOU'RE PROBABLY RIGHT.
WELL... THE MAINLAND IS DEVELOPED AND FAIRLY SAFE.
AS LONG AS YOU DON'T LEAVE THE CAPITAL, YOU SHOULDN'T RUN INTO ANY DANGER.
HOPEFULLY, THEY WON'T NEED THEIR TRAINING.
WELL, I GUESS THAT MAKES SENSE.
IS IT TRUE ?

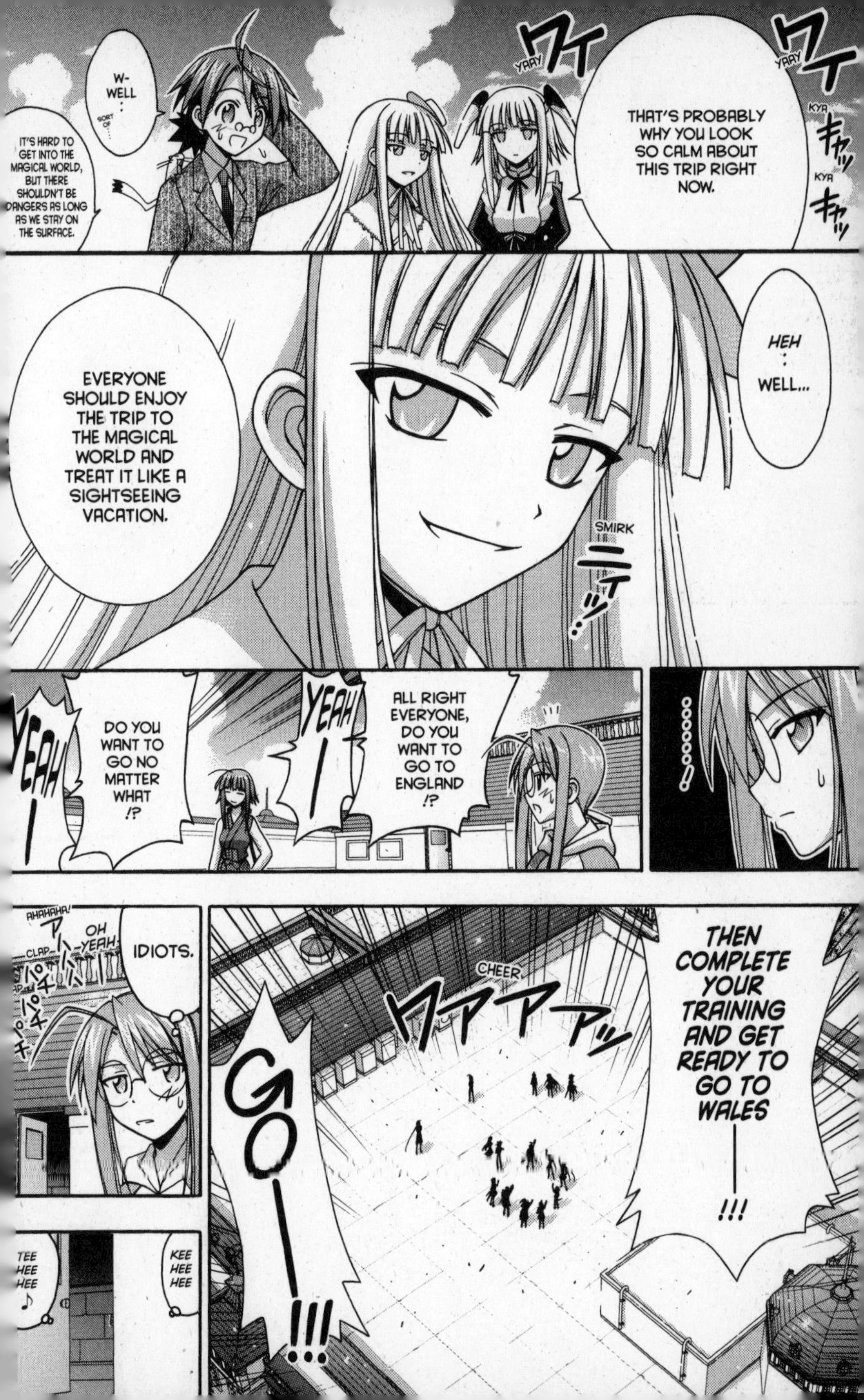
YAAY
KYA
KYA
YAAY
THAT'S PROBABLY WHY YOU LOOK SO CALM ABOUT THIS TRIP RIGHT NOW.
W-WELL: SORT OF...
IT'S HARD TO GET INTO THE MAGICAL WORLD, BUT THERE SHOULDN'T BE DANGERS AS LONG AS WE STAY ON THE SURFACE.
HEH: WELL...
SMIRK
EVERYONE SHOULD ENJOY THE TRIP TO THE MAGICAL WORLD AND TREAT IT LIKE A SIGHTSEEING VACATION.
OOOOOO!
ALL RIGHT EVERYONE, DO YOU WANT TO GO TO ENGLAND!?
YEAH!
DO YOU WANT TO GO NO MATTER WHAT!?
YEAH!
THEN COMPLETE YOUR TRAINING AND GET READY TO GO TO WALES—!!!
CHEER
GO—!!!
IDIOTS.
OH YEAH
AHAHAHA!
CLAP
KEE HEE HEE
TEE HEE HEE ♪

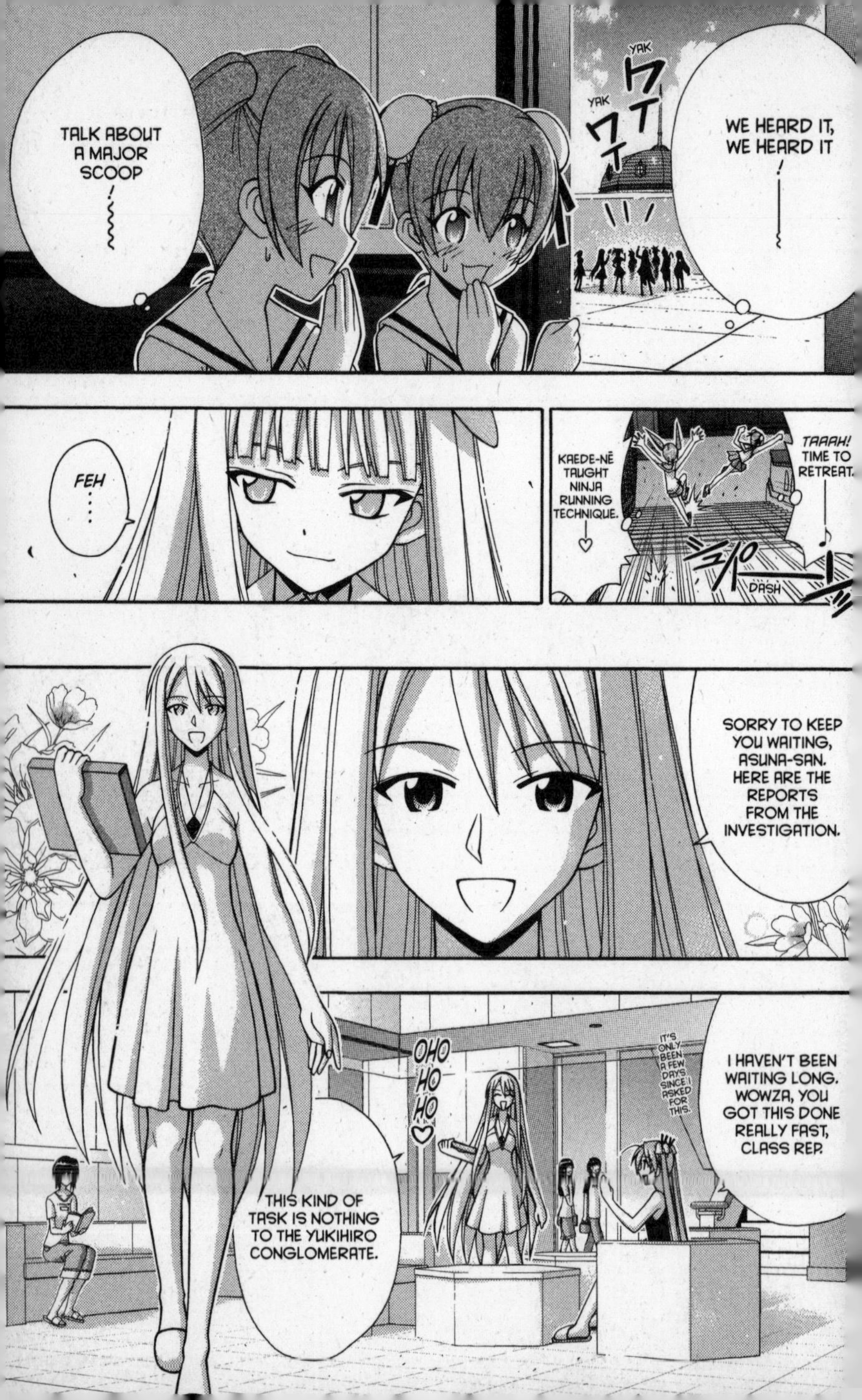
WE HEARD IT, WE HEARD IT!
YAK
YAK
TALK ABOUT A MAJOR SCOOP!
TAAAH! TIME TO RETREAT.♪
KAEDE-NĒ TAUGHT NINJA RUNNING TECHNIQUE. ♡
DASH
FEH...
SORRY TO KEEP YOU WAITING, ASUNA-SAN. HERE ARE THE REPORTS FROM THE INVESTIGATION.
I HAVEN'T BEEN WAITING LONG. WOWZA, YOU GOT THIS DONE REALLY FAST, CLASS REP.
IT'S ONLY BEEN A FEW DAYS SINCE I ASKED FOR THIS.
OHO HO HO ♡
THIS KIND OF TASK IS NOTHING TO THE YUKIHIRO CONGLOMERATE.

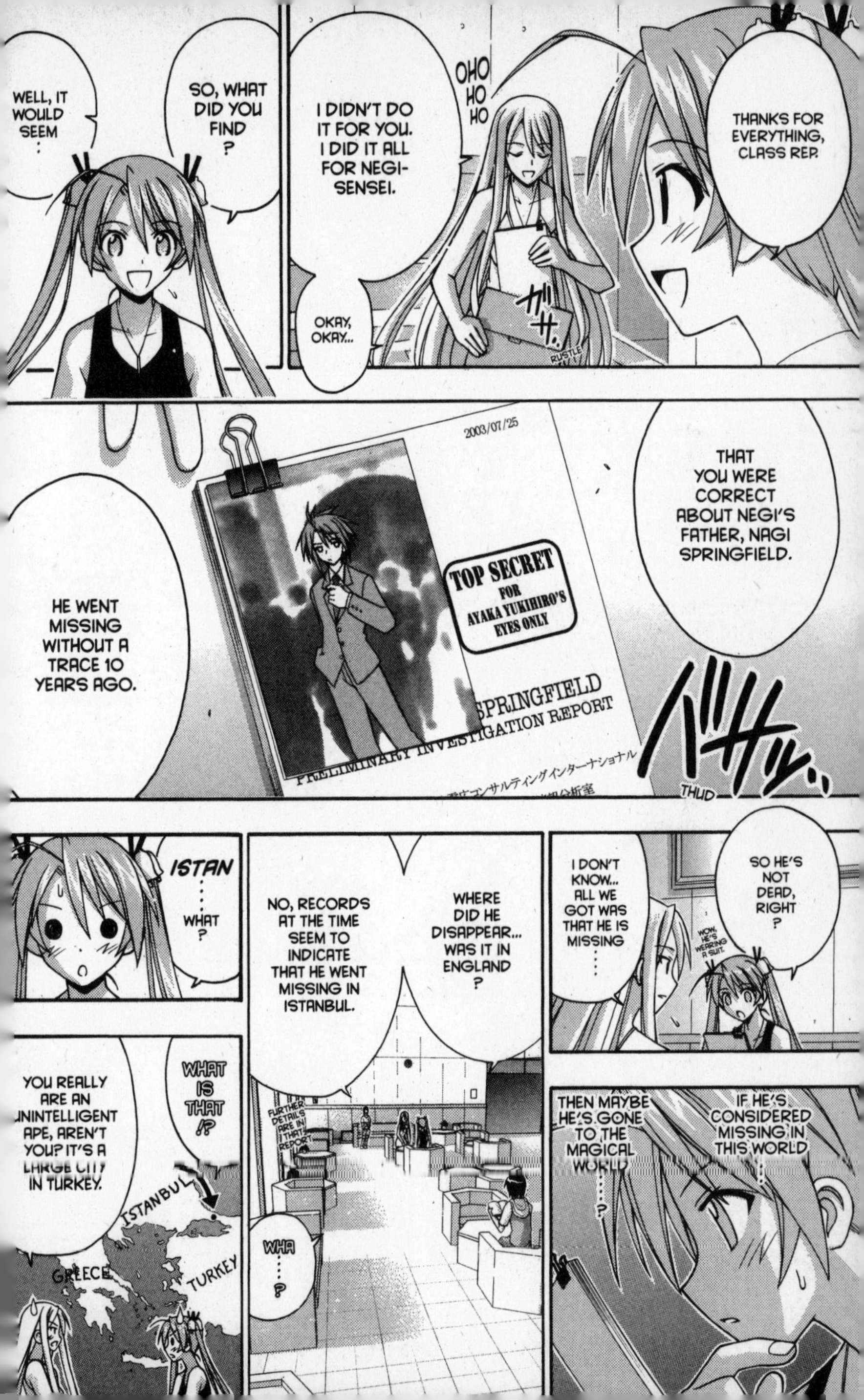
THANKS FOR EVERYTHING, CLASS REP.
OHO HO HO
I DIDN'T DO IT FOR YOU. I DID IT ALL FOR NEGI-SENSEI.
OKAY, OKAY...
RUSTLE
SO, WHAT DID YOU FIND?
WELL, IT WOULD SEEM...
THAT YOU WERE CORRECT ABOUT NEGI'S FATHER, NAGI SPRINGFIELD.
THUD
2003/07/25
TOP SECRET FOR AYAKA YUKIHIRO'S EYES ONLY
SPRINGFIELD
PRELIMINARY INVESTIGATION REPORT
コンサルティングインターナショナル
HE WENT MISSING WITHOUT A TRACE 10 YEARS AGO.
SO HE'S NOT DEAD, RIGHT?
I DON'T KNOW... ALL WE GOT WAS THAT HE IS MISSING...
WOW, HE'S WEARING A SUIT.
WHERE DID HE DISAPPEAR... WAS IT IN ENGLAND?
NO, RECORDS AT THE TIME SEEM TO INDICATE THAT HE WENT MISSING IN ISTANBUL.
ISTAN... WHAT?
IF HE'S CONSIDERED MISSING IN THIS WORLD...
THEN MAYBE HE'S GONE TO THE MAGICAL WORLD...?
FURTHER DETAILS ARE IN THAT REPORT.
WHA...?
WHAT IS THAT!?
YOU REALLY ARE AN UNINTELLIGENT APE, AREN'T YOU? IT'S A LARGE CITY IN TURKEY.
ISTANBUL
GREECE
TURKEY

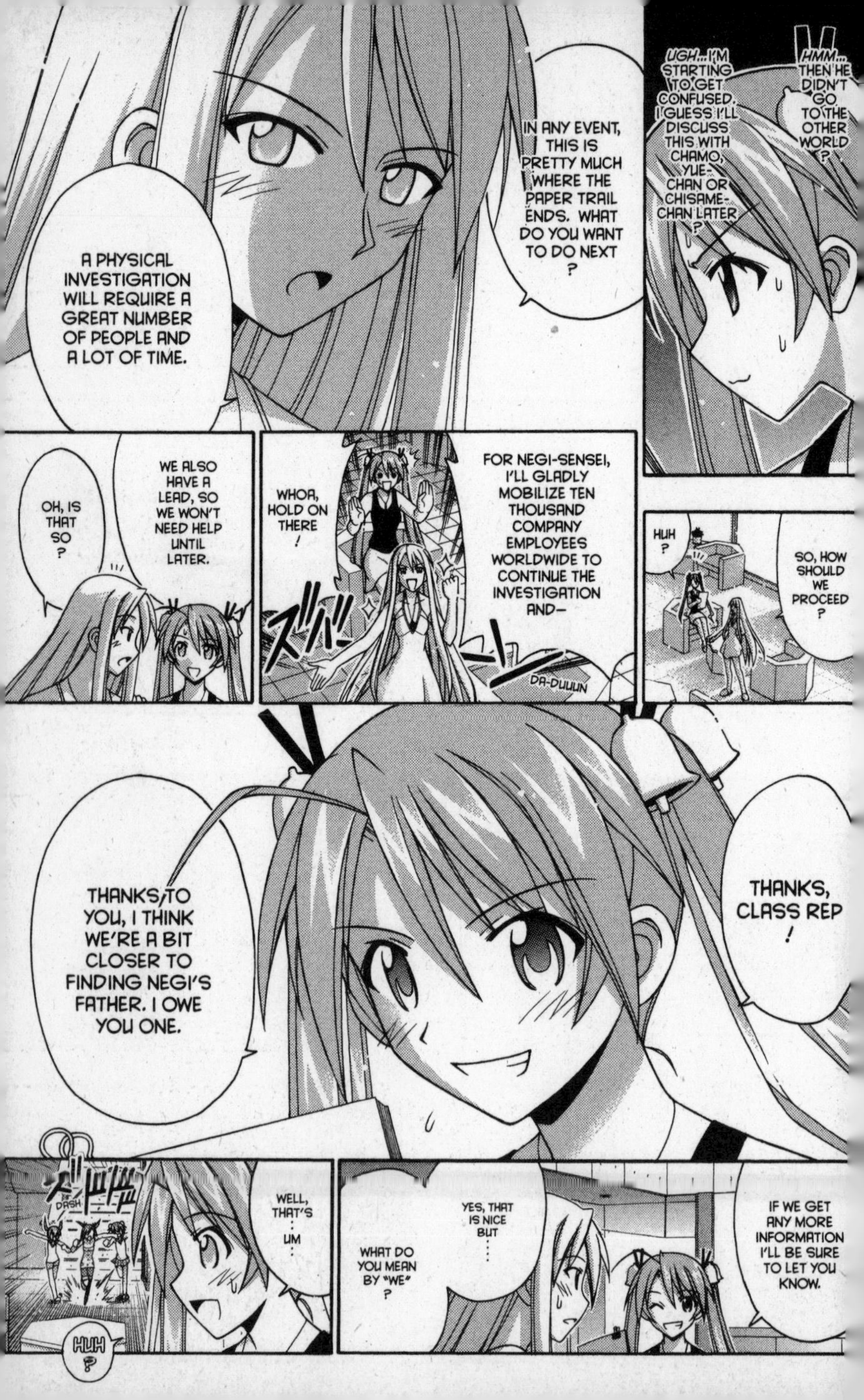
HMM... THEN HE DIDN'T GO TO THE OTHER WORLD?
UGH... I'M STARTING TO GET CONFUSED. I GUESS I'LL DISCUSS THIS WITH CHAMO, YUE-CHAN OR CHISAME-CHAN LATER?
IN ANY EVENT, THIS IS PRETTY MUCH WHERE THE PAPER TRAIL ENDS. WHAT DO YOU WANT TO DO NEXT?
A PHYSICAL INVESTIGATION WILL REQUIRE A GREAT NUMBER OF PEOPLE AND A LOT OF TIME.
SO, HOW SHOULD WE PROCEED?
HUH?
FOR NEGI-SENSEI, I'LL GLADLY MOBILIZE TEN THOUSAND COMPANY EMPLOYEES WORLDWIDE TO CONTINUE THE INVESTIGATION AND–
DA-DUUUN
WHOA, HOLD ON THERE!
WE ALSO HAVE A LEAD, SO WE WON'T NEED HELP UNTIL LATER.
OH, IS THAT SO?
THANKS, CLASS REP!
THANKS TO YOU, I THINK WE'RE A BIT CLOSER TO FINDING NEGI'S FATHER. I OWE YOU ONE.
IF WE GET ANY MORE INFORMATION I'LL BE SURE TO LET YOU KNOW.
YES, THAT IS NICE BUT.....
WHAT DO YOU MEAN BY "WE"?
WELL, THAT'S... UM...
DASH
HUH?

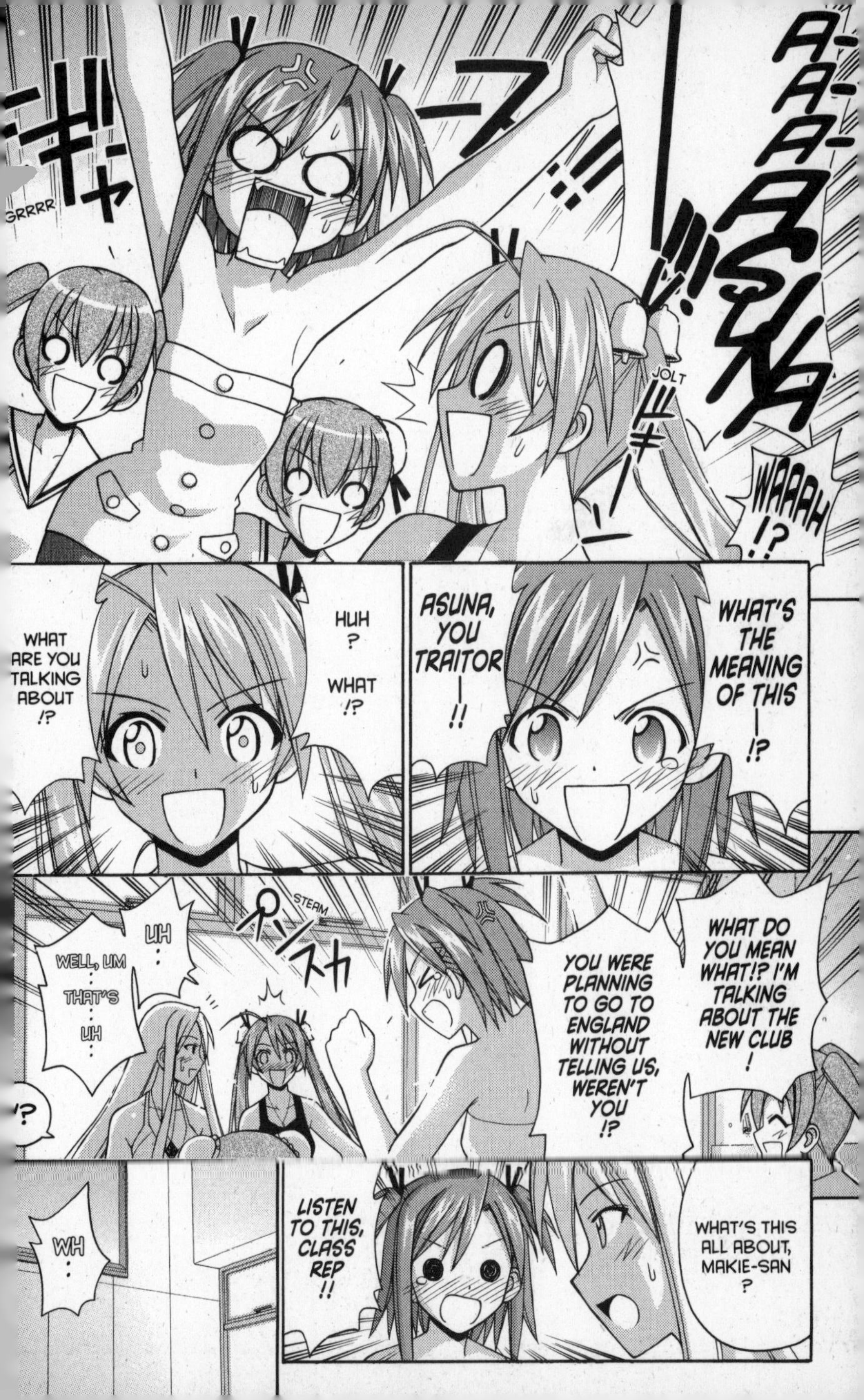
WAAAH!?
JOLT
GRRRR
WHAT'S THE MEANING OF THIS—!?
ASUNA, YOU TRAITOR—!!
HUH? WHAT!?
WHAT ARE YOU TALKING ABOUT!?
WHAT DO YOU MEAN WHAT!? I'M TALKING ABOUT THE NEW CLUB!
YOU WERE PLANNING TO GO TO ENGLAND WITHOUT TELLING US, WEREN'T YOU!?
STEAM
UH...
WELL, UM... THAT'S... UH
!?
WHAT'S THIS ALL ABOUT, MAKIE-SAN?
LISTEN TO THIS, CLASS REP!!
WH...

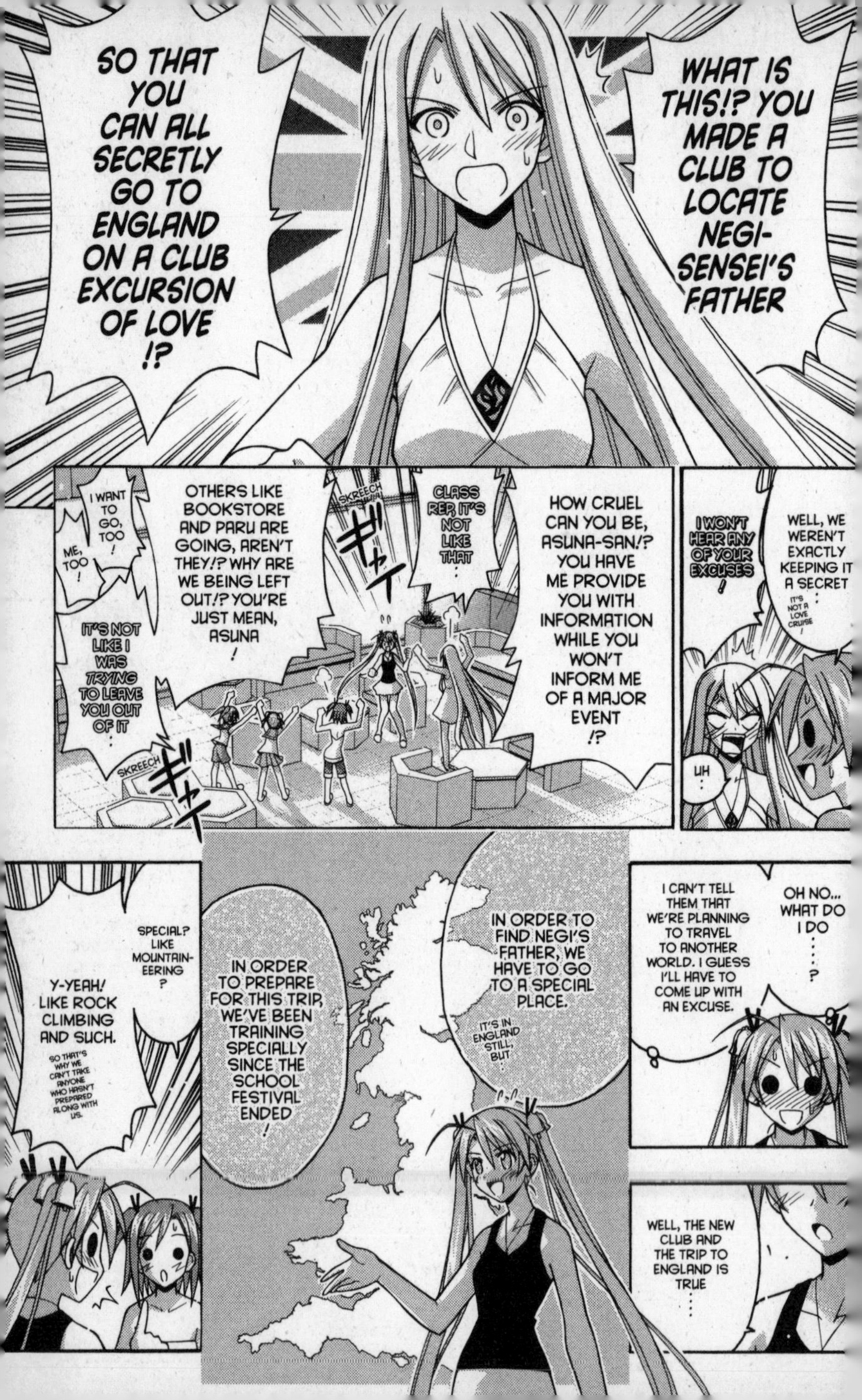
WHAT IS THIS!? YOU MADE A CLUB TO LOCATE NEGI-SENSEI'S FATHER
SO THAT YOU CAN ALL SECRETLY GO TO ENGLAND ON A CLUB EXCURSION OF LOVE !?
WELL, WE WEREN'T EXACTLY KEEPING IT A SECRET :
IT'S NOT A LOVE CRUISE !
I WON'T HEAR ANY OF YOUR EXCUSES !
UH ..
HOW CRUEL CAN YOU BE, ASUNA-SAN!? YOU HAVE ME PROVIDE YOU WITH INFORMATION WHILE YOU WON'T INFORM ME OF A MAJOR EVENT !?
CLASS REP, IT'S NOT LIKE THAT :
SKREECH
OTHERS LIKE BOOKSTORE AND PARU ARE GOING, AREN'T THEY!? WHY ARE WE BEING LEFT OUT!? YOU'RE JUST MEAN, ASUNA !
I WANT TO GO, TOO !
ME, TOO !
IT'S NOT LIKE I WAS TRYING TO LEAVE YOU OUT OF IT :
SKREECH
OH NO... WHAT DO I DO ...?
I CAN'T TELL THEM THAT WE'RE PLANNING TO TRAVEL TO ANOTHER WORLD. I GUESS I'LL HAVE TO COME UP WITH AN EXCUSE.
WELL, THE NEW CLUB AND THE TRIP TO ENGLAND IS TRUE :
IN ORDER TO FIND NEGI'S FATHER, WE HAVE TO GO TO A SPECIAL PLACE.
IT'S IN ENGLAND STILL, BUT
IN ORDER TO PREPARE FOR THIS TRIP, WE'VE BEEN TRAINING SPECIALLY SINCE THE SCHOOL FESTIVAL ENDED !
SPECIAL? LIKE MOUNTAINEERING ?
Y-YEAH! LIKE ROCK CLIMBING AND SUCH.
SO THAT'S WHY WE CAN'T TAKE ANYONE WHO HASN'T PREPARED ALONG WITH US.

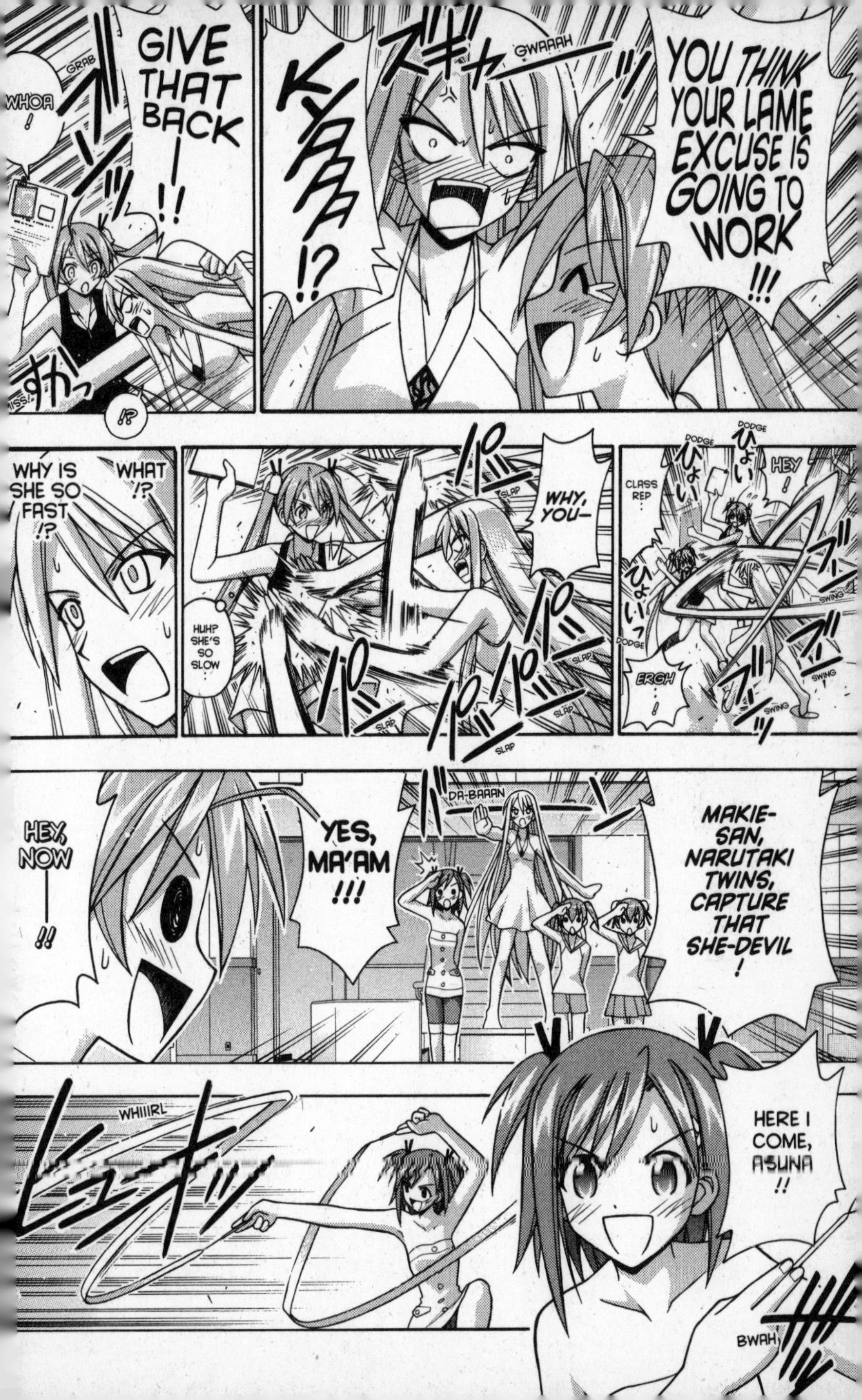
YOU THINK YOUR LAME EXCUSE IS GOING TO WORK!!!
GWAAAH
KYAAA!?
GIVE THAT BACK—!!
GRAB
WHOA!
MISS!
!?
DODGE
DODGE
HEY!
CLASS REP...
SWING
SWING
SWING
DODGE
ERGH...!
WHY, YOU—
SLAP
SLAP
SLAP
SLAP
SLAP
HUH? SHE'S SO SLOW...
WHAT!?
WHY IS SHE SO FAST!?
MAKIE-SAN, NARUTAKI TWINS, CAPTURE THAT SHE-DEVIL!
DA-BAAAN
YES, MA'AM!!!
HEY, NOW—!!
HERE I COME, ASUNA!!
BWAH
WHIIIRL

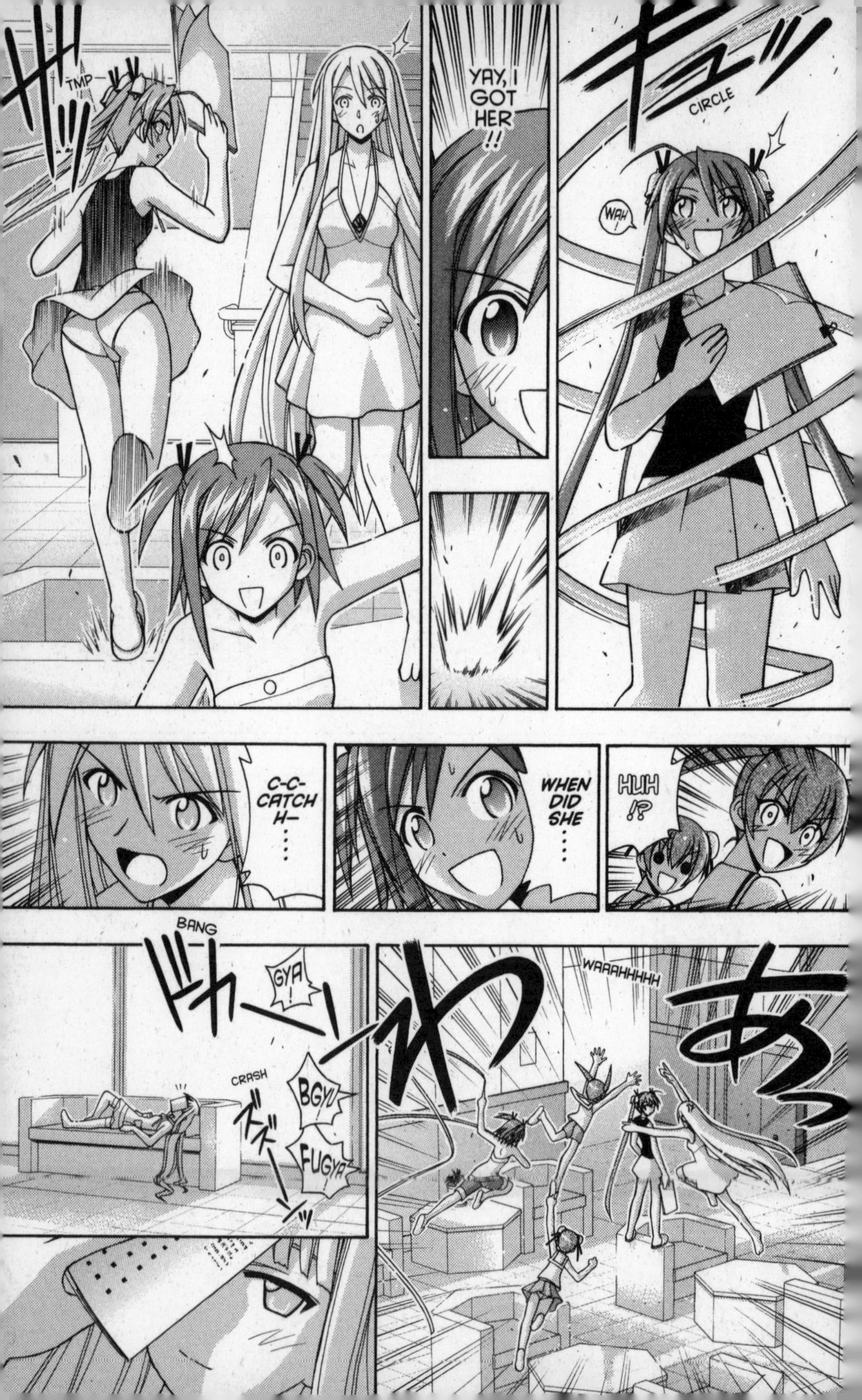
CIRCLE
WAH!
YAY, I GOT HER!!
TMP
HUH!?
WHEN DID SHE....
C-C-CATCH H-....
WAAAHHHHH
BANG
GYA!
CRASH
BGYU
FUGYA

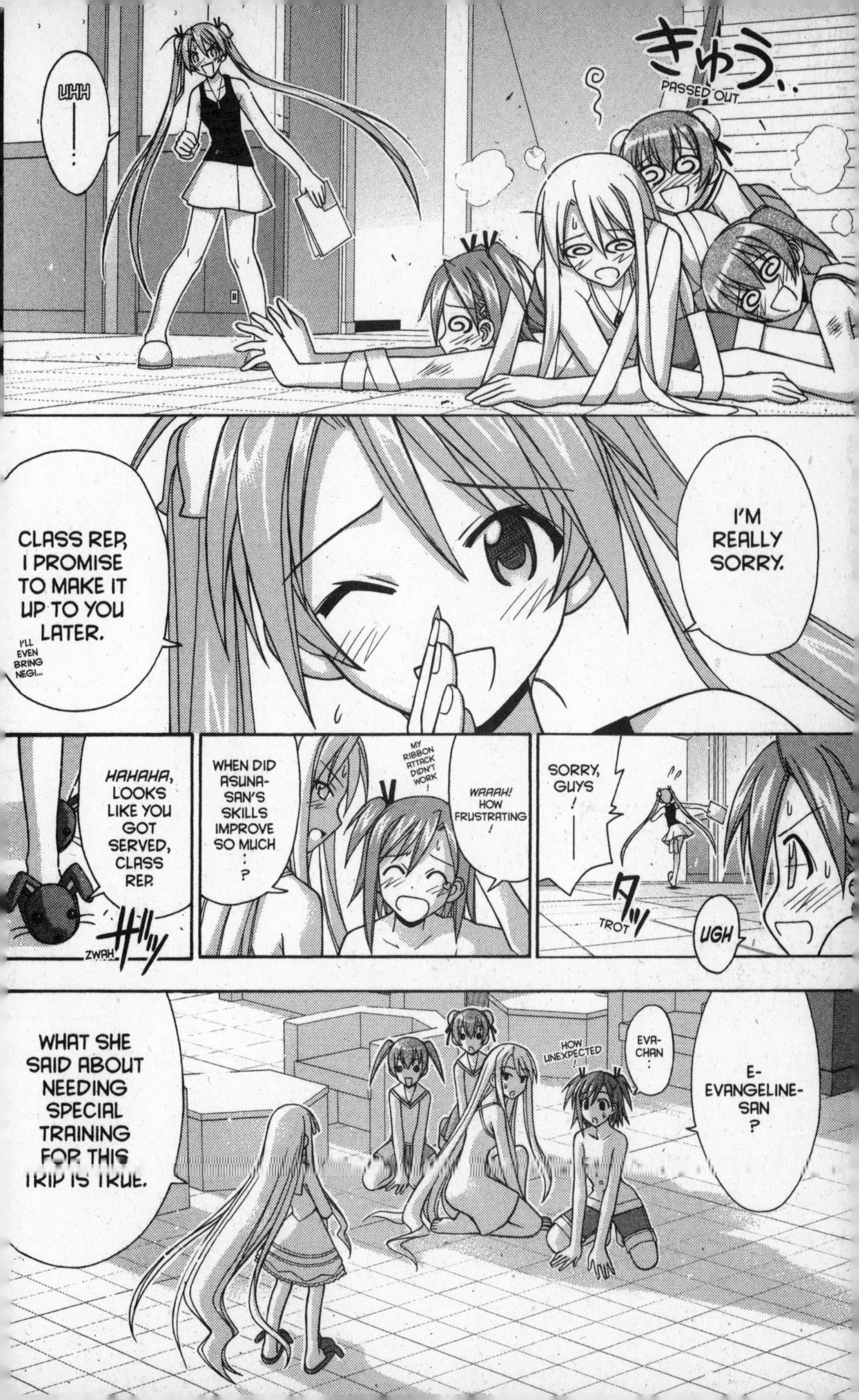
きゅう
PASSED OUT
UHH—!!
I'M REALLY SORRY.
CLASS REP, I PROMISE TO MAKE IT UP TO YOU LATER.
I'LL EVEN BRING NEGI...
UGH
SORRY, GUYS!
タッ
TROT
WAAAH! HOW FRUSTRATING!
MY RIBBON ATTACK DIDN'T WORK!
WHEN DID ASUNA-SAN'S SKILLS IMPROVE SO MUCH..?
HAHAHA, LOOKS LIKE YOU GOT SERVED, CLASS REP.
ザッ
ZWAH
E-EVANGELINE-SAN?
EVA-CHAN..
HOW UNEXPECTED!
WHAT SHE SAID ABOUT NEEDING SPECIAL TRAINING FOR THIS TRIP IS TRUE.

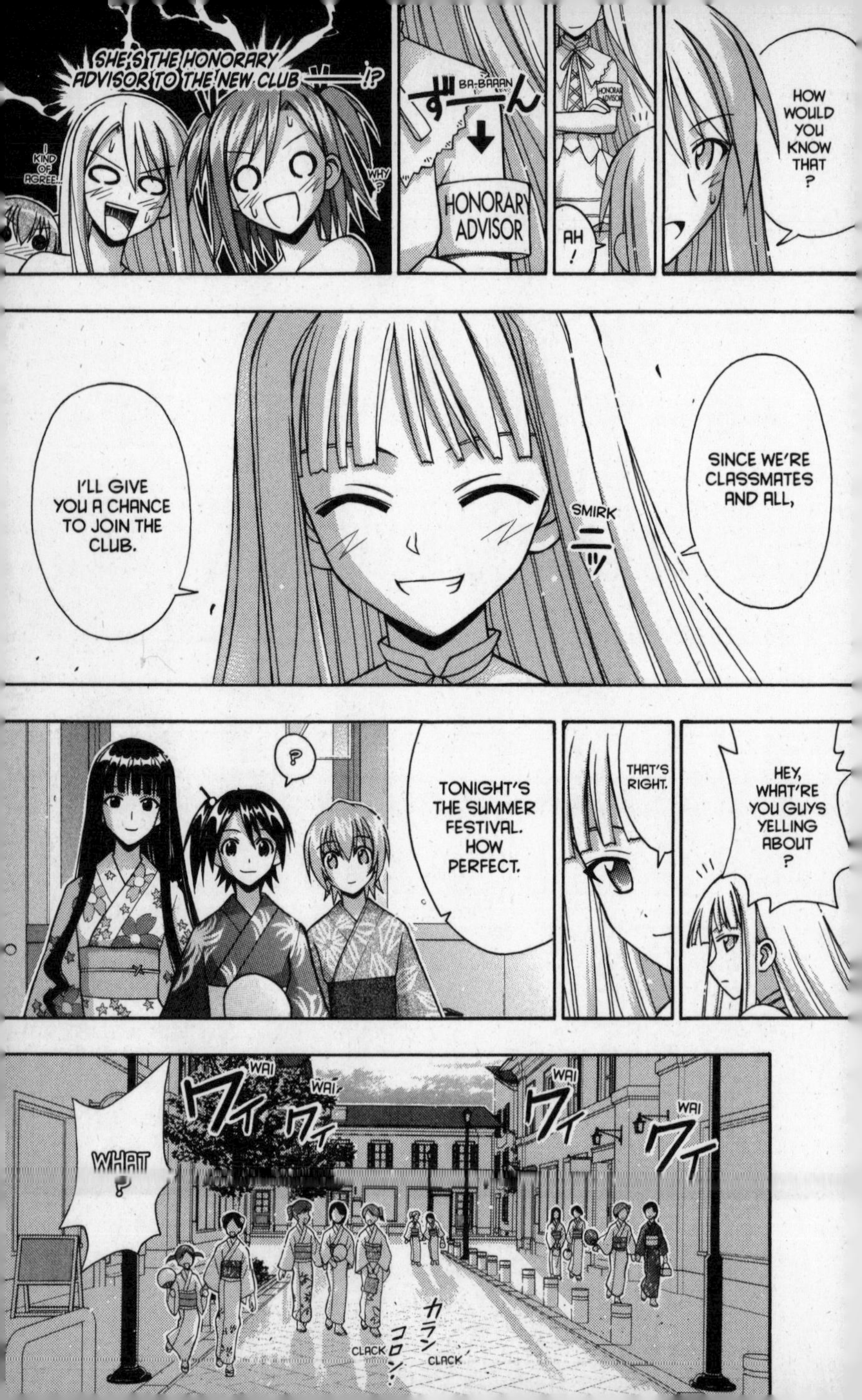
HOW WOULD YOU KNOW THAT?
AH!
HONORARY ADVISOR
BA-BAAAN
ずーん
HONORARY ADVISOR
SHE'S THE HONORARY ADVISOR TO THE NEW CLUB—!?
WHY?
I KIND OF AGREE...
SINCE WE'RE CLASSMATES AND ALL,
SMIRK
ニーッ
I'LL GIVE YOU A CHANCE TO JOIN THE CLUB.
HEY, WHAT'RE YOU GUYS YELLING ABOUT?
THAT'S RIGHT.
TONIGHT'S THE SUMMER FESTIVAL. HOW PERFECT.
?
WAI
ワイ
WAI
ワイ
WAI
ワイ
WAI
ワイ
WHAT?
カラン
CLACK
コロン
CLACK

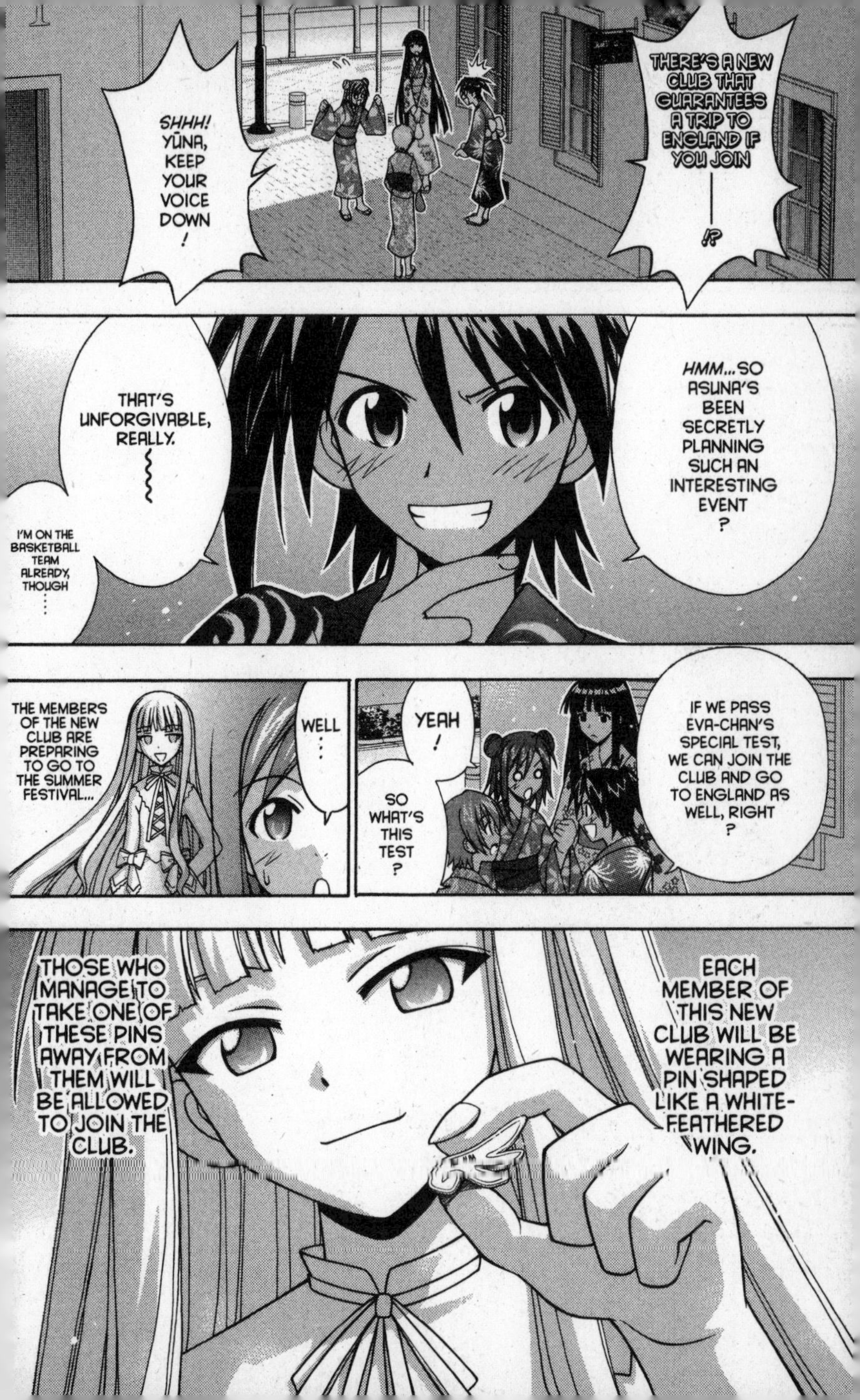
THERE'S A NEW CLUB THAT GUARANTEES A TRIP TO ENGLAND IF YOU JOIN —— !?
SHHH! YŪNA, KEEP YOUR VOICE DOWN!
HMM...SO ASUNA'S BEEN SECRETLY PLANNING SUCH AN INTERESTING EVENT?
THAT'S UNFORGIVABLE, REALLY.
I'M ON THE BASKETBALL TEAM ALREADY, THOUGH...
IF WE PASS EVA-CHAN'S SPECIAL TEST, WE CAN JOIN THE CLUB AND GO TO ENGLAND AS WELL, RIGHT?
YEAH!
SO WHAT'S THIS TEST?
WELL...
THE MEMBERS OF THE NEW CLUB ARE PREPARING TO GO TO THE SUMMER FESTIVAL...
EACH MEMBER OF THIS NEW CLUB WILL BE WEARING A PIN SHAPED LIKE A WHITE-FEATHERED WING.
THOSE WHO MANAGE TO TAKE ONE OF THESE PINS AWAY FROM THEM WILL BE ALLOWED TO JOIN THE CLUB.

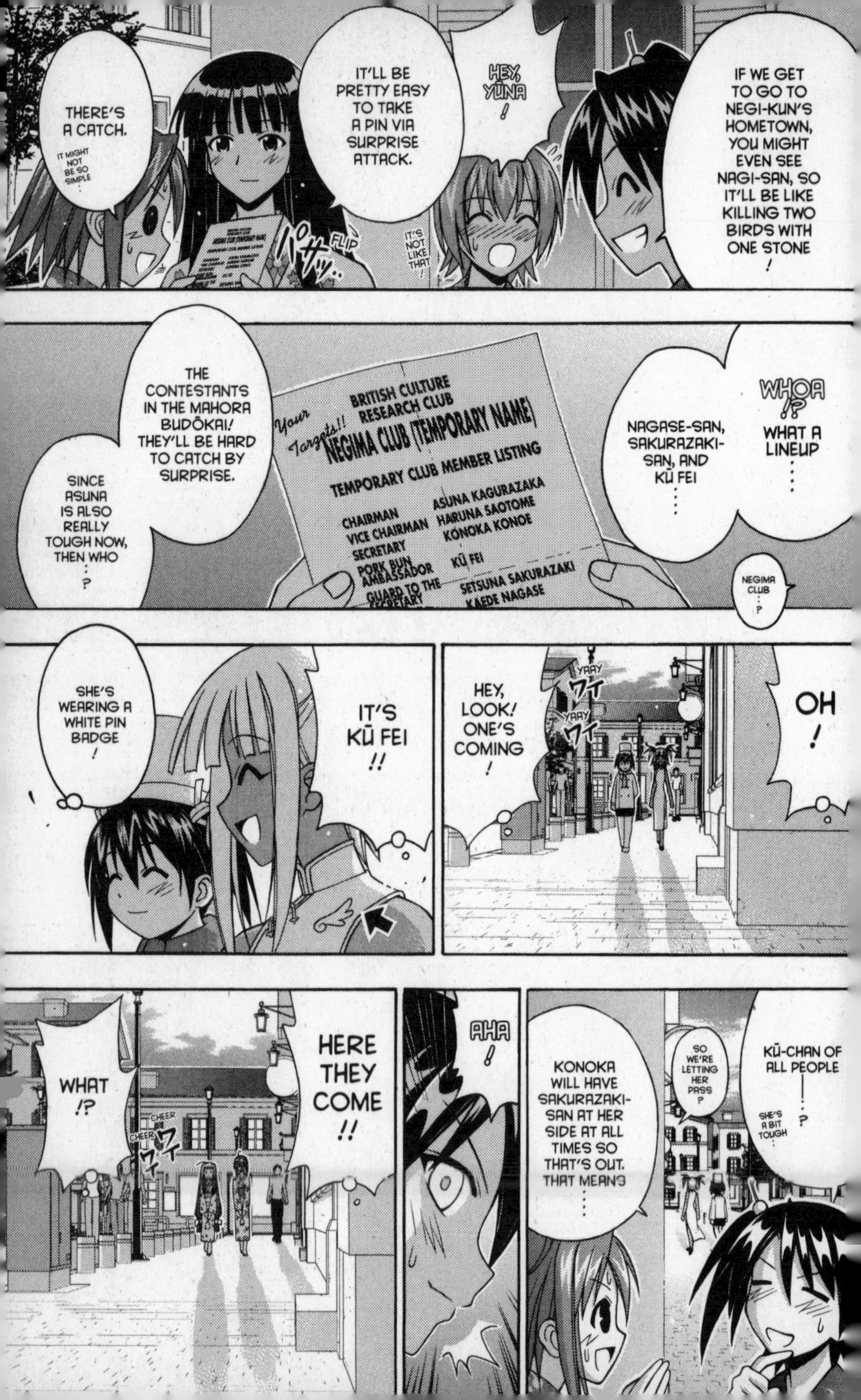
IF WE GET TO GO TO NEGI-KUN'S HOMETOWN, YOU MIGHT EVEN SEE NAGI-SAN, SO IT'LL BE LIKE KILLING TWO BIRDS WITH ONE STONE!
HEY, YŪNA!
IT'S NOT LIKE THAT!
IT'LL BE PRETTY EASY TO TAKE A PIN VIA SURPRISE ATTACK.
FLIP
THERE'S A CATCH.
IT MIGHT NOT BE SO SIMPLE...
WHOA!? WHAT A LINEUP...
NAGASE-SAN, SAKURAZAKI-SAN, AND KŪ FEI...
NEGIMA CLUB...?
Your Targets!!
BRITISH CULTURE RESEARCH CLUB
NEGIMA CLUB (TEMPORARY NAME)
TEMPORARY CLUB MEMBER LISTING
CHAIRMAN ASUNA KAGURAZAKA
VICE CHAIRMAN HARUNA SAOTOME
SECRETARY KONOKA KONOE
PORK BUN AMBASSADOR KŪ FEI
GUARD TO THE SECRETARY SETSUNA SAKURAZAKI
KAEDE NAGASE
THE CONTESTANTS IN THE MAHORA BUDŌKAI! THEY'LL BE HARD TO CATCH BY SURPRISE.
SINCE ASUNA IS ALSO REALLY TOUGH NOW, THEN WHO...?
OH!
HEY, LOOK! ONE'S COMING!
YAAY
YAAY
IT'S KŪ FEI!!
SHE'S WEARING A WHITE PIN BADGE!
KŪ-CHAN OF ALL PEOPLE...?
SHE'S A BIT TOUGH...
SO WE'RE LETTING HER PASS?
KONOKA WILL HAVE SAKURAZAKI-SAN AT HER SIDE AT ALL TIMES SO THAT'S OUT. THAT MEANS...
AHA!
HERE THEY COME!!
WHAT!?
CHEER
CHEER

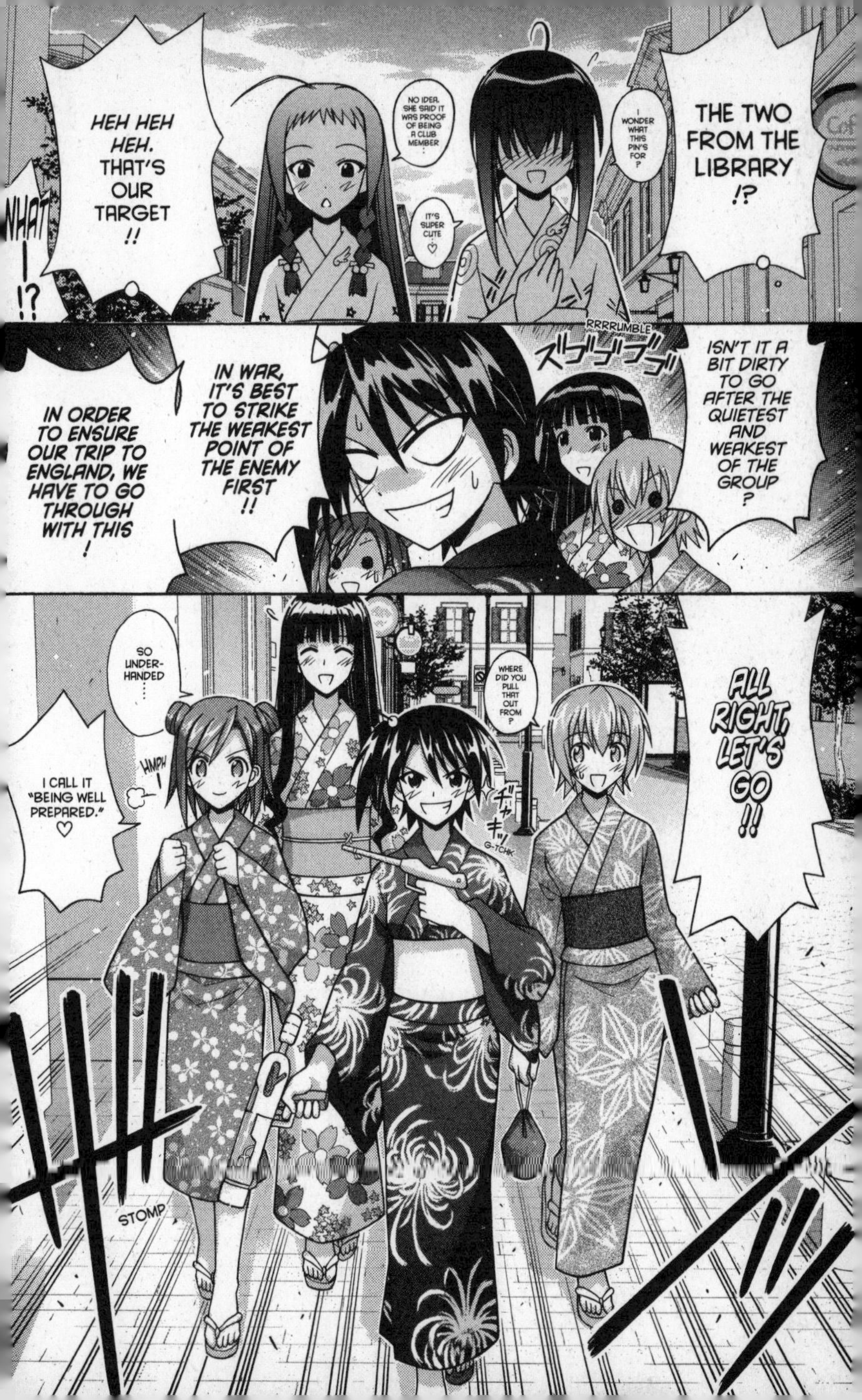
THE TWO FROM THE LIBRARY !?
I WONDER WHAT THIS PIN'S FOR ?
NO IDEA. SHE SAID IT WAS PROOF OF BEING A CLUB MEMBER …
IT'S SUPER CUTE ♡
HEH HEH HEH. THAT'S OUR TARGET !!
WHAT !?
RRRRUMBLE
ISN'T IT A BIT DIRTY TO GO AFTER THE QUIETEST AND WEAKEST OF THE GROUP ?
IN WAR, IT'S BEST TO STRIKE THE WEAKEST POINT OF THE ENEMY FIRST !!
IN ORDER TO ENSURE OUR TRIP TO ENGLAND, WE HAVE TO GO THROUGH WITH THIS !
ALL RIGHT, LET'S GO !!
WHERE DID YOU PULL THAT OUT FROM ?
G-TCHK
SO UNDER-HANDED …
HMPH !
I CALL IT "BEING WELL PREPARED." ♡
STOMP

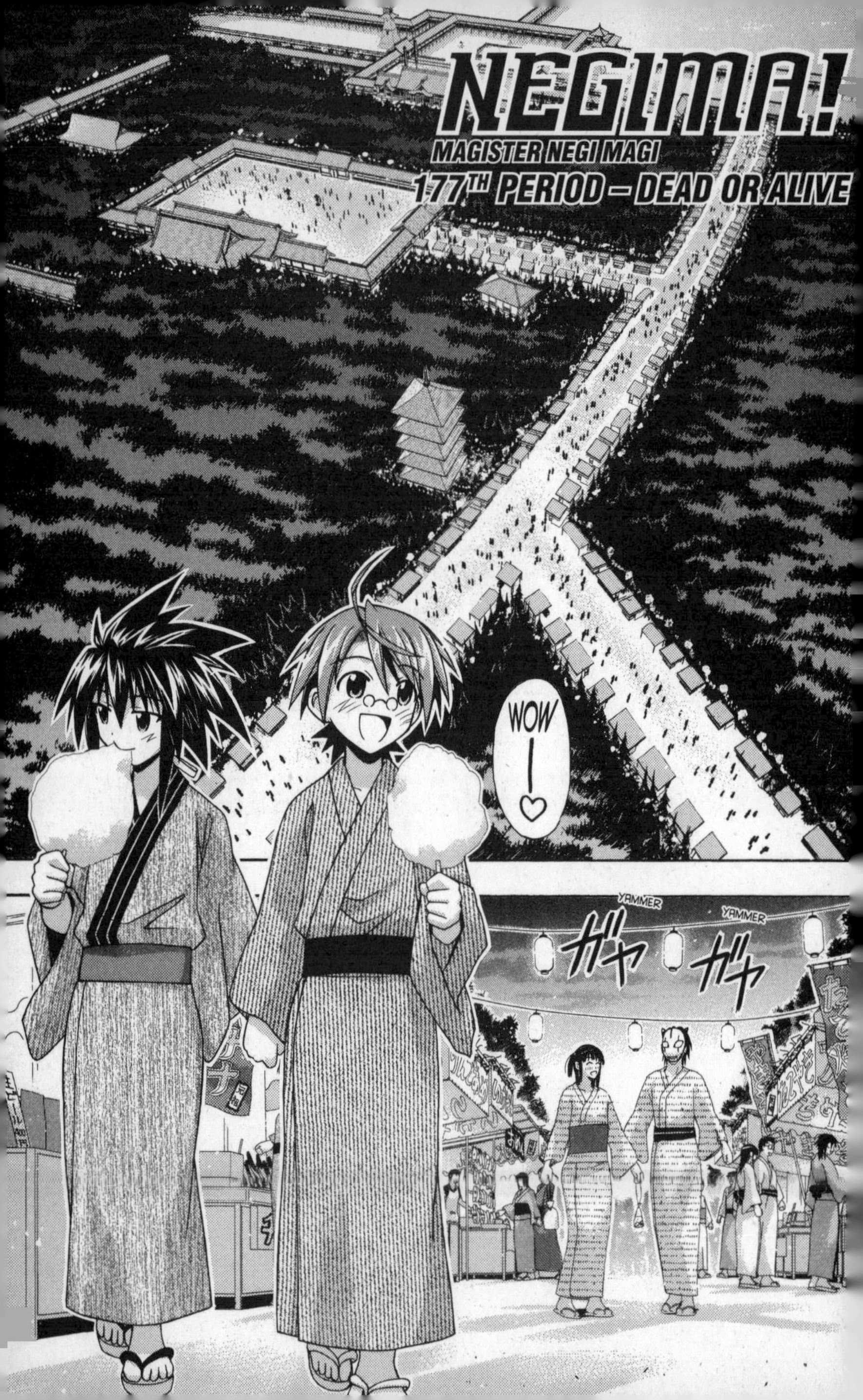
NEGIMA!
MAGISTER NEGI MAGI
177TH PERIOD – DEAD OR ALIVE
WOW! ♡
YAMMER
YAMMER

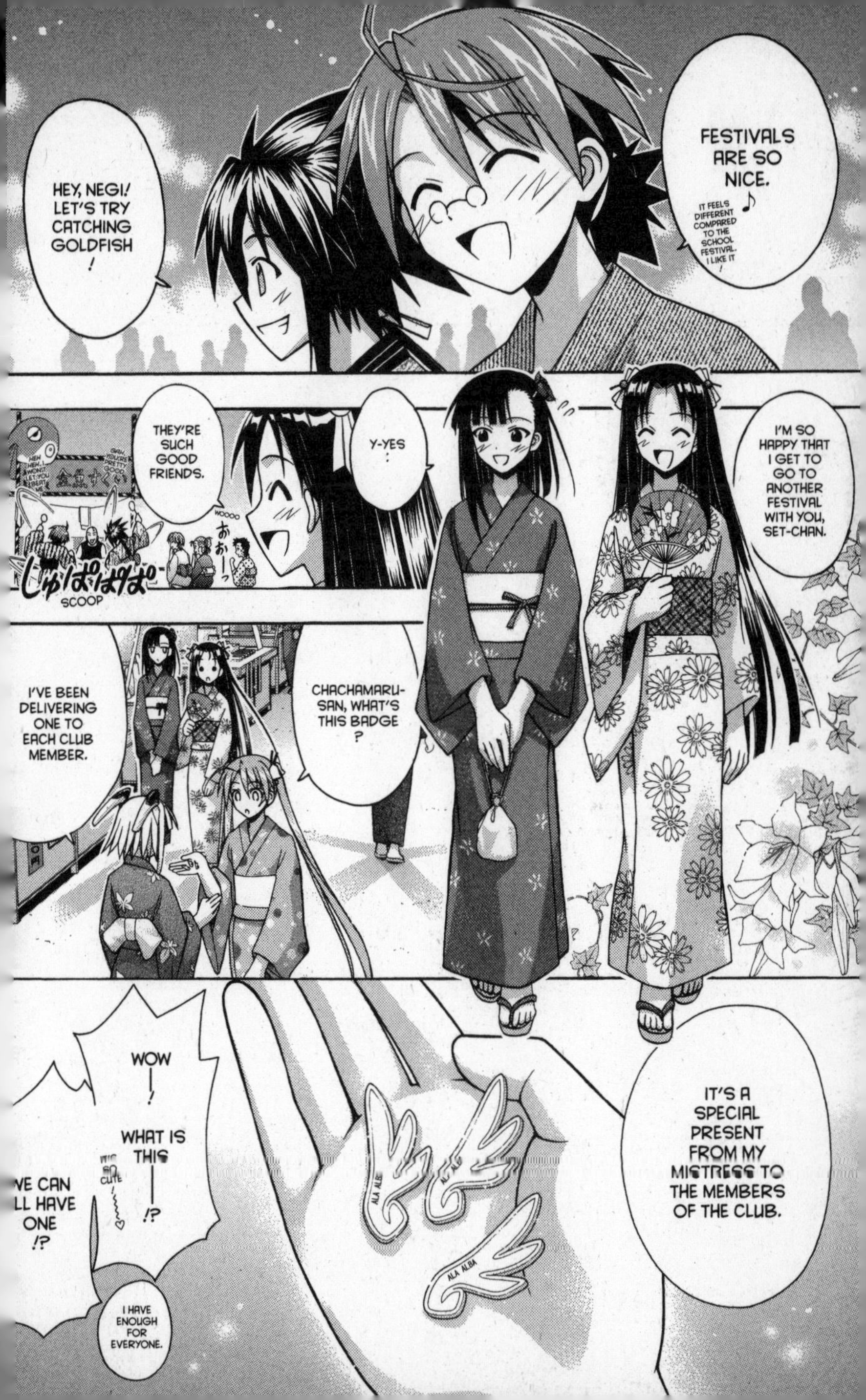
FESTIVALS ARE SO NICE. ♪
IT FEELS DIFFERENT COMPARED TO THE SCHOOL FESTIVAL. I LIKE IT!
HEY, NEGI! LET'S TRY CATCHING GOLDFISH!
I'M SO HAPPY THAT I GET TO GO TO ANOTHER FESTIVAL WITH YOU, SET-CHAN.
Y-YES...
THEY'RE SUCH GOOD FRIENDS.
WOOOO
おおーっ
GAH, YOU'RE PRETTY GOOD
HEH HEH, I WON'T LET YOU BEAT ME
金魚すくい
しゅぱぱぱ
SCOOP
CHACHAMARU-SAN, WHAT'S THIS BADGE?
I'VE BEEN DELIVERING ONE TO EACH CLUB MEMBER.
IT'S A SPECIAL PRESENT FROM MY MISTRESS TO THE MEMBERS OF THE CLUB.
WOW! WHAT IS THIS—!?
SO CUTE~♡
VE CAN LL HAVE ONE !?
ALA ALBA
ALA ALBA
ALA ALBA
I HAVE ENOUGH FOR EVERYONE.

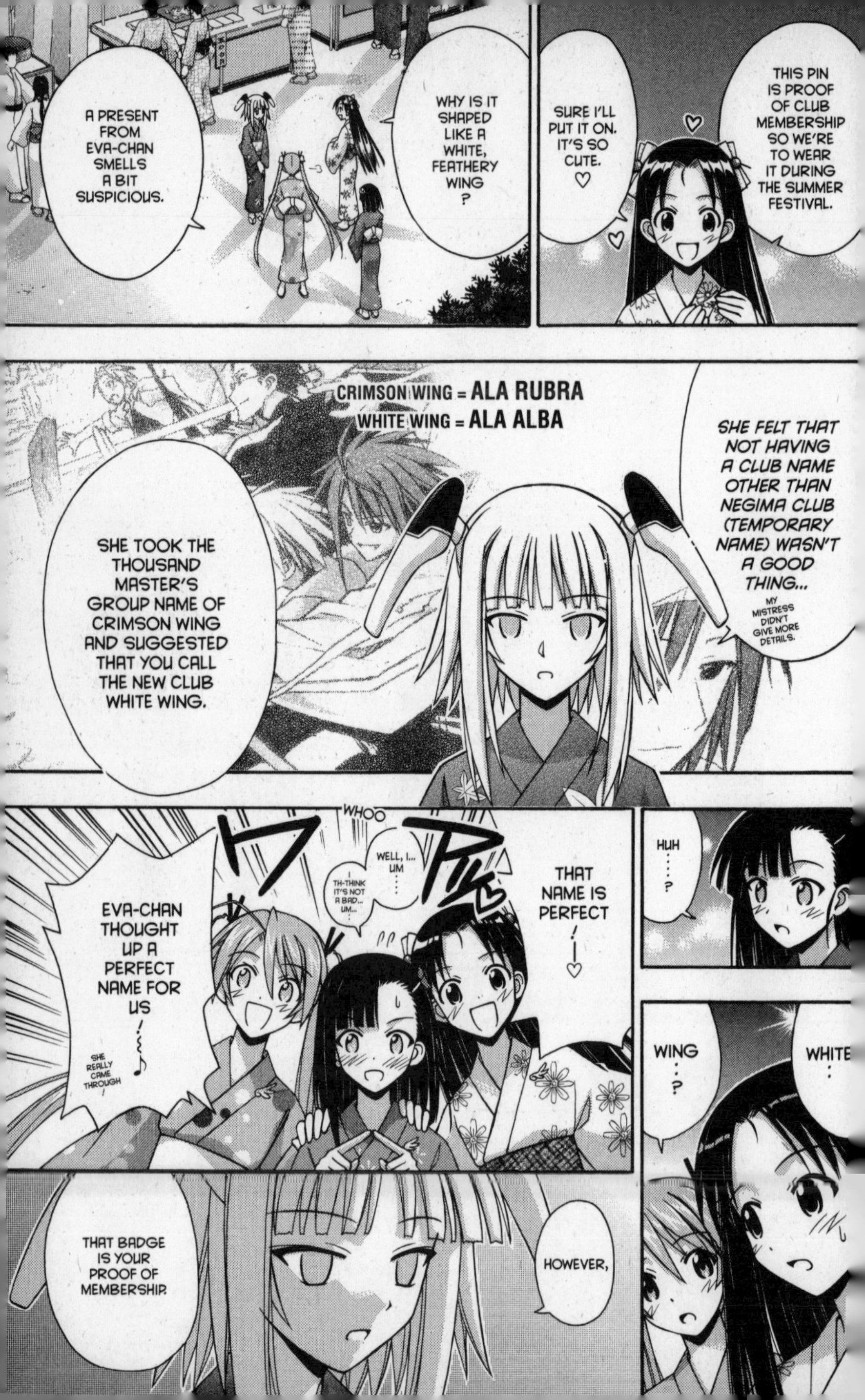

THIS PIN IS PROOF OF CLUB MEMBERSHIP SO WE'RE TO WEAR IT DURING THE SUMMER FESTIVAL.
SURE I'LL PUT IT ON. IT'S SO CUTE. ♡
WHY IS IT SHAPED LIKE A WHITE, FEATHERY WING?
A PRESENT FROM EVA-CHAN SMELLS A BIT SUSPICIOUS.
SHE FELT THAT NOT HAVING A CLUB NAME OTHER THAN NEGIMA CLUB (TEMPORARY NAME) WASN'T A GOOD THING...
MY MISTRESS DIDN'T GIVE MORE DETAILS.
CRIMSON WING = ALA RUBRA
WHITE WING = ALA ALBA
SHE TOOK THE THOUSAND MASTER'S GROUP NAME OF CRIMSON WING AND SUGGESTED THAT YOU CALL THE NEW CLUB WHITE WING.
HUH....?
WHITE...
WING...?
WHOO
THAT NAME IS PERFECT!! ♡
WELL, I... UM...
I TH-THINK IT'S NOT A BAD... UM...
EVA-CHAN THOUGHT UP A PERFECT NAME FOR US!! ♪
SHE REALLY CAME THROUGH!
HOWEVER,
THAT BADGE IS YOUR PROOF OF MEMBERSHIP.

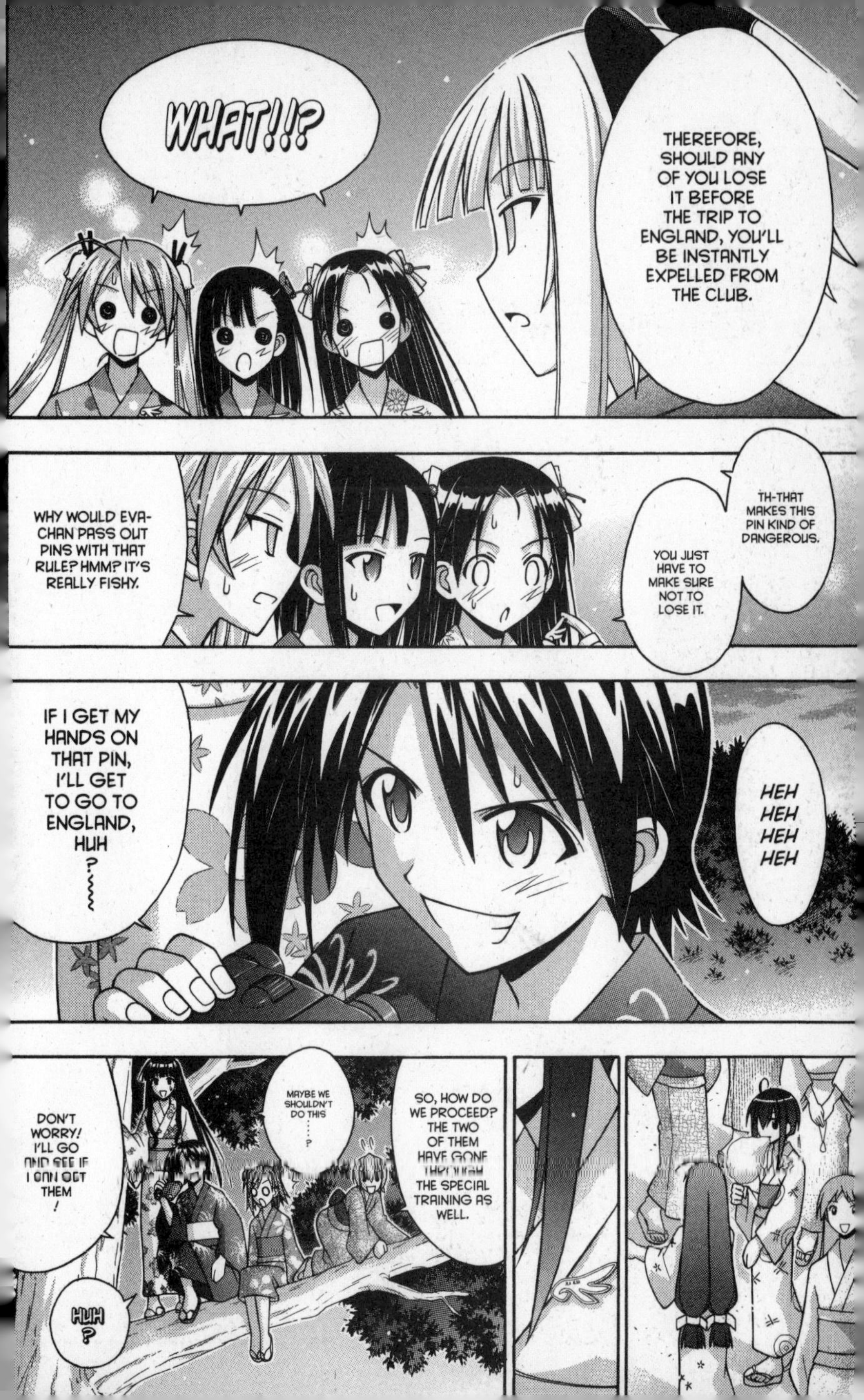
THEREFORE, SHOULD ANY OF YOU LOSE IT BEFORE THE TRIP TO ENGLAND, YOU'LL BE INSTANTLY EXPELLED FROM THE CLUB.
WHAT!!?
TH-THAT MAKES THIS PIN KIND OF DANGEROUS.
YOU JUST HAVE TO MAKE SURE NOT TO LOSE IT.
WHY WOULD EVA-CHAN PASS OUT PINS WITH THAT RULE? HMM? IT'S REALLY FISHY.
HEH HEH HEH HEH
IF I GET MY HANDS ON THAT PIN, I'LL GET TO GO TO ENGLAND, HUH?
SO, HOW DO WE PROCEED? THE TWO OF THEM HAVE GONE THROUGH THE SPECIAL TRAINING AS WELL.
MAYBE WE SHOULDN'T DO THIS....?
DON'T WORRY! I'LL GO AND SEE IF I CAN GET THEM!
HUH?

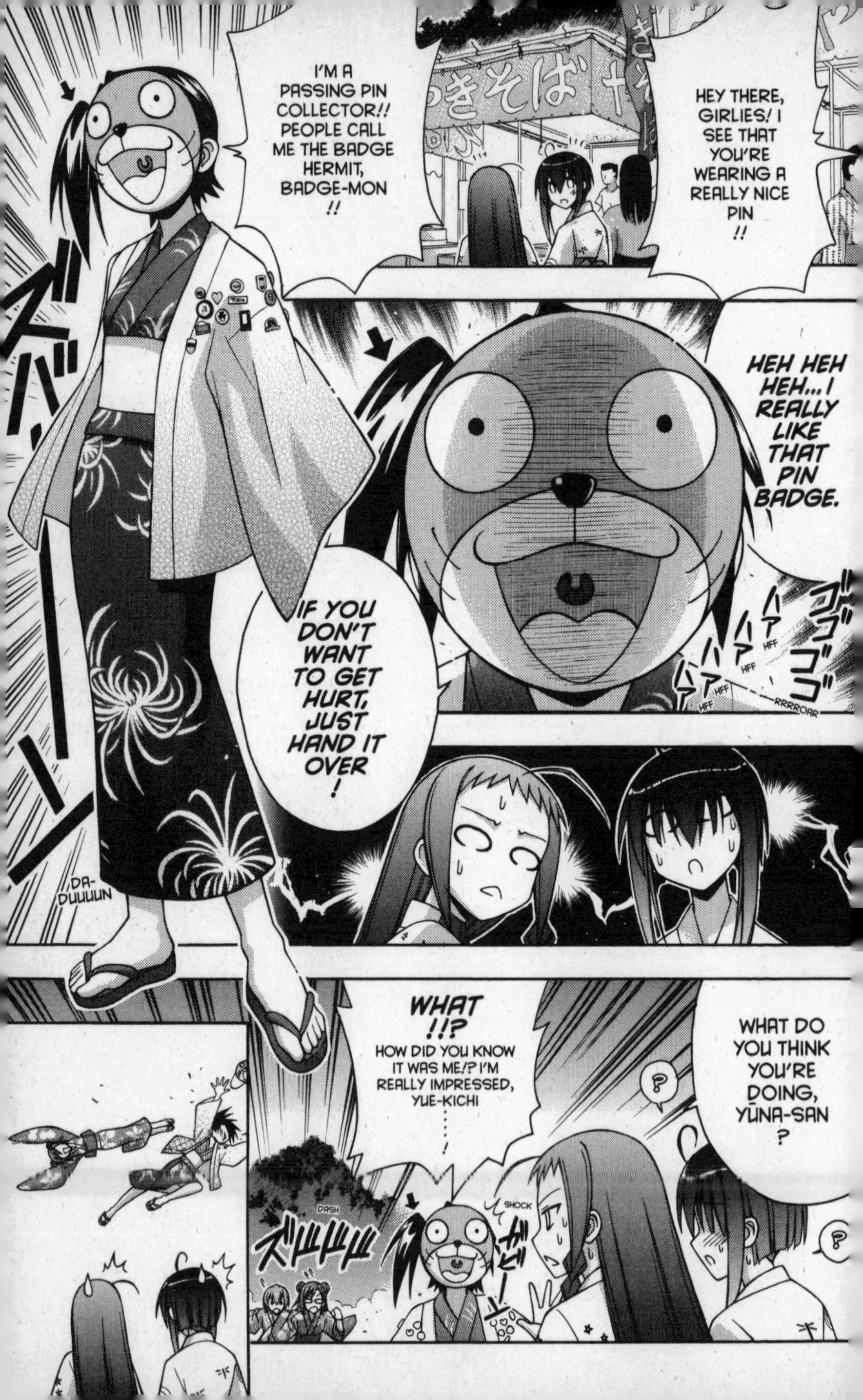
HEY THERE, GIRLIES! I SEE THAT YOU'RE WEARING A REALLY NICE PIN!!
I'M A PASSING PIN COLLECTOR!! PEOPLE CALL ME THE BADGE HERMIT, BADGE-MON!!
DA-DUUUUN
HEH HEH HEH...I REALLY LIKE THAT PIN BADGE.
HFF HFF HFF HFF
RRRROAR
IF YOU DON'T WANT TO GET HURT, JUST HAND IT OVER!
WHAT DO YOU THINK YOU'RE DOING, YŪNA-SAN?
?
?
WHAT!!? HOW DID YOU KNOW IT WAS ME!? I'M REALLY IMPRESSED, YUE-KICHI...!
SHOCK
DASH

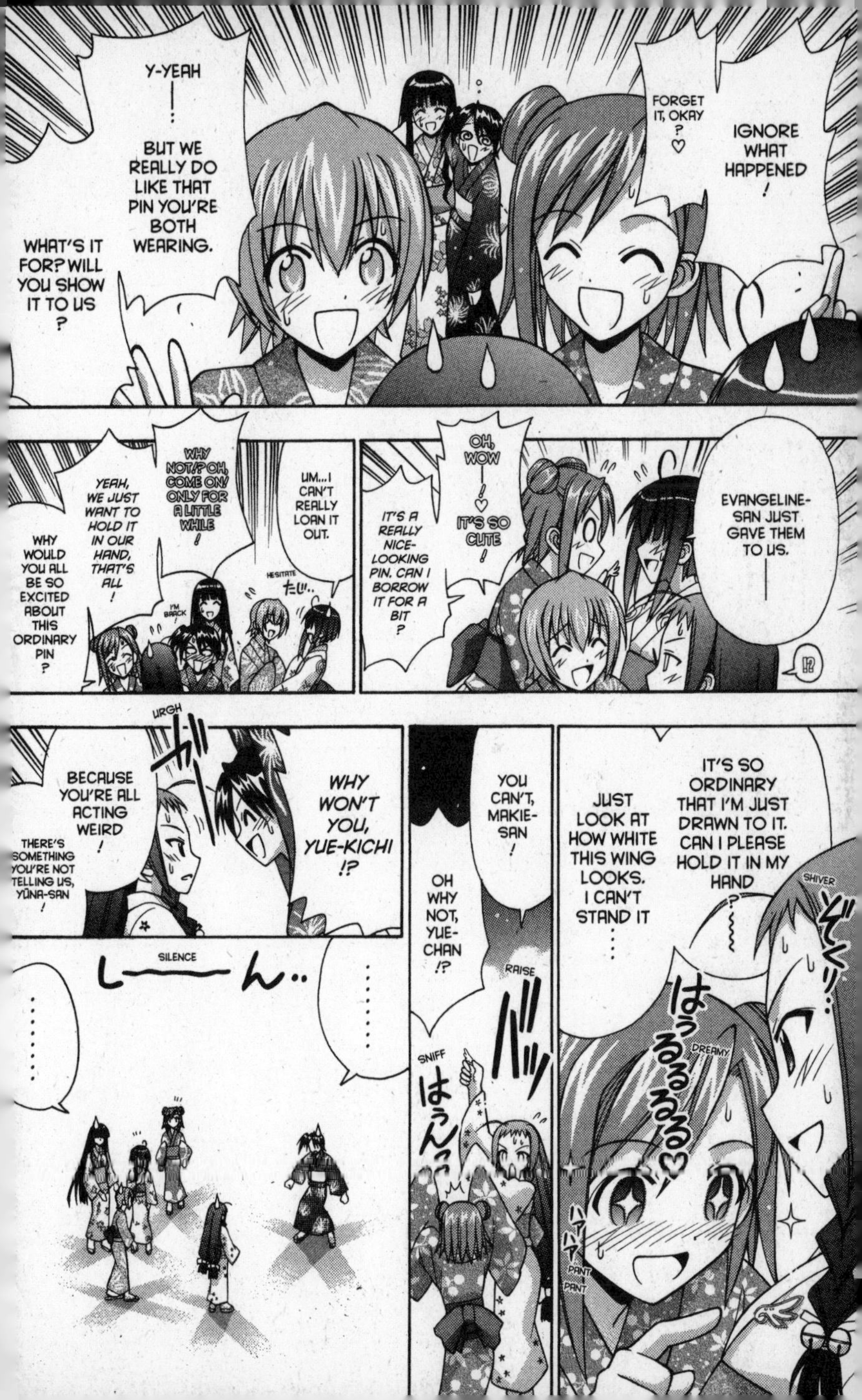

IGNORE WHAT HAPPENED!
FORGET IT, OKAY?♡
Y-YEAH—BUT WE REALLY DO LIKE THAT PIN YOU'RE BOTH WEARING.
WHAT'S IT FOR? WILL YOU SHOW IT TO US?
EVANGELINE-SAN JUST GAVE THEM TO US.—
!?
OH, WOW—!♡
IT'S SO CUTE!
IT'S A REALLY NICE-LOOKING PIN. CAN I BORROW IT FOR A BIT?
UM...I CAN'T REALLY LOAN IT OUT.
HESITATE
WHY NOT!? OH, COME ON! ONLY FOR A LITTLE WHILE!
YEAH, WE JUST WANT TO HOLD IT IN OUR HAND, THAT'S ALL!
I'M BAACK
WHY WOULD YOU ALL BE SO EXCITED ABOUT THIS ORDINARY PIN?
IT'S SO ORDINARY THAT I'M JUST DRAWN TO IT. CAN I PLEASE HOLD IT IN MY HAND?~~
SHIVER
JUST LOOK AT HOW WHITE THIS WING LOOKS. I CAN'T STAND IT...
DREAMY
PANT PANT
YOU CAN'T, MAKIE-SAN!
OH WHY NOT, YUE-CHAN!?
RAISE
SNIFF
WHY WON'T YOU, YUE-KICHI!?
URGH
BECAUSE YOU'RE ALL ACTING WEIRD!
THERE'S SOMETHING YOU'RE NOT TELLING US, YŪNA-SAN!
......
SILENCE
......

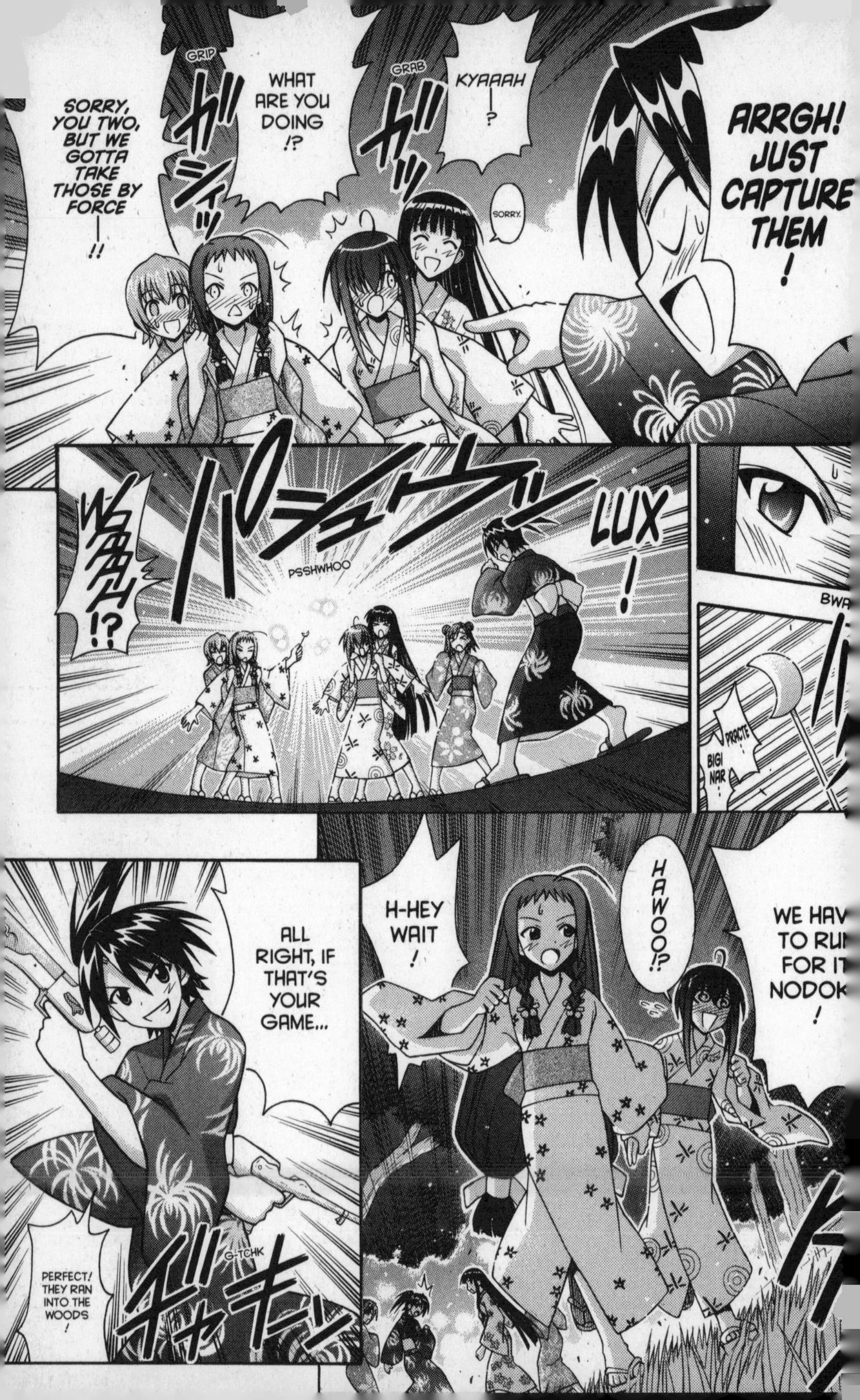
ARRGH! JUST CAPTURE THEM !
KYAAAH —?
GRAB
SORRY.
WHAT ARE YOU DOING !?
GRIP
SORRY, YOU TWO, BUT WE GOTTA TAKE THOSE BY FORCE —!!
BWA
PRACTE !
BIGI NAR !
LUX !
PSSHWHOO
WAAAH !?
WE HAV TO RU FOR IT NODOK !
HAWOO!?
H-HEY WAIT !
ALL RIGHT, IF THAT'S YOUR GAME...
G-TCHK
PERFECT! THEY RAN INTO THE WOODS !

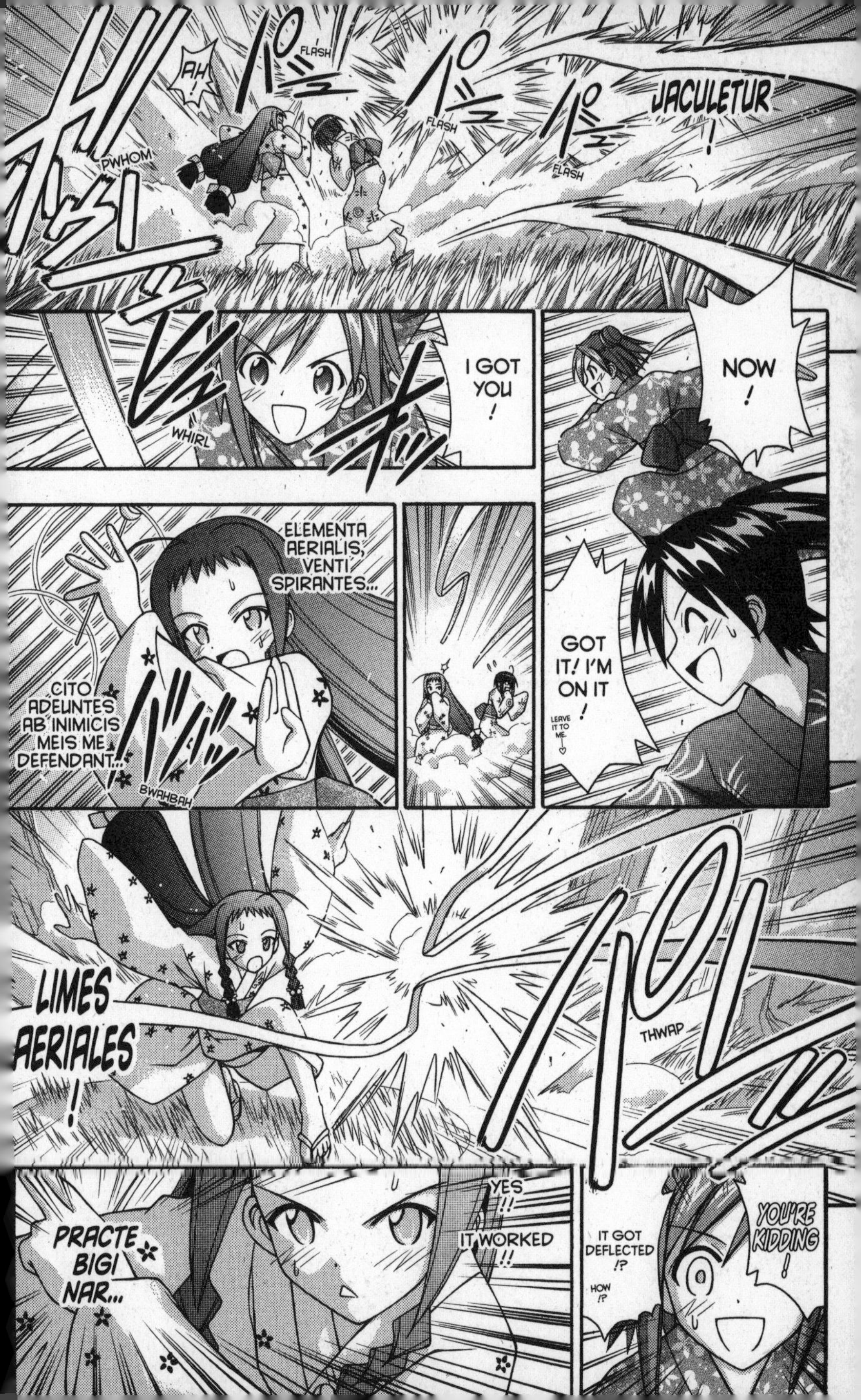
JACULETUR!
FLASH
FLASH
FLASH
AH!
PWHOM
NOW!
I GOT YOU!
WHIRL
GOT IT! I'M ON IT!
LEAVE IT TO ME. ♡
ELEMENTA AERIALIS, VENTI SPIRANTES...
CITO ADEUNTES AB INIMICIS MEIS ME DEFENDANT...
BWAHBAH
THWAP
LIMES AERIALES!
YOU'RE KIDDING!
IT GOT DEFLECTED!?
HOW!?
YES!!
IT WORKED!!
PRACTE BIGI NAR...

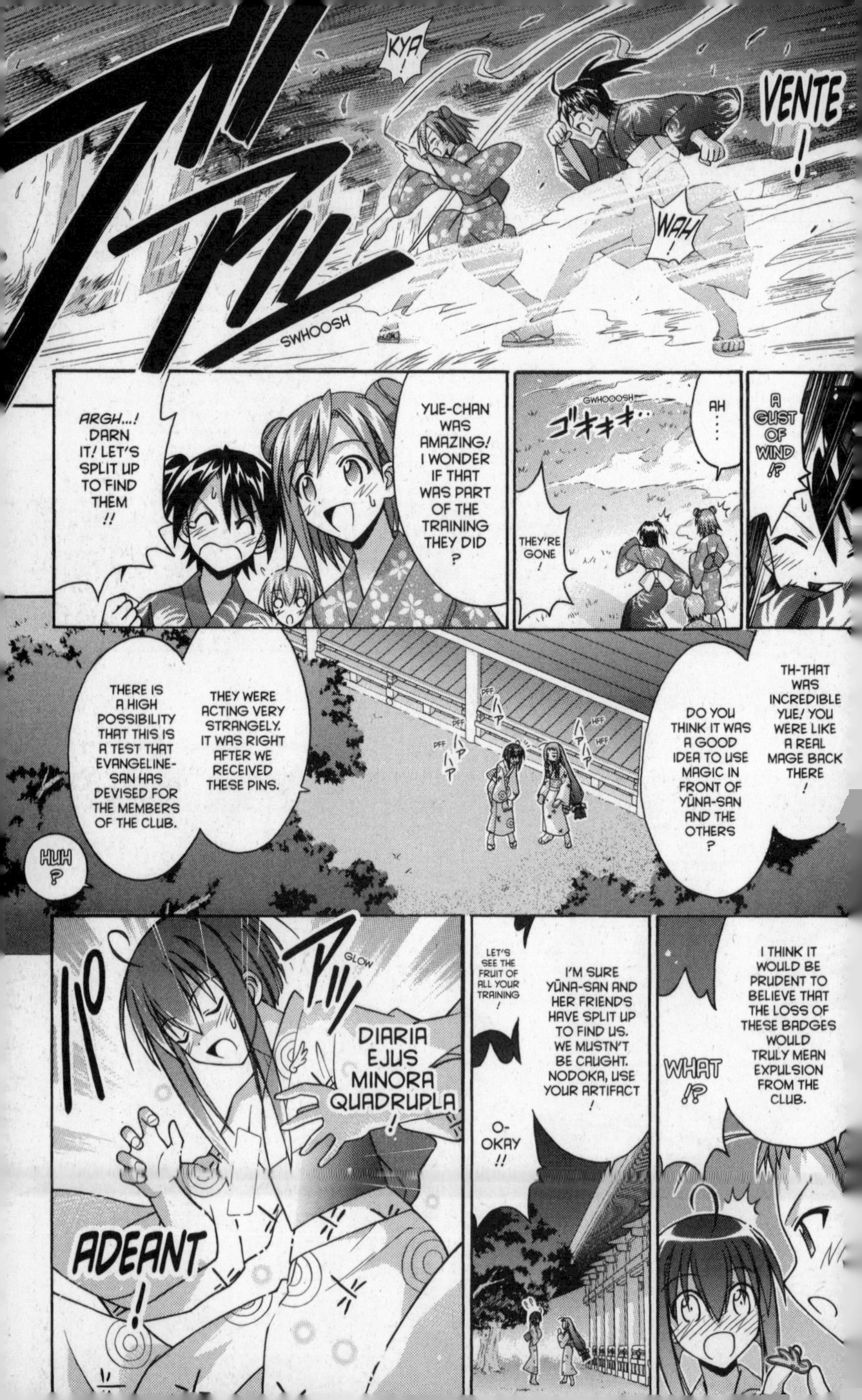
VENTE!
KYA!
WAH!
SWHOOSH
A GUST OF WIND!?
AH...
GWHOOOSH
THEY'RE GONE!
YUE-CHAN WAS AMAZING! I WONDER IF THAT WAS PART OF THE TRAINING THEY DID?
ARGH...! DARN IT! LET'S SPLIT UP TO FIND THEM!!
TH-THAT WAS INCREDIBLE YUE! YOU WERE LIKE A REAL MAGE BACK THERE!
DO YOU THINK IT WAS A GOOD IDEA TO USE MAGIC IN FRONT OF YŪNA-SAN AND THE OTHERS?
HFF HFF
PFF PFF PFF
THEY WERE ACTING VERY STRANGELY. IT WAS RIGHT AFTER WE RECEIVED THESE PINS.
THERE IS A HIGH POSSIBILITY THAT THIS IS A TEST THAT EVANGELINE-SAN HAS DEVISED FOR THE MEMBERS OF THE CLUB.
HUH?
I THINK IT WOULD BE PRUDENT TO BELIEVE THAT THE LOSS OF THESE BADGES WOULD TRULY MEAN EXPULSION FROM THE CLUB.
WHAT!?
I'M SURE YŪNA-SAN AND HER FRIENDS HAVE SPLIT UP TO FIND US. WE MUSTN'T BE CAUGHT. NODOKA, USE YOUR ARTIFACT!
LET'S SEE THE FRUIT OF ALL YOUR TRAINING!
O-OKAY!!
GLOW
DIARIA EJUS MINORA QUADRUPLA!
ADEANT!

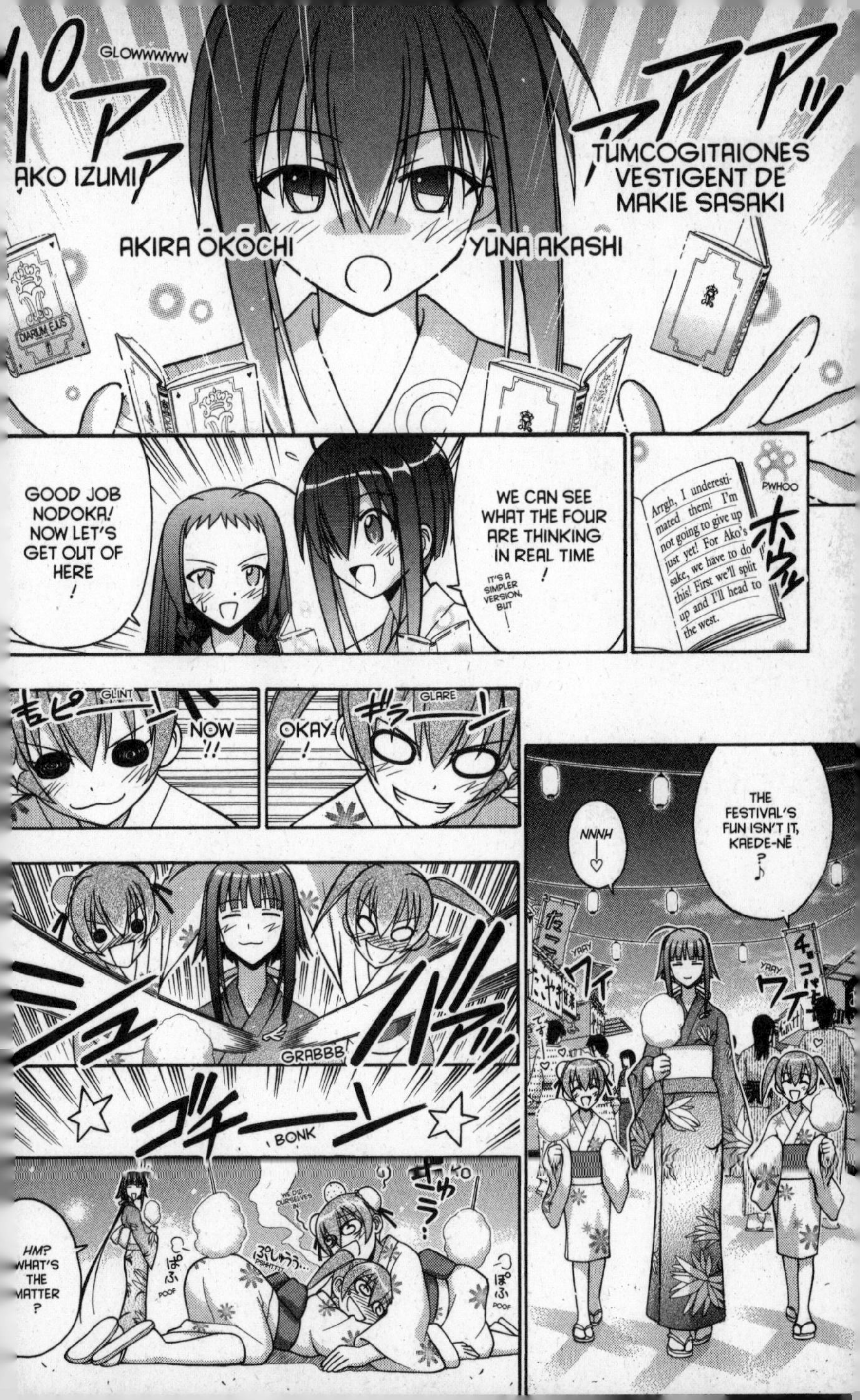
TUMCOGITAIONES VESTIGENT DE MAKIE SASAKI
YŪNA AKASHI
AKIRA ŌKŌCHI
AKO IZUMI
GLOWWWWW
PWHOO
Arrrgh, I underestimated them! I'm not going to give up just yet! For Ako's sake, we have to do this! First we'll split up and I'll head to the west.
WE CAN SEE WHAT THE FOUR ARE THINKING IN REAL TIME!
IT'S A SIMPLER VERSION, BUT!
GOOD JOB NODOKA! NOW LET'S GET OUT OF HERE!
GLARE
OKAY!
GLINT
NOW!!
GRABBB
BONK
THE FESTIVAL'S FUN ISN'T IT, KAEDE-NĒ? ♪
NNNH ♡
YAAY
YAAY
KO
WE DID OURSELVES IN~
PSHHHH
POOF
POOF
HM? WHAT'S THE MATTER?

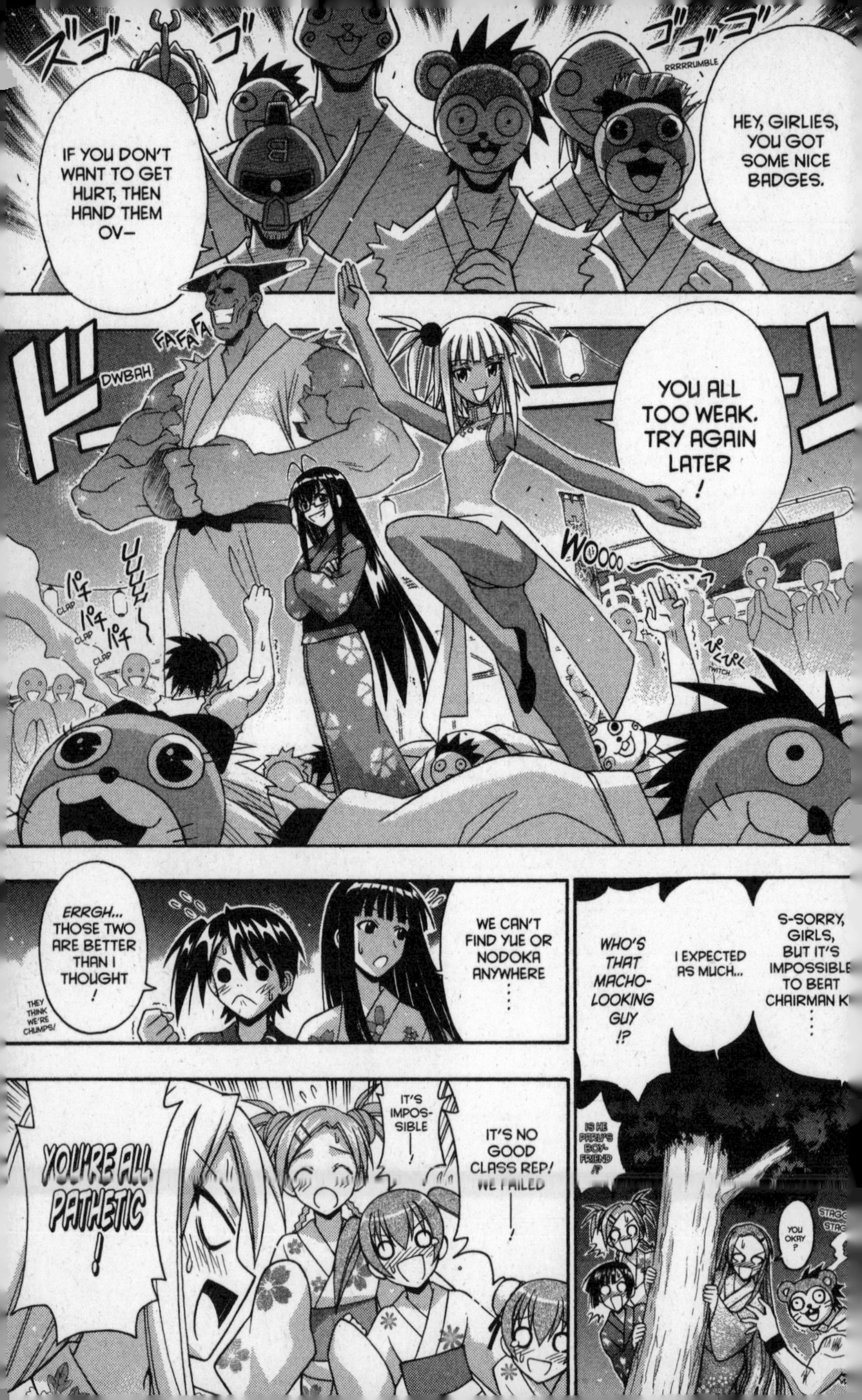
RRRRRUMBLE
HEY, GIRLIES, YOU GOT SOME NICE BADGES.
IF YOU DON'T WANT TO GET HURT, THEN HAND THEM OV–
FAFAFA
DWBAH
YOU ALL TOO WEAK. TRY AGAIN LATER!
WOOOO
CLAP
CLAP
CLAP
TWITCH
S-SORRY, GIRLS, BUT IT'S IMPOSSIBLE TO BEAT CHAIRMAN K...
I EXPECTED AS MUCH...
WHO'S THAT MACHO-LOOKING GUY!?
IS HE PARU'S BOY-FRIEND!?
YOU OKAY?
STAGG
STAG
WE CAN'T FIND YUE OR NODOKA ANYWHERE...
ERRGH... THOSE TWO ARE BETTER THAN I THOUGHT!
THEY THINK WE'RE CHUMPS!
IT'S NO GOOD CLASS REP! WE FAILED!
IT'S IMPOS-SIBLE!
YOU'RE ALL PATHETIC!

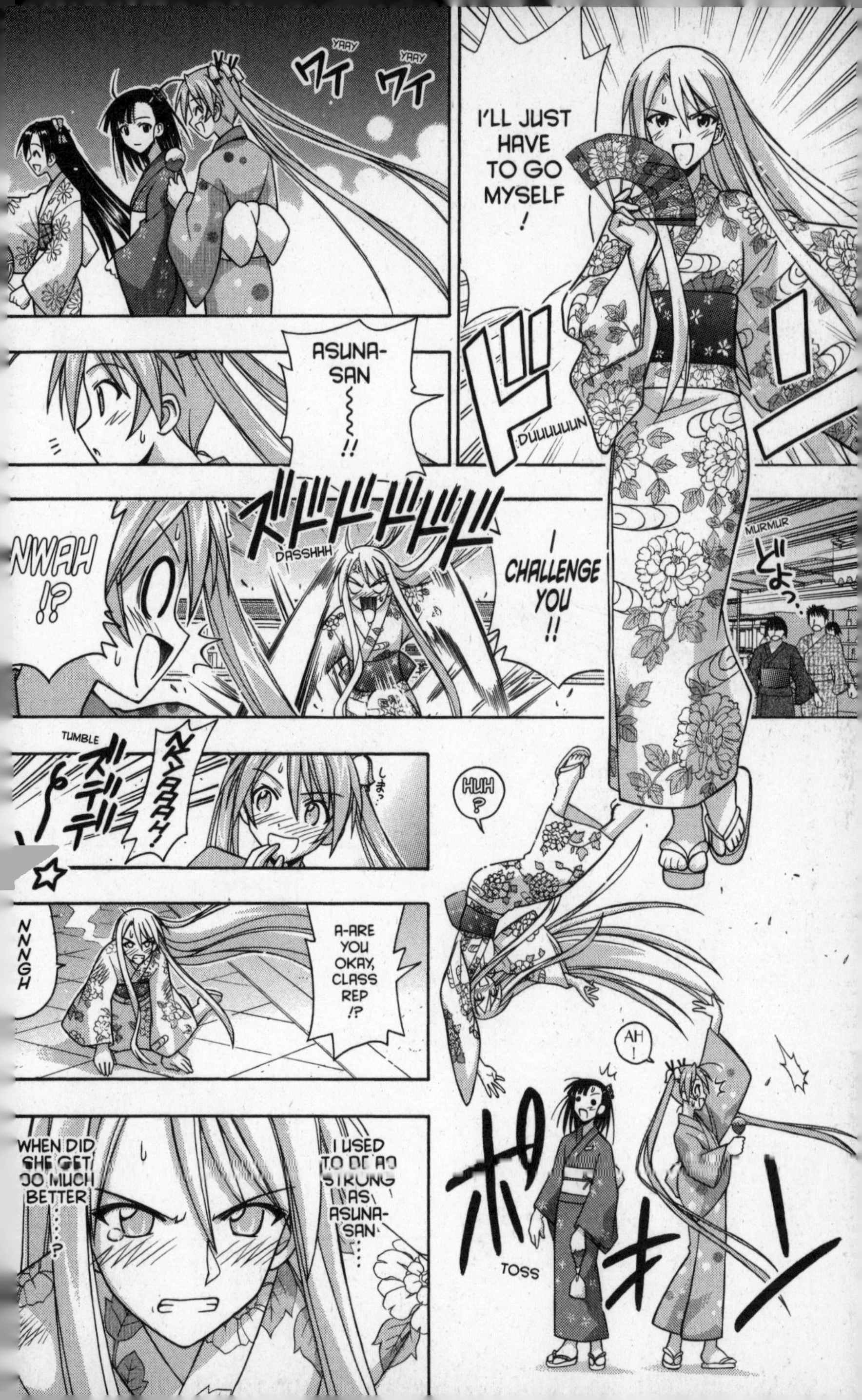
I'LL JUST HAVE TO GO MYSELF !
ドーン
DUUUUUUN
I CHALLENGE YOU !!
どよっ…
MURMUR
ワイ
YAAY
ワイ
YAAY
ASUNA-SAN ~~~ !!
ズドドドドド
DASSHHH
NWAH !?
HUH ?
AH !
ポーン
TOSS
しま…
NKYAAAH!
ズデデデ
TUMBLE
A-ARE YOU OKAY, CLASS REP !?
NNNGH
I USED TO BE AS STRONG AS ASUNA-SAN …
WHEN DID SHE GET SO MUCH BETTER …?

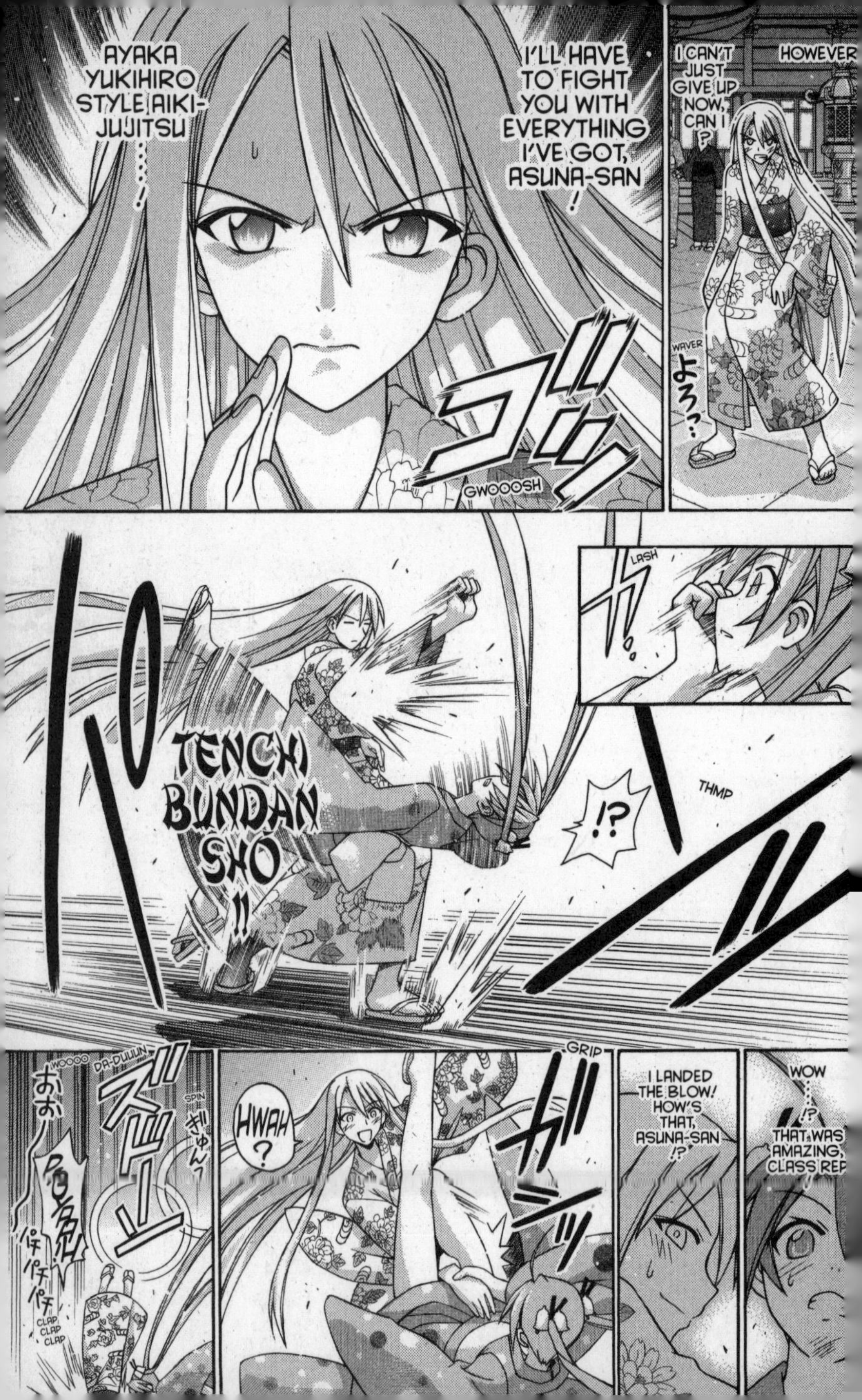

HOWEVER
I CAN'T JUST GIVE UP NOW, CAN I ?
WAVER
よろっ…
I'LL HAVE TO FIGHT YOU WITH EVERYTHING I'VE GOT, ASUNA-SAN !
AYAKA YUKIHIRO STYLE AIKI-JUJITSU ...!
GWOOOSH
LASH
THMP
!?
TENCHI BUNDAN SHO !!
WOW ...!?
THAT WAS AMAZING, CLASS REP
I LANDED THE BLOW! HOW'S THAT, ASUNA-SAN !?
GRIP
HWAH ?
SPIN
DA-DUUUN
WOOOO
CLAP CLAP CLAP

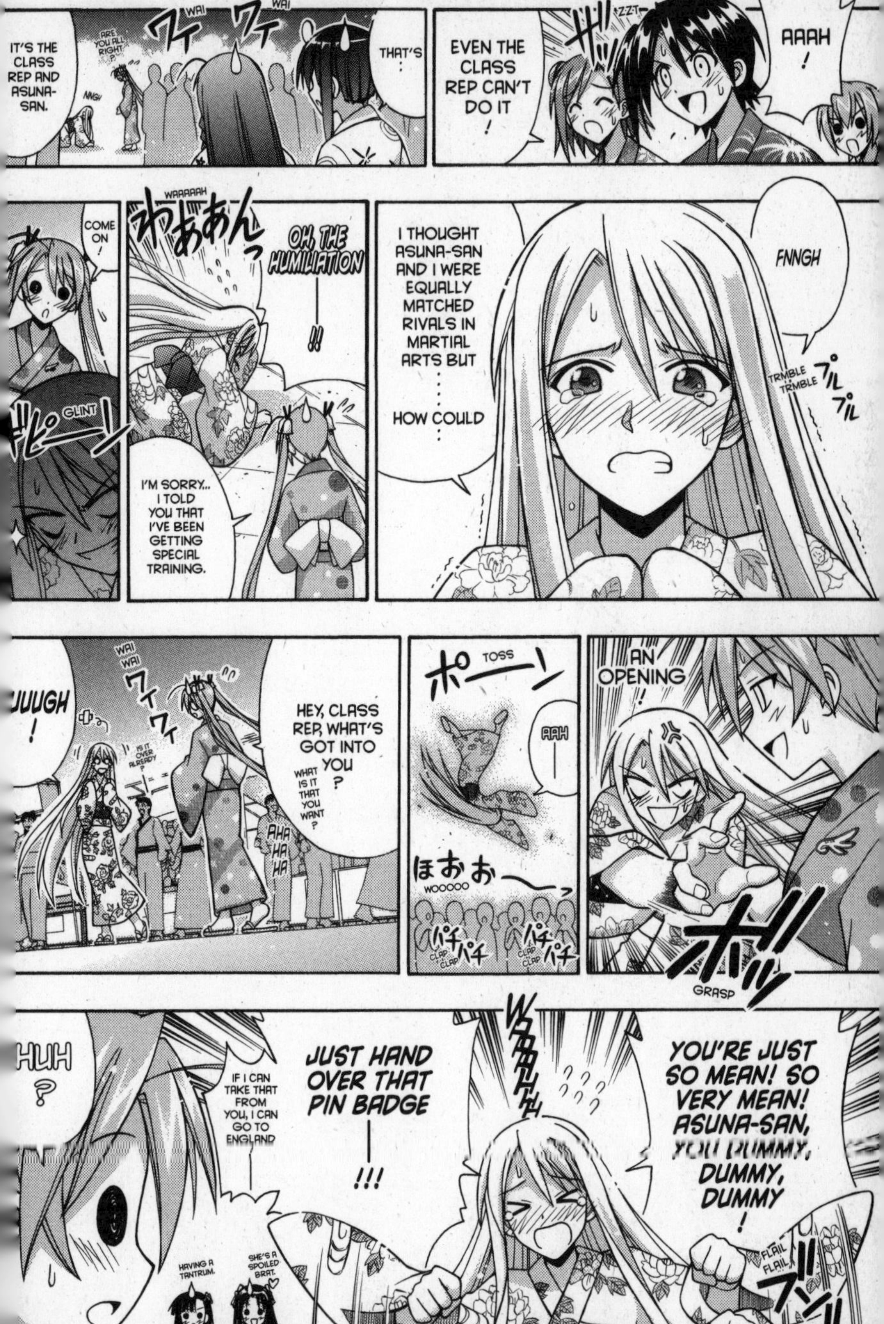
AAAH!
ZZZT
EVEN THE CLASS REP CAN'T DO IT!
THAT'S...
WAI WAI
ARE YOU ALL RIGHT?
NNGH
IT'S THE CLASS REP AND ASUNA-SAN.
FNNGH
TRMBLE TRMBLE
I THOUGHT ASUNA-SAN AND I WERE EQUALLY MATCHED RIVALS IN MARTIAL ARTS BUT...... HOW COULD......
WAAAAAH
OH, THE HUMILIATION —!!
I'M SORRY... I TOLD YOU THAT I'VE BEEN GETTING SPECIAL TRAINING.
COME ON!
GLINT
AN OPENING!
GRASP
TOSS
AAH —
WOOOOO
CLAP CLAP
CLAP CLAP
HEY, CLASS REP, WHAT'S GOT INTO YOU?
WHAT IS IT THAT YOU WANT?
AHAHAHA
IS IT OVER ALREADY?
WAI WAI
UUUGH!
YOU'RE JUST SO MEAN! SO VERY MEAN! ASUNA-SAN, YOU DUMMY, DUMMY, DUMMY!
FLAIL FLAIL
JUST HAND OVER THAT PIN BADGE —!!!
IF I CAN TAKE THAT FROM YOU, I CAN GO TO ENGLAND
SHE'S A SPOILED BRAT.
HAVING A TANTRUM.
HUH?

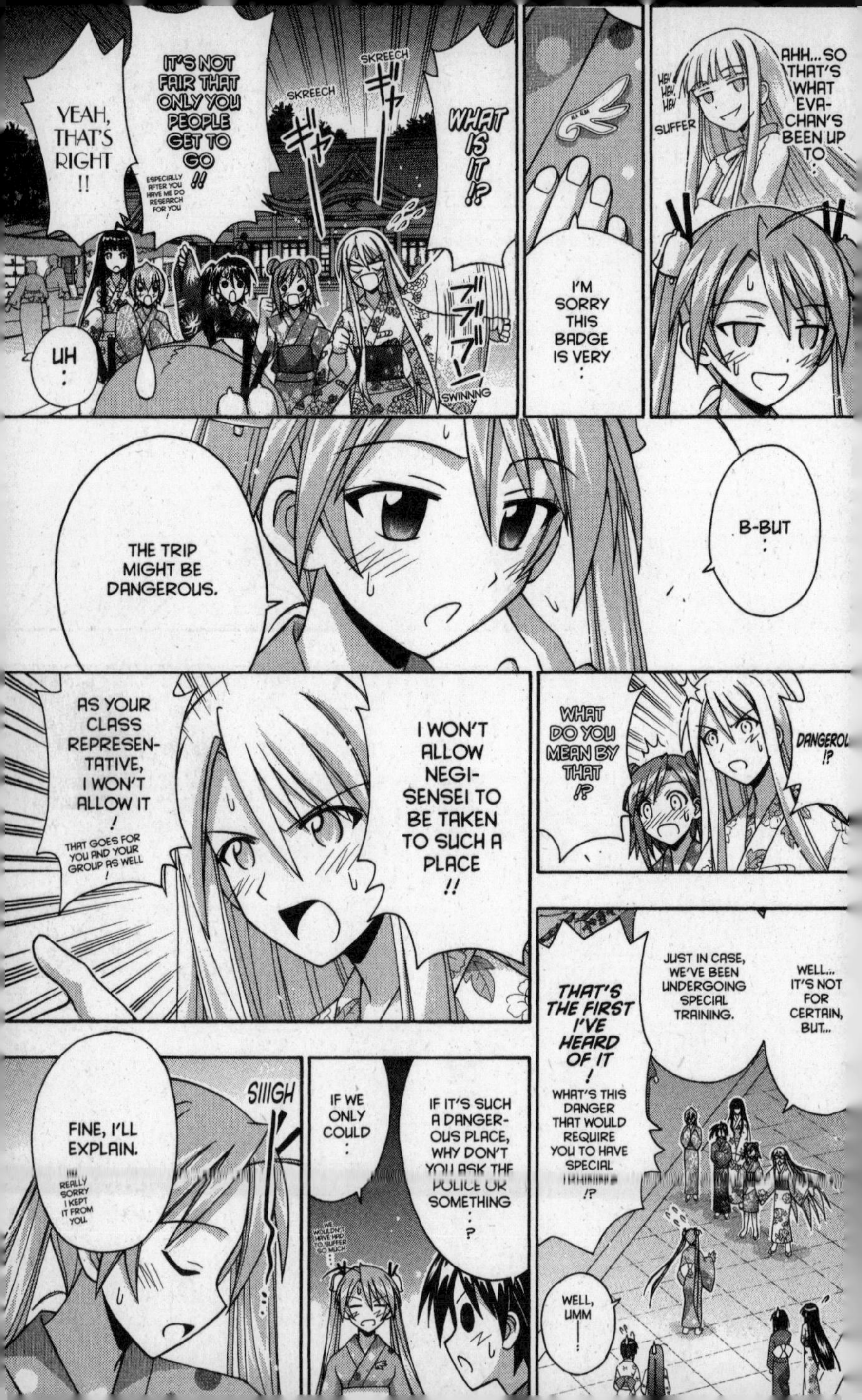
AHH... SO THAT'S WHAT EVA-CHAN'S BEEN UP TO :
HEH HEH HEH
SUFFER
I'M SORRY THIS BADGE IS VERY :
WHAT IS IT !?
SKREECH
SKREECH
IT'S NOT FAIR THAT ONLY YOU PEOPLE GET TO GO !!
ESPECIALLY AFTER YOU HAVE ME DO RESEARCH FOR YOU !
YEAH, THAT'S RIGHT !!
SWINNNG
UH :
B-BUT :
THE TRIP MIGHT BE DANGEROUS.
DANGEROU !?
WHAT DO YOU MEAN BY THAT !?
WELL... IT'S NOT FOR CERTAIN, BUT...
JUST IN CASE, WE'VE BEEN UNDERGOING SPECIAL TRAINING.
THAT'S THE FIRST I'VE HEARD OF IT !
WHAT'S THIS DANGER THAT WOULD REQUIRE YOU TO HAVE SPECIAL !?
WELL, UMM !
I WON'T ALLOW NEGI-SENSEI TO BE TAKEN TO SUCH A PLACE !!
AS YOUR CLASS REPRESENTATIVE, I WON'T ALLOW IT !
THAT GOES FOR YOU AND YOUR GROUP AS WELL !
IF IT'S SUCH A DANGEROUS PLACE, WHY DON'T YOU ASK THE POLICE OR SOMETHING ..?
IF WE ONLY COULD :
WE WOULDN'T HAVE HAD TO SUFFER SO MUCH
SIIIGH
FINE, I'LL EXPLAIN.
REALLY SORRY I KEPT IT FROM YOU.

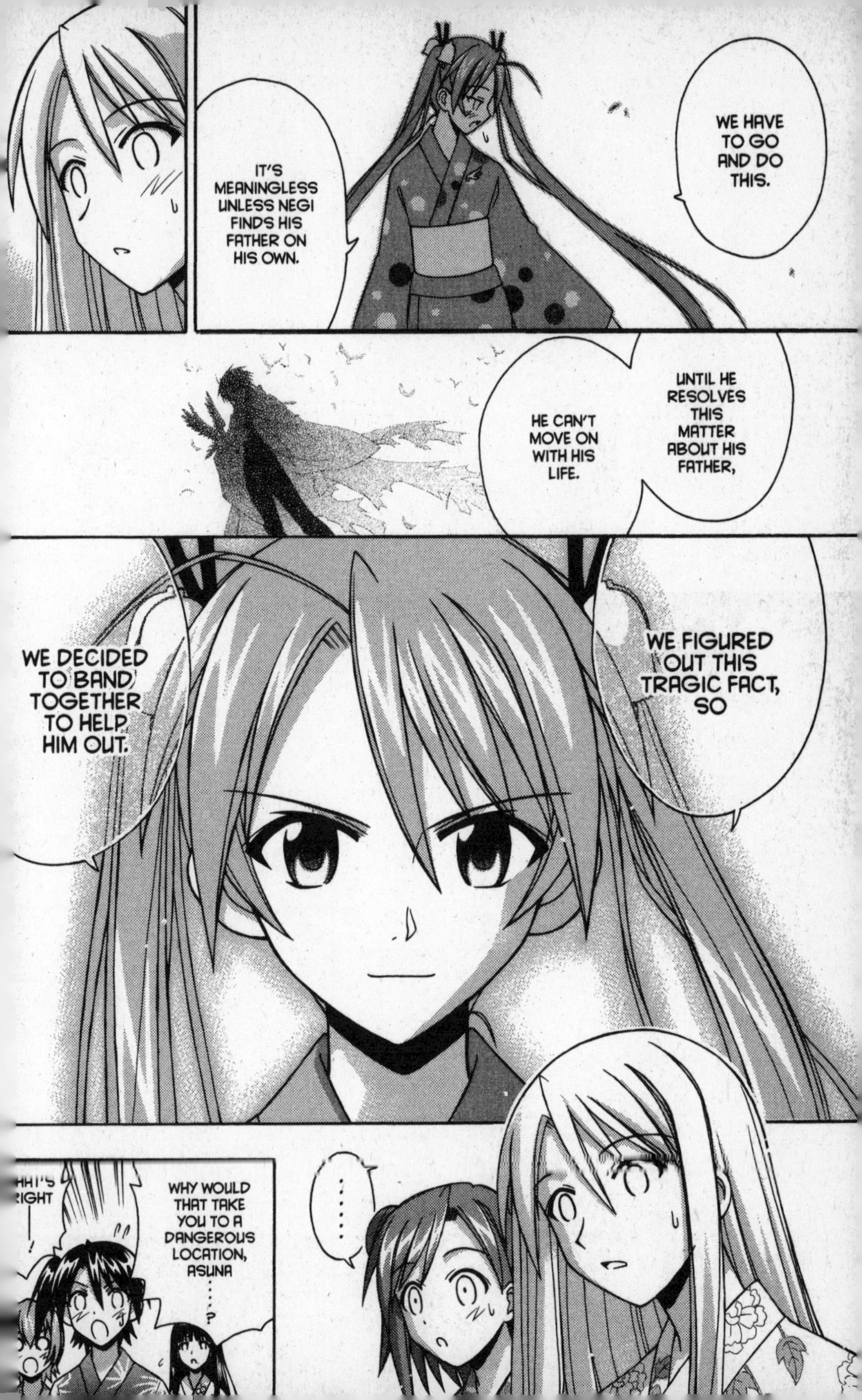
WE HAVE TO GO AND DO THIS.
IT'S MEANINGLESS UNLESS NEGI FINDS HIS FATHER ON HIS OWN.
UNTIL HE RESOLVES THIS MATTER ABOUT HIS FATHER,
HE CAN'T MOVE ON WITH HIS LIFE.
WE FIGURED OUT THIS TRAGIC FACT, SO
WE DECIDED TO BAND TOGETHER TO HELP HIM OUT.
......
WHY WOULD THAT TAKE YOU TO A DANGEROUS LOCATION, ASUNA
.....?
HAT'S RIGHT
—!

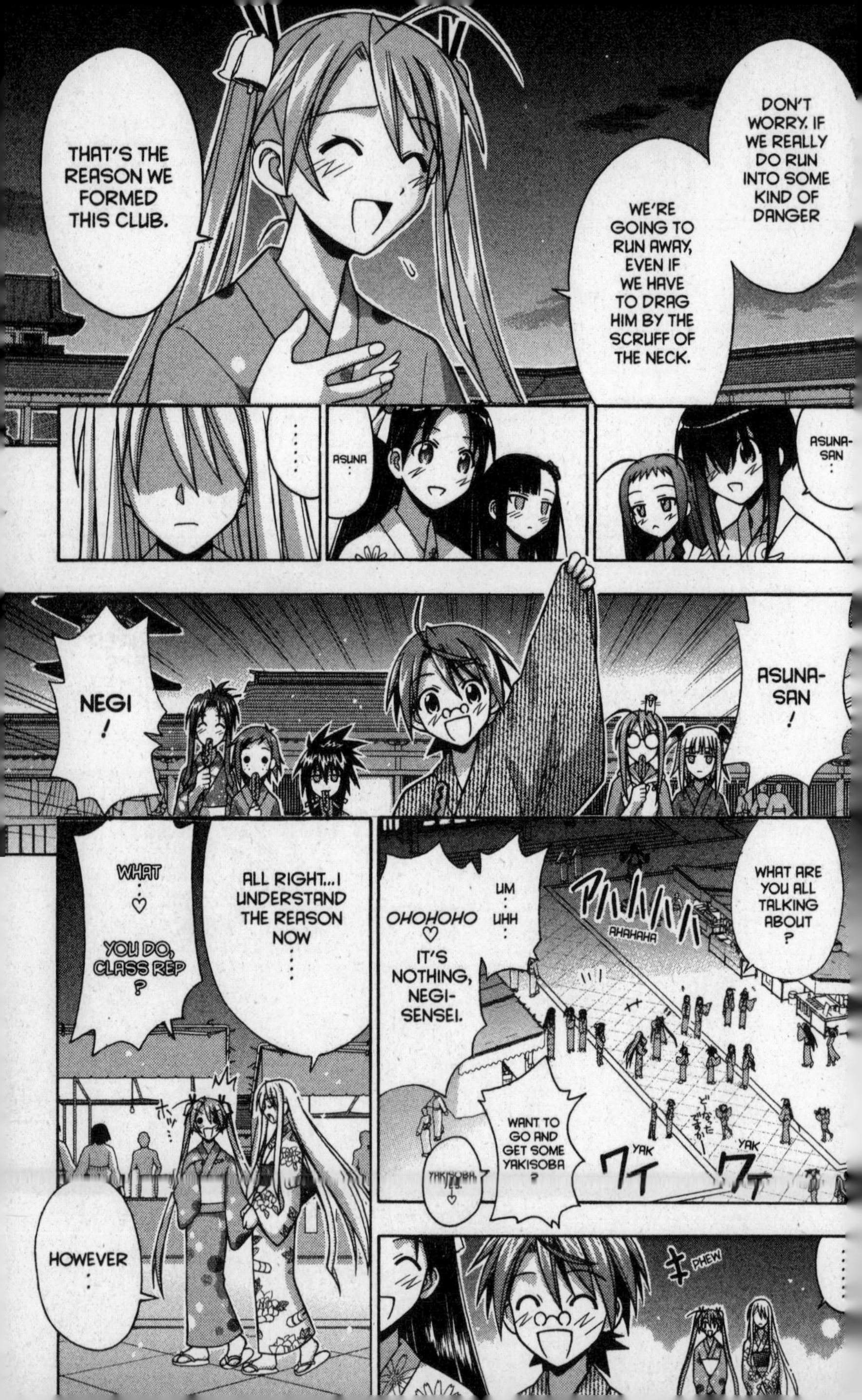
DON'T WORRY. IF WE REALLY DO RUN INTO SOME KIND OF DANGER
WE'RE GOING TO RUN AWAY, EVEN IF WE HAVE TO DRAG HIM BY THE SCRUFF OF THE NECK.
THAT'S THE REASON WE FORMED THIS CLUB.
ASUNA-SAN...
ASUNA...
......
ASUNA-SAN!
NEGI!
WHAT ARE YOU ALL TALKING ABOUT?
AHAHAHA
UM... UHH...
OHOHOHO ♡ IT'S NOTHING, NEGI-SENSEI.
WANT TO GO AND GET SOME YAKISOBA?
YAKISOBA YES. ♡
YAK
YAK
PHEW
...
ALL RIGHT...I UNDERSTAND THE REASON NOW...
WHAT...♡ YOU DO, CLASS REP?
HOWEVER...

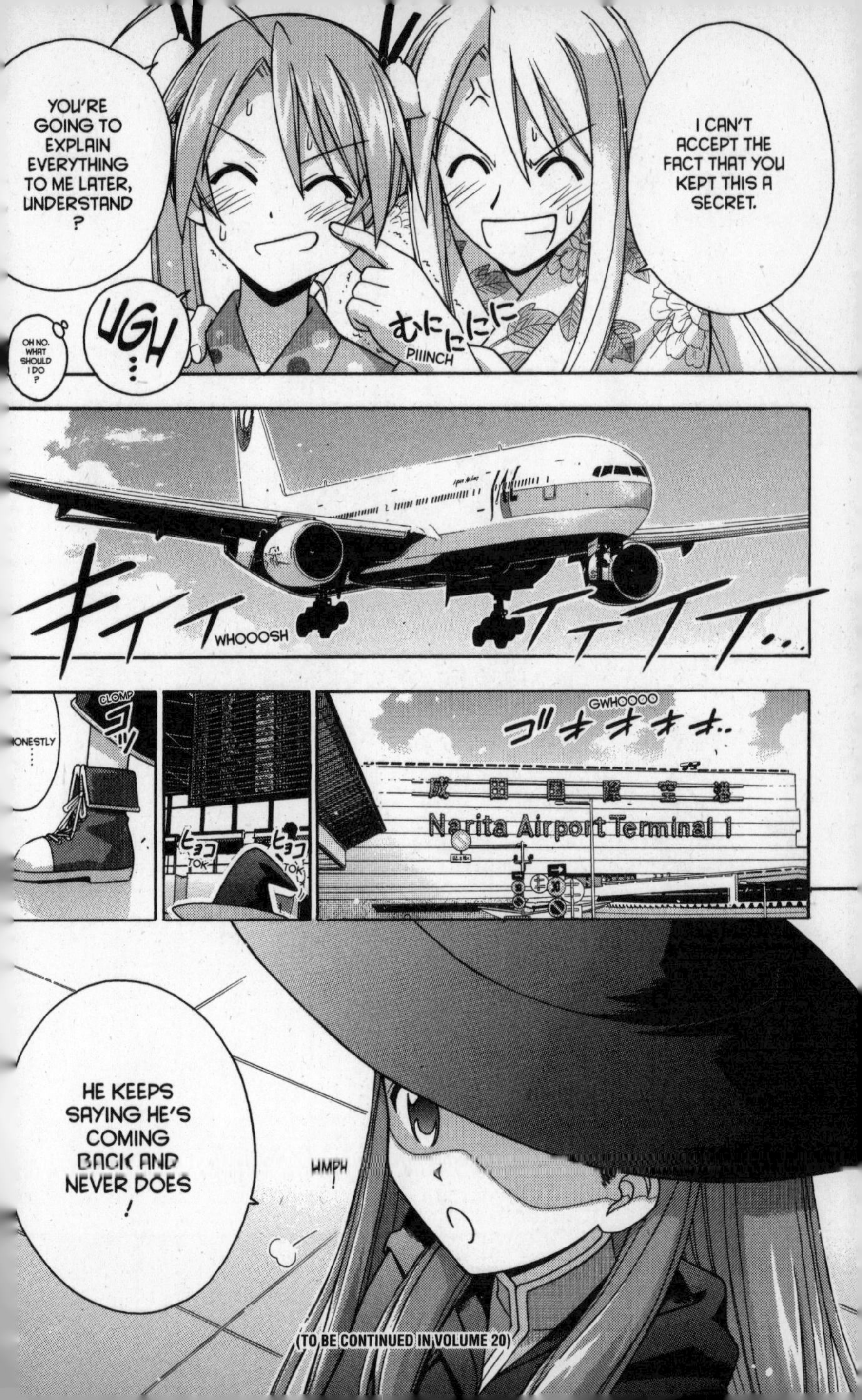
I CAN'T ACCEPT THE FACT THAT YOU KEPT THIS A SECRET.
むにににに
PIIINCH
YOU'RE GOING TO EXPLAIN EVERYTHING TO ME LATER, UNDERSTAND?
UGH...
OH NO. WHAT SHOULD I DO?
キイイイイイ..
WHOOOSH
GWHOOOO
ゴォォォォ..
成田国際空港
Narita Airport Terminal 1
ヒョコ
TOK
ヒョコ
TOK
CLOMP
ゴッ
HONESTLY...
HE KEEPS SAYING HE'S COMING BACK AND NEVER DOES!
HMPH!
(TO BE CONTINUED IN VOLUME 20)

- STAFF -

Ken Akamatsu
Takashi Takemoto
Kenichi Nakamura
Masaki Ohyama
Keiichi Yamashita
Tadashi Maki
Tohru Mitsuhashi

Thanks To

Ran Ayanaga

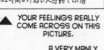

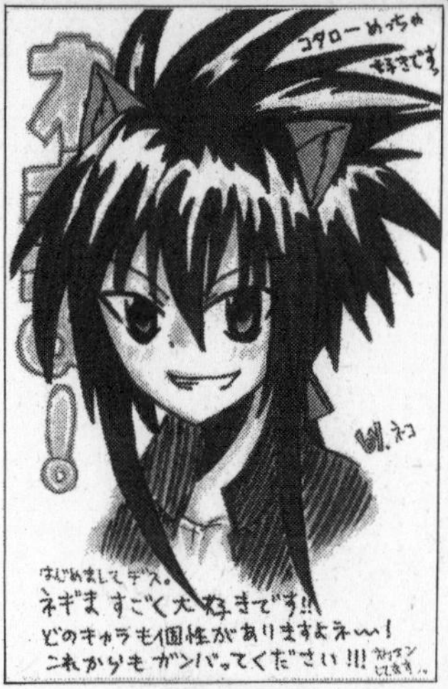
コタロー めっちゃ好きです
はじめましてデス。
ネギま すごく大好きです!!
どのキャラも個性がありますよネ～!
これからもガンバってください!!!

A VERY MANLY LOOKING KOTARŌ.

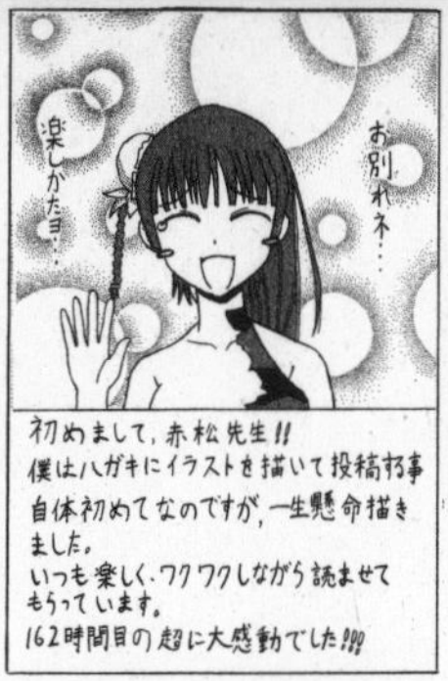
お別れネ…
楽しかたヨ…
初めまして，赤松先生!!
僕はハガキにイラストを描いて投稿する事
自体初めてなのですが，一生懸命描きました。
いつも楽しく，ワクワクしながら読ませてもらっています。
162時間目の超に大感動でした!!!

YOUR FEELINGS REALLY COME ACROSS ON THIS PICTURE.

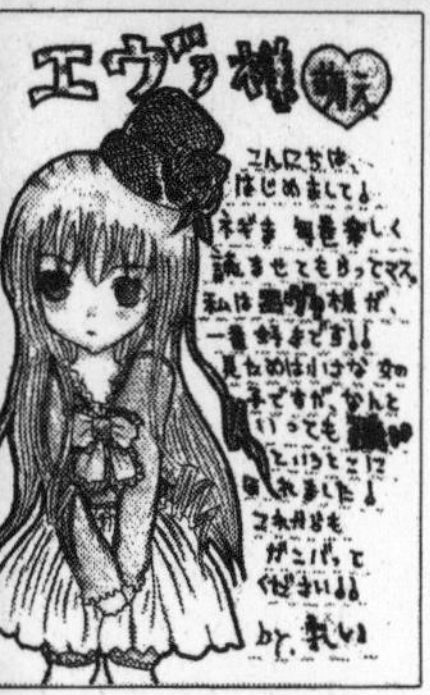
エヴァ様 萌え
こんにちは。
はじめまして。
ネギま 毎巻楽しく読ませてもらってマス。

A VERY CUTE OUTFIT!

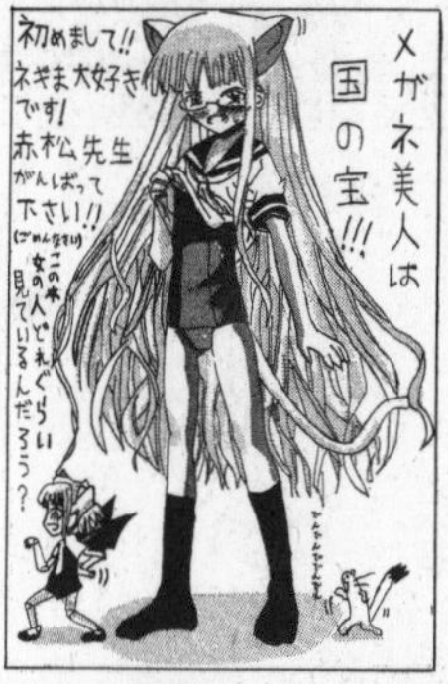
メガネ美人は国の宝!!!
初めまして!!
ネギま大好きです!
赤松先生がんばって下さい!!

I CAN FEEL YOUR PASSION IN THIS PICTURE!

NEGIMA!

FAN ART CORNER

I HAVE A HARD TIME ORGANIZING THIS SECTION IN EVERY VOLUME. (^^;) THERE ARE SO MANY PIECES OF ARTWORK I WANT TO INCLUDE, BUT I CAN'T! ☆ RECENT TRENDS: I'VE NOTICED LOTS OF PICTURES OF PEOPLE SAYING GOODBYE TO CHAO AND CUTE VERSIONS OF EVA. I REALLY ENJOY IT WHEN THE ARTWORK PEOPLE SEND IN ARE RELATED TO THE STORYLINE. ☆ PLEASE SEND YOUR CONTRIBUTIONS TO THE EDITORIAL OFFICES OF KODANSHA COMICS! ☆

TEXT BY ASSISTANT MAX

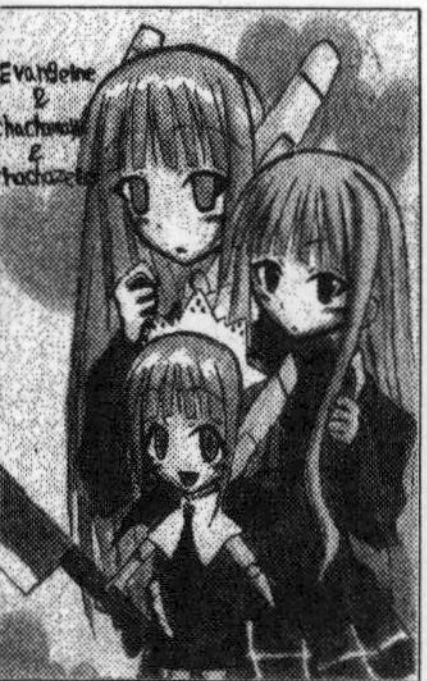

CHACHAZERO LOOKS REALLY CUTE! ★

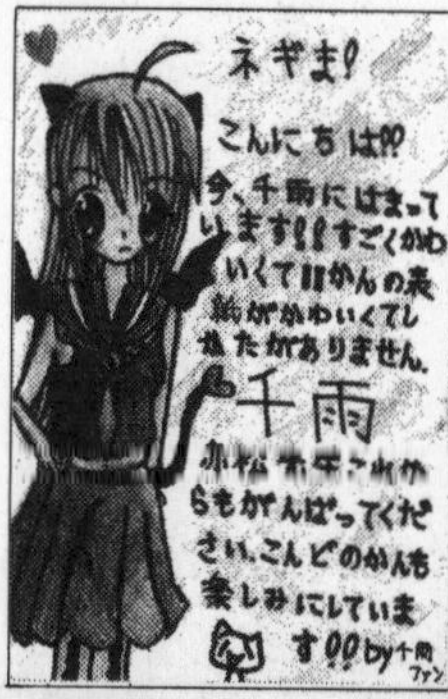
ネギま!
こんにちは!?
今、千雨にはまっています!!すごくかわいくて!!かんの表紙がかわいくてしかたありません。
千雨
赤松先生これからもがんばってください。こんどのかんも楽しみにしています!!
by千雨ファン

A FAN OF CHIU, HUH?

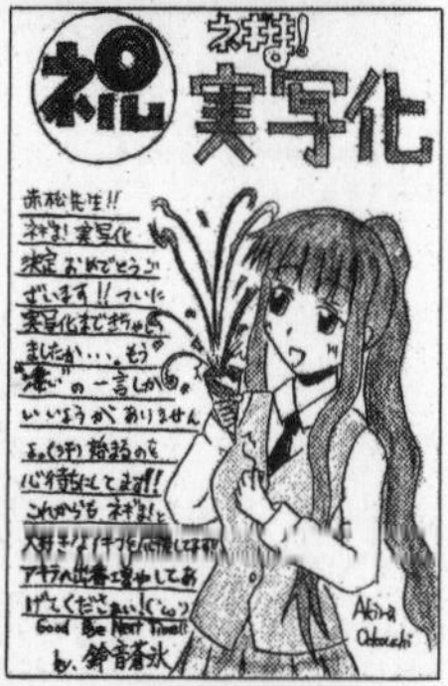
ネギま! 実写化
赤松先生!!
Akira Okochi

I HOPE AKIRA GETS SOME ACTION SOON, TOO!

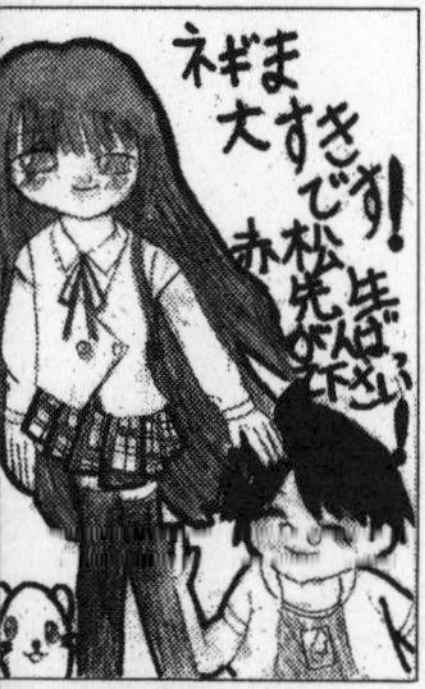
ネギま 大すきです! 赤松先生がんばって下さい

NEGI SEEMS VERY HAPPY.

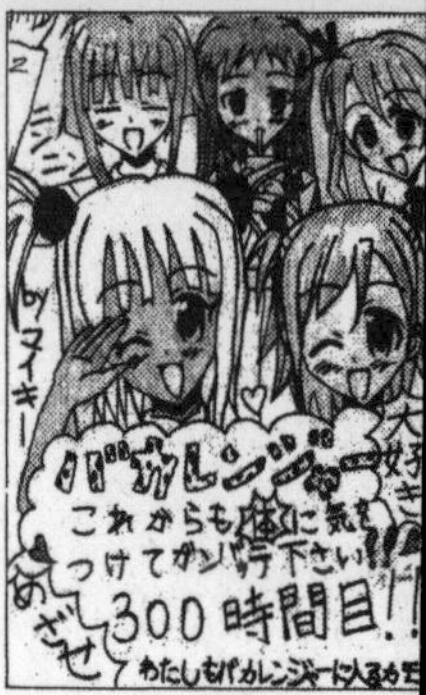
バカレンジャー
これからも体に気をつけてガンバって下さい!!
300時間目!

▲ LOOKS LIKE THEY'RE HAVING FUN. ★

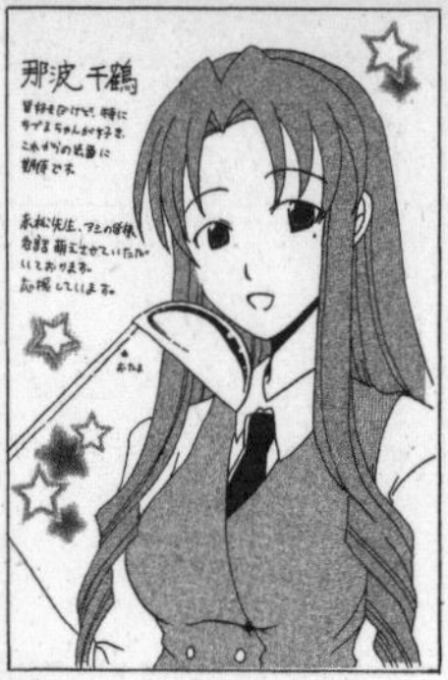
那波千鶴

◀ THIS IS VERY NEATLY DRAWN.

▼ THE ULTIMATE TEAM-UP. (^^)

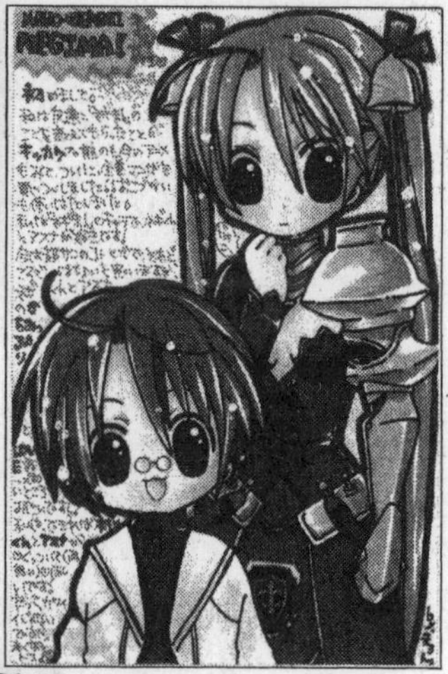

▶ THERE'S AN ELEGANT QUALITY TO THIS PICTURE.

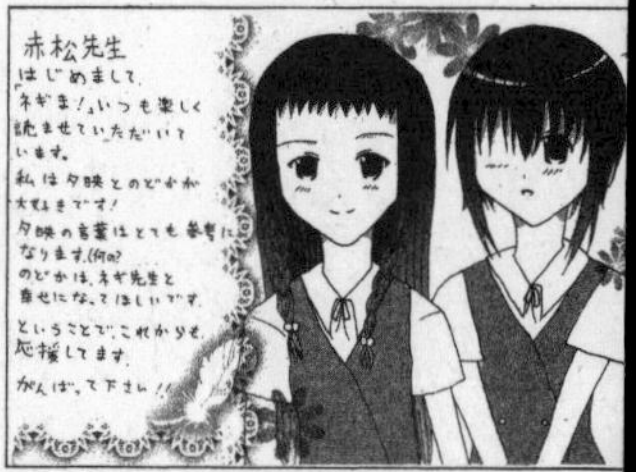
赤松先生
はじめまして
「ネギま!」いつも楽しく読ませていただいています。
私は夕映とのどかが大好きです!
がんばって下さい!!

▼ THEIR EXPRESSIONS ARE LOVELY.

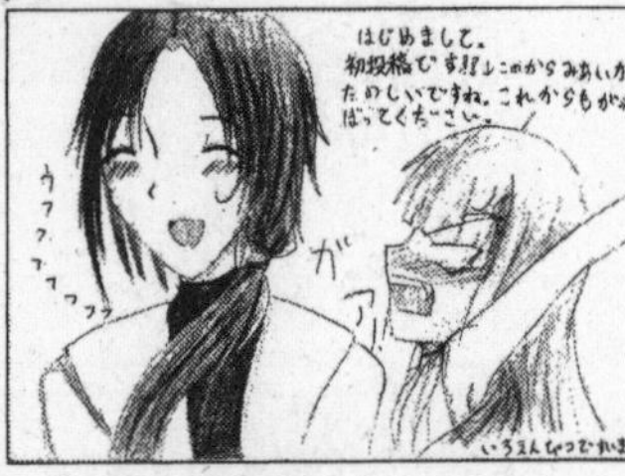
はじめまして。

▶ LET'S AVOID THE REALLY STRANGE BEVERAGES. (LAUGHS)

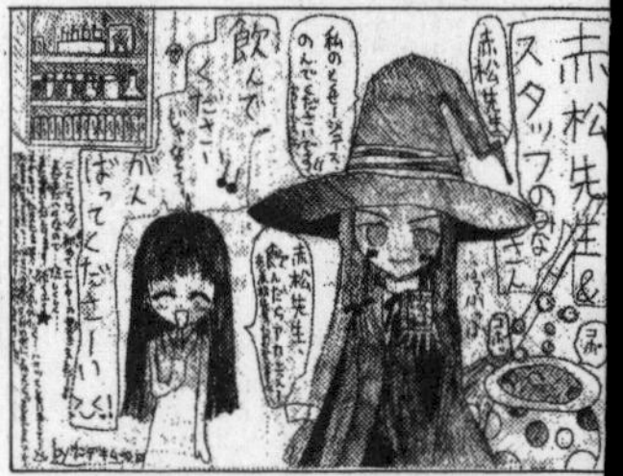
赤松先生&スタッフのみなさん
飲んでください
がんばってください

▼ NOW THIS IS AN INTERESTING TRIO.

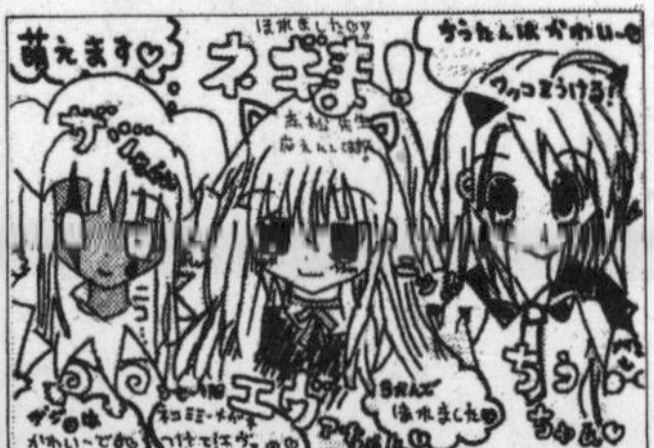
萌えます♡
ネギま!

▶ HAPPY BIRTHDAY! ★

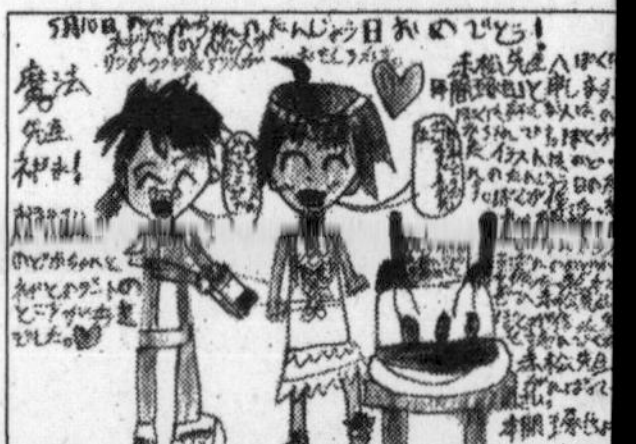
魔法先生ネギま!

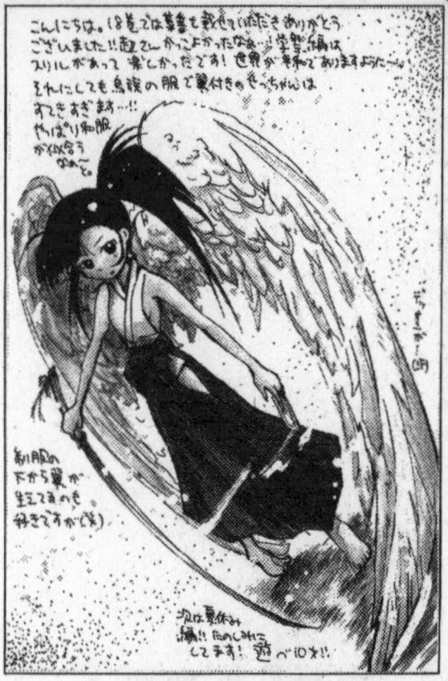

THE GENTLE USE OF COLOR IS WONDERFUL.

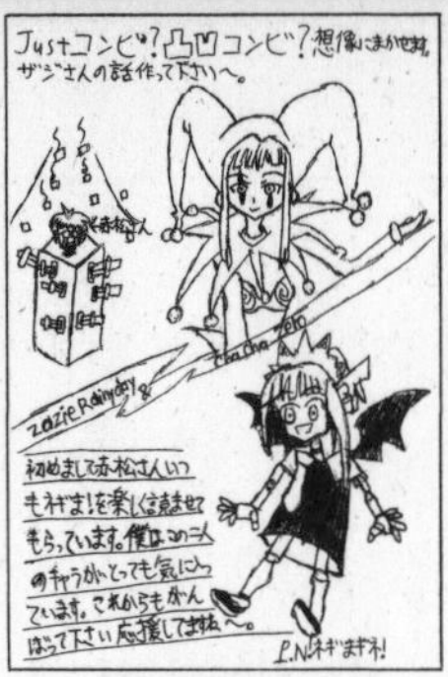

THEY MIGHT ACTUALLY MAKE A REALLY GOOD TEAM...

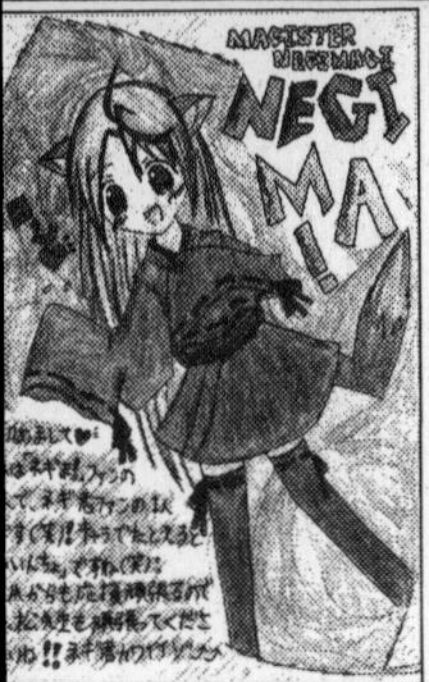
MAGISTER NEGI MAGI
NEGI MA!

THIS NEGI LOOKS VERY CUTE IN PINK!

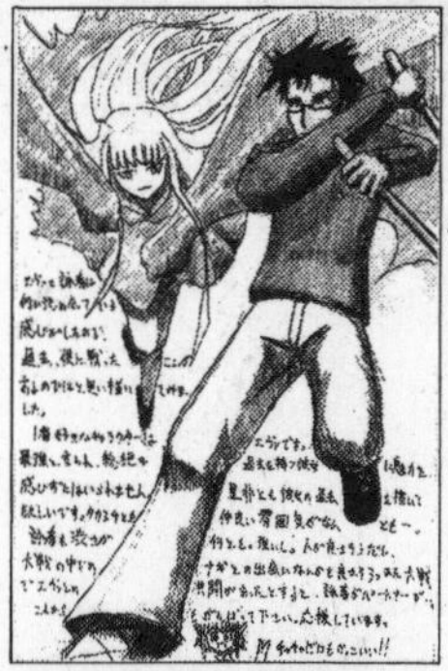

YOU CAN REALLY GET THE SENSE OF MOTION IN THIS PICTURE.

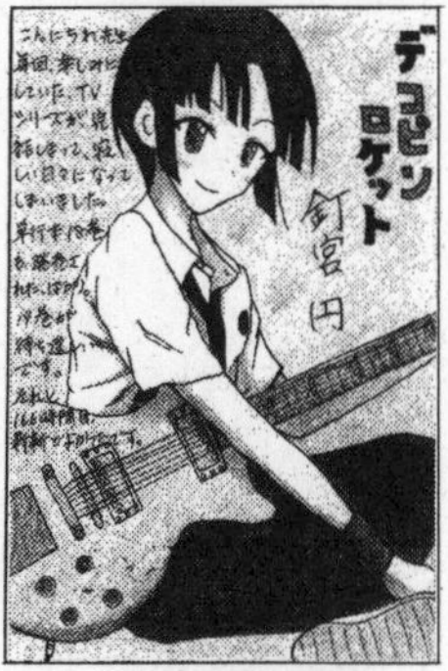
デコピンロケット
釘宮円

THE GUITAR REALLY SUITS HER IN THIS PICTURE. ★

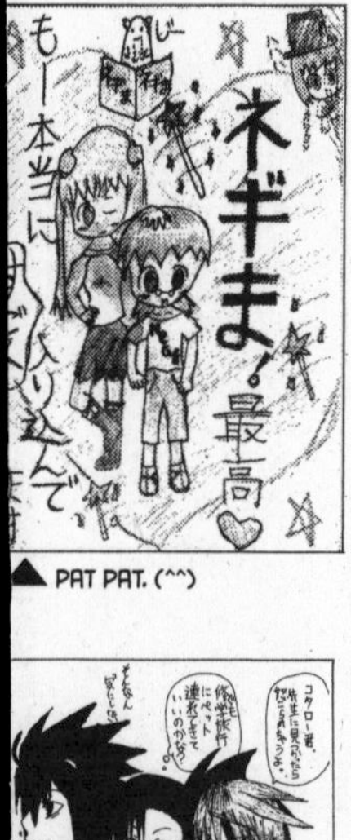
ネギま！最高

PAT PAT. (^^)

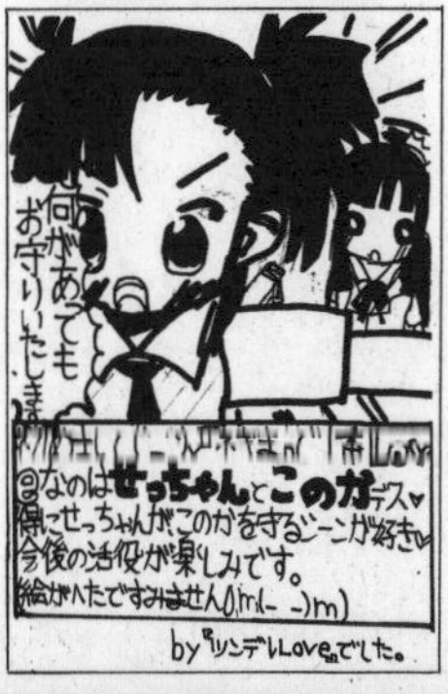
何があってもお守りいたします
今後の活役が楽しみです。
by「ツンデレLove」でした。

A VERY HEROIC-LOOKING SETSUNA.

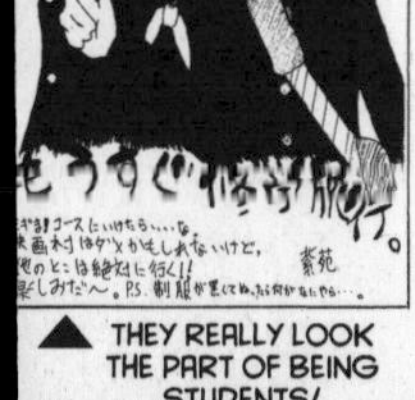

THEY REALLY LOOK THE PART OF BEING STUDENTS!

NEGI MA!

NEGI MAGI

MAGISTER

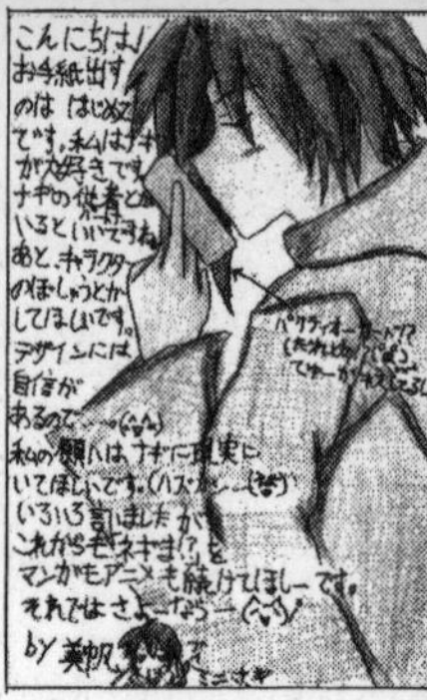
こんにちは!

▲ NAGI'S EXPRESSION IS VERY NICE.

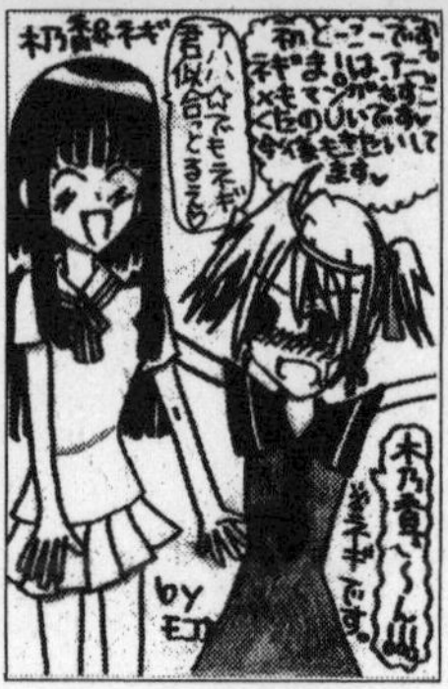
by モエ

▲ WE DIDN'T REALIZE THIS WAS NEGI...

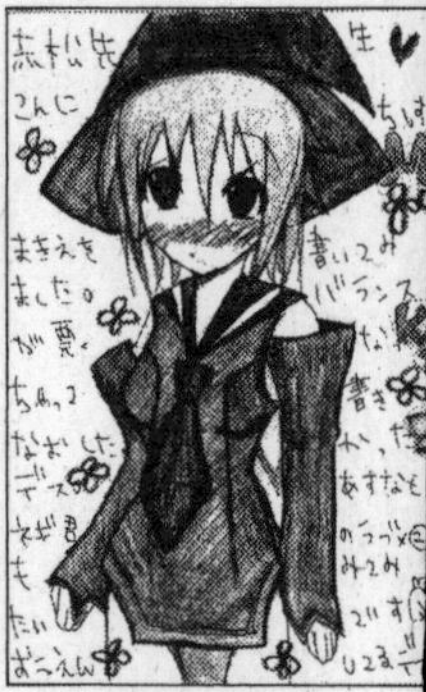

▲ MAKIE LOOKING VERY TIRED.

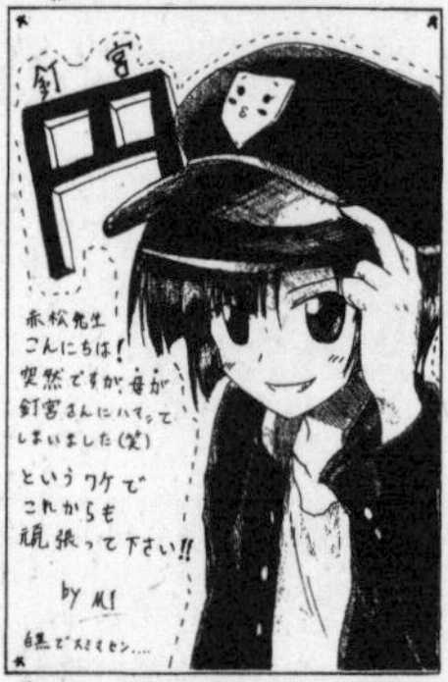
赤松先生
こんにちは!
というワケで
これからも
頑張って下さい!!
by M!

▲ A VERY COOL-LOOKING MADOKA!

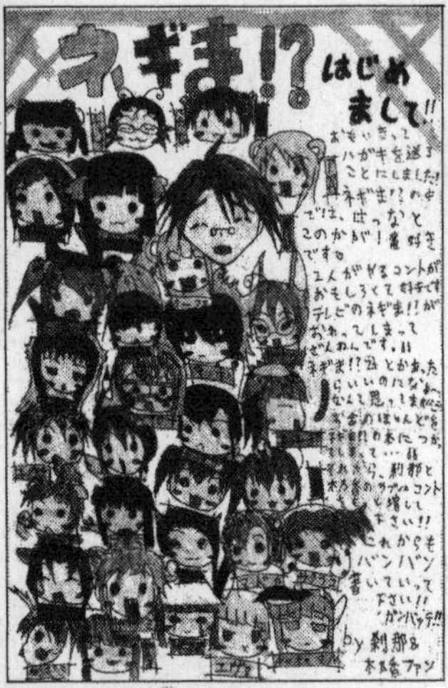
ネギま!?
はじめ
まして!!

▲ EACH FACE IS SO CUTE. ★

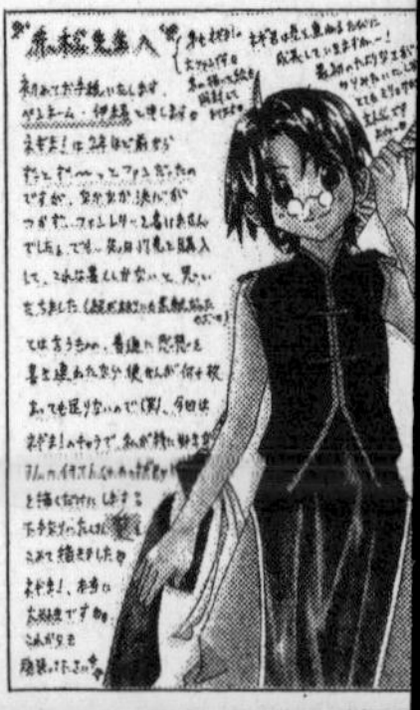

▲ A VERY MATURE-LOOKING NEGI.

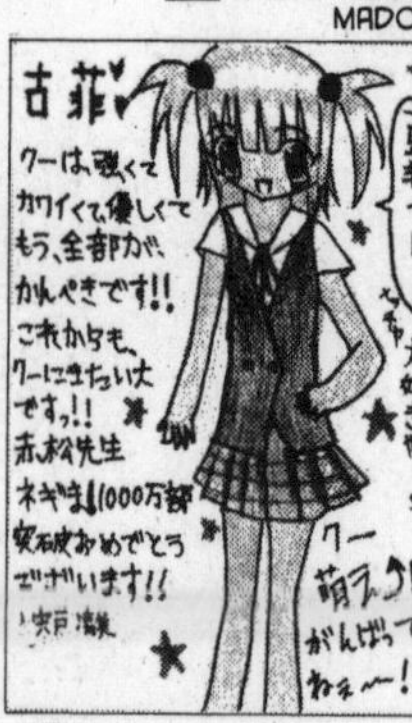
古菲
古菲アルッ★
がんばってねぇ~!!

▲ KEEP ON CHEERING FOR KŪ! ★

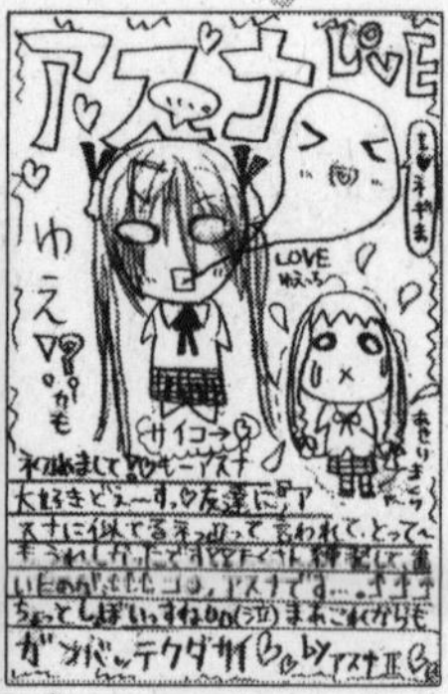
アスナ
LOVE

▲ WE REALLY LOVE THIS ASUNA! (LAUGHS)

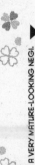

3-D BACKGROUNDS EXPLANATION CORNER

IN THIS VOLUME, WE HAD A VARIETY OF VERY BIG STRUCTURES AND VERY SMALL ITEMS.

• LEBENS SCHULD CASTLE

SCENE NAME: EVA'S CASTLE

POLYGON COUNT: 576,479

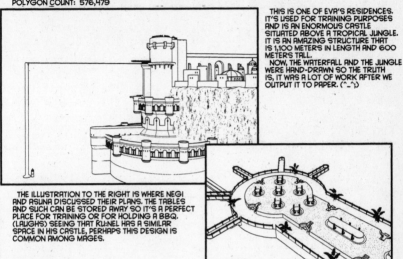

THIS IS ONE OF EVA'S RESIDENCES. IT'S USED FOR TRAINING PURPOSES AND IS AN ENORMOUS CASTLE SITUATED ABOVE A TROPICAL JUNGLE. IT IS AN AMAZING STRUCTURE THAT IS 1,100 METERS IN LENGTH AND 600 METERS TALL.

NOW, THE WATERFALL AND THE JUNGLE WERE HAND-DRAWN SO THE TRUTH IS, IT WAS A LOT OF WORK AFTER WE OUTPUT IT TO PAPER. (^_^;)

THE ILLUSTRATION TO THE RIGHT IS WHERE NEGI AND ASUNA DISCUSSED THEIR PLANS. THE TABLES AND SUCH CAN BE STORED AWAY SO IT'S A PERFECT PLACE FOR TRAINING OR FOR HOLDING A BBQ. (LAUGHS) SEEING THAT KU:NEL HAS A SIMILAR SPACE IN HIS CASTLE, PERHAPS THIS DESIGN IS COMMON AMONG MAGES.

YŪNA'S HOUSE

CENE NAME: YŪNA'S ROOM

OLYGON COUNT: 70,150

THIS IS THE APARTMENT THAT YŪNA'S FATHER, WHO IS A PROFESSOR AT MAHORA UNIVERSITY, RESIDES IN AND IS YŪNA'S HOME.

THE DESIGN INSIDE IS VERY COMMON LOOKING, BUT FOR THE STORY, THERE WERE SEVERAL ROOMS THAT WERE CREATED. YŪNA'S ROOM, THE STUDY, KITCHEN AND DINING ROOM, AND SO ON.

• KITCHEN & DINING ROOM

A KITCHEN THAT LOOKS LIKE IT CAN MAKE BETTER THINGS THAN JUST BOIL-A-BAG CURRIES. (LAUGHS)

AND AGAIN, A LOT OF THE MODELS USED IN THIS ROOM ARE FROM A ROOM THAT WASN'T USED PREVIOUSLY.

• YŪNA'S ROOM

IT'S A RATHER GIRLY ROOM WITH TEDDY BEARS AND ALL. THE TRUTH IS, MANY OF THE ITEMS IN THIS ROOM ARE RECYCLED FROM A ROOM THAT DIDN'T GET USED PREVIOUSLY. BUT THIS ISN'T A BAD-LOOKING ROOM, IS IT? (LAUGHS)

• GIRLS' DORMITORY LOBBY
SCENE NAME: LOBBY
POLYGON COUNT: 27,696

THIS IS THE SPACIOUS LOBBY LOCATED ON THE FIRST FLOOR OF THE GIRLS' DORMITORY. THIS IS WHERE THE RESIDENTS READ, EAT SNACK FOODS AND WHATNOT, DEPENDING ON THE STUDENT.

THERE'S A LARGE WINDOW IN THE ROOM AND IT MIGHT BE A NICE PLACE TO NAP NEAR AS EVANGELINE WAS DOING. (LAUGHS)

• SUMMER FESTIVAL
SCENE NAME: SUMMER FESTIVAL
POLYGON COUNT: 971,088

THIS IS THE ANNUAL SUMMER FESTIVAL HELD AT TATSUMIYA SHRINE. SHOPS LINE THE PATH FROM THE GATE ALL THE WAY TO THE TEMPLE AND ARE VISITED BY THE MANY PEOPLE LIVING IN MAHORA.

IN TRUTH, THERE WERE SEVEN DIFFERENT MODELS OF SHOPS AND THEY WERE ARRANGED RANDOMLY AND THEN DETAILS LIKE BANNERS AND SIGNS WERE DRAWN BY HAND AFTERWARD.

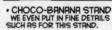

• SHOOTING GALLERY
IF YOU LOOK CAREFULLY, YOU MIGHT RECOGNIZE THE PRIZES... (LAUGHS)

• CHOCO-BANANA STAND
WE EVEN PUT IN FINE DETAILS SUCH AS FOR THIS STAND.

POLY-MEN AND POLY-WOMEN WEARING *YUKATA*. THEN AGAIN, WITHOUT HAIR ON THEM, IT'S HARD TO TELL THEM APART. (^^;)

- BONUS -

• HAND BELL
IT'S A HASSLE TO DRAW THE FINE LINES EACH TIME SO WE MADE A 3-D VERSION. (LAUGHS)

• ALA RUBRA CLUB MEMBER PIN BADGE
SEE EXPLANATION TO THE LEFT. (LAUGHS)

PRELIMINARY DESIGN COLLECTION
~ CHARACTER ROUGH SKETCHES ~

NAME: YŪKO AKASHI
PERSONALITY: SORT OF RANDOM AND NOT FOCUSED
OCCUPATION: PRESCHOOL ASSISTANT (PART-TIME)

VERY INTENSE AT SCHOOL BUT TENDS TO BE A LITTLE UNFOCUSED ABOUT WHAT SHE DOES.

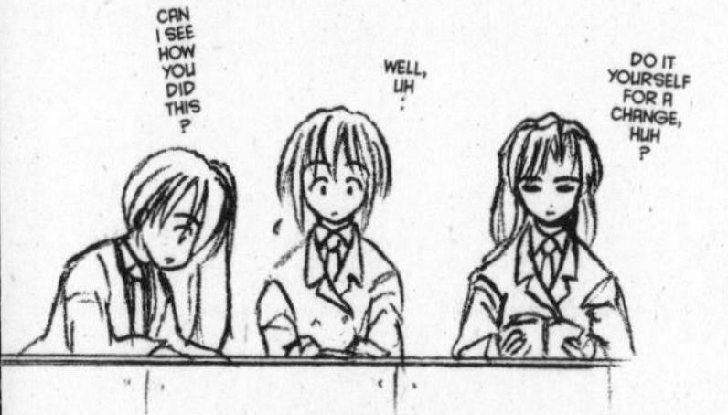
CAN I SEE HOW YOU DID THIS?
WELL, UH...
DO IT YOURSELF FOR A CHANGE, HUH?

[YŪKO AKASHI]

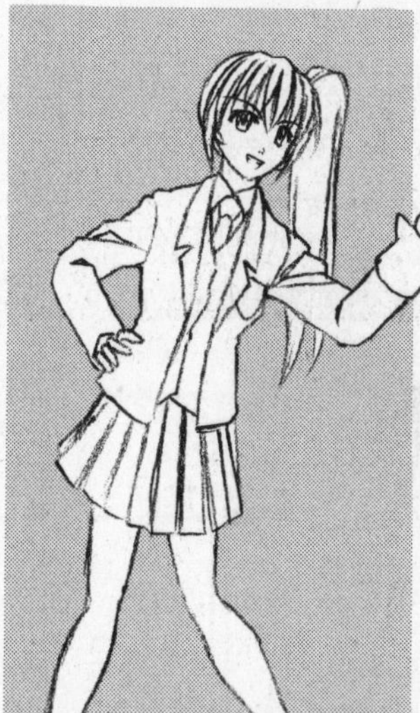

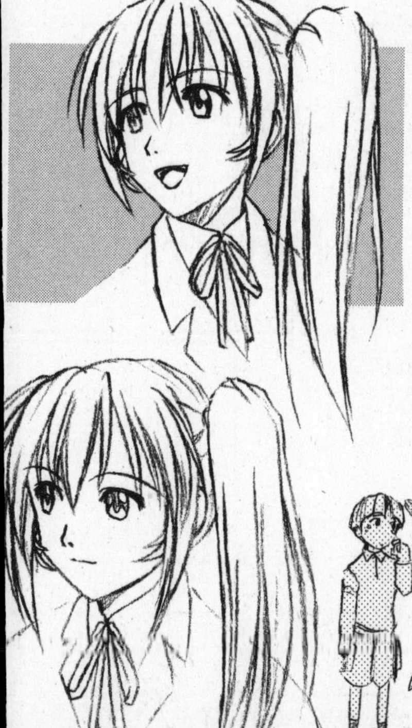

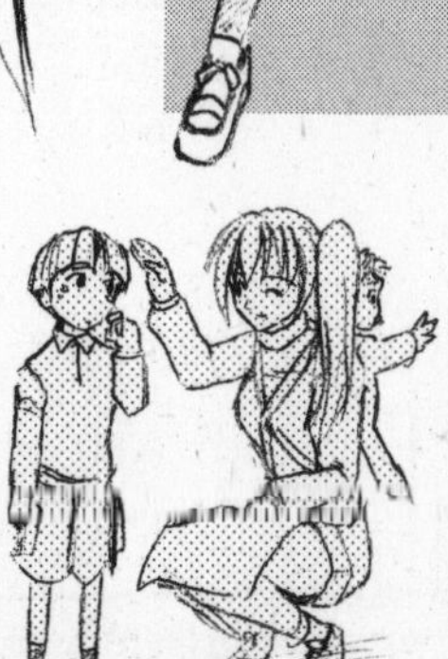

WHETHER SHE'S SERIOUS OR NOT, SHE'S WORKS PART-TIME AT A PRESCHOOL. SHE'S ACTUALLY REALLY GOOD WITH CHILDREN.

THE PRESCHOOL (BECAUSE OF TIME CONSTRAINTS SHE WORKS AT A PRESCHOOL INSTEAD OF A KINDERGARTEN) ACTUALLY COUNTS ON HER QUITE A BIT.

NEGI MA!

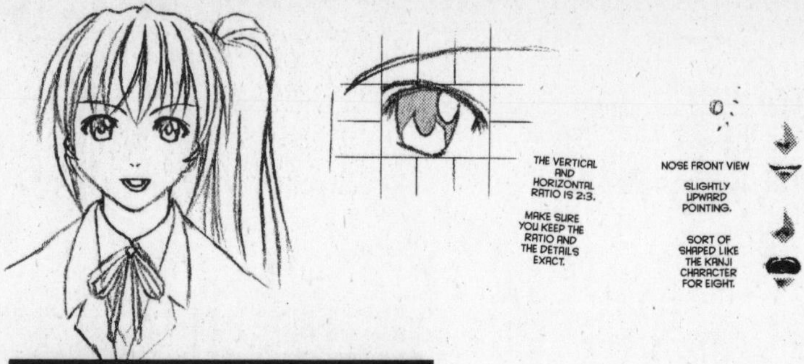

THE VERTICAL AND HORIZONTAL RATIO IS 2:3.
MAKE SURE YOU KEEP THE RATIO AND THE DETAILS EXACT.
NOSE FRONT VIEW
SLIGHTLY UPWARD POINTING.
SORT OF SHAPED LIKE THE KANJI CHARACTER FOR EIGHT.

THESE TWO BECOME YŪNA AND CHIZURU... BUT SOMETHING IS WRONG HERE! THE SECRET OF THAT IS ON THE NEXT PAGE. (LAUGHS) ACTUALLY THINGS LIKE THIS HAPPEN ALL THE TIME.

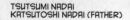

magister negi magi

TSUTSUMI NADAI
KATSUTOSHI NADAI (FATHER)

A DAUGHTER WHO HAS AN EXTREME FATHER COMPLEX, AND HER FATHER. THE FATHER IS A TEACHER AT THE SCHOOL WHERE THE MAIN CHARACTER TEACHES. POSSIBLY HAS A CONNECTION TO THE MAIN CHARACTER'S FATHER AS WELL?

IT'S A FATHER-DAUGHTER-ONLY FAMILY AND DESPITE THE CONSTANT COMPLAINING, SHE ENJOYS TAKING CARE OF HER FATHER. BECAUSE OF THAT, SHE'S VERY GOOD AT COOKING AND OTHER HOUSEHOLD CHORES. HER DREAM FOR HER FUTURE IS BECOMING HER FATHER'S WIFE (HEY NOW!). BUT HER FATHER'S SCHOOL HAS MANY FEMALE TEACHERS, AND THEY ARE A CONSTANT SOURCE OF JEALOUSY FOR HER.

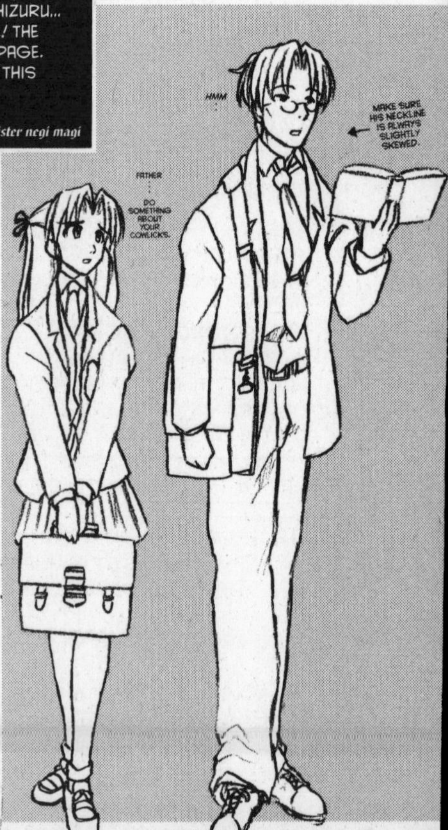

HMM
MAKE SURE HIS NECKLINE IS ALWAYS SLIGHTLY SKEWED.
FATHER
DO SOMETHING ABOUT YOUR COWLICKS.

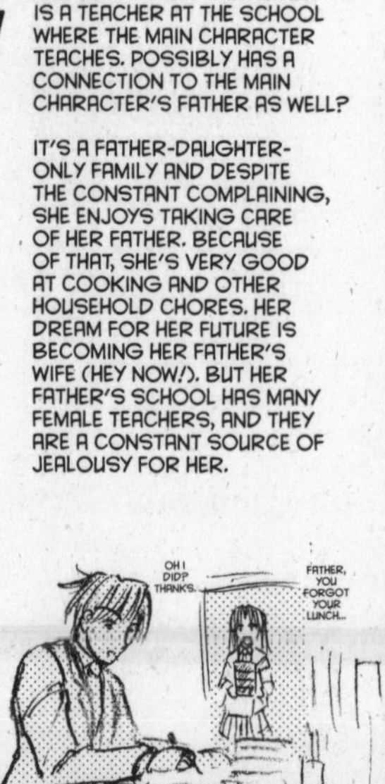

FATHER, YOU FORGOT YOUR LUNCH...
OH! DID? THANKS.

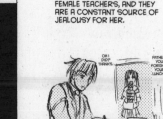

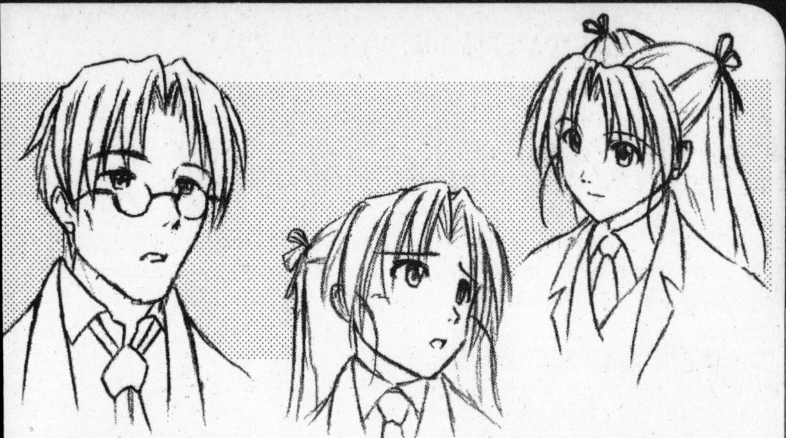

character design INSIDE STORY YŪNA AND CHIZURU WERE CREATED AFTER A PERSONALITY SWAP

THE TWO CHARACTERS FEATURED IN THE PRELIMINARY DESIGN SECTION WERE BASICALLY BUILDING BLOCKS FOR THE FINAL CHARACTERS. THE ENERGETIC CHARACTER OF YŪKO AKASHI BECAME THE BASIS FOR YŪNA AKASHI, BUT SHE TAKES CARE OF CHILDREN FOR HER PART-TIME JOB! IN THE STORY, IT'S ACTUALLY CHIZURU NABA WHO IS THE VOLUNTEER NANNY. AND ON THE OTHER HAND, THE CONCEPT CHARACTER OF TSUTSUMI NADAI HAS YŪNA'S FATHER COMPLEX BUT ISN'T WELL PROPORTIONED OR ENERGETIC.

THE TRUTH IS, THE TWO CONCEPT CHARACTERS BECAME THEIR FINAL FORMS BY SWAPPING OUT THE "NANNY" AND "FATHER COMPLEX" TO END UP WITH:

THE ENERGETIC YET UNFOCUSED GIRL: YŪNA AKASHI

THE VOLUNTEER NANNY WHO WANTS TO TAKE CARE OF OTHERS: CHIZURU NABA.

LEXICON NEGIMARIUM

[*Negima!* 169th Period Lexicon Negimarium]

■ (Let hundreds and thousands combine, run forth lightning. THOUSAND LIGHTNING BOLTS)

• An extremely destructive lightning-based attack spell that has a large area of effect. The spell is incanted in ancient Greek. From the highly destructive power of the spell, it is believed that it requires a great amount of magical power to cast.

[*Negima!* 177th Period Lexicon Negimarium]

■ *lux*

(light)

• An entry-level spell that emits a small light. It is one of the first spells to be taught to a student mage. With experience and practice, the light can be maintained for a prolonged length of time, but for someone with Yue's experience level, only a momentary flash can be achieved. But in darkness, the sudden light can be used to blind an opponent.

■ *elementa aerialis, venti spirantes cito adeuntes ab inimicis meis me defendant LIMES AERIALES*

(Spirits of the air, breath of the winds, come forth and protect us from the enemy. BARRIER OF WIND)

• This is the barrier magic used by Negi in *Negima!*, vol. 16, 145th Period. In this volume, the full incantation has appeared so it's listed here. For the description of the spell, see the lexicon in vol. 16

■ *Diaria Ejus Minora Quadrupla adeant tumcogitaiones vestigent de Makie Sasaki, Yūna Akashi, Akira Ōkōchi, Ako Izumi*

(Picture Diary of ID, four miniature simplified volumes, come forth. Follow the thoughts of Makie Sasaki, Yūna Akashi, Akira Ōkōchi, and Ako Izumi)

• This spell allows Nodoka's artifact, Diarium Ejus (Picture Diary of ID), to separate to read the thoughts of multiple individuals. Adeant is the plural form of Adeat as she is calling forth multiple copies of her artifact. When reading the thoughts of multiple targets, the diary no longer contains pictures but is very effective when dealing with many opponents. Even still, it is difficult for the caster to follow the thoughts of multiple people.

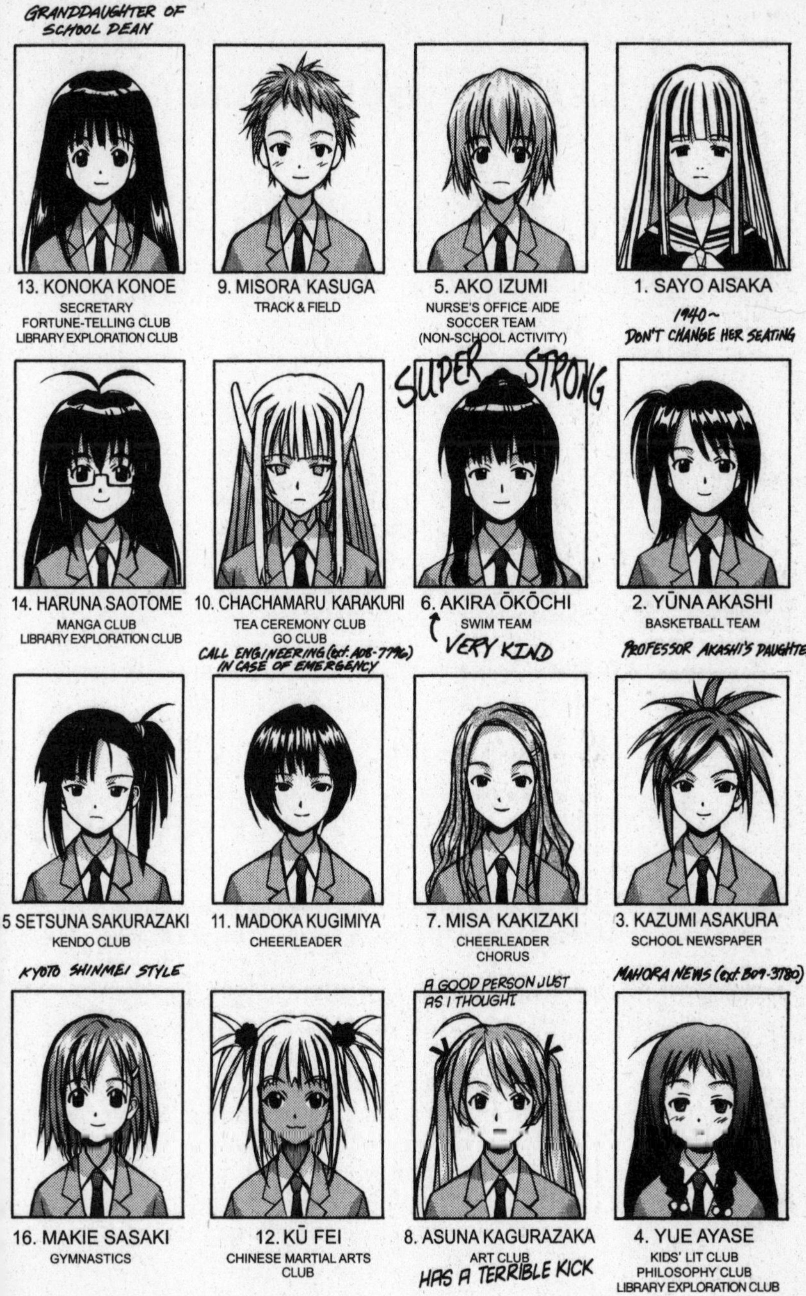

1. SAYO AISAKA
1940~
DON'T CHANGE HER SEATING
5. AKO IZUMI
NURSE'S OFFICE AIDE
SOCCER TEAM
(NON-SCHOOL ACTIVITY)
9. MISORA KASUGA
TRACK & FIELD
GRANDDAUGHTER OF SCHOOL DEAN
13. KONOKA KONOE
SECRETARY
FORTUNE-TELLING CLUB
LIBRARY EXPLORATION CLUB
2. YŪNA AKASHI
BASKETBALL TEAM
PROFESSOR AKASHI'S DAUGHTER
SUPER STRONG
6. AKIRA ŌKŌCHI
SWIM TEAM
VERY KIND
10. CHACHAMARU KARAKURI
TEA CEREMONY CLUB
GO CLUB
CALL ENGINEERING (ext. A08-7796) IN CASE OF EMERGENCY
14. HARUNA SAOTOME
MANGA CLUB
LIBRARY EXPLORATION CLUB
3. KAZUMI ASAKURA
SCHOOL NEWSPAPER
MAHORA NEWS (ext. B09-3780)
7. MISA KAKIZAKI
CHEERLEADER
CHORUS
11. MADOKA KUGIMIYA
CHEERLEADER
5 SETSUNA SAKURAZAKI
KENDO CLUB
KYOTO SHINMEI STYLE
4. YUE AYASE
KIDS' LIT CLUB
PHILOSOPHY CLUB
LIBRARY EXPLORATION CLUB
A GOOD PERSON JUST AS I THOUGHT.
8. ASUNA KAGURAZAKA
ART CLUB
HAS A TERRIBLE KICK
12. KŪ FEI
CHINESE MARTIAL ARTS CLUB
16. MAKIE SASAKI
GYMNASTICS

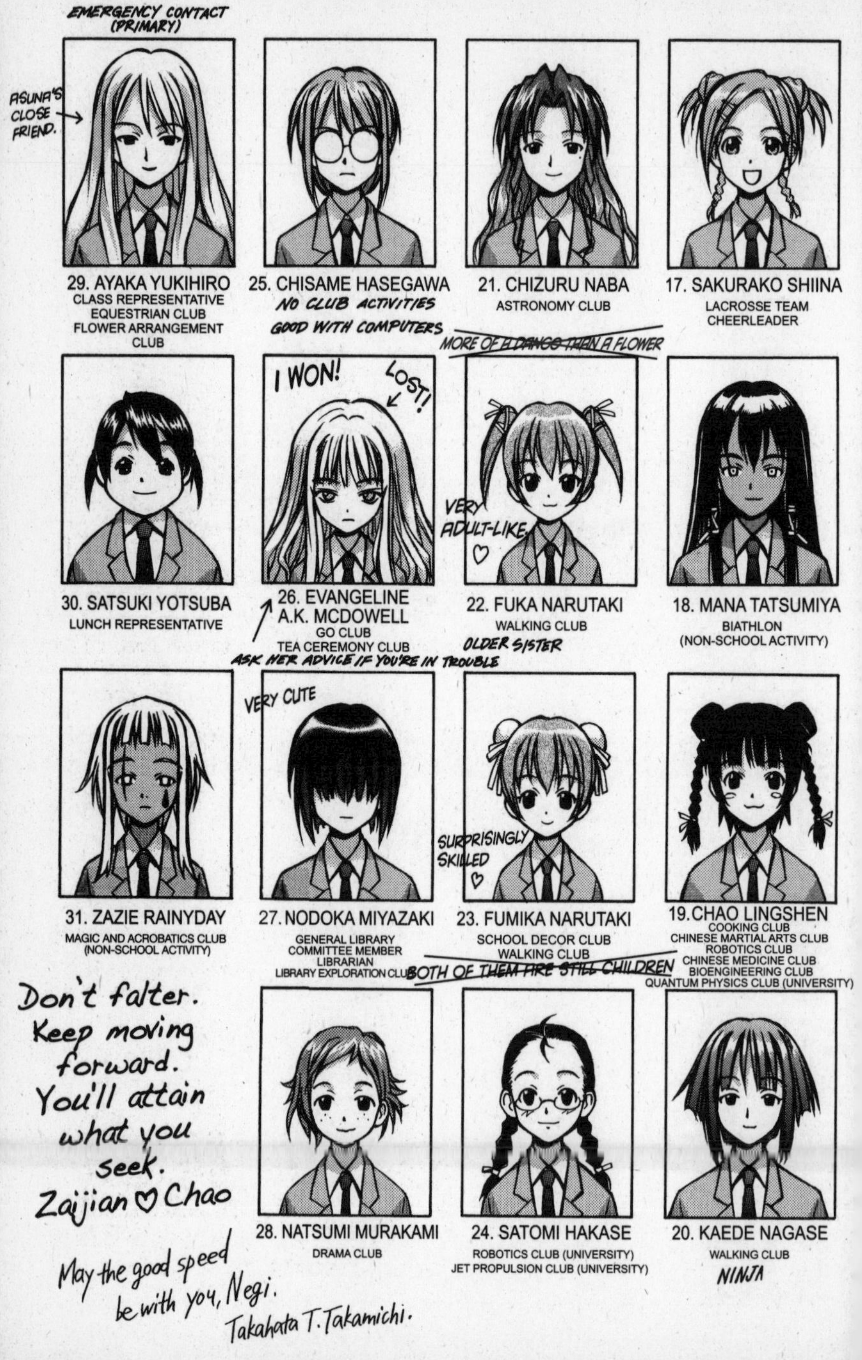

17. SAKURAKO SHIINA
LACROSSE TEAM
CHEERLEADER
21. CHIZURU NABA
ASTRONOMY CLUB
MORE OF A DANGO THAN A FLOWER
25. CHISAME HASEGAWA
NO CLUB ACTIVITIES
GOOD WITH COMPUTERS
EMERGENCY CONTACT (PRIMARY)
ASUNA'S CLOSE FRIEND.
29. AYAKA YUKIHIRO
CLASS REPRESENTATIVE
EQUESTRIAN CLUB
FLOWER ARRANGEMENT CLUB
18. MANA TATSUMIYA
BIATHLON
(NON-SCHOOL ACTIVITY)
VERY ADULT-LIKE. ♡
22. FUKA NARUTAKI
WALKING CLUB
OLDER SISTER
I WON!
LOST!
26. EVANGELINE A.K. MCDOWELL
GO CLUB
TEA CEREMONY CLUB
ASK HER ADVICE IF YOU'RE IN TROUBLE
30. SATSUKI YOTSUBA
LUNCH REPRESENTATIVE
19. CHAO LINGSHEN
COOKING CLUB
CHINESE MARTIAL ARTS CLUB
ROBOTICS CLUB
CHINESE MEDICINE CLUB
BIOENGINEERING CLUB
QUANTUM PHYSICS CLUB (UNIVERSITY)
SURPRISINGLY SKILLED ♡
23. FUMIKA NARUTAKI
SCHOOL DECOR CLUB
WALKING CLUB
BOTH OF THEM ARE STILL CHILDREN
VERY CUTE
27. NODOKA MIYAZAKI
GENERAL LIBRARY COMMITTEE MEMBER
LIBRARIAN
LIBRARY EXPLORATION CLUB
31. ZAZIE RAINYDAY
MAGIC AND ACROBATICS CLUB
(NON-SCHOOL ACTIVITY)
20. KAEDE NAGASE
WALKING CLUB
NINJA
24. SATOMI HAKASE
ROBOTICS CLUB (UNIVERSITY)
JET PROPULSION CLUB (UNIVERSITY)
28. NATSUMI MURAKAMI
DRAMA CLUB
Don't falter. Keep moving forward. You'll attain what you seek. Zaijian ♡ Chao
May the good speed be with you, Negi.
Takahata T. Takamichi.

魔法先生 ネギま!
MAGISTER NEGI MAGI

赤松 健 SHONEN MAGAZINE COMICS
KEN AKAMATSU

19

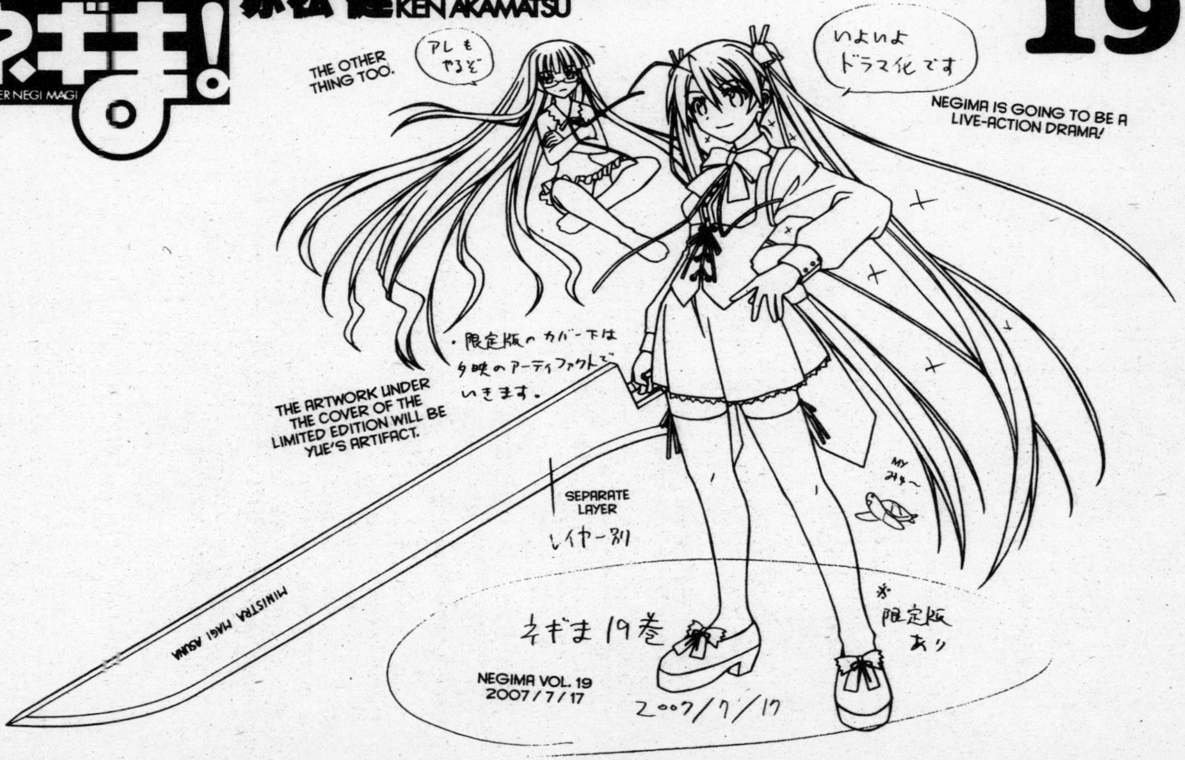
いよいよ ドラマ化です
NEGIMA IS GOING TO BE A LIVE-ACTION DRAMA!
アレも やるぞ
THE OTHER THING TOO.
・限定版のカバー下は 夕映のアーティファクトで いきます。
THE ARTWORK UNDER THE COVER OF THE LIMITED EDITION WILL BE YUE'S ARTIFACT.
MY みゅ〜
SEPARATE LAYER
レイヤー別
MINISTRA MAGI ASUNA
※限定版あり
ネギま19巻
NEGIMA VOL. 19
2007/7/17
2007/7/17

キャラ解説

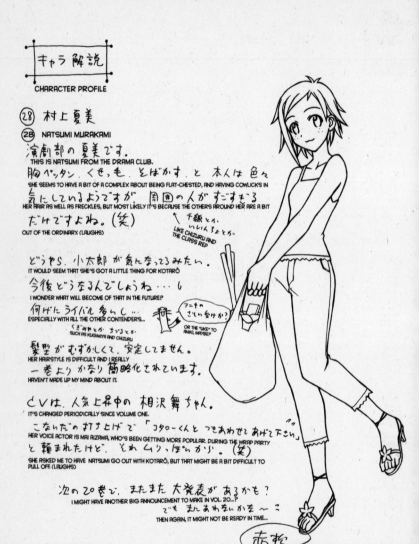

CHARACTER PROFILE

㉘ 村上夏美

㉘ NATSUMI MURAKAMI

演劇部の夏美です。

THIS IS NATSUMI FROM THE DRAMA CLUB.

胸ペッタン、くせっ毛、そばかす、と 本人は色々

SHE SEEMS TO HAVE A BIT OF A COMPLEX ABOUT BEING FLAT-CHESTED, AND HAVING COWLICKS IN

気にしているようですが、周囲の人がすごすぎる

HER HAIR AS WELL AS FRECKLES, BUT MOST LIKELY IT'S BECAUSE THE OTHERS AROUND HER ARE A BIT

だけですよね。(笑)

OUT OF THE ORDINARY. (LAUGHS)

↑ 千鶴とか いいんちょとか

LIKE CHIZURU AND THE CLASS REP

どうやら、小太郎が気になってるみたい。

IT WOULD SEEM THAT SHE'S GOT A LITTLE THING FOR KOTARŌ

今後どうなるんでしょうね…

I WONDER WHAT WILL BECOME OF THAT IN THE FUTURE?

何げにライバル多いし…

ESPECIALLY WITH ALL THE OTHER CONTENDERS...

くぎみやとか ちづるとか

SUCH AS KUGIMIYA AND CHIZURU

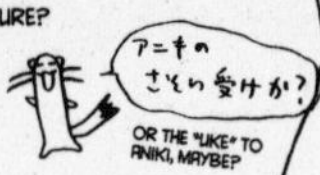
アニキの さそい受けか?

OR THE "UKE" TO ANIKI, MAYBE?

髪型がむずかしくて、安定してません。

HER HAIRSTYLE IS DIFFICULT AND I REALLY

一巻よりかなり簡略化されています。

HAVEN'T MADE UP MY MIND ABOUT IT.

CVは、人気上昇中の相沢舞ちゃん。

IT'S CHANGED PERIODICALLY SINCE VOLUME ONE.

こないだの打ち上げで「コタローくんとつきあわせてあげて下さい」

HER VOICE ACTOR IS MAI AIZAWA, WHO'S BEEN GETTING MORE POPULAR. DURING THE WRAP PARTY

と頼まれたけど、それムリっぽいから。(笑)

SHE ASKED ME TO HAVE NATSUMI GO OUT WITH KOTARŌ, BUT THAT MIGHT BE A BIT DIFFICULT TO PULL OFF. (LAUGHS)

次の20巻で、またまた大発表があるかも?

I MIGHT HAVE ANOTHER BIG ANNOUNCEMENT TO MAKE IN VOL. 20...?

でも まにあわないかな〜

THEN AGAIN, IT MIGHT NOT BE READY IN TIME...

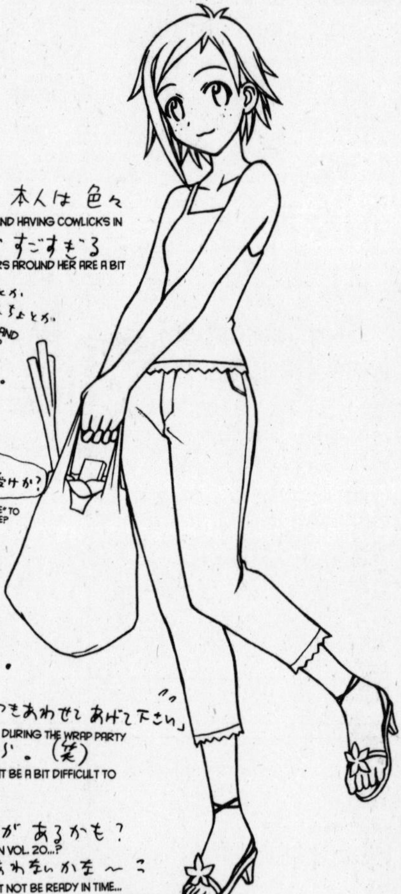

赤松

AKAMATSU

Translation Notes

Japanese is a tricky language for most Westerners, and translation is often more an art than a science. For your edification and reading pleasure, here are notes on some of the places where we could have gone in a different direction or where a Japanese cultural reference is used.

Yakitori eaters,
page 21

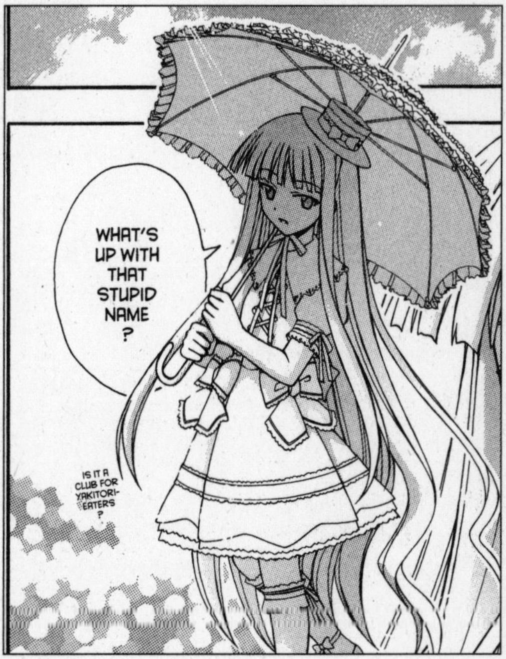
WHAT'S UP WITH THAT STUPID NAME ?
IS IT A CLUB FOR YAKITORI-EATERS ?

Negima is a common *yakitori* (BBQ) dish where meat is skewered alternately with sections of leeks or green onions.

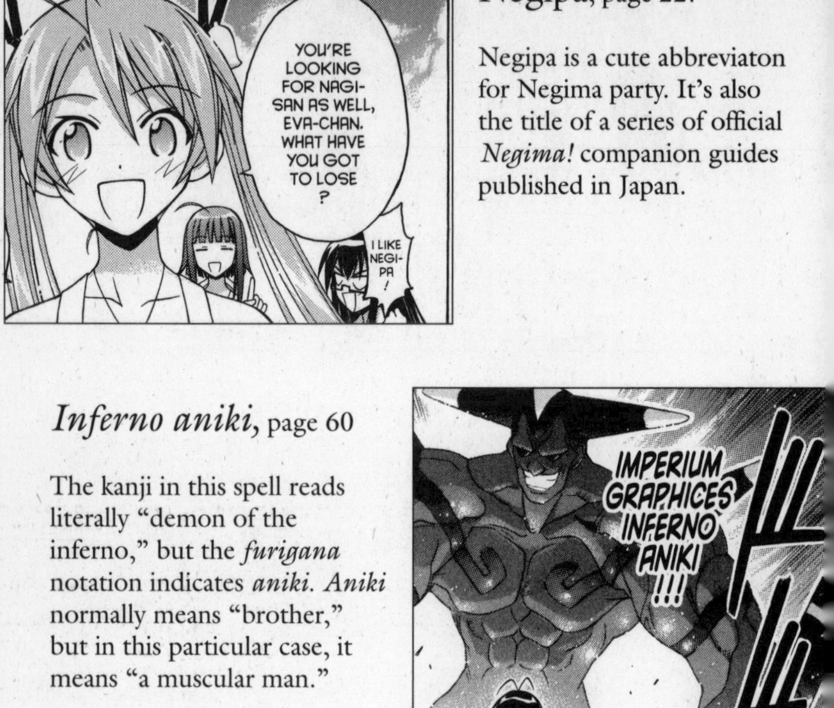
YOU'RE LOOKING FOR NAGI-SAN AS WELL, EVA-CHAN. WHAT HAVE YOU GOT TO LOSE ?
I LIKE NEGI-PA !

Negipa, page 22.

Negipa is a cute abbreviaton for Negima party. It's also the title of a series of official *Negima!* companion guides published in Japan.

Inferno aniki, page 60

The kanji in this spell reads literally "demon of the inferno," but the *furigana* notation indicates *aniki*. *Aniki* normally means "brother," but in this particular case, it means "a muscular man."

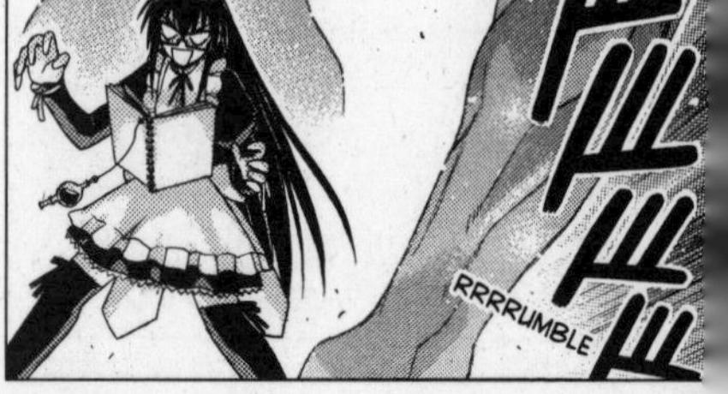
IMPERIUM GRAPHICES INFERNO ANIKI !!!
RRRRUMBLE

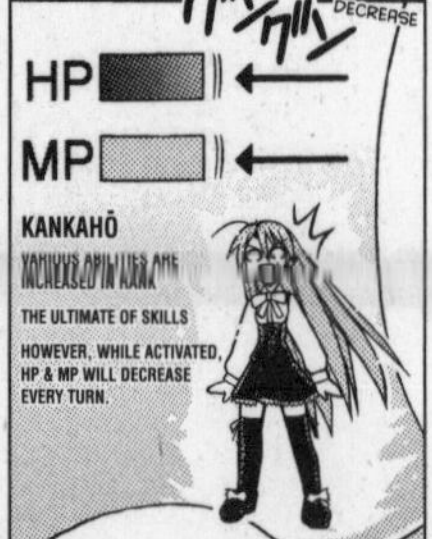
DECREASE
DECREASE
HP
MP
KANKAHŌ
THE ULTIMATE OF SKILLS
HOWEVER, WHILE ACTIVATED, HP & MP WILL DECREASE EVERY TURN.

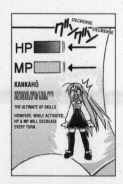

HP and MP, page 68

Video-game fans will recognize this notation right away: It's "hit points" and "magic points," as used in an RPG.

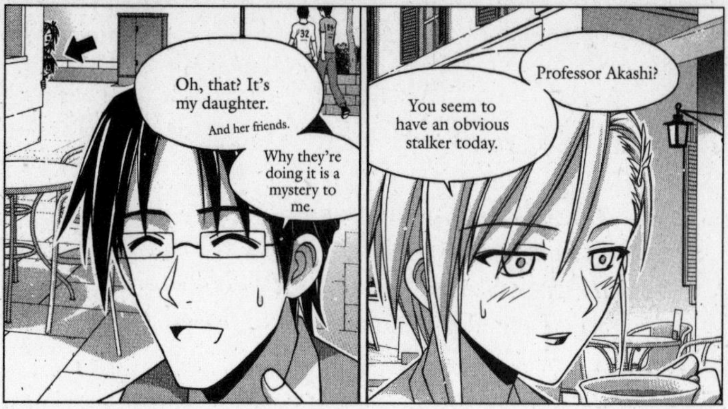
Professor Akashi?
You seem to have an obvious stalker today.
Oh, that? It's my daughter.
And her friends.
Why they're doing it is a mystery to me.

Donet and Akashi's conversation, page 102

Donet and Akashi's conversation was set in a special font in the Japanese edition to indicate that they were speaking in English, a convention which we've imitated here.

VA: Mamiko Noto, page 116

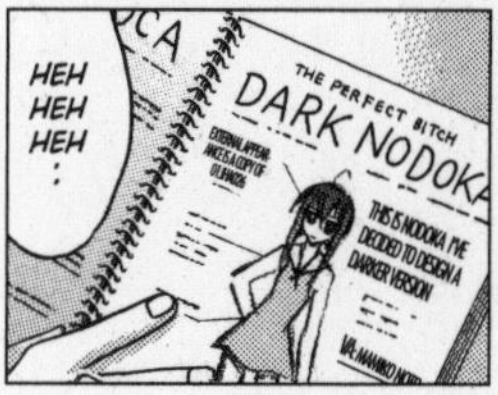
THE PERFECT BITCH
DARK NODOKA
THIS IS NODOKA I'VE DECIDED TO DESIGN A DARKER VERSION
HEH HEH HEH
:

VA stands for "voice actor." Mamiko Noto plays Nodoka in the *Negima!* anime; American *Negima!* fans know Leah Clark as the voice of Nodoka in the English-dubbed version.

About the Creator

Negima! is only Ken Akamatsu's third manga, although he started working in the field in 1994 with *AI Ga Tomaranai* (released in the United States with the title *A.I. Love You*). Like all of Akamatsu's work to date, it was published in Kodansha's *Shonen Magazine*. *AI Ga Tomaranai* ran for five years before concluding in 1999. In 1998, however, Akamatsu began the work that would make him one of the most popular manga artists in Japan: *Love Hina*. *Love Hina* ran for four years, and before its conclusion in 2002, it would cause Akamatsu to be granted the prestigious Manga of the Year award from Kodansha, as well as going on to become one of the best-selling manga in the United States.

FROM HIRO MASHIMA, CREATOR OF *RAVE MASTER*

FAIRY TAIL

FAIRY TAIL 1
Hiro Mashima Creator of Rave Master

FAIRY TAIL 2
Hiro Mashima Creator of Rave Master

Lucy has always dreamed of joining the Fairy Tail, a club for the most powerful sorcerers in the land. But once she becomes a member, the fun really starts!

Special extras in each volume! Read them all!

VISIT WWW.DELREYMANGA.COM TO:

- Read sample pages
- View release date calendars for upcoming volumes
- Sign up for Del Rey's free manga e-newsletter
- Find out the latest about new Del Rey Manga series

RATING T AGES 13+

DEL REY MANGA デルレイ

The Otaku's Choice™

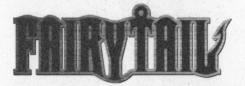

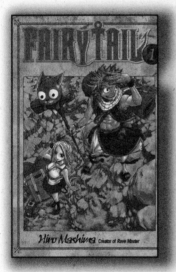

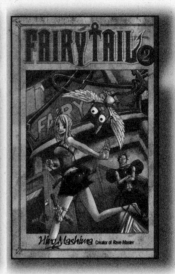

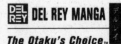

STORY BY KIO SHIMOKU
ART BY KOUME KEITO

FROM THE PAGES OF *GENSHIKEN*!

The Genshiken gang have long obsessed over a manga called *Kujibiki Unbalance*, the story of an average boy who becomes class president at a ritzy academy. Now *Kujibiki Unbalance* is a real-life manga for every fan's enjoyment!

• The eagerly awaited spin-off to the bestselling *Genshiken* series!

Special extras in each volume! Read them all!

TOMARE!

[STOP!]

You're going the wrong way!

Manga is a completely different type of reading experience.

To start at the *beginning*, go to the *end*!

That's right! Authentic manga is read the traditional Japanese way—from right to left, exactly the *opposite* of how American books are read. It's easy to follow: Just go to the other end of the book, and read each page—and each panel—from right side to left side, starting at the top right. Now you're experiencing manga as it was meant to be.